N

EDONIAN CANAL
VER NESS

INVERNESS

RIVER
ENRICK

RIVER
COILTIE

Urquhart Cas

ANNET   700

500

RIVER
INVERFARIGA
pier

The Monsters
of
Loch Ness

The Monsters

of

Loch Ness

Roy P. Mackal

THE SWALLOW PRESS INC.
CHICAGO

First Edition
First Printing

Published by
The Swallow Press Incorporated
811 West Junior Terrace
Chicago, Illinois 60613

ISBN 0-8040-0703-9
Library of Congress Catalog Card Number 76-3139

Contents

Illustrations

Maps

Introduction

The questions I am most frequently asked about the Loch Ness phenomenon are: "Do you really believe there is a monster?" "How did you get involved with the monster?" "Have you seen it?" The first and last questions are answered in the chapters that follow. In fact, whether or not there are large animals in Loch Ness—and what they are—is what this book is all about. A great deal of nonsense has been written about the notorious "Loch Ness monster." As a result no one can be blamed for regarding the whole matter as a silly-season joke. I have tried to present the facts without embellishments, believing that the plain, unadorned truth is one of the most exciting challenges in human experience. The reader must judge whether my conclusions are reasonable.

I became involved in this matter because of a circumstance that many travelers sooner or later encounter: too many cities, too many bright lights, too much bustle. Finding myself in London, feeling surfeited, in the fall of 1965, I was searching for something new, refreshing, different. As I walked idly down Oxford Street, I noticed a poster depicting a lovely mountain scene. It described the Scottish Highlands as remote and breathtakingly beautiful. In my frame of mind, I did not take much convincing, and a few days later I found myself high on a Scottish mountainside overlooking Loch Ness at the place known as Urquhart Bay.

The view below me certainly lived up to the poster's promise. Except for the slit of black-topped road a few yards below, the land sloped without interruption 200 feet down to the black water, which, I was aware, was claimed to be the habitat of the "Loch Ness monster."

The loch at this point was over a mile wide. The opposite shore rose in a cliff of brownish igneous rock to a tree-topped crest. Movements of the earth's crust long ago displaced the two shores, so that the rocks originally on this side of the deep gorge were now 65 miles to the southwest; the resulting fissure, gouged and deepened by later glacial action, accounted for what now is known as Glen More—the

Great Glen—a water-filled valley extending clear across Scotland, with Loch Ness at its northeasterly end, passing out through the Ness River and Moray Firth into the North Sea.

The Loch is deceptively ordinary looking. In fact, the hillsides are merely the above-water portion of a cliff 1,000 feet high—the edges of the volcanic and glaciated slit in the rock—and some 700 feet of cliffs extend to the bottom of the gorge below the water's surface. A body of water nearly 25 miles long, a mile wide, and as much as 700 feet deep contains about 263 billion cubic feet.

These few facts had been gleaned from the reading I had done prior to embarking on this Highlands adventure. Like anyone else, I had been titillated from time to time by new "monster sightings," and having decided to go to the Highlands, it was not hard to decide to pay Loch Ness a visit.

Thus it was that I found myself that morning in a nest of bracken fern. I had a breathtaking view of Urquhart Bay and 2-3 miles of loch surface in either direction. The loch was flat calm, a black mirror; the sky overcast. I scanned the loch through binoculars. Nothing disturbed the calm surface, though occasional vagrant air currents produced many odd surface effects. After a half hour or so, it began to rain gently. It was warm, and the rain did not disturb me. I dozed fitfully, rousing myself periodically to scan the loch. After a couple of hours the rain stopped, and the sun broke through the cloud cover, lifting my spirits. A little later my eye caught a van boasting a tripod and camera mounted on its roof parked beside the road.

Deciding to investigate, I worked my way through the giant bracken to the van and introduced myself to the two men in attendance. One of them explained that this was one of the vehicles sent out daily by the "Bureau." In exchange, I told him I was a biologist. It didn't seem necessary to say I was an American tourist.

They were interested in my scientific background, although they lost interest when I told them that my field was research with infectious viral deoxyribonucleic acid—a form of submicroscopic life.

What I learned then and later about the Bureau persuaded me that reasonable men and women might indeed hope to ascertain whether or not large animals lived in Loch Ness, and that reasonable persons were already hard at work in what seemed to be an intelligent, if acutely limited, effort to find out.

Illus. 1 Main camera rig at LNPIB headquarters, Achnahanet, Scotland, along the western shore of Loch Ness, 1965.

Illus. 2 Main camera rig: 35mm movie camera with 36″ lens and two F24 still photo cameras with 20″ lenses mounted one of each side of central camera. The two F24 cameras were so arranged as to automatically take pairs of sequential stereo photos when the central camera was activated. *LNIB photo.*

The Loch Ness Phenomena Investigation Bureau (LNPIB) had expedition headquarters on the shore of Loch Ness about 8 miles from where I encountered the van. Its terminology initially seemed strange to me, even pretentious. "Bureau" to an American ear suggested an arm of the government, but all of LNPIB's money and manpower and much of its equipment are volunteered. Over the years, the Bureau has had only one or two full-time paid workers. The word "Phenomena" seemed to me outside the popular vocabulary, though far preferable to the wholly misleading "monster." At least it had the virtue of refusing to presume that what caused all the gossip was some kind of animal or even anything living at all. And a group of trailers parked on a cliffside less than an hour's drive by paved road from the largest city in northern Scotland, Inverness, hardly seemed to me an "expedition." But this was headquarters for successive groups of dedicated amateurs, men and women of widely varying interests, who did indeed serve time, from dawn to dusk, monitoring the lake, motion picture cameras at hand, hoping to gain more knowledge of what might be in the water.

In 1965 the Bureau's volunteers were making do with what they could afford (which was by no means what they could imagine). Every two weeks, almost the entire crew, some 20 men and women, almost all on summer vacations, departed, and a new group moved in. Days when the visibility was poor, because of rain or mist, or when high winds and turbulent waves made surface sightings impossible, no one went out on station. Nights were free. For the privilege of being accepted as a volunteer, each worker paid a modest fee to cover his or her own room and board. What each offered was workhours, plus at least a rudimentary understanding of a 16-millimeter motion picture camera.

There were farmers and tradesmen, schoolteachers and housewives, students from several lands, and white-collar workers from an assortment of Scottish and British cities—presided over by the hovering presence of a monk turned camera technician, Clem Skelton.

The real leader of the expedition, I learned, was, and is, David James: author, publisher, World War II torpedo-boat skipper, hero of a notable escape from a Nazi prison camp, resident of Torosay Castle on the Island of Mull 80 miles to the southwest, and Member of Parliament. Before I left Scotland, I met David James and became permanently infected with his forthright attitude toward the search.

Part One

THE SEARCH

SCOTLAND

Scale of Miles
0   50

ORKNEY ISLANDS

John o'Groat's

NORTH SEA

Thurso

Wick

Isle of Lewis

North Minch

HEBRIDES

NORTHWEST HIGHLANDS

Dornoch

Braemore

Moray Firth

Elgin

Banff

Nairn

Peterhead

Isle of Skye

Inverness

Loch Ness

LOCH NESS AREA OF INVERNESS

Fort Augustus

Caledonian Canal

INNER HEBRIDES

Fort William

△ *Ben Nevis 4406 ft.*

HIGHLANDS

□ Balmoral Castle

Aberdeen

GRAMPIAN MOUNTAINS

HIGHLANDS

Montrose

Mull I.

Oban

Firth of Lorne

Dundee

Firth of Tay

Perth

St. Andrews

Kinross

Loch Lomond

Stirling

Firth of Forth

Jura I.

Dunbarton

Falkirk

Dunbar

Greenock

Clydebank

EDINBURGH

Paisley

■ **GLASGOW**

Berwick-on-Tweed

Islay I.

Sound of Jura

Motherwell

L O W L A N D S

Kilmarnock

Lanark

Peebles

Arran I.

Firth of Clyde

Selkirk

Ayr

Prestwick

Campbeltown

SOUTHERN UPLANDS

CHEVIOT HILLS

NORTHERN IRELAND

North Channel

Dumfries

Stranraer

Solway Firth

ENGLAND

I
Operation Bootstrap
1965-1966

Over the years reports of observations of unusual and unidentified aquatic animals have been made in Canada, Ireland, Scotland, Scandinavia, and the Soviet Union. Usually these observations have been made at lakes geographically located between 50° and 60° N latitude. The most famous of these sites is Loch Ness, located in northern Scotland about 56° N latitude. All of the lakes concerned, including Loch Ness, have a relationship to the sea that permits migratory fish, such as salmon and eels, to enter them.[1]

In the case of Loch Ness the northeast sea connection consists of the Caledonian Canal, containing 7 locks, and the River Ness, which runs roughly parallel to the canal, both of which empty into Moray Firth. The southwest connection consists of the Caledonian Canal, containing 17 locks, which connects Loch Ness with Loch Oich and the sea loch, Loch Linnhe, via Loch Lochy. Loch Ness itself is a tectonic lake, that is, a lake resulting from the movement of the earth's crust. The Great Glen, which contains Loch Ness, is a gigantic wrench-cleft or tear in the earth's surface that cuts clear across Scotland.

Loch Ness is 24¼ miles long and includes its northern extremity, called Loch Dochfour. The loch proper, from Fort Augustus to the narrows at Bonaferry, extends some 22⅔ miles along its axis of maximum depth. Before 1970 its greatest known depth was 754 feet, its mean depth 433 feet. In 1969 exploration by Vickers Ltd. found

---

[1] Some of the lakes involved in these observations are (with bibliographical references in parentheses): Lake Okanagan, British Columbia (Lyons); Lake Störsjo, Sweden (Skjelsvik); Lake Varota, Lake Labynkyr, Lake Khaiyr, Siberia (Dinsdale [1966]). See Chapter III (opening paragraph) for a list of lakes in Ireland.

7

two deeper holes. The deeper location, in the vicinity of Urquhart Bay, measured at least 850 feet and possibly as much as 920 feet.

Biologically, the lake is classified as oligotrophic, or "little nourishing," in contrast to a eutrophic lake. An oligotrophic lake is one in which the hypolimnion—that is, the lower layer of cold water—never becomes completely depleted of oxygen. Oxygen in the hypolimnion is consumed as organic material settling from the epilimnion—upper warmer layer—decays. There are two kinds of oligotrophic lakes: in one kind there is little production of organic matter in the surface water; in the other the lake itself is deep and contains a large hypolimnion. In this latter type, of which Loch Ness is an example, although there is a substantial production of life in the epilimnion, the oxygen of the hypolimnion is never used up because there is so much of it.

The water in Loch Ness is very cold, about 42°F in the lower layers, and is filled with a very fine suspension of particles of peat. As a result, underwater visibility is very poor, and plant life dependent on light from photosynthesis is confined to the upper 20 to 30 feet of water. Because of the low temperature, which is constant in the hypolimnion throughout the year (the loch never freezes), and because of a slightly acid condition, which is caused by the percolation of the feeder rivers and streams through a peaty soil prior to their discharging into Loch Ness, the microscopic life forms known as plankton are found in lower concentrations in Loch Ness than is the case in more hospitable lakes, such as, for example, Lake Windemere in the Lake District of England. However, despite the low temperature and the humic acid content, a complete biological cycle is present.

The basic cycle begins with the sun's energy, which is used by chlorophyll-containing phytoplankton, and leads through a chain of successively larger predators to the largest animals in Loch Ness. The basic cycle of life, however, is greatly augmented by the millions of salmon and eels that migrate annually into the loch from the sea. (See Chapter XII for more on the food supply in Loch Ness. For more details of the physical and biological characteristics of the loch, see Appendix K; also Appendix J.)

Such are the bare physical conditions of the lake that has been the site of strange observations for over 1,400 years. The earliest record of a "fearsome beastie" in Loch Ness is found in Book 2, Chapter 27 of *The Latin Life of the Great St. Columba*, written in the year 565

A.D. According to the manuscript (preserved in the library of Schaff-hausen, Switzerland), the ferocious monster killed one of the local inhabitants of the loch area. Later, when another man seemed threat-ened, St. Columba, Abbot of Iona, caused the "fearsome beastie" to cease and desist by commanding, presumably in a loud voice, "Go thou no further nor touch the man; go back at once." On hearing the word of the saint, so the account goes, the monster was terrified and fled away more quickly than if it had been dragged off by ropes, even though it had come within about 10 feet of Lugne, the saint's com-panion, who had swum out into the loch after a boat.

Since the sixth century, reports have continued to this day, increas-ing in the years 1933-1934, when prolonged blasting in the area during road building is alleged to have increased sightings.

The information above represented the sum total of my knowledge about the Loch Ness mystery when I received an invitation, during my 1965 Scotland vacation, to visit David James. We met at Oban, the mainland port opposite the Island of Mull.

My first impression of David James was of a medium, sandy man, given to honest woolens, without the false heartiness sometimes seen in politicians. He exhibited what I had come to expect as the usual Scottish politeness, which might be taken for meekness, unless one remembered that a German commander once termed his kilt-clad enemy "the ladies from Hell." He approached his subject with knowl-dege and energy, and he had a ready wit. Acquaintance added many dimensions, especially David's inbred adventurousness and his con-tempt for stupidity; indeed, our first encounter quickly ripened into close acquaintance and, finally, into warm friendship.

Initially, we sought to measure each other. I was still curious—as a scientist on holiday. David had an ulterior reason: as a man accus-tomed to leading—and therefore to taking advantage of all that fell in his path—he immediately saw in me a door that could perhaps be an entrance into the orthodox and therefore respectable scientific community.

Thus one of his questions was: "You're a scientist. What is your general impression?"

"I have a lot of impressions, all unscientific and all offhand," I told him. "Principally this. Your people are great, but if they learn anything, it will be by accident. A real search would be an enormous project, costing enormous sums. And after thousands of man-hours, and perhaps hundreds of thousands of dollars, you still may find nothing, or that there was nothing there in the first place."

"But what if we could establish that there is?"

"You mean, would science be interested? Biologists, zoologists? Of course, they would. We live on the land; we think by now we pretty well know about the land animals. But we're only coming to explore what may be under water."

"What difference would it make," he asked, "if large animals did live in Loch Ness—to science, I mean?"

"Who can tell? At the least, scientists are curious like everyone else. Practical objectives? They're not always necessary. Anyway," I said, "as a Member of Parliament, you surely don't have to rely on an American tourist, who happens to be a molecular biologist, to learn how science would evaluate a discovery like that. You must have connections enough to canvass any number of wholly competent scientists in the United Kingdom."

"I have," he admitted. "They say the same thing. Many of them are quite curious. But just about all of them want nothing *publicly* to do with Loch Ness."

"I see why," I told David, "and I share their reservations."

Then he wanted to know more about my work, and asked some especially good questions about how a researcher such as I had his work financed.

"Mostly by going around, hat in hand, when the present grant runs out," I told him.

Going around, he wanted to know, to whom? Foundations? Individuals? Corporations that perhaps might benefit from my research? All of these, I said, might be possible donors. David is a fine man, but one with transparent motives. I could easily see his drift—an American, a scientist, and a man who perhaps knew where to look for money! Well, I said to myself, why not? What's to lose? In fact, I didn't leave David and his family until two days later, spent at his estate at Torosay Castle on Mull. The days were well spent. Wildlife abound—seals on the rocks, deer on the high ridges, fat trout amazingly abundant in the cold streams, sea birds everywhere—and the island, like the mainland opposite, is scarce in population. In short, it is an idyllic spot for a two-day vacation, and those days were particularly enjoyable because some of the Bureau's resources are stored in David's library—sighting reports from Loch Ness, correspondence with a few of the great and more of the lowly, and an abundance of printed materials, some of which might and some that evidently did not bear on what might exist in Loch Ness—and because the stay gave us a chance to get to know each other better and to discuss "monster" possibilities.

As a biologist, I was, in short order, able to dismiss: *sea serpents* (in all of evolution, no serpent ever made it in water as cold as the 42° of Loch Ness) and *reptiles* (in general, for the same reason).

In the discussion, I was prompted to raise a question that did then, and still does, seem fundamental. If there were large animals living in Loch Ness, why should they *ever* be seen at the surface? These Loch Ness things were seen so rarely that I could detect no pattern to their surfacing.

"Give us enough time and enough film—maybe we'll find a pattern," said David.

"Unless they actually surface much more often but rarely expose whatever it is they do expose," I was thinking aloud. "Your people see things mostly on flat, calm days—no waves. Most days there are waves, and something barely emerging might simply not be seen."

Nature encourages incredible adaptations. Years later I was to acquire a snail that lives underwater and procures its air by means of an elastic protuberance that barely breaks the water, for all the world like the snorkel of a submarine. This little creature was only 2 inches long, but the wondrous world of mollusks offers thousands of known varieties and—who knows?—maybe as many more still unknown, and they come in size from the microscopic to the 50-foot giant squid, an adaptation almost beyond belief. Of this family almost anything could be believed.

In any case, I couldn't accept something that, from all the reports, added up to a creature perhaps 20 feet long—with a 6-foot neck ending in a snake-like head, a back like an overturned boat, marked shoulder to tail by an apparent dorsal fin—that propelled itself by its tail, sometimes basked and sometimes thrashed the surface but never seemed to come up on any regular schedule at all, unless it crawled out on the land in the dark. Such an animal never was. Yet, if the evidence of eyewitnesses was worth pursuing at all, some or all of these details would have to be explored.

It was, to say the least, food for thought. Certainly, I came away from Mull thinking that the Bureau was no conglomerate of crazies.

These were solid, serious—if undertrained and underfinanced—lay researchers.

The films finally made me a supporter of the Bureau, though not of the idea of a "monster." When we arrived back in London, David arranged for me to view all the film then existing of the phenomena at Loch Ness. Afterward, especially after viewing Tim Dinsdale's film, I emerged increasingly persuaded that the Bureau might really be onto something substantial.

During my return to Chicago and the months that followed, I had time for considerable soul searching. Did I really want to get involved in this project? If so, what really were the odds that all of this was not simply nonsense? Such questions plagued me, permitting no peace of mind. The crux of the matter lay in whether or not there were unusual phenomena present at Loch Ness: not necessarily unidentified animals, but something which could not be explained in ordinary terms, by known processes and objects. Even something trivial, if unusual, might be worthwhile. If I could honestly answer yes, well and good, I'd go ahead; if not, I'd forget the whole thing. I did not of course require any guarantees, only a finite possibility that somewhere buried in the data something unusual was lurking.

What was at hand to help me decide? First, the published material relating to Loch Ness and its alleged monster, none of it "scientific" in nature, mainly anecdotal. A few still photographs and film sequences, some of which were not really available but were only alleged to exist. Such then was the picture. To be sure it would take a long time, perhaps years, to analyze all of the data completely, but what little I had seen seemed singularly unconvincing.

Then there was the Bureau and its modest experience; some alleged successes, but most failures, must weigh heavily in the scale of my judgment. A group of dedicated, sincere people no doubt, but in the main amateurs lacking funds, scientific talent, and technology. It was obvious why a scientist-engineer was sorely needed: someone to weigh the evidence, sort it out, pass it through the sieve of open-minded but hard-nosed skepticism, and plan experiments and future activities with a view as to what constituted valid data, valid scientific evidence. To the extent that I qualified, there was no question that I was needed, but did I need this problem of an alleged Loch Ness monster? I read and reread the published material available to me, searching for decisive factors, pro or con. No amount of effort affected the answer which always came out the same: inconclusive, nothing convincing for or against. A really open question, with just enough smoke to prevent me from dropping it completely.

What about the Bureau experience and its evidence? They had spent a few summers at Loch Ness watching the surface of the lake from various vantage points, cameras at the ready. I had looked at the film obtained, some of it convincing. Also a collection of sighting reports prepared by a variety of people. More material such as had already been published: perhaps valuable if properly analyzed and studied, but that would also take years and could not be of immediate help. A few other Bureau activities: wires strung along the shoreline to detect the passage of a large object, large searchlights at night in case some denizen of Loch Ness might be attracted by a bright light. No results, and nothing to make me decide anything—except to forget the whole matter. If this had been all there were, I am convinced that at this point I would have washed my hands of Loch Ness permanently.

The one thing that would not go away was the Dinsdale film sequence. Although it was grainy in quality because of the great distance involved in the photography, I could not explain it, try as I would. It alone was sufficient for me. One unexplained film sequence —extremely meager indeed to stick my neck out for world ridicule and perhaps even worse. Nevertheless, it seemed to me that regardless of this, no area of human experience should be taboo. Even Loch Ness and its alleged phenomena should be subject to investigation by honest and reasonable men and women.

I had only my own judgment to go by, but I saw no reason not to undertake the task David had intended for me from the beginning: to see if I could stir up both interest and money from U.S. resources to further the Bureau's searches.

It would take at least a year of thought, study, and actual experience at Loch Ness to make an educated judgment and perhaps formulate a master plan for an attack on the Loch Ness problem. I had to determine what was possible, what the major technical problems might be, and what criteria would be needed to settle this matter.

From what I had seen of the Bureau and its organization, it seemed a good place to begin. I decided I would go along for a year and see how things went. If the activities of the coming year (1966) should produce nothing but mistaken identification of ordinary objects floating around in the loch, I could always withdraw discreetly to the side lines—or at least so I thought.

Early on, David and I agreed on a modest approach, an effort to raise thousands of dollars rather than unlikely and unjustified scores of thousands. Even given a majestic windfall, we would not at first have known what technology to buy with it; and costly items we could visualize we knew we could not staff. Thus I began my search for modest funding.

The obvious first prospects seemed to be museums and zoos. The first reactions, invariably, were that I must be joking. Loch Ness? Why, everybody knew those monster stories were a farce. And so I came to recite, almost automatically, my litany about the need at least to look at what evidence existed, about the unfortunate lasting effects of popular magazine "exposures" on the public mind (including that of my listener), about the value of any find if one occurred, about my own concessions that there might be no animals there at all. Those at each zoo and aquarium who heard me out at least ended up with open minds—but not with open pocketbooks. (These included the Bronx Zoo, the New York Aquarium, the Brookfield Zoo just west of Chicago, and Chicago's Shedd Aquarium.)

Commander Encil E. Rains, USN (Ret.), Director of the Chicago Zoological Park at Brookfield, summed up the reactions of all such institutions: "My directors can understand a request for money for a new lion. If they authorize the money for one, eventually we'll get one. But zoos simply don't pay for animals that very well may not ever be caught, and quite possibly may not exist at all."

The reaction of William Braker, Director of the Shedd Aquarium, was similar. But he did steer me to an effective donor, the Chicago Adventurers' Club. The club was begun in 1911, when Major W. Robert Foran, who had served as the Associated Press correspondent attached to Colonel Theodore Roosevelt's African big-game expedition in 1909 and 1910, came to Chicago and shortly thereafter became acquainted with Charles Dawell. Dawell was the proprietor of St. Hubert's Old English Grill, and a group of adventurers, explorers, big-game hunters, and military men had taken to meeting informally in his establishment. Foran, an author and journalist, with a background in big-game hunting, ivory poaching, and military and police service, was a welcome addition to the group. He proposed a formal organization, and a society of swashbucklers emerged with the motto "To provide a hearth and home for those who have left the beaten path and made for adventure." Theodore Roosevelt was elected first honorary member. The roster has also included such distinguished names as Sir Ernest Henry Shackleton, pioneer of Arctic and oceanic explorations; Sir Francis Younghusband, explorer of Tibet; Roald Amundsen, explorer of both polar regions; Carl F. Akely, explorer and naturalist; Thor Heyerdahl, sea explorer and ethnologist; and Sir Edmund Hillary, first climber of Mount Everest.

A. R. ("Rush") Watkins, a member of the club, sounded out other members for me and returned with enthusiasm. It was agreed that David James should come over in January 1966, to make the presentation with me before the club's entire membership of our plan for a May-October search (14 two-week tours of duty by successive crews of volunteers).

Success! First, the club adopted our plan for extended surveillance of the loch's surface with much improved camera equipment and agreed to provide financial support; second, the club promptly offered membership to David for his adventurous escape from a Nazi prison and for his work as a cartographer in the Antarctic (and to me —perhaps for daring to adventure out of the secure laboratory!).

The Adventurers' Club support enabled the Bureau to continue its work, though our efforts were severely threatened two weeks later, in late February 1966, when word was leaked to the British press that one of its government's principal military intelligence units had been devoting serious time to the study of films of the notorious "Loch Ness monster." The public reaction, particularly in Britain, was wondrous in the extreme.

The facts were simple and inoffensive. Britain's Joint Air Reconnaissance Intelligence Centre—JARIC—had been prevailed upon to look at Dinsdale's film and return an evaluation. Totally obscured in the initial hubbub was the simple fact that the photo interpreters had said they could only conclude the film showed an object that was not a boat and probably was a large animate object moving on the surface of Loch Ness at a speed of about 11 mph. Totally present to the public mind was that some kind of hoax had been perpetrated on one of the most sensitive of Britain's military agencies, and that if this were the way the military was defending the realm, things were in a very bad state indeed.

When the press and public did get around to looking at what the

JARIC report actually said, a new division immediately occurred. On the one hand were those who said, "I always knew there was something in Loch Ness!" On the other were those who said, "Oh! That our finest military minds could be thus deceived!"

In fact, as I was learning, those with closed minds will never accept any evidence, from any source, that Loch Ness animals are anything but a poor joke.

Here was filmed evidence, viewed by experts, with a firmly if cautiously stated conclusion. These experts were working in the tradition of photo interpreters who repeatedly saved the Free World from peril during World War II. The Battle of Britain (film was in there ahead of radar), the *Bismarck* episode, the analysis of the heavy-water sites in Scandinavia, the discovery of the V-bomb sites in Western Europe—these occur as examples. And yet, if one simply would not believe large animals existed in Loch Ness, one could not even believe some of the world's most expert interpreters of photography.

For myself, and speaking as a scientist, the JARIC report—when the "scandal" blew over—was gratifying but, of course, inconclusive. Nothing would be absolutely conclusive except the taking of an actual specimen.

Other than the scientific information offered, the JARIC flap had positive and negative effects. First, it made money raising easier. Second, it added to our troubles by indirectly giving a new dimension to the monster myth. The JARIC report mentioned that by their techniques and under the given circumstances a body of about 92 feet would be about the ultimate limit of what they *might* measure. This figure was taken up in press reports as "the actual length of the Loch Ness Monster." Such jumping to wrong conclusions was patently absurd. The biggest animal that ever lived, the blue whale, is approximately that size, and certainly nothing approaching that dimension was in Loch Ness.

David on his side of the Atlantic and I on mine spent months setting right this total misconception. The 92-foot figure kept emerging in discussions with scientific colleagues as evidence that the interpreters had to be wildly wrong. And I learned another lesson: once an error is perpetrated in public, it may never be possible to correct.

On February 7, 1966, I received a letter from David containing two proposals. The first was an invitation from the Board of Directors of the Loch Ness Phenomena Investigation Bureau Ltd. to become a director, which of course delighted me and which I immediately accepted. The second proposal came from Norman Collins, President of LNPIB. This was the idea of an International Committee of top people (mostly scientists but not exclusively so) to convene in Scotland at a conference to exchange ideas concerning the Loch Ness phenomena. Included in this prospect of international cooperation was the suggestion that I set up a branch of LNPIB in the U.S. I thought the ideas of the conference and a U.S. branch of the Bureau were good. However, I had considerable misgivings as to whether we could get suitable people to participate and whether financial backing for both projects could be obtained.

During David's visit, we had conducted press conferences, sat for a few TV interviews, and noted that publicity brought reactions from both extremes: disparagement amounting almost to hate mail on the one hand, and expressions of intense interest on the other. Welcome if modest contributions came in, including one from Catholic Girls Junior College in Springfield, Illinois, but it was the Adventurers' Club with "Rush" Watkins assisted by Arthur L. Myrland, George Laadt, and Frank Kolbe that underwrote the work of 1966.

Meanwhile, I set to thinking and planning. All sorts of ideas—from draining the loch to seining it to setting off explosive devices—passed through my mind, all to be quickly discarded. But explosives held my attention more than briefly. Underwater explosives, thanks to compression shocks, can collapse a submarine; they would certainly bring to the surface—dead—any animals large or small in the vicinity. This would include, of course, all the fish in an area where many inhabitants depended on fishing; and quite conceivably a vertebrate protected by an Act of Parliament might be a victim of the blast. It was no go. Ultimately, I agreed that in spite of my impatience to bring modern scientific technology into the picture, photography probably was the best way to spend our limited funds in the immediate future.

The Bureau directors met in September, generously on a date tied in to my next visit to Loch Ness. Tim Dinsdale was the honored guest. Present besides David and me as directors were Norman Collins, Director of Associated Television; Peter Scott, Director of the World Wild Life Fund and a noted naturalist; and Richard Fitter, an ornithologist from the London Zoo. I was gratified to learn that Scott was urging a complete ecological survey of Loch Ness, and that Fitter would pursue this matter. It moved forward projects to which I had recently assigned some priority: food surveys, water-temperature findings, and study of the walls and bottom of the Great Glen.

Scott related how the spreading story of new evidence at Loch Ness was eliciting offers from kindred souls, and many ideas were kicked about, including the use of a silent observation platform. Both Thor Heyerdahl with the Kon Tiki and the Ra, and Captain John Ridgway and Sargent Chay Blyth in their rowboat crossing of the Atlantic, frequently observed marine life close at hand, and both groups reported observations of huge and possibly unknown marine animals.

Any such scheme lay in the future, but it was encouraging to see and note evidence of serious scientific interest. This development was matched by interest in the loch. Even as late as September, the number of visitors was substantial, and at one point I even held a news conference at the Bureau's loch headquarters.

As a result, I experienced first hand the Loch Ness Frustration Phenomenon. In 16 of the 19 stories ensuing from that press conference, my careful use of "animal" became "monster." The figure 12 once became 1200; 55 feet became 55 tons; and a general discussion of what determines where and how animals of any sort live— food, reproduction, water temperature—emerged as "Scientists Say Loch Ness Monster Could Be Caught with a Giant Hot Plate." We learned. Preconceptions simply will not change.

And now I had a new one to live down with my colleagues—the report that I had assuredly identified the "monster" as a giant sea slug. In discussing what evidence might fit which kinds of animals, I had pointed out that sighters often reported what seemed to be a variable back contour. I mentioned that this was not uncharacteristic of animal life, giving the sea slug as an example. Needless to say, I had not identified the Loch Ness animal (if any) as a sea slug.

I spent the next few days on the surface of the loch, surveying the shore line, as I familiarized myself with the entire area, and observing wind effects, wave forms, wakes of our own and passing craft, the inlets, the geology of the banks. Igneous rocks made caves unlikely, but I looked into a couple. The larger was some 12 feet deep; if there are caves below water, they are hardly large enough to conceal much of anything.

Trying to participate in everything, I went out on a camera watch, and successfully filmed, instead of the monster, a fishing cormorant. The day dawned flat calm but overcast; it was a Sunday morning, quiet since no local craft are to be found on the loch on the Sabbath. David Field and I moved out early to the southernmost station above Invermoriston, approximately the location where Kenneth Wilson, a London surgeon, had snapped his two pictures in 1934. The day continued flat calm, although now and then a slight breeze produced some ripples. Visibility was good even though the overcast was extensive.

About 10:30 I noted a ring of ripples some 300-400 yards out in the loch. Suddenly I saw a black head and slender neck pop up out of the water for a moment only, immediately submerging. I alerted Field, who focused a pair of 10X binoculars on the area. A few seconds later the head-neck appeared again, and I began to run the film. This transient surfacing continued for several minutes, sometimes as much as 30 to 50 feet from the last appearance. We watched with upwelling excitement. Finally, a body appeared, and with some disturbance and flapping the object soared off into the sky.

Illus. 1 Author just before filming a fishing cormorant near Invermoriston. *David Field photo.*

Had we been interrupted prior to the bird's takeoff, we could easily have come away with the idea that we had observed and filmed the monster. Such experiences are invaluable in developing judgment as to what may be the cause of a given observation. In some cases the sheer intensity of belief produces persons who may be classified as "seers." This is not to exclude the possibility that such persons may make a genuine observation; but the very frequency of their experiences is so contrary to statistical probability that one can be certain they are reporting many erroneous observations, however honestly.

My own next episode occurred during a watch on the main camera rig, on the slope below the base camp on September 17. Elizabeth Logan and I were carefully scanning the surface when I noted two 15-foot-long patches of brown scum or debris some 200 yards northeast of the camera rig. Carefully sweeping over every square inch of the area with 12X binoculars, I made out a round, black object about the size of a dinner plate riding low in the water, its convex surface barely protruding above the surface. The object rode heavily as though part of a greater mass, a suggestion supported by the fact that the small wavelets were breaking over it rather than raising it with their passing. A few inches away from the edge of the darker object and 4-6 inches apart were two much smaller objects. These objects retained exactly this relationship for about 10 minutes, at which time they vanished below the surface. Logan filmed a few minutes with the 16mm hand-held Bolex, but the range was too great.

What this object may have been is, of course, unknown, and the episode was not recorded as a sighting. This experience, while interesting in the overall context of Loch Ness, cannot be included in the category of evidence.

The only other events of moment during my stay at Loch Ness that year occurred on September 25. I was once again engaged in a tour of duty at the main camera rig. About 10:30 Clem Skelton drove off to Drumnadrochit on an errand. While returning along the road to our headquarters, he noted a black, hump-like object, similar in appearance to an overturned boat, just inshore below the main camera rig. He estimated the object was about 30 yards offshore, well below the tree line and thus screened from observation from the main camera platform.

Roaring back to base, Skelton leaped out of the car and rushed down the side of the loch, pointing and gesturing toward the water.

I remained at the camera in case the object should move out far enough to be filmed. When Skelton broke through the tree line near the shore, he observed a large spreading circle of ripples—and nothing more.

This near-miss put everyone in an expectant mood, especially since the loch was flat calm with a bright sun overhead. Nothing more occurred during the afternoon, however, except that two visitors stopped to report seeing a black convex hump from a point about 2 miles south of our headquarters. The object submerged after remaining stationary for several minutes; the approximate time: 5:10. The loch had been covered with small waves up to about 4:30, after which the surface again had become flat calm.

Our watch continued without incident until about 5:50 when Peter Hodge, who had moved off to the middle of a field south of headquarters where he had a good view of the loch, suddenly beckoned vigorously. Skelton scooped up a Bolex. Since intervening trees again made the main rig camera useless, I abandoned my post and hurried toward Hodge. We all observed a rather substantial disturbance in the water.

Hodge described a black "back" breaking the surface, moving forward, and simultaneously diving. The sequence was repeated several times. Size was hard to estimate, since the object was never stationary, but Peter thought it was too large for an otter. The episode was so rapid that although film was exposed, the camera missed the mark.

During the early evening, with the light failing, we watched four small black objects moving about, separated by between 30 and 80 feet from one another. These objects were not positively identifiable because of poor light, but they had all the characteristics of birds and were so classified.

Such a concentration of activity was never to be repeated during my subsequent visits to Loch Ness, and while all of these experiences were inconclusive, they did contribute to my determination to get to the bottom of the matter.

I returned home in October, wondering what impact the summer's mass of printed nonsense might have had on my colleagues at the University of Chicago. I found the administration very sophisticated about the matter; they were fully aware of the fallibility of the popular press. Further, they had a high regard for academic freedom, and no serious difficulties arose regarding my interest in Loch Ness. A few colleagues were critical at times, but they were only a handful and represented personal views rather than official policy.

In the mail I found many requests for speaking engagements and television appearances. One, to appear on "To Tell the Truth," I was advised to accept because it would mean income for Loch Ness research. And indeed it did: that program, aired on Sunday, October 23, provided some $750 for LNPIB.

Another invitation was even more gratifying. It was from Ralph Buchsbaum, an invertebrate zoologist at the Universtiy of Pittsburgh. Professor Buchsbaum had been contacted earlier in the year about the seminar of zoologists we had hoped to hold at Loch Ness during the summer but simply had not been able to afford. However, as a result of the correspondence that ensued I presented a seminar at Pittsburgh on April 29, 1967. For the first time, a group of professional scientists, zoologists, listened seriously and began to think of Loch Ness in terms other than as a funny story. And my discussions with Buchsbaum did much to clarify the problems and ramifications involved in the idea of a large, freshwater mollusk. He felt strongly that the invertebrate idea was not viable and raised a number of valid objections.

Time for Loch Ness activities was always at a premium. After all, I was primarily pursuing laboratory research at the university, and I had to turn down many opportunities that might have meant income for the Bureau and could not readily attend to some matters that were pressing. However, I produced for publication a summary of where things stood at the end of 1966 representing the Bureau's and my identical viewpoints:

1. After a year's consideration, including several months at the scene, we concluded that unusual phenomena had been and were occurring at Loch Ness.

2. Of the possible explanations, we regarded as most probable the idea that living creatures were involved.

3. Further than that we did not know. Our purpose was to obtain objective evidence. We had no favorite view of what kinds of creatures might be there, and individuals were free to form any opinion they wished.

Again under questioning as to what I thought personally, I admitted a very slight bias toward one kind of animal—mollusks.

II
Scotland 1967-1968

This book is about a continuing search—and about the tedious trial-and-error that goes into any scientific project. It is about many frustrations as well as about some successes. It is an effort to chronicle what lies behind the "Loch Ness monster" story. It is about the evidence and what it may mean, subject always to that final hoped-for achievement: the actual isolation of a live specimen for identification and study.

Certain basic questions were always in our thoughts. Were there large unidentified animals in Loch Ness? Would we be able to explain scientifically all of the evidence accumulated? Would we accumulate new evidence? If we were to discover large animals, what would be their identity?

The questions were obvious. Arriving at answers was to prove more difficult. Essentially, we had two problems. The first involved working with the evidence we had, and the evidence we had was incredibly mixed—possibly good, probably largely faulty, unknown. We simply did not know at first how reliable our data were, and one of the first tasks was devising tests to assess them.

In this connection, an episode comparable to Loch Ness in some ways is instructive—not least because the tests devised finally led to the identification of the beast known as Pelorus Jack, the popular name given to a dolphin that used to meet and accompany ships as they crossed Admiralty Bay between North and South Islands of New Zealand between the years 1888 and 1912. Many articles appeared about him in magazines, and he became world famous through picture postcards that described him as "the only fish in the world protected by Act of Parliament"—actually an Order in Council by New Zealand Governor Plunket prohibited the taking of Risso's dolphin in Cook Strait.

Descriptions of Pelorus Jack varied, especially as to color and size. The most striking discrepancy involved his being described as much lighter in color than a Risso's dolphin, which led to his original and erroneous identification as a beluga or white whale. Since the beluga has no dorsal fin and Pelorus Jack did, he could not be a whale. Indeed, as more and more observations were recorded and a range of photographs became available, some showing the tail, others the head, some the outline under the water, and even one on his side, identification finally was made.

Reverend D. C. Bates of the Meterological Office in Wellington used the eyewitness observations and photographs made by non-expert individuals as a basis to make the identification. The Pelorus Jack data include hundreds of eyewitness reports, a half dozen or so still photographs, and at least one short movie film sequence. This information is comparable to much of the early data from Loch Ness. Thus it may serve as a useful comparative case, especially since the actual animal was finally and positively identified as Risso's dolphin (*Grampus griseus*), whose known characteristics accorded with the various descriptions. Even the perplexing light color was explained, since Risso's dolphin turns gray with age.

Our second Loch Ness problem was, as usual, money. All research takes money, a lot of it, and at the Bureau we were in dire need. Fortunately, we found another angel. While pursuing the idea of a conference of zoologists at Loch Ness, I had been referred to Dr. William H. Nault, executive vice-president and editorial director of Field Enterprises Educational Corporation in Chicago, publishers of, among other items, the *World Book Encyclopedia, Childcraft,* and several yearbooks, including *Science Year.*

At first, I suggested that the seminar would make a good story for *Science Year.* What ensued was better than that. World Book, which is associated through its parent company, Field Enterprises, Inc., with such other communications media as the Chicago *Daily News* and the Chicago *Sun-Times,* was no stranger to adventurous promotions, having, for example, sustained one of Sir Edmund Hillary's expeditions to the Himalayas in search of the "Abominable Snowman." And World Book executives saw in our Loch Ness proposals another opportunity to foster science and garner good publicity. To cut a long story short, after prolonged but always friendly negotiations, an agreement between the Bureau and World Book was signed in Chicago on

May 13, 1967.

The unanswered question still was: Are there unusual, unexplained phenomena in Loch Ness? I had concluded a year earlier on the basis of Dinsdale's film sequence and anecdotal evidence that such might be the case. Now I had no additional evidence, only my first-hand experience at Loch Ness during September of 1966 and a personal acquaintance with local eyewitness observers. I was fully aware of how subjective this experience was, but I also realized that all human activities, including those labeled scientific, must begin with an observation by a human being. This was true regardless of the subject, be it the needle on a dial in a laboratory or an unknown animal in the field. In any case we intended to formulate our plans and activities based on the assumption that there was something strange at Loch Ness. Our future activities would be aimed at accumulating data which might lend support to this idea. At least in theory no amount of failure could disprove our basic assumption. However, in practice, human nature being what it is, continued and total failure would be equivalent to disproof. One would eventually become tired and discouraged, funding would be unavailable, and the effort would come to an end. While I do not recall that this eventuality was voiced by others, it certainly was conspicuous in my thinking. Of course, if further positive evidence such as a good film sequence were to be obtained, we would need to design further experiments with a view to identifying the phenomena. This was the ultimate purpose of all future activities at Loch Ness. We needed to consider every possible explanation and plan experiments to test each hypothesis. In practice this can never be done completely because of the limitations of time, money, and human resources. One, or at most a few, of the more probable hypotheses are generally pursued. In our case the most reasonable explanation for the observations in Loch Ness seemed to be animals, perhaps an unknown species. Our approach was designed to test this working hypothesis while we remained conscious of the ever-present possibility that our initial assumption might be partially or entirely wrong. We proceeded with this sequence of questions in mind:

1. Are there unusual phenomena in Loch Ness? If the answer is no, stop all activity and go home; if yes, on to the next question.

2. Are the phenomena inanimate or animate in nature? If inanimate, pack up and go home, unless the inanimate phenomena were

sufficiently unusual to warrant further attention. If animate, on to the next question.

3. What kind of animal is involved? If we obtained an answer to this last query, our investigation would be finished. We never lost sight of the fact that for some people, i.e., the doubting Thomases, the only completely satisfactory answer to this question would be an actual specimen, either living or dead. Some of the members of the Bureau, myself included, were of that persuasion, and many toasts were drunk to a carcass on the beach. Since only one such event had ever been reported and that not even at Loch Ness (but in Ireland, as described in the next chapter), the probabilities for this kind of luck were close to zero.

A realistic list of possible projects was a long one, and each activity had to be carefully considered as to time, cost, probability of success, and, most important, the kind of information it was capable of providing. The following projects were considered and many actually carried out with varying degrees of thoroughness and enthusiasm.

Baiting with traps or lines to capture a living specimen.

Dredging for animal remains.

Attempting to obtain tissue samples by means of a biopsy harpoon so that the kind of animal could be identified immunologically.

Night drifting to see if surfacing occurred more frequently at night and if so to obtain photographic film and/or a tissue sample.

Tagging the animal with a small radiotransmitter (biotelemetry). Information obtained by such a procedure might lead to identification by observing behavior and perhaps ultimate capture by permitting us to keep track of a particular specimen.

Patrolling the lake from the air with a view to clearer vertical photography.

Patrolling the lake from surface vessels for possible close-up photography.

Expanding the visual inspection and filming from stations ashore to improve our odds for a good film sequence.

Setting up a fixed sonar beam from shore to record any large objects swimming through the energy beam. This procedure might yield information as to behavior and size.

Carrying out mobile sonar searches (by means of a device fixed to the prow of a research vessel) yielding similar data as the fixed sonar procedure. The advantage over the fixed method would be exploration of a much larger volume of water.

Midget submarine employing sonar equipment, biopsy device, etc.

Skin diving to make visual and/or photographic contact with the objects in question.

Stroboscopic photography of the subsurface by a towed underwater sled which might yield a picture of animal remains.

Stroboscopic photography underwater coupled with a sonar trigger, designed to operate the camera only when a large moving object entered the sonar beam at a suitable range.

Recording an audiotape by means of hydrophones of any underwater animal sounds.

Finally, additional data-gathering projects were proposed to give us a better understanding of the animal's enviornment:

Mapping the loch's bottom and sides, including a search for anomalies.

Measuring water inflow and outflow and temperatures.

Food resources of the loch.

Other aquatic animals found in Loch Ness: a continuing attempt to catalog and study the various kinds.

Only 2 years earlier, in 1965, when we were planning our 1966 search, some of these proposals would not even have been technically feasible. However, since then the Bureau's own associates and volunteers had created technology for implementing some of the projects. Nonetheless, there was no way we could possibly staff all the projects at once. We had to choose only a few for our 1967 investigation.

As a first step, we decided to expand the photographic effort to a really adequate level, especially since David felt photography had not had a fair trial. Additional photographic equipment was purchased, including a number of 16mm Bolex hand-held cameras with 6″ lenses and a reflex camera with a 36″ lens, releasing the older headquarters camera for operation at Fort Augustus. In addition, a surface craft suitable for night drifts and stable operations on the loch, even in rough weather, was considered essential and was purchased. Other projects, requiring extra planning, were held over for 1968. The wisdom of this decision was confirmed by a spectacular success early in the year.

On June 13, 1967 the first really acceptable photographic success of the Bureau was achieved. A technically excellent film sequence was obtained of an object—a length of 7 feet was visible—moving at

5 mph, finally submerging. (See Chapter VIII, F 15, for details of this filming.) Tim Dinsdale, viewing the film a few days later, commented on the clarity of the sequence and emphasized two points: the wake characteristic was similar to the one he had filmed in 1960, and the animal appearing in both film sequences used its tail as a primary source of propulsion. Dinsdale, calling attention to the foreshortening effect caused by the large telephoto lens, suggested running a boat of known size and speed over the course taken by the filmed object and filming this run for comparison.

This photographic evidence was particularly satisfying to me, because it confirmed Dinsdale's original film, which had weighed so heavily in my decision to become involved in this problem. This kind of evidence tended not only to reinforce our assumption that something unusual was in the lake, but also that the "something" was alive. This respectable success produced a much needed boost in morale in all active LNPIB members and interested parties, including World Book executives.

As per schedule, I arrived at Loch Ness on September 8. By that time four films had been obtained, but during my tour of duty at Loch Ness, no further filming opportunities arose.

However, on September 18, John Matheson, a local technical engineer from Fort Augustus, reported a sighting. Matheson lived in Fort Augustus at the southwest end of Loch Ness. One would not expect him—forthright, respected, totally familiar with the lake—to be deceived. And yet I believe he was deceived—by that most persistently confusing natural effect resulting from the peculiar shore structure of the loch, the standing wave.

When a boat passes through Loch Ness, it develops a bow wave that trails behind in the customary long "V." When this wave strikes the rocky shores, two waves are reflected back to the center, one from each bank, reversing the "V." It takes quite some time for the reflected waves to return to the center of the mile-wide lake. When they do, one reflected from each shore, the result is a standing wave—a line of turbulence that continues to be drawn in the direction the boat is traveling, though by now so far behind the boat that caused it as not to be associated with the boat at all. A similar effect is produced close inshore when the shore-reflected bow wave interacts with the incoming stern wave, produced by the stern of a large boat. The progress of these reflected lines of turbulence is fairly continuous and

looks for all the world like the disturbance caused by a partially submerged creature swimming in a straight line.

The standing wave is the most ubiquitous of all the Loch Ness mirages. Quite early, the Bureau began keeping a record of any and all
boats passing through the lake, so as more readily to discount sightings that were really reports of the standing waves.

In contrast to Matheson's report was that of John Cameron, 61,
and for many years head lock keeper at Fort Augustus, where Loch
Ness ends and the canal to Loch Oich begins. John had spent his entire adult life, 40 years, in attendance at Loch Ness, including his
share of that time salmon fishing on its surface. In those four decades,
he said, he had never seen anything unusual entering or leaving the
locks, and nothing he would definitely label as the "monster" in Loch
Ness itself. Until this incident he simply did not believe large, unknown animals existed in the lake, on the grounds that if he had not
seen one in 40 years, they simply were not there to see.

Such a man would certainly have experienced all the curious effects
of sun, wind, light and shade, and turbulent water that contributed
to erroneous "monster" reports. Neither was he rushing forward, eager to tell his story. He was a shy, earnest, sincere man.

His story concerned a fishing expedition he had made six months
earlier. There was a strong wind with 3-foot waves on the loch, so that
he was more or less occupied with keeping his fishing gear in trim.
Suddenly he saw, no more than 35 yards away, a brownish "back"
cleaving the waves. More of the animal became visible when it passed
through a wave trough. He noted a "mane" beginning at a place on
the back that he called the "shoulder." The creature continued back-
ward, without interruption, into the water. He saw nothing suggesting
a possible head or neck.

During the sighting, a salmon struck his line; when he turned back,
the object was lost to view.

Clearly his proximity (about 100 feet—and lock keepers would
know something of distances and dimensions) was responsible for the
details of his observation. And crediting his 40 years on the water, I
surmised that he would not mistake a floating object, say, a log, for
an animal.

What he described was within the realm of zoological possibility.
The "mane" could surely be a continuous dorsal fin or similar structure, but Cameron rejected the notion that what he had seen was any

of the known animals in the loch with which he was familiar. So did I, though as yet I could offer no solution.

The remainder of my stay at Loch Ness was uneventful. I concerned myself with visiting and interviewing other locals and going over written sighting reports. Both the quality and thoroughness of the photographic surveillance of the Loch's surface were much improved in 1967, mainly as a consequence of the financial support provided by Field Enterprises.

My evaluation of the 1967 Loch Ness investigation was as follows: A group of phenomena are present that, in the mind of the general public, are popularly known as the "Loch Ness monster." A large number of sightings involve a combination of animate and inanimate artifacts, and there is clearly a strong psychological bias to see the unusual. However, there appears to be a substantial number of phenomena that cannot be explained in these terms. On the basis of evidence so far accumulated, a group of living creatures is the most probable explanation.

* * *

Although photographic surveillance of the loch's surface continued the next year, 1968 was the year of new approaches—especially the use of sonar.

Our sonar source was one of the world's leading developers and experts on sonar devices, Professor D. G. Tucker, chairman of the Department of Electronic and Electrical Engineering at the University of Birmingham, England. Tucker was planning a 1968 spring test at Loch Ness of a new kind of sector-scanning sonar with a range of 600-800 meters (650-875 yards). David had earlier requested Tucker's help at Loch Ness, proposing a sonar gate. While Tucker thought David's suggestion of using transit sonar to provide an acoustic screen was feasible, he wondered whether a non-scanning sonar could possibly give enough information to identify anything that might be detected. The two men met and worked out a collaborative effort. LNPIB would supply manpower (one or two persons), some funds, and film stock. (Since constant human surveillance of the sonar oscilloscope screen would be prohibitively tedious and expensive, a 16mm movie camera would instead photograph the oscilloscope display at 10-second intervals; thus, a permanent record would be obtained, and very little, if anything, would be missed.) The sonar equipment would be furnished by the university. Tucker suggested that their new digital sonar, different in its electronic principles from other existing sonar types, be tried simultaneously with an older kind, so that comparison of results and experience could be made. He summarized the plan:

The Department of Electronic and Electrical Engineering at the University of Birmingham has a long experience of sonar research, and among other sophisticated sonar devices has two of particular relevance to the Loch Ness investigation. These are both instruments, which, for every sonar pulse transmitted, plot on a cathode-ray tube the range and bearing of echoing objects within the sector under observation. One instrument [the older one] virtually swings a narrow receiving beam over a wide insonified sector 10,000 times per second. The other [more recent] uses microelectronic digital circuitry to give essentially the same result but without forming beams, rather by analyzing [by means of a small and cheap on-line computer] the sound field at the receiver. Since the object being looked for is large, there is a chance of its shape being roughly portrayed by the sonar, especially if it comes within a few hundred feet of the sonar equipment.

The Department has agreed to assist the investigation because it feels that in the search for a creature which spends nearly all its time wholly submerged, a means of underwater observation can be expected to add materially to the data available.

April field trials were successfully completed, paving the way for a 2-week sonar search during August. As it turned out, these sonar searches were the most successful and worthwhile experiments of the entire 1968 effort. The results (See Chapter IX and Appendix E.) were so important that I was anxious to discuss them with Tucker personally during my second 1968 visit to Loch Ness. In the fall we went over all of the results, which were very exciting indeed. Briefly, they had tracked an object several yards in length diving rapidly, and had tracked what was presumably a group of these objects diving to and fro from the bottom of the loch. In one swoop the range of possible animals was greatly reduced. The diving profiles indicated non-air breathers, which reduced the list of possible candidates markedly. All kinds of fish with closed swim bladders were also eliminated since these animals would not be able to make such rapid depth changes. This breakthrough was very strong support for the animal hypothesis.

It was agreed that nothing should be publicly released until a scientific paper had been published in a scientific journal. The plan was to publish in *Nature* and hold a joint press conference in London, including David, Tucker, and me, as soon as *Nature* came off the press. By November 8, I had a preliminary copy of Tucker's proposed paper, which I found excellent. He was conservative in his interpretation and did not go beyond the evidence. At this point, the first setback, albeit temporary, occurred. Although having earlier accepted the Tucker paper for publication, the editors of *Nature* at the last minute refused to publish it. The decision took me by surprise even though I was well aware that anything associated with the "Loch Ness monster" was regarded as not respectable by many in the international scientific community. This setback produced considerable delay. However, the *New Scientist* published the paper, "Sonar Picks Up Stirrings in Loch Ness," in its December 19, 1968 issue.

Plans for the joint press conference aborted because of a news leak about Tucker's paper. All we could do was hold immediate, separate press conferences on December 18, the day before publication, to explain what the results really meant. Reactions were mixed, ranging from casual dismissal as ridiculous to such strong statements as "existence of Loch Ness monster proved beyond a shadow of a doubt."

Nature, which for its own inscrutable reasons had refused to publish Tucker's results, printed in its December 28, 1968 issue an unsigned editorial, "Monsters by Sonar." Aside from the polemical content of the piece, reminiscent of 19th-century rhetoric against Darwin's theory of evolution, it stated that Tucker's sonar gear had been tested by the Fisheries Laboratory at Lowestoft and found to be prone to ambiguities, whereas in fact Tucker's digital sonar had at that time never been anywhere near the Fisheries Laboratory, much less tested there; the test referred to by *Nature* involved another, completely different, earlier sonar unit. The article closed on the note that Tucker and his assistant Hugh Braithwaite (leaders in the sonar field, with the highest scientific and academic credentials) were not to be taken seriously.

An admirable defense of Tucker was provided by a letter to the editor from Dr. Peter F. Baker of Emmanuel College, Cambridge, and published in *Nature*, January 11, 1969.

The sonar work actually took only two weeks in August, but we were busy in other areas in 1968. For a start I had worked on and designed a biopsy (tissue sampling) plan. The biopsy cutting head

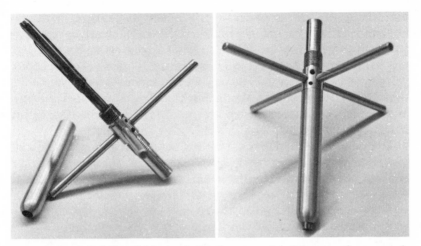

Illus. 1 Author-designed biopsy device for removing 2-3 gram tissue sample from large animal. *James Gregorio photo.*

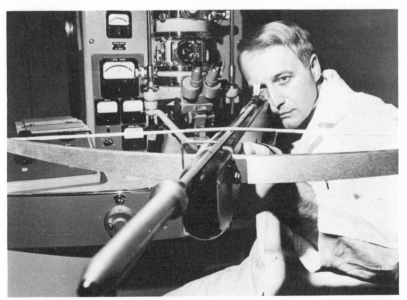

Illus. 2 Author in his laboratory holding a crossbow with a bolt tipped with a modified biopsy device. A crossbow, less powerful than a Greener harpoon gun, does not require the large right-angled stops (as shown in Illus. 1) used to prevent excessive penetration. *Courtesy World Book Encyclopedia.*

I developed and tested was attached to crossbow arrows and to the head of a Greener harpoon gun. Then there was the little matter of success—and what to do with it. While our greatest concern was improving our chances of obtaining a tissue sample, we also had to be prepared in the event of being successful. No special preparations were required for histological and biochemical studies of tissue. However, I wanted to have suitable antisera on hand for serological and immunological studies.[1]

In case we were able to procure a sample, I arranged to obtain antisera of the main groups of animals that might be related to the animals in Loch Ness, and by the time I left for Europe I had access to the following list of animal groups: Sirenia, Pinnipedia, Cetacea, Apodes, Amphibia, Reptilia, Mollusca.

When David and I arrived at customs at the London airport, both of us looked like pack horses, loaded down with so much gear. The inspector was very businesslike in going through our effects. Suddenly he came to our crossbows, the arrows of which were fitted with the rather strange looking biopsy devices. To the customs official's query as to what these might be, David answered, "These are to get a sample of the Loch Ness monster." The official said not a word, passing next to David's electronic fish finder, asking again what this might be. David: "This is to *find* the Loch Ness monster." Again, no

---

[1] Higher animals have the ability to protect themselves against invasions of pathogenic microorganisms by the production of antibodies. When any material containing a foreign protein, such as viruses or bacteria, is introduced into the bloodstream, chemical substances (also proteins) appear in the bloodstream. These substances or antibodies can react with, neutralize, or kill substances (if alive) of the same kind that induced the formation of the particular antibody. Experimentally, this protective mechanism can be used to obtain information bearing on the similarity or dissimilarity between different species of animals. If one injects mouse blood or tissue into the bloodstream of a rabbit, antibodies against mouse tissues would form in the rabbit. If one later takes some of the rabbit's blood, removes the blood cells, leaving only the serum, and adds mouse serum, an "immune reaction" would be observed as a precipitate. If serum from a frog is added, no precipitate will form, showing that the frog (an amphibian) is not closely related. If, however, hamster serum were added, only slightly less precipitate would form, showing that hamsters are close relatives of mice. Generally the less closely related the animal serum to be tested is, the less the precipitate; conversely, the serum from the animal that is most closely related will produce the most precipitate.

change of expression or comment from the official. He then picked up my case labeled "Greener Harpoon Gun." Taking up David's cue, I said "To shoot the Loch Ness monster with." The official's facial muscles twitched, then he waved us through the gate, arms gesticulating, shaking his head and muttering unintelligibly.

After this stunning reception, I appeared on a most unsatisfactory BBC-TV program on "The Loch Ness Monster." After that, I left for Scotland. I was anxious to begin the planned night drifting activities. We had plenty of volunteers, and I spent a number of days instructing and practicing with the biopsy crossbows and biopsy harpoon. Enthusiasm was very great, but the effective range was only about 80 feet. The drop of the dart was about 12-14 inches at this range, resulting mainly from the drag engendered by the attached line; if aimed at the upper edge of a silhouette, the drop would place the projectile in a suitable position in the target.

We decided on crews of three, requiring at least this number to carry the equipment up and down the 180-foot height between the surface of the loch and our headquarters installation. The equipment consisted of crossbows and harpoon gun, two car storage batteries (for powering the silent electric trolling motor), life preservers, portable lights, flash cameras, and a supply of rum. This latter was a most necessary item since the nights on the loch's surface were often bitterly cold, and remaining adrift was made bearable only by an infusion—one swallow—of rum every half hour or so.

Unfortunately, nothing much was discovered, although the drifts were continued after I left the loch.

At least World Book was pleased with the overall success of the sonar effort, realizing that in probing the unknown, not all approaches can be expected to yield results. By the end of October they had agreed in principle to provide further funds, and a new contract was prepared and presented to us for consideration on November 15, 1968.

New developments were in the offing, even before the new contract with World Book was signed, however. On November 1, I received a phone call from Nixon Griffis, one of the directors of the New York Aquarium, regarding cooperation with us in a mobile sonar search to be based on a proposal by Robert Love and paid for in large part by the Griffis Foundation. We were of course most anxious to cooperate. By the end of November, a feasibility study prepared by Bob Love was in our hands. Both David and I were greatly impressed by the thoroughness with which the project had been worked out; this marked the beginning of my own and the Bureau's invaluable and continuing relationship with Bob.

David pursued the possibility of mounting a suitable dredging project in 1969, since this idea had to be shelved temporarily in 1968; by December he had interested Dr. N. B. Marshall of the Natural History Museum in London in the project and hoped that Marshall might actually be prevailed upon to take charge of the dredging operation. The British Natural History Museum had always been decidedly aloof about Loch Ness, and now it seemed that interest had finally developed in that quarter.

Thus the progress in 1968 was most gratifying, especially the highly successful sonar probes carried out by Tucker and colleagues. The year's activities were briefly summed up for the press as follows:

> The solution to the question of whether or not unusual phenomena exist in Loch Ness, Scotland, and if so, what their nature might be, was advanced a step forward during 1968, as a result of sonar experiments conducted by a team of scientists under the direction of D. Gordon Tucker. . . .
>
> Professor Tucker reported that his fixed beam sonar made contact with large moving objects sometimes reaching speeds of at least 10 knots. He concluded that the objects are clearly animals and ruled out the possibility that they could be ordinary fish. He stated: "The high rate of ascent and descent makes it seem very unlikely [that they could be fish], and fishery biologists we have consulted cannot suggest what fish they might be. It is a temptation to suppose they might be the fabulous Loch Ness monsters, now observed for the first time in their underwater activities!"

Even these data were still quite inadequate to decide the matter. A great deal of further investigation with more refined equipment was needed before definite conclusions could be drawn.

III
Ireland 1968

Captain Lionel A. D. Leslie, whom I visited on the Island of Mull in 1965, was a member of the LNPIB. However, Lionel was most keenly interested in Loch Ness-like phenomena along the west coast of Ireland in the Galway region of Connemara. He spent the three years before 1968 investigating and checking data and observers there, and he had established that observations of unusual unidentified aquatic animals had been reported from quite a number of Irish lakes (loughs) in that area. The list includes Loughs Shanakeever, Auna, Gowlan, Derrylea, Glenda, Nahillion, Waskel, Ree, Mask, Derg, Fadda, Neagh, Nahooin, Kylemore, Abisdealy, Claddaghduff, and Glendalough.

One of the most interesting reports, which was made also to the Irish Fisheries Board, had been made by Rev. Richard Quigley. Father Quigley stated that on May 18, 1960, at about 9:30 P.M., he and two other priests were sitting quietly in a rowboat on Lough Ree some 50 to 60 yards offshore from St. Mark's Wood on the east of the Leinster side of the lake, waiting for the expected evening rise of trout. Visibility was excellent, and the lake surface was a flat, calm mirror. One of the priests spotted an object moving slowly on the surface, about 80 to 100 yards away. Two parts of the object were visible simultaneously, a forward section of uniform girth, stretching quite straight out of the water, and inclined to the plane of the surface at about a 30° angle, in length 1½ to 2 feet with a diameter of about 4 inches. The extremity tapered rather abruptly, like a serpent's head. Between the leading and the following section of this creature, there was about two feet of water. Then a portion like a loop or hump about 1½ feet high at the water line followed. The object was seen in silhouette, so no color could be determined. The object was observed for about two or three minutes as it moved in a northeasterly

37

direction toward the shore. Then it submerged gradually, rather than in an abrupt dive, and disappeared from view completely. A few minutes later, it reappeared, moving quite leisurely to the surface, showing the same two parts of its body in the same attitude, and continued to move in the same direction at the same slow speed, perhaps one mile per hour. It maintained its heading for about two minutes more until it reached a point about 30 yards from shore, where it submerged and was seen no more.

A second observation reported a serpent-shaped creature swimming with its body projecting in two sections above the surface of the water. This sighting was made at a greater distance, and the overall impression of size was somewhat greater than in the first observation. Lough Ree, the center lake of three great Shannon lakes, where these episodes took place, is an irregularly shaped lake, perhaps 17 miles in length. It is a limestone lake, rich in aquatic life, and has a maximum depth of 120 feet.

Further detailed descriptions of observations would be tedious; rather, I will give brief summaries of additional observations that influenced my thinking and my conclusions about the Irish phenomena. These descriptions will round out the picture as to the character of the phenomena for later comparison with those at Loch Ness.

Teige O'Donovan reported observations going back as far as 1914 from Lough Abisdealy, which translates from the ancient Irish to "The Lake of the Monster." A man, driving home in his horse-drawn cart very late one moonlit night along the lakeside, suddenly saw in front of him a huge creature like an eel crawling out of the lake. Men who lived near the lake said there was an eel in it "the size of a man's thigh." Another group of observers saw a strange creature swimming rapidly down the center of the lake. It had a small flat head and a long neck, with three large loops sticking out of the water. The object appeared dark brown in color and was estimated to be 25 feet in length overall. There is another report from this lake of an object swinging part of its body out of the water in a 2-foot arc; this portion was dark brown in color, looking exactly like the tail end of a huge conger eel. Lough Abisdealy is about one mile long by ¼-mile wide and about 2 miles from the sea.

At Lough Fadda, Georgina Carberry saw a black object moving slowly toward her and her three friends at a distance of 150-200 yards, approaching to within 20 yards and then submerging. She described a black skin color, head-neck region about 3 feet long, sticking out of the water, humps about 2 feet, with an overall length estimate of 6-8 feet. This observation occurred in 1953 or 1954 on a June evening. Lough Fadda is about 2½ miles long by 1 mile wide, 29 feet above sea level, unsurveyed, shallow in parts with some deep holes. Divers report a muddy bottom at depths of 32 feet, rocky bottom in some spots with clear water.

Lionel, impressed with Carberry as a witness, decided in 1965 to try an experiment. At the point on the west side of Lough Fadda where she had her experiences, 7 pounds of gelignite were detonated among the rocks on the shore. About 10 seconds after the blast, at a distance of 50 yards, something violently broke the surface of the lake. However, no clear impression of the object was obtained. A tantalizing but inconclusive result.

Michael Coyne reported that in about 1956 he saw in Lough Claddaghduff what he thought at first to be a bullock swimming. Upon closer observation, he saw it was an eel-like creature with at least 10 feet showing as it turned over, displaying a white underside.

Loughs Gowlan and Derrylea are connected by a gully about 100 yards in length. Many residents in the area state that about 80 years ago an eel-like creature got stuck in this gully, died, and was left to decay. When David and I checked the area, we found an ancient-looking culvert and supposed that this was what probably had trapped the creature. If this is true, the animal must have been at least 18 inches in diameter, based on measurement of the culvert.

Finally, fishermen from Lough Neagh reported that in 1956 their net was damaged by a "thing like a giant eel."

Although Lionel has collected quite a number of additional reports, these representative accounts should suffice to give a general impression of the Irish situation as it stood in December 1967.

Our experience of 1965-1967 emphasized for us the formidable difficulties at Loch Ness in terms of its size alone, so that both David and I looked with longing at the relatively small lakes in Ireland where the chances of taking a specimen, dead or alive, were far better. In due course these considerations were made known to Field Enterprises, and in December 1967 they agreed to support an Irish expedition, if two conditions were met: first, there would be no sacrifice of attention to Loch Ness since a considerable amount of time, money, and effort had already been expended there; second, specific plans for a particular enterprise with some semblance of scientific-mechanical sense must be developed.

We decided on Loughs Auna and Shanakeever. Lough Auna is a glacial lake about one mile long with an uncharted depth, secluded and unfrequented, except by occasional fishermen. Lionel indicated that sighting reports in the lough dated back 30 years and described a creature 15 feet in length, similar in appearance to the Lough Fadda specimen. A trap, constructed on eel-trap principles, was to be lowered into the lake, baited with fish offal and small eels. The trap was to be maintained for the summer season, being raised and rebaited periodically.

Lough Shanakeever is also a small, bottle-shaped lake, connected with Lough Auna (1 mile away) and by a stream to the sea (3 miles distant). The depth was uncharted (it turned out to be not much more than 15 feet). A small creature, similar in description to the ones observed in Loughs Auna and Fadda, had been reported during the last 4 years during the summer periods. Lionel proposed to stretch a net across the narrow portion of the lake, and by making disturbances underwater attempt to drive the alleged animal into the net opening. Cine cameras would also be mounted at suitable locations to photograph any interesting activity. David also procured an electronic fishing device, the Cybertronic MK 12 Electro Fisher. My contribution to preparations consisted of my Greener harpoon gun, which fired a 1-pound harpoon attached to 100 feet of 1,000-pound test line. This device is ideally suited for taking a moderate-size aquatic animal and is routinely used to take sharks up to 10 or 12 feet in length; however, it can be easily modified for harmlessly getting a tissue sample.

Since both David and Lionel had gained the impression from the locals that the so-called horse eels burrowed into the mud at times and were assumed to spend periods of time in a dormant state, David suggested that it might be wise to obtain permission to set off small seismic charges of gelignite to stir things up a bit. Lionel obliged by arranging with the manager of Clyden marble quarry to execute suitable detonations when called for. At the same time the necessary netting permits and a firearms certificate for the harpoon gun were obtained.

Joining us for the Ireland expedition were Howard Phalin, chief executive officer at World Book, and Dick Lewis, the Chicago *Sun-*

Times science reporter who had done a masterful job of covering events at Loch Ness the previous year.

At the last minute, we altered our plans and went to Lough Nahooin because of a new sighting there. An inspection of the lough was the first order of business. I unpacked my harpoon gear, checked my supply of .38 caliber ammunition, and joined David, Dick, and Howard for our trek to the lake. We were in a remote part of Ireland, but in spite of the poor condition of the few roads that were available, we were able to negotiate part of the distance by car. The final leg of the journey was made on foot through peat bogs. The lake itself was a small body of water, about 250 yards long by 150 yards wide. Across the center were stretched brightly colored buoys supporting a net stretched straight across the lake, dividing it into two compartments. I experienced a sinking feeling as I contemplated this small body of water; not even one substantial animal could have more than a transient relation with this little pond, even if one assumed a maximum of possible food sources. I could only assume that the animals were at least partially amphibious and could move from one lake to another, especially during the wet season when small streams become rivers and dried-up gullies become streams.

Still, we were here and we decided to continue the program. However, we soon grew disillusioned. David's electric fish finder proved of no value and we saw nothing. We then took to exploring the area on foot, and to talking with the generally shy local inhabitants. Finally, we posted a notice offering a reward. With no more success than before, we broke up.

David and I left for London to appear on the BBC. We were quite discouraged. Our Irish expedition, which had used up valuable funds, had established nothing helpful, except more anecdotal evidence. Still, investigation continued there for several more years. It confirmed our worst fears: if it was so difficult to catch something in the dinky Irish lakes, it was going to be even more difficult than we had expected to work Loch Ness.

IV
Science and Submarines
1969

The rather spectacular success of the Tucker-Birmingham sonar experiments assured the continued funding and participation of World Book. The question was: What direction should we take for 1969? The projects discussed included use of three submarines, a small one-man submarine privately built by Dan Taylor, the *Deep Star III* submarine built by General Dynamics, and a 2-man submarine built by Westinghouse; three sonar experiments, including a repeat performance by the Tucker-Birmingham team, Bob Love's mobile sonar search, and a sonar effort under sponsorship of the British Independent Television News (ITN), involving Plessey Ltd. Ocean Systems, Inc. suggested the use of acoustic disturbances in the depths of Loch Ness designed to stimulate surfacing. The idea did not appeal to us, but an unconfirmed rumor was that *Life* magazine had recently requested from Ocean Systems a cost estimate for a thorough search. The estimate of $500,000 minimum was presumably too steep for *Life*, since nothing ever developed. ITN also planned to bring into Loch Ness an offshore mine sweeper equipped with sonar, radar, and underwater cameras. A captive balloon, from which vertical photographic coverage could be obtained was to be moored over the center of the loch.

David planned to continue photographic surface surveillance and the night drift program and to carry out the long-talked-about dredging and longlining project as well as to give support to Tim Dinsdale's personal effort, whimsically labeled "Water Kelpie."

Each project was carefully analyzed with respect to chances of success, which was set as being the acquisition of "hard evidence"—an actual tissue sample. Visual observation, still and motion picture photography, and sonar devices naturally could not produce tissue samples. Dredging and surface surveillance by boats carrying biopsy

Illus. 1 Submarine *Viperfish*, Dan Taylor (left), Harry Ruecking (World Book executive), and author (standing). *Courtesy World Book Encyclopedia.*

Illus. 2 Dan Taylor preparing for a dive with the *Viperfish* in Urquhart Bay at Loch Ness. *Stuart Markson photo. Courtesy LNIB/World Book.*

Illus. 3 Underwater photo of *Viperfish* showing twin biopsy harpoons ready for firing. *Robert Love photo. Courtesy LNIB/World Book Encyclopedia.*

devices offered little chance of success. That left submersibles. All the evidence suggested their use. Estimates of probability of success ranged from low to good, depending on the animal's behavior. Ultimately World Book and the Bureau agreed on this approach. As we narrowed the choice, the following submarine activities were debated intensely:

1. General underwater investigation and exploration of Loch Ness.
2. Search of the bottom for evidence of large animal remains.
3. Search of the loch with a submarine-mounted sonar to approach any large target for identification and/or tissue sampling.
4. Attempt to obtain a tissue sample and identify a large target located either by land-based or water-based external sonar.

While we worked up our plans, we also selected the Dan Taylor craft as the most adaptable to our purposes. Dan set to work to rebuild his submarine with the special problems of operating in Loch Ness in mind. Sonar was a must, as were biopsy devices to collect tissue samples in the event that one of the animals could be approached. Everyone recognized that approach depended entirely on the behavior of the animals. No small submarine could be designed to equal 10-12 knots, at least not within budgets available to us, and if the animals took off at high speed there was no way the sub could catch them. On the other hand, I pointed out to Dan, these animals had lived in Loch Ness a long time free of danger from predators and therefore would be unlikely to be fearful. Also, as is the case with some aquatic animals, such as sharks, they might be curious and approach the submarine quite closely. We ardently hoped that such would be the case.

I designed a modification of my biopsy harpoon, and two harpoons, powered by compressed air, were mounted on the upper part of the bow of Dan's submarine. After tests and further modifications, the harpoons (with an underwater range of 10-15 feet) were passed as acceptable to the team.

World Book and LNPIB originally planned to have Dan's submarine in Scotland and operational sometime in August. However, ITN's schedule and available shipping dates made it necessary that Dan get his submarine to Loch Ness by June 1. As a result, Dan began working night and day. Even then, he could not get ready in time, and the submarine had to be taken to Scotland in an incomplete state and, of course, without having undergone any preliminary field trials.

Innumerable difficulties seemed to arise at every point, not the least
of which was the problem of an export license for the submarine and
guarantees relative to its return. However, through the efforts and
good offices of World Book, these problems were solved one by one,
and by June 1 Dan and his submarine were at Loch Ness, accompanied by unprecedented publicity. As a result, both Dan and I were
swamped with stamped envelopes from philatelists who wanted us to
inscribe the letters and carry them on the first dive the *Viperfish*, as
Dan named his vehicle, might make.

The project was so widely discussed, debated, commended, and/or
condemned, as the case may be, that it finally attracted the attention
of the House of Lords, where it was duly debated. The debate struck
a high comic note at times, as when Lord Blyton protested, "My
Lords, is my noble friend aware that it will be an act of sacrilege to
take away from the Scottish Tourist Board the myth of the monster
of Loch Ness by which they get many gullible tourists each year?"

Lord Hughes answered, "I do not know on what scientific grounds
my noble friend says that the monster is a myth."

It had been made clear that the expedition hoped to secure a tissue
sample. This prompted Lord Hawke to say, "My Lords, how would
the noble [Lord Hughes] like to be 'potted' by an airgun to take samples of his tissue?"

Lord Hughes replied, "My Lords, provided that the relevant part
of my tissue was no greater than the small amount, in proportion,
that was taken from the bulk of the whale, I doubt whether I should
notice it."

The debate also had a serious side, and it illustrates the official
ambivalence that surrounds Loch Ness and its phenomena: an attitude that regards the phenomenon as a myth in one context and as
reality in another. At least some of the noble lords found it possible
to embrace both views at one and the same time. In any case, the defense of our biopsy program by Lord Hughes was successful, and Dan
and the Bureau were permitted to go about their business.

August was the period when maximum effort would be mounted
at the loch, and I arrived the first week in the month. The immediate
problems involved getting the *Viperfish* ready. For one of the earlier test dives, it was decided that I would man the surface control,
including hydrophone communication with Dan. This was a never-
to-be-forgotten experience; at one point it appeared that we had lost

Dan and his submarine in the depths of Urquhart Bay. His dive had been postponed for several days because of last-minute operational difficulties or poor weather. Finally, however, the day dawned sunny and flat calm, with good weather prospects for the rest of the day, and the *Viperfish* was deemed ready. Dan and his craft, after taking on a suitable charge of compressed air in his reservoirs, were towed out to a point 300 feet deep in Urquhart Bay. (We had decided to save his batteries for the more important underwater propulsion, using a surface craft for positioning the submarine at a suitable location. The same procedure was employed even by the much more sophisticated Vickers submersible, *Pisces*.)

Cameras at the ready, Dan closed down the hatch preparing to dive. When communications checked out as satisfactory, he went down nose first. Voice communications continued more than adequate, Dan relaying each operational move as he made it. Suddenly, however, there was complete silence; for the next 20 minutes there was not a sound from Dan. I worked frantically to reestablish communication, but as the minutes ticked by, the thought that we would never see Dan alive at the surface became more and more obtrusive.

Of slight comfort was the fact that a safety device, the Acoustic Locater System, loaned by the Dukane Corporation, had been installed on Dan's sub. The device provided a means of surface tracking the submarine when it was submerged, and in the event of a submarine accident, it gave an indication at the surface of a flooded condition and a means of accurately locating the disabled vessel at any time within a period of 30 days thereafter. The thought that at least we would know where Dan ended his career was not much consolation.

We had just about given up hope, when the submarine shot up and surfaced like a cork popped from a bottle. Diving precipitously, Dan had buried the nose of the submarine in the silt of the bottom, effectively blocking the hydrophone transducer in the mud. After unsuccessfully trying to back the vehicle out of the mud with reverse propeller, he finally blew ballast, making the sub so buoyant that it partially leaped from the water like a flying fish. Dan, fortunately, was no worse for the experience.

Most of Dan's other dives were more routine, although very few trouble-free dives were made; Loch Ness was indeed a formidable and treacherous body of water. No positive results were obtained by this experiment, in spite of Dan's brave and daring excursions below the dark surface of Loch Ness. Apparently the animals were not curious about the strange yellow visitor intruding into their domain.

Of the other submarines, the *Deep Star III* and the Westinghouse submersible were never deployed in Loch Ness. A fourth submarine, the *Pisces* (six-man capacity, owned by Vickers, Ltd.), was operated in the loch and produced some exciting results. It had been brought into Loch Ness for reasons other than monster hunting. A film about Sherlock Holmes and the Loch Ness monster was being made, and the submarine was used in making this film. In addition, Vickers regarded this excursion as an excellent opportunity for field trials, and although it was never officially acknowledged, there was interest in the Loch Ness phenomena among crew and some Vickers executives who were fully aware of what Loch Ness allegedly contained. This permitted the field trials to serve a dual purpose.

Early in the filming of the movie, the artificial monster broke loose from its towing cable and sank irretrievably to the bottom, ensuring that everyone knew the remains of at least one monster were most certainly on the floor of Loch Ness. With the demise of the artificial monster, the *Pisces* was free to probe the depths of the loch to see what might be lurking there.

Illus. 4 Submarine *Pisces* about to be lowered into Loch Ness by crane. *Courtesy World Book Encyclopedia.*

During one cruise, the *Pisces* sonar contacted a large moving target about 50 feet above the loch bottom some 200 yards off. Pisces moved forward cautiously, reducing the distance by 100 yards. A few feet closer the target began to recede, moving off and rapidly leaving the *Pisces* and its sonar beam. It was a near miss and very disappointing. A close-up view by such an experienced crew might have answered the 1,400-year-old question about the identity of the large animals in Loch Ness.

However, the fact that submarine-mounted sonar had also contacted a large moving object was still extremely important from a scientific point of view. One of the basic considerations in scientific experimentation is that the results be reproducible by different investigators. Just as the Bureau film obtained early in 1967 corroborated the Dinsdale film, this sonar contact reinforced the Birmingham sonar results.

Several fish including eels were observed, especially in the bay areas. However, nothing was seen that could account for this sonar contact.

Otherwise, we had not much success to report. Ken Peterson of Walt Disney Productions shot a 90-minute documentary (eventually it was cut to a 20-minute educational film) under an agreement with the Bureau and World Book involving a substantial cash contribution to LNPIB.

The grandiose ITN scheme which involved the use of a minesweeper, produced nothing whatsoever in the way of positive evidence. During the initial phases of planning and discussion, cooperation among everyone concerned was excellent. However, as the project progressed, a go-it-alone attitude seemed to develop, and I was particularly concerned that the project as finally executed took practically no account of possible zoological factors.

David had anticipated that the latter part of the season would be filled with so many experiments that any dredging to be done should be initiated early in the season. At the end of 1968 it seemed likely that Freddy Marshall, a scientist of high reputation, would take command of the dredging project. However, to everyone's disappointment he found it impossible to participate. In the circumstances David decided to go ahead with the experiment but to concentrate on trawling and attempting to hook relatively large animals on so-called longlines, lines some 1,800 feet in length, to which at regular intervals various sizes of hooks were attached by means of shorter lines attached to the longlines. To carry out the project the 49-foot drifter *Penorva* was chartered in early May. The results were disappointing. Although some channel wall and bottom topography was charted, the longlines and trawls themselves produced nothing significant, although three hooks were torn off the long lines and a few trout were hooked. Extensive dredging in various depths of silt was never carried out.

The Loch Ness efforts kept us very busy, but not so busy that we were not highly intrigued when we heard of a new incident at Loch Morar, some 70 miles to the southwest of Loch Ness. From this loch, phenomena identical to those in Loch Ness have been regularly reported, and on August 18, the Bureau headquarters at Achnahannet received a call from Mallaig, near Loch Morar. Although the information was confused, its essence was that two fishermen had rammed a large unidentified animal in Loch Morar. We decided to pay an immediate visit to the two fishermen to obtain first-hand information— and, we hoped, the first hard evidence, a tissue sample possibly still adhering to the hull of their craft.

After a recklessly fast drive to Morar from Loch Ness, we soon learned that we were probably too late. The encounter had actually occurred on August 16, so that when we arrived, the boat had been in the water 48 hours after the contact, making the possibility of tissues adhering to the hull rather remote. Duncan McDonell, one of the two fishermen involved, was away, but the other, William Simpson, described what actually happened.

Duncan and William had been out fishing that day on Loch Morar in an 18-foot cabin cruiser. As they were returning at about 15 mph to Morar village, their craft rammed a large animal that apparently surfaced nearby. The collision, though only a glancing blow, was violent enough to spill water out of the heating water kettle, extinguishing the gas flame. While Duncan was engaged with the animal above deck, William was below deck frantically trying to shut off the gas supply to the burner. Duncan first attempted to push the boat away from the animal with one of the boat's oars, but it was somewhat rotten and broke. After succeeding in turning off the gas, William rushed above deck just in time to see the animal submerge as Duncan fired a rifle in its general direction.

Contrary to the wild press stories—stories of a battle with a "60-foot monster" circulated—the portion of the animal observed at the

surface was definitely less than the length of the boat. Simpson estimated the animal at 6 to 7 feet in diameter at the thickest part of the
body. He described the color as "dirty brown" with a flecked surface
like coke. When I asked him what animal in his experience most resembled what he saw, he answered, "A monkfish." Monkfish, also
called angel fish, are a familiar sight around Mallaig. They are taken
in great numbers and are discarded as junk fish. The fish reaches
lengths up to 7-8 feet, belongs to the group including sharks and rays,
and is considered to be a transitional form or link between the sharks
and the rays. Simpson, of course, was not saying that the animal was
a giant monkfish, only that this was the best comparison he could
make on the basis of his limited zoological knowledge.

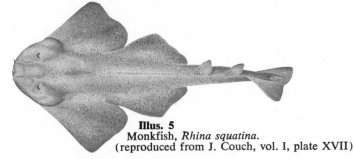

Illus. 5
Monkfish, *Rhina squatina.*
(reproduced from J. Couch, vol. I, plate XVII)

Unfortunately, the hull of the boat was very smooth, and no trace
of organic material was evident at the point of impact, which was
marked by scratches and missing paint.

All in all, the Morar incident was interesting but disappointing,
especially since by the end of August it was clear that no other successes were coming our way. Left were the two submarines, *Viperfish*
and *Pisces*, and Bob Love with his mobile sonar probe which was
just becoming operational.

Fortunately, Bob Love's period of operation extended well beyond
August, or the most sophisticated and extensive investigation of Loch
Ness would have (with the exception of the *Pisces* sonar contact)
drawn a complete blank. Love's detailed plan of action for a mobile
sonar search using Honeywell equipment, jointly supported by the
Griffis Foundation and World Book, was exceptionally well conceived. Bob had spent three weeks during early summer at Loch
Ness making a preliminary survey, including an examination of the
channel wall and bottom topography, temperature and light absorp-

tion measurements at various depths, bottom sampling, and general limnological observations of surface conditions of the loch. This kind of preliminary work was characteristic of Bob's professional approach, invaluable under any circumstances.

In October, Bob made contact with a large, moving object at a point slightly over a mile northeast of Foyers at a range of 500 yards. While movie cameras whirred, automatically recording time, the spots on the oscilloscope screen, and other data, Bob had frantically switched to manual control, so that he could hold the sonar beam on the target as long as possible. In fact, he was able to track the object for 3 minutes while it moved in a large loop at speeds between 1 and 4 mph, approaching as close as 800 feet.

The excitement at expedition headquarters was electric. How large was the target? Did it dive vertically or remain at constant depth? Eagerly we spent the next few days making prints from the film record of this contact and analyzing the data, which were very impressive. While exact size estimates were not possible from such sonar data, preliminary calculations based on comparing target-strengths of equivalent air volumes suggested about twice the intensity expected if the target were, say, a 10-foot pilot whale, clearly suggesting a substantial animal, possibly 20 feet in length. More careful calculations made in Chicago confirmed the earlier estimates.

In short, Bob's success had turned what had been a disappointing year into a year of great success—so much so in fact that at the annual meeting of the Bureau's Board of Directors later in October, it was agreed that the full scale of the scientific effort was now beyond the capability of any one director in the field. Therefore, the next year's team would be divided into two separate but cooperating groups, one concerning itself with underwater activities, the other with surface activities such as surveillance and night drifts. Each of the two groups would have its own director in the field. Bob Love and Tim Dinsdale were unanimously elected for these tasks in 1970. Thus we closed out a year which had taught us that fewer, carefully conceived and executed projects were more likely to yield results than a great number of hastily thrown together experiments.

We now had three independent sonar experiments all saying that relatively large objects were moving around in the depths of Loch Ness.

V
The Big Expedition 1970

Before sonar contact with a large animate target was first made in 1968, we had often doubted if there really *were* unexplained creatures in Loch Ness. With this corroboration and the sonar confirmation of 1969, our thinking shifted more and more toward *what* kind of animals these might be. Clearly, the next step in the underwater investigation was to develop techniques that might lead to identification.

The difficulties still were formidable. Our data from surface sightings and sonar contacts indicated that the animals were dispersed throughout the entire expanse of Loch Ness—2 cubic miles of water —though they seemed to spend most of their time along the sides and bottom. We had no precise knowledge of their habitat and behavior patterns in water as deep as 850 feet. Overall the peat-stained water made a visual search *very* difficult.

However, in 1970 we had two advantages. First, the publicity resulting from sonar contacts was generating serious interest even in some scientific circles in the United States, and as a result new suggestions for methods of investigation were beginning to come in. Second, World Book offered to provide financial support for an expanded underwater research program, allowing us time to develop a well-planned approach to the problem.

The questions we asked ourselves were formidable in difficulty. Loch Ness has a reputation of never giving up its dead. The bodies of humans who drown in its deep waters are not recovered. But what happens to the remains of the unknown animals when they die? Are the 42° waters of the bottom cold enough to prevent bloating and a rise to the surface, as happens in shallow lakes? The soft parts undoubtedly are devoured by the voracious eel population, but what about less palatable parts of the carcass, such as bone. These must remain at the bottom of the loch. Skeletal remains—if indeed there is a skeleton—could undoubtedly provide a clue to identification.

How could we get at the bones? Minimally a detailed survey of a large expanse of bottom area beneath hundreds of feet of dark water was called for.

Fortunately, calculations based on estimates of population, life span, bottom area, and silting rates indicated that there was a small but still finite probability of obtaining a photograph of at least one section of bottom containing skeletal remains during the time we allotted. Thousands of exposures with a deep-water camera and a powerful stroboscopic flash would be required.

It was here that our new scientific respectability reaped fruitful results. The chief source of the necessary photographic equipment, Dr. Harold E. Edgerton, Professor of Electrical Engineering at Massachusetts Institute of Technology, invited us to address, as he christened it, the "First Monster Hunting Seminar" at MIT. In addition, Paul J. Perkins of the Narragansett Marine Laboratory of the Univeristy of Rhode Island wrote urging that since many aquatic creatures produce characteristic acoustic calls, we might think of monitoring the waters of Loch Ness with hydrophones (underwater microphones) and record the calls for study. Our 1967 list of possible projects had included hydrophone work, but we could not afford it. Now it was financially feasible. Further, Nat Pulsifer, President of Listening, Inc., a company that had done work in communication between dolphins, offered the help of his scientific staff.

Jim Colvin, of World Book, and I set off on a whirlwind trip to learn what we could from these experts. The MIT seminar was attended by several dozen interested "monster hunters" from industry as well as the university, who had much to offer, particularly with regard to underwater techniques, though Professor Edgerton was unable to promise use of his camera gear because he had already made commitments to Jacques Cousteau. Nat Pulsifer's staff produced numerous ideas that later were incorporated into equipment designed for use at Loch Ness. Paul Perkins demonstrated techniques that were used to analyze and identify calls of aquatic creatures. Dr. Winn, who had been working with eels, was quite taken with our suggestion that some form of giant freshwater eel was a contender for the position as the Loch Ness "monster" and described the effect of the lunar cycle on eel behavior. Such behavioral patterns could provide a clue to identification if we could monitor any associated sounds.

That scientists of note were so interested in a project that had often evoked only amusement was very encouraging. As Edgerton said, "If I believed the statistics, I never would have started most of the things I have done." But while we returned from our trip filled with new ideas, the problems confronting us were as great as ever.

It seemed clear that we had to develop means of detecting and monitoring as many animal characteristics as possible. The detection systems had to be flexible and capable of deployment at various locations and depths, if chances of contact were to be maximized. They had to be capable of gathering data with a minimum of human attention if they were to be effective during periods of rough weather and darkness. The equipment had to be able to record the most complete data, possibly automatically, if meaningful interpretations were to be made later. The underwater research program, as planned, consisted of six fundamental lines of investigation: 1) bottom photography, 2) acoustic monitoring, 3) mobile sonar search, 4) fixed sonar screens, 5) baited underwater cameras, and 6) specimen collection of the fauna in Loch Ness.

1. Photography of the bottom for possible skeletal remains depended on our being able to borrow one of Edgerton's deep-water stroboscopic cameras. A sled was designed to tow such a camera across the bottom, but at the last moment we were forced to cancel this project when two of the cameras were lost at sea, leaving none available for use at Loch Ness.

2. Acoustic monitoring of bioacoustic "calls" produced by aquatic creatures offered great promise, for two reasons: the range at which such calls could be detected was considerably greater than the maximum range for visual surveillance, and the nature of the calls might provide identification of the creatures producing them. However, the calls had to be recorded for analysis, and a tape recorder running continuously would consume several miles of tape each day —clearly an impossible expense. No solution to this problem was commerically available, so we developed a system that would operate only when sounds were detected. A two-channel Aiwa tape recorder proved adaptable to such a system. The amplifiers were left in operation continuously, providing inputs to a sound-operated electronic switching system, which turned on the tape drive motor when sounds were detected.

The sound detectors for such a monitoring system, the underwater hydrophones, are built primarily for military application and proved to be extremely expensive. After much search, a hydrophone was procured for testing purposes from Marine Research, Inc. The great depth of Loch Ness meant that as much as 1,000 feet of cable would be needed to connect a hydrophone to the recorder on the surface; such long cables would require a preamplifier near the hydrophone to boost the signal along its way, and a small solid state amplifier was designed and sealed in a section of copper tubing near the hydrophone. The device was powered from the surface to eliminate need for batteries under water.

Only time would tell whether all these newly developed components could be made to function together as an effective monitoring system. Of course, we tested the system carefully, though our tests provoked much amusement and some embarrassment. The first time the system was turned on, it was swamped with a loud hum from the speaker. Tests showed that the equipment was ultrasensitive, picking up hum from household wiring. Clearly, the hydrophone required shielding. To test the shielding apparatus we built, the hydrophone was dropped into our kitchen sink filled with water—at which point human sounds were detected. The hydrophone was picking up voices from neighboring apartments, carried through the plumbing to the sink! We inadvertantly mentioned the results to a member of the press. Imagine our chagrin to find the incident faithfully reported in a feature article in newspapers delivered the following Sunday to the neighbors.

Field tests in Lake Michigan were next. On a bright summer afternoon, the hydrophone was lowered over the side of a boat a few miles out of harbor. The clamor issuing from the speakers was indescribable. Water pumps in a city pumping station a mile away and the engine of a freighter a mile and a half out were detectable, as was the breaking of waves against the hull of our own boat. As we moved into the lee of a breakwater to reduce wave noise, we picked up the sound of an air hammer at a construction site on shore. This was soon drowned out by a "cowboy" in a speedboat two miles away! At best, we were encouraged to know that we had a sensitive acoustic monitoring system.

We next made deep-water tests. Natural wave noise increases many fold when surface winds pick up. We hoped to record this sound level in order to design automatic noise level compensation into the sound operated switches, so they would not trigger the tape recorder drive as wind conditions changed.

At a distance of ten miles from shore we stopped all machinery on board, lowered the hydrophone, and listened—to the slow throb of a distant freighter. At twenty miles out, the hydrophone was lowered in 200 feet of water and initially picked up the low level noise of waves on the surface, the sounds we had come to record. However, these were soon punctuated by a series of stacatto knocks, repeated at irregular intervals. The crew checked the boat and reported that the master switch was disengaged and that the boat was dead silent. A radar check revealed no other boats within fifteen miles. Then the knocks died away, and we again started the recorder. Within minutes we were greeted by a new series of knocks, sounding like a group of crazy carpenters. After drifting for an hour, during which the intensity of the knocks rose and fell, we turned back toward shore, perplexed by these strange sounds.

The next day, after a thorough check of the equipment had revealed nothing unusual, we began to study the recordings. The knocks did not have a regular cycle, and there was an indication of multiple sound sources joining in unison. Recalling reports of fish choruses, we began to suspect that these sounds might be of biological origin. We called upon Dr. Arthur Hassler at the University of Wisconsin. Hassler had done work on calls produced by a variety of freshwater fish. After listening to the recording, he identified the sound as belonging to *Aplodinotus grunniens*, a species of freshwater drum-fish he had studied in Lake Winnebago several years before but had not previously been reported in Lake Michigan.

This first—and unexpected—success in recording and identifying bioacoustic calls was most gratifying, and we next taped the sounds of other aquatic creatures in the Shedd Aquarium. Calls of dolphins and other creatures were easily distinguishable.

After completing all these tests we proceeded with the final design, adding a clock to record a time code every hour so that the time of calls recorded could be determined. We were now confident that we had a sensitive new tool, capable of bugging not only a human dwelling but, we hoped, the lair of the animals in Loch Ness.

3. We planned to contnue the mobile search with Honeywell Scanar sonar and recording cameras mounted on a surface vessel continually traversing the length of the loch. Acoustic monitoring and

recording equipment were added to the capability of this vessel, and a sensitive depth finder was obtained on loan from Ross Laboratories so that we could make a continuous record of fish shoals and bottom profiles below the vessel. An intercom system was installed to connect the wheelhouse and the sonar operator's position so that all operational commentary and positional information could be recorded. Finally, a time code system was worked out so that time data on the voice recorder and depth recorder charts could be recorded. We wanted to be sure that all data would be recorded in such a form that it could later be integrated and analyzed.

In addition, we felt that the sonar search vessel could be used to help secure a biopsy sample of tissue from one of the unknown creatures. Some tissue would permit a biochemical and immunological analysis, certainly a great aid in identification. Two methods for obtaining such a tissue specimen were evaluated.

The first involved use of a small, self-powered underwater vehicle that could be launched from the search vessel in the event of a sonar contact. It would home on the sonar target and fire recoverable biopsy darts when within range of the target. Preliminary design of the vehicle indicated it to be technically feasible, though beyond our present financial means.

The second approach employed a quantity of expendable biopsy darts that could be dropped from the air. The idea was to saturate the expanse of water in which a sonar target was contacted with several hundred such darts, which would sink toward the loch bottom. This concept was very attractive because it reduced the intercept problem to one of two dimensions rather than three. (The darts were designed such that if in its descent through the water a dart touched an animal, contact would activate a propulsion strong enough to penetrate and obtain a tissue sample; then the unit would self-inflate and float the sample to the surface for recovery.)

We hoped to drop the darts from the Wallis autogyro which was to be employed in connection with Tim Dinsdale's surface surveillance program. With such a joint air-sea effort the darts could hardly fail to make an "impression" on our friends beneath the surface. Our plans were frustrated, however, when Commander Wallis advised that anyone dropping anything from the air over the British Isles should be prepared to go to jail, a prospect not at all to his liking. Obviously, more lawful schemes for identification had to be devised!

4. Arrangements were made with Professor Tucker of the University of Birmingham to employ his digital sonar on shore for a third year. To the original equipment which measured increment in a vertical plane and range and which had successfully contacted several moving targets in 1968, a second display to monitor azimuth movements was added for 1970.

5. Photography as a means of identification was an obvious approach, but with a few exceptions surface photography had proved disappointing. The infrequent appearance of the creatures on the surface, the great distances involved, and bad weather conditions compounded the problems of manned camera surveillance. Underwater photography to be even minimally effective had to employ a flash to provide illumination and the subject must be within a few feet of the camera. However, if a sufficient number of cameras, capable of automatically taking a photograph when a subject was in range, could be deployed throughout the lake, perhaps the animals could be made to take their own pictures. Therefore we devised underwater cameras with baited lines, designed so that a tug on the bait a few feet away from the camera would trigger the shutter producing a picture of our predator in action.

The idea was appealingly simple, but, as with most such ideas, a number of problems arose. The first problem involved development of a waterproof housing that would withstand the great pressures at depths of 800 feet in Loch Ness and yet be easily opened for servicing. When an adequate housing was designed, we had the problem of the camera to face. We built a prototype of the baited camera using a spring-wound instamatic camera enclosed in the waterproof housing with electrical circuits and batteries. The bait line was attached to a magnet outside so that a pull on the bait would close a sensitive magnetic switch, applying power to an electromagnet and triggering the camera. The camera was weighted to hang downward with the bait line below and could be moored at any depth in the loch. Tests in Lake Michigan showed that with a fresh flash cube the camera was capable of taking four color photographs without human attention. At last we had a tool for potential portraits of the animals in their watery habitat.

(Biopsy darts, underwater cameras, etc. . . . We bothered with inventing or constructing certain equipment simply because at the time we needed it, it did not exist or existed in a form too sophisticated and expensive for our use and our budget. Fortunately, our less-than-spectacular success with some of our tools at Loch Ness is not the total story for such technology. For instance, after 1970 the biopsy equipment was adopted by marine scientists and has been successfully used since for obtaining tissue samples from whales in a program of conservation for these endangered species.)

6. Finally, while we were interested in all means for identification of large creatures, we were also interested in gaining knowledge of *all* the fauna inhabiting Loch Ness, since these things might be related in some way to our main problem. A program therefore was planned to collect specimens of whatever species of eels and fish might be encountered at various depths in the loch. Baited lines and passive and active traps of several sizes were designed, and chemicals were prepared for preservation of any unusual specimens that might be collected. (See Appendix G.)

By the end of May most of the equipment prototypes had been tested. We now were able to estimate costs and to decide how many of each prototype to build. It was decided to build 6 underwater camera units and 5 hydrophone listening and recording units. Production began in earnest at once, with the sounds of construction continuing far into the night. The apartment began to resemble a combination warehouse, machine shop, and electronics laboratory. Our concern about complaints from neighbors was relieved when, prompted by publicity and promise of a bowl of "monster fin soup," they good-naturedly offered their assistance in the production effort. Hectic days followed as equipment was built, tested, debugged, and retested. There seemed no end to the growing list of supplies and spare parts required.

By the end of June a mountain of underwater gear and supplies had been assembled. After several days of packing, almost a ton of equipment was loaded into a trailer for delivery to the shipping dock of World Book, where it was airbilled to be flown to Scotland. Bob Love and his associates followed speedily.

They arrived at Loch Ness to find the photographic surveillance effort led by Tim Dinsdale in full swing along the shores. As in the previous year we established the headquarters for our underwater research effort in small house trailers parked at Temple Pier on the shore of Loch Ness. This provided access from the Inverness Road to the water and docking facilities for the vessels we would be using.

Recruiting of a staff had begun in the United States. An eager new member, Jeffrey Blonder, joined up in New York. Photographer Stuart Markson with his wife Susette also were from the United States. In Scotland, LNIB was joined by veterans of the Loch Ness search Ron Mercer and Ivor Newby, whose fast cabin cruiser was to be used to service equipment in more distant locations on the loch. Don Boddington brought in his motor sailer *Rangitea*, which we had chartered as our sonar search vessel, and introduced Captain James Skinner, who would be her master. Tim Dinsdale made available the LNIB work boat, *Fussy Hen*, from the Achnahannet site.

It was with a sigh of relief that we checked off the 50-odd crates of equipment that arrived on the truck from the airport. The recording equipment was to be floated in sealable 55 gallon steel drums, ballasted to float upright and anchored to the bottom with the hydrophones hanging down into the water below. The first such system was towed into position during calm weather late one afternoon. A voice commentary was recorded at the start of the tape to provide identification, and the system was then set to record automatically any sounds detected during the night.

The next evening our crew gathered in the trailer to listen to this first tape, recording sounds originating in the depths of Loch Ness. Would there be exotic animate sounds or would the noise level be so high that it obscured everything else? At first, occasional outboard fishing boats were detected. These sounds had died out by 6:00 P.M., however, as the fishermen returned to shore for supper. Then ensued four hours of quiet, interrupted at about 10:00 P.M. by sounds like an outboard boat passing in the distance. This was baffling indeed. Who fishes at night? The solution came suddenly. Poaching of deer from the loch under cover of darkness is considered a traditional right by local residents. The monitoring systems had faithfully recorded this clandestine activity!

With confidence in the capability of the acoustic monitoring systems to record distant calls, we anchored the first drum in deep water with hydrophones hanging hundreds of feet below. Our mooring of the drum coincided with an end to the unusual period of calm weather, and Loch Ness again became its usual tempestuous self, with 20-knot (23-mph) winds and 5-foot waves, making it impossible to approach the bouncing drum for three days. When we could reach it, we found the hydrophone cables and anchor line had become hopelessly entangled, requiring that the entire system be hauled into shore to be re-rigged. The recording tape had run out, but a replay revealed only sounds of turbulence as the hydrophones surged up and down with the bobbing of the drum. We were a trifle discouraged, but at least we were spared the realization that this incident was going to be entirely typical and that it marked the beginning of a continuing struggle to keep our equipment operating in and on Loch Ness.

Obviously the hydrophones required anchoring at fixed distances above the bottom to prevent their surging with the surface waves. This was accomplished by attaching a plastic soccer ball to the line to serve as a float, so that when the anchor reached the bottom, the soccer ball float would be pulled about 10 feet below the surface, thus keeping the anchor line taut. Two hydrophones were fastened to the anchor line at fixed depths of 300 and 600 feet so that the relative intensity of calls recorded simultaneously on the two channels would give some indication of the depth of their source. The drum containing the recording equipment was tethered loosely to the sub-surface buoy with 40 feet of line so that it could float on the waves without moving the hydrophones below.

Illus. 1 Ron Mercer (left) and Bob Love preparing hydrophone recording unit for deployment in Loch Ness. *Stuart Markson photo. Courtesy LNIB/ World Book Encyclopedia.*

Illus. 2   Hydrophone servicing equipment: Ivor Newby's boat and platform. Note U-shaped cutout on servicing platform. *Stuart Markson photo. Courtesy LNIB/World Book Encyclopedia.*

Illus. 3   Bob Love servicing a hydrophone unit. The U-shaped cutout of the work platform Love is on fits around the drum in order to nest the drum and platform firmly next to one another so the two can ride the waves together and permit changing of tapes on other than calm days. *Stuart Markson photo. Courtesy LNIB/World Book Encyclopedia.*

Using a special boom mounted on the *Fussy Hen*, this rig was anchored in 700 feet of water near Urquhart Castle early in August, and we returned to shore with great expectations. Two days later the tape was recovered. The tape had recorded bird-like chirps, which were picked up with greater intensity on the deep hydrophone than on the one 300 feet below the surface. Since we had no idea as to what had produced these calls, the following day we moored a camera baited with cut fish near the hydrophone station. A chunk of iron was used to anchor the camera above the bottom with a taut line extending to a buoy 10 feet below the surface.

At dawn the next morning we discovered that the camera rig, buoy and all, was missing. A confusion of thoughts raced through our minds. What could that camera tell us—if we could ever recover it? Had the wind simply blown it from its mooring into deeper water? If so, the two buoys still should float the whole camera rig. Could some creature have taken the bait and made off with the camera? Had the bait line frayed and allowed the camera to float to the surface? Or had the rig been pulled so deep that the floats had collapsed, never to rise again? Lunch table talk was filled with such speculations. After lunch, further search revealed nothing. We all dreamed that night of "Nessie" lying in her lair, puzzling over the strange contrivance attached to that delicious piece of fish. And maybe even chuckling!

The next morning the winds began to drop, and by afternoon the waves were reduced to one foot swells. Captain Jim motored out in *Rangitea* in search of the camera. The boat returned that evening with the missing camera, which had been found floating in the middle of the loch. We were elated to find that a number of pictures had been taken, but Loch Ness does not give up her secrets easily. Not one of the photographs revealed anything but the baited line hanging below.

The camera had apparently been blown from its mooring into deeper water by a change in wind direction. But what could have tugged on the bait to expose the pictures? Mooring tests with the camera provided the answer. As the camera was lowered from a rolling boat, the water surging against the bait as the mooring line rose and fell caused an intermittent pull on the bait line and triggered the camera several times before it reached the bottom.

What was needed was a method to deactivate the trigger mechanism until the camera was anchored on the bottom. Obviously the simplest scheme was to block the trigger arm with some solid material

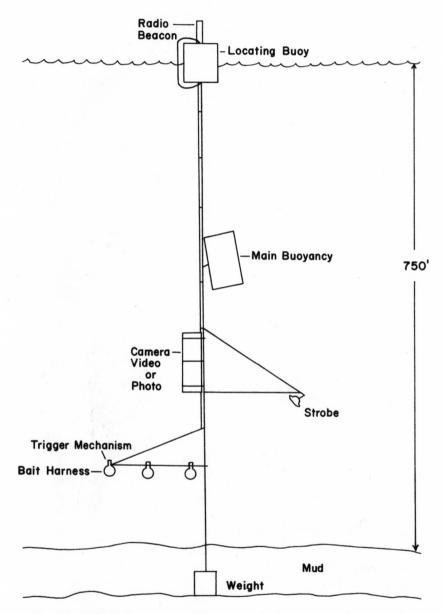

Illus. 4 Rig for underwater photography at Loch Ness. Based on Scripps Institution of Oceanography designs.

that would dissolve after being lowered into the water. Tests of several such materials were soon underway in our field kitchen, to the great amusement of our culinary staff. Sugar cubes dissolved after 1 minute, not long enough for a camera to be lowered to the bottom. Cough drops lasted 10 minutes but got sticky and were expensive in quantity. The ultimate solution was use of a stack of mints similar to Lifesavers; these took 15 minutes to dissolve and free the trigger arm for motion. One staff member was heard to remark, "I never dreamed I would be gluing mints together when I joined this expedition."

With some of the preliminary problems solved, we began to deploy automatic equipment throughout the loch. Four acoustic monitoring systems were moored at Invermoriston, Strone Point, Tychat, and Dores. Six baited underwater cameras were anchored near these locations and in Urquhart Bay. Unfortunately, we were frequently beset by periods of high winds and rough water, which made it virtually impossible to change recorder tapes. With stations located 5 to 10 miles from our Temple Pier headquarters, the servicing difficulties were considerable.

Illus. 5   LNIB equipment at Temple Pier after one of Loch Ness' storms. Note *Viperfish* behind trees. *Stuart Markson photo. Courtesy LNIB/World Book Encyclopedia.*

One unwelcome respite developed when winds reached 30 knots (35 mph) and blew for three days. Such an extended storm was unusual even for Loch Ness, and by the time it was obvious that we were in for a real blow, the waves had reached such a magnitude that there was no hope of recovering the moored equipment. After the second night a survey from shore confirmed our worst fears. The recording station at Invermoriston was missing, and four of the camera buoys could not be spotted in the six foot waves. When the wind dropped, one camera was recovered, but loss of three cut our photographic capability in half. The recording station drum was found a week later, washed ashore with both hydrophones missing.

Stronger moorings and heavier anchors with more floatation were added to the remaining equipment, but Mother Nature had clearly won this round.

I arrived with my wife in September to initiate the specimen collection program. Two small creel-type traps, "mini-traps," were set at depths of 20 to 100 feet in Uruqhart Bay, along with three larger "midi-traps." They were all passive traps with funnel-shaped entrances designed for sampling the fish and eel populations.

Four larger traps with spring-loaded covers also were installed. The first such trap was built in the form of a cone with its apex anchored to the bottom. It stood 6 feet high and measured 5 feet across its circular top, dimensions that led it to be dubbed the "great trap." A frame carrying the chicken wire cover could be opened against springs and held open by a trigger mechanism inside the trap near the apex. An aquatic predator entering the open cover could reach a bait pouch attached to the trigger mechanism that, if tugged, would cause the cover to spring shut. With such traps we hoped to catch large and perhaps unknown animals.

The nearby town of Inverness provided an adequate, if sporadic, supply of most of the materials we needed for our operations. Our requirement for soccer balls as floats and markers for our equipment rapidly exceeded the supply. Curiosity of the local merchants began to mount when we had consumed all the orange soccer balls in town, yet still wanted more. They could not understand our penchant for the orange balls, which were, of course, much more visible in the water, and they were quite taken aback when Ron Mercer returned to Woolworth's to buy 6 white soccer balls and a can of orange paint!

Ron did much of the shopping and became adroit at dodging questions, even when he purchased 12 spools of sewing thread. The spools were to be used for the trigger mechanism of the "great trap." Maybe we were crazy. As Ron said, "Sane people use thread and throw away the spools. We use the spools and throw away the thread."

The spools proved to be hollow plastic and collapsed under the force of springs in the trap. So Ron returned the next day to the same store with a request for 12 more spools of thread, this time specifying that the spools be of wood. With a puzzled look the clerk explained to the store manager that she had a customer who wanted 12 "wooden" spools of thread. He thought there were wooden spools of thread in the warehouse if Ron could come back after lunch and, by the way, what color did he want? Ron replied, "It really doesn't matter." And left it at that. However, he did request a reprieve from shopping duties, pleading concern that his sanity was being questioned by his friends and neighbors.

Captain Jim provided three "great lines" (longlines) as used by coastal fishermen, for deployment along with traps. These 1,800-foot lines were fixed up with 100 short lines, with large hooks, at 18-foot intervals and were laid on the bottom from shore into deeper water.

The theory was that this system would provide an indication of the depth distribution of species taken. However, although some baits were mangled, nothing was caught. We began to suspect that eels were to blame, and when the large hooks were replaced with smaller ones, the lines began to hook eels. After trying various kinds of bait, we switched to kippered herring, with a sizable increase in the catch.

These freshwater eels (*A. anguilla*) were of great interest since the idea that giant eels might be the Loch Ness monsters had some appeal, because such creatures could conceivable account for most of the reported characteristics of the monsters. (Long-time residents of the area, indeed, report catches of 10-16-foot specimens when the eel fishing industry was at its peak many years ago.) Traps were run morning and evening, with no apparent difference in the number of eels taken during periods of daylight and darkness. One notable discovery was their strong preference for newly attached bait. In a trap containing kippered herring from the evening before as well as from the morning, the entrapped eels gorged themselves on the newer bait while ignoring the older.

Most of the eels collected were taken in the mini-traps and were under 3 feet in length, probably because these smaller traps did not

favor entry by larger specimens. Weight, length, girth, and other dimensions were measured, and they were marked by notching the dorsal fin before being returned to the loch. Some degree of territorial
preference among eels may be indicated by the fact that occasionally
the same eels were caught a second time within a ½-mile radius of
where they had been released.

With so many activities and such a small staff our program was
seriously overextended. However, the arrival in September of Peter
Hodge, an experienced electronic engineer, permitted the initiation
of the mobile sonar search program. The sonar, fathometer, time
code, and intercom systems had been installed earlier in *Rangitea*,
but numerous adjustments and refinements were made by Peter before all systems worked together as intended. A tape recorder and
hydrophone system were installed. The drag chute was hung at the
stern, where it could be rapidly launched to stop the boat during a
sonar contact. Thrusters were mounted on the bow and stern to maintain heading. A battery charger and plug-in cables were installed on
the pier so that batteries could be recharged between search traverses.
Bristling with all this equipment, *Rangitea* began to resemble a clandestine electronics surveillance ship.

Sonar search traverses were normally begun at Fort Augustus and
ended at Dores, taking full advantage of the prevailing winds. Traverses were made both during the day and at night, in case the creatures for which we searched displayed a nocturnal pattern of activity.
The time of passing of each of 14 check points on shore was recorded. The recording cameras photographed each scan of the sonar
screen along with a time check in the control console so that the position of a sonar target could be determined after each contact. Despite
bad weather and lack of definite contact with a moving target, the
sonar search was continued by Jeff when Peter's tour of duty ended.

In September the University of Birmingham sonar team under the
direction of Hugh Braithwaite arrived, to set up their fixed sonar
screen across the loch. Full-time monitoring of the sonar screens was
not practicable, but the cameras recorded many thousand feet of film
that required processing and viewing before the results of the experiment could be made known.

Whenever surface conditions permitted, tapes were changed on the
hydrophone monitoring recorders. While servicing one of these stations, I observed a disturbance about 6 feet in diameter, about 30 feet

away. The disturbance was caused by what appeared to be some animal roiling about. My first thought was that a mighty salmon was playing tricks in the water. Unfortunately, I had the same disadvantage most Loch Ness observers have: I was close to the water's surface, giving me an extremely poor viewing angle; therefore, I could see only that portion of the animal projecting above the surface. (Peat-saturated though the loch is, the top foot or so of water is clear enough to permit seeing part of an animal underwater *if* one could ever view from above or at least get a more favorable angle than is usually the case.) Jeff and Bob both saw what I saw, a black, triangular, blunt-pointed, rubbery-looking object, like the tip of an appendage, that appeared every few seconds within the disturbance. The entire episode lasted less than a minute, concluding with a complete and final submergence.

Although I have often viewed live salmon and sea trout, no anatomical feature of these fish corresponds with what I observed at the surface. This experience is a typical example of a tantalizing, suggestive yet inconclusive observation. The believer can interpret the object as the tip of a flipper of one of the Loch Ness animals, the skeptic as the unidentified portion of a very large salmon or sea trout.

Loch Ness was buzzing with activity during September, since four other groups of investigators were conducting operations from Temple Pier. A group from the National Institute of Oceanography was conducting a study of the internal wave, or seiche, that occurred at the thermocline in the loch. Since their findings could help us understand the deep loch currents, we assisted them by deploying a thermistor chain for measuring temperatures at various depths in Urquhart Bay.

The results of the study indicated that a somewhat irregular 2-3-day cycle of wind produces surface currents. The surface currents cause a mass movement of surface water along the length of the loch, raising the level at one end by several inches. The water returns in the opposite direction above the thermocline 200 feet below the surface. The returning flow induces a slower current below the thermocline, which, in turn, results in a counter flow along the bottom of the loch. (See Illus. 6.) We had frequently been plagued with hydrophone cables that became entangled for no apparent reason. With our knowledge of four zones of current reversal at different depths, all of which change when the wind shifts, the tangling was easy to understand, and future moorings were made taking these currents into account.

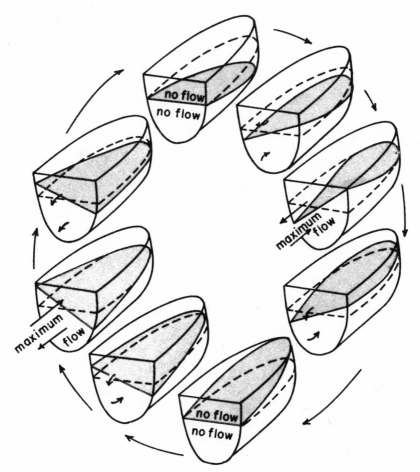

Illus. 6 Schematic depiction (not to scale) of the periodic change of position of the thermocline in Loch Ness. The rocking of the temperature interface (57-60-hour period) is much like a seesaw which also has a supporting pivot tilting regularly from left to right. (from Hutchinson)

Another group, working in tandem with the Bureau, was organized by Robert Lewis, an account executive with Carl Byoir and Associates. Lewis had become interested in the possible application of detection equipment produced by some of his clients to the investigations at Loch Ness, and after learning the broad scope of efforts we were planning, he began to put together a group of interested observers and photographers under the direction of expeditionary veteran Jack Ullrich. One of his clients, the Black and White Distilleries, made a generous contribution to the Bureau. Another, the Asahi Camera Company, made available a very sensitive infra-red camera system to be used to monitor the surface of the loch by night.

The team consisted of photographers, divers, and infra-red camera specialists. They were soon indoctrinated in the lore of Loch Ness and became enthusiastic "monster" hunters. Jack organized observers in shifts to man the infra-red camera, and nocturnal vigils of Urquhart Bay got underway. The rainy, overcast weather during this period greatly reduced visibility at night, and despite several reports of unusual disturbances in the water no conclusive evidence was recorded on film.

Other experiments directly related to our main purpose began when Robert H. Rines, Ike Blonder, and Marty Klein of the Academy of Applied Science arrived. Bob Rines, president of the academy, had attended our seminar of "monster hunters" at MIT, had been intrigued by the problem, and later had informed us the academy had decided to join forces with the surface and underwater research teams of the Loch Ness Investigation Bureau (now LNIB, having dropped the "Phenomena" from its name). With the assistance of several university, governmental, and industrial laboratories, the academy had developed a number of sensory attractants, which everyone hoped would appeal to the creatures' senses. In addition they had obtained the services of Marty Klein, president of Klein & Associates, and his new model of side-scan sonar with which to monitor selected portions of Loch Ness. The attractants, which were deployed in areas under surveillance in an attempt to increase the frequency of sightings in these areas, were classified as food, visual cues, scents, sounds, and sexual stimulants. One sighting of a telephone-pole-like object protruding from the water was reported by Tim Dinsdale in a baited area, but the episode was too transient to be filmed.

The Klein side-scan sonar produced more interesting results. When

first installed in a fixed mode at Temple Pier, it indicated a number
of small targets, probably fish. On another occasion three echos were
received from a moving target(s), remaining in the beam for 15 seconds. Detected at a range of 250 feet these echos could have been
caused by three large fish or, conceivably, three portions of a single
large moving object. Assisted by Tim Dinsdale with his boat, the side-
scan sonar was also used in the conventional mobile mode with its
transducer towed 100 feet below the surface. Again small echos of
what may have been fish were detected, as well as occasional larger
objects, which were not identifiable. (See Chapter IX for a discussion
of various sonar results.)

The international press took an avid interest in the "sex lures"
being used by the Academy of Applied Science, and when word
leaked out about the sonar contacts, we were beseiged by reporters
from all the British newspapers. Upon announcement of a press conference each paper doubled its efforts to obtain an advance copy of
the sonar photographs in order to scoop the other papers. Some sizable rewards must have been offered, since a number of local residents, including our friendly mail carrier, showed up with likely stories contrived to obtain a copy of the photographs. Stuart Markson,
our photographer, locked himself in the darkroom trailer and slept
with the prints under his mattress that night.

The press conference was widely covered by the media as Bob
Rines described the sonar results; also, samples of some of the equipment being employed in the investigation, including one of the baited
cameras, were displayed. A reporter from the BBC who taped an interview in which the use of pepsin mints to block the camera triggers
was described, provided the next day's headlines, "Monsters, Mints,
and Mouth Organs," to the obvious delight of the Polo Mint Company. The managing director of the company immediately wrote, offering to provide a free supply of Polo Mints for our research program. How could our scientific expedition fail with such help?

At the end of September, almost everyone departed, leaving the
field to Tim's surface surveillance team and the underwater research
team.

Loch Ness has been described as being the only place in the world
where one can experience all four seasons in a single day, and October was a month of such variable weather. Yet, despite the inescap-
able feeling that Nature held all the trump cards and that she wasn't

on our side, we continued to use all the detection and collection systems at our command. Sonar traverses with the search boat were made day and night, limited only by the time necessary to recharge batteries. Captain Jim's years at sea had conditioned him to lack of sleep, and he kept this pace going. And finally all the efforts paid off.

Sonar contact was made and maintained for 4 minutes with a moving mid-water target. The location was near Invermoriston, about 3 miles north of the 1969 contact at Foyers. Unfortunately, the short duration of the contact did not permit use of hydrophone equipment, while the photographic record of the sonar screen was lost due to a film jam in the camera during this contact. Thus the exact target behavior was impossible to ascertain, but as in the 1969 contact, target strength determinations ruled out fish schools and the fathometer recorded a flat bottom in this area. We were again left with the conclusion that the target was a large animate creature. This contact provided a tantalizing piece of evidence for the theory that large creatures existed in Loch Ness.

The three remaining baited underwater cameras, moored at depths of 200 to 600 feet, were producing pictures, but the pictures were raising more questions than providing answers. In some of the photographs the bait was not visible within the field of view. Could current be triggering the cameras or was something else pulling on the bait? In other pictures the bait pouch could be seen, but there was no clear view of any creature near the bait. If the cameras were being triggered while being raised to the surface, this did not explain why a number of pictures were taken by cameras that were raised slowly only on calm days.

Moreover, interpretation of the photographs was difficult since the dark water reflected little light from the flash, and an animal with dark pigmentation would be almost invisible against such a poor background. However, since many aquatic creatures have developed a protective coloration with lighter undersides, which render them less visible to predators below who view them against the lighted surface of the water above, we inverted the rigging on the baited underwater cameras so that they were aimed upward at the bait suspended above them. But again we had little success, especially since it was increasingly difficult to rebait the cameras with *fresh* bait now that we knew it to be a key factor in attracting eels.

Altogether, the baited cameras recorded some pictures in which indistinct smaller objects—possibly eels—were visible, but they did not provide conclusive identification of the quarry we sought. The secret of Loch Ness was not to be unlocked at this time by self portraits.

The specimen collection program yielded some surprises. Biometric measurements were made on over 125 specimens of eels (*A. anguilla*), and subsequently a statistical analysis revealed a highly skewed size distribution, suggesting, but not proving, that large eels might exist in the population. Of great interest was the finding that as the eels increased in length, they became relatively thicker. Such data when extrapolated to an eel 20 feet long were consistent with the general impression that the largest Loch Ness animals had a maximum body diameter of 5 or 6 feet. (See Appendix G.) Whether large thick-bodied eels could be the explanation for the Loch Ness animals was hotly debated.

Early on in the expedition our depth recorder had revealed shoals of fish at depths of 400-600 feet. These were presumed to be arctic char, a migratory fish occasionally caught by local fishermen at great depth in the loch. As autumn temperatures fell, the char moved into the shallower bays to spawn, and three, full of roe, were taken in our traps in 80 feet of water. Later, as migration of salmon and other fish into the River Enrick became visible from the surface, we undertook a qualitative population survey using a depth (and fish) recorder on a boat in Urquhart Bay. Passage of individuals under the boat was recorded at several points in the bay, with increasing density as the head of the bay was approached. Our captain, a professional fisherman experienced in use of depth recorders in the location of herring, estimated the size of one shoal near the river as representing a catch of 8-10 tons. Loch Ness obviously supports a far more prolific fauna than is generally recognized. (Cf. Chapter XII.)

As the days got shorter and the weather rougher, it became obvious that we had to abandon water-based stations. With two weeks in October remaining, we moved the drum ashore and anchored only the hydrophones out in the loch. In spite of the problem of climbing down the cliff to the shore—Ron with alpining experience was best at it—servicing the stations by land proved easier than by water. The recorders were now producing tapes at a far faster rate. We knew from the tapes that had been audited so far that most had recorded uninteresting sounds such as motor boats. But as time grew short we audited less, and therefore didn't know whether we had recorded anything of significance on the miles of tape—other than the earlier "chirp" sounds.

On the evening of a cold but calm October 28, we set out on the loch to record the water-borne sounds of our own outboard motors. This would be useful in the future for designing filters to eliminate the recording of such noise. Reaching the mouth of Urquhart Bay in *Fussy Hen*, we lowered a hydrophone 50 feet into the water, while Ivor proceeded several hundred yards farther in his cruiser so that test runs could be made. Despite the calm water the hydrophone was picking up an unusual kind of noise, an irregular series of "clicks" loud enough to be heard over the sound of the distant outboard motor.

As Ivor made the first run past the recorder in *Fussy Hen*, the clicking sounds died away, but then they resumed with still greater intensity. Clearly they were not produced by either of our two boats, so Ivor ran down the loch to see if any other boats were present. Again the clicking sounds stopped, then resumed as the sound of the outboard motor faded in the distance. We raised the hydrophone to 30 feet, and the sound intensity increased, seeming to indicate that they originated near the surface. When Ivor returned to report no other boats on the loch, the clicking sounds were now loud enough to interfere with the outboard recording; they seemed to come from multiple sources, rising and falling in intensity. Suddenly we realized that these were not mechanical sounds but calls—produced by living creatures in the water below.

Alone in a small boat with darkness falling it was an awesome feeling. Somewhere nearby were unseen animals who were calling to each other. How big were the animals responsible and how close were they? Were there many? What could they be? How long would the chorus continue? Minute after minute the calls continued to be recorded. At last we had it—an extended recording of calls from unknown animals in Loch Ness.

A rare treat of charcoal barbecued steaks had been planned for the evening meal, and as we entered the dining trailer carrying this precious recording, everyone sensed that we now had a real cause for celebration. Even the steaks took second place to excited questions as we played the tape over and over again. How do aquatic animals make calls? Can they hear each other? Do they have a common language? What behavior accompanies the calls? Could we identify the callers? We were confronted with many unanswered questions. But no matter, we had in the eleventh hour succeeded in obtaining new evidence of the presence in Loch Ness of some unidentified species of animal.

This unexpected success kindled a burst of enthusiasm among the expedition. Despite temperatures near the freezing mark, the staff agreed to extend their efforts two more weeks in November. Perhaps we could record more of the strange calls.

Before breakfast the following day, *Fussy Hen*, loaded with recording equipment and shivering staff members, was underway into Urquhart Bay. We were not disappointed. Similar clicking calls were picked up by a hydrophone lowered into the water at three locations in the bay. Again the sounds were louder with the hydrophone near the surface than when lowered below 100 feet. Apparently the callers preferred lesser depths. Perhaps this explained why such click calls had not been heard before on the tapes we had played back from the deep-water hydrophones on the moored recording stations.

But the sheer abundance of locations where calls were recorded was puzzling. Could there be so many individual callers dispersed throughout the bay or was some unexplained multiple propogation of sounds responsible? We laid out an imaginary grid of 12 listening positions in the bay to try to answer this question. Results, however, were inconclusive. On some days calls were recorded at a number of stations, although the intensity varied. On other days virtually no calls were detected at any station.

A surprising phenomenon was noted during these experiments. As in the outboard motor tests, exposure to a period of loud noise from a motor tended to suppress the calls for a short time, followed by resumption with increased intensity. This led us to wonder if we could stimulate the callers by playing back the recorded calls into the water. In this experiment one tape recorder was used to play back the sounds while another recorder with hydrophone attached was used to record the response. Again, results were inconsistent. In many cases a change in calling pattern occurred after playback; sometimes calling seemed to be intensified, while at others it was suppressed.

Of course, the different responses might reflect reactions to different messages since we were playing back recordings indiscriminantly, not having the slightest inkling what the messages "said." As we listened to the responding calls, Ron quipped, "I can already see the headlines in the British papers, 'American Scientists Drive Nessie Nuts.' " One wondered, with an apprehensive glance over the gunnel of the small boat, whether one has played back a love song or a war dance!

This recording program marked the end of the expedition, but as we began to pack up the other equipment, we could not resist the temptation to leave one hydrophone moored in Urquhart Bay, connected to a recorder in a trailer on shore. In the quiet of the trailer other faint calls could sometimes be heard. Some of these resembled the squeaks we had heard as traps containing eels had been raised to the surface, and we gave this tentative identification to the squeaks. However, on the last morning of operation yet another type of sound was picked up by this hydrophone: loud "knocks" spaced at irregular intervals a second or more apart. This kind of sound pulse is produced by some aquatic creatures, presumably for use in echo-location. Then, during the afternoon the "knocks" were sometimes accompanied by turbulent "swishing" sounds like those that would be produced by tail motion of some animal propelling itself through the water. At times the knocks and swishes seemed to be articulated; periods of high activity in both sounds were interspersed with periods of quiet. It was as if some animal were feeding, using echo-location to find its prey.

As we listened through the evening meal our curiosity knew no bounds. Could the sounds really be originating from some unseen animal or had the hydrophone become tangled so as to rub on its mooring and mechanically produce such sounds? After supper we decided to answer the question.

If animate in origin, perhaps the pattern would change when a noise stimulus was introduced nearby. After some discussion, Jeff and Stuart volunteered to produce the stimulus and boarded *Fussy Hen*. When the outboard motor was started, the rhythm of the sounds slowed. Then as motor noise grew louder with the approach of the boat the knocks and swishes ceased entirely, only to resume with vigor 15 minutes after the boat had returned to Temple Pier. Our question was answered. Alteration of the sound pattern in response to motor noise argues strongly for some living source of the knocks and swishes. In any case, they continued at a rate of activity higher than that prior to the disturbance, perhaps as a behavioral response by animals conditioned to avoid or overcome interference from natural sources. Creatures living under conditions of perpetual darkness need some non-visual means of communication, navigation, feeding, and mating. Many marine mammals have developed sophisticated acoustic systems. Perhaps similar capabilities have been evolved by animals in the peat-stained water of Loch Ness.

The end of 1970 left us in a paradoxical situation. Two new sonar contacts added to the evidence for the existence of unknown, and apparently large, creatures in mid-water. Specimens collected began to provide an insight into the prolific fauna in the loch and some of their unusual characteristics. And most importantly, acoustic monitoring had yielded recordings of 5 different categories of calls and sounds. At least 3 of these suggest the involvement of multiple, animate, sound-producing sources capable of a varied repertoire of sound and response to artificial stimuli. One category is eels; the others represent calls unlike any of the hundreds of known species sounds. More specifically, competent authorities state that none of the known forms of life in the loch has the anatomical capabilities of producing such calls. It is tempting, therefore, to make the assumption that some of these calls come from the very "monster" that has been observed and photographed on the surface of Loch Ness and tracked by sonar beneath the surface. For this there is no absolute proof. But there were certainly a lot of pieces beginning to fit together. The puzzle seemed tantalizingly near to showing us some picture.

However, 1970 also saw the retirement of Jim Colvin, our most valuable World Book proponent of the search at Loch Ness. With Jim's retirement and with recessionary economic pressures at home, World Book reluctantly advised that they had reached the end of their financial support.

Realistically, we knew that we had to make do with the information we had already gathered. Scientifically, identification of the Loch Ness monster would have to be accomplished with the data at hand. Ideally, a theory should be formulated when *all* the data are in; at least lip service is paid to this concept. In practice, it almost never works that way except in the simplest cases. One can always do more experiments. At some point one must sit back and say, "What have we got?" and "Where do we go from here?" Actually, we had a vast amount of data which would seem compelling to some and "rubbish" to the ultra-skeptics. I was sure that any analysis attempting a solution short of the specimen in a trap would be labeled by many as a premature effort based on wishful thinking and inadequate evidence, unless perchance it concluded that the whole Loch Ness matter was much ado about nothing. After considerable soul searching, I decided that somebody ought really to make an attempt at sorting things out. The results of such an attempt follow in the remainder of this book. Months were spent in classifying and organizing data into categories. There were two historical classes of data: one consisting of evidence obtained by the Bureau and associated groups working from 1962 on, the other everything accumulated prior to that date. I felt that as far as was humanly possible every scrap of relevant information ought to be considered. To summarize, the first class of material—that resulting from efforts by the Bureau and associated groups—stacked up as follows:

1. First-hand anecdotal evidence, verbal and written sighting reports, and taped interviews. (The only difference between these and the earlier material was that these were first-hand rather than second- or third-hand or even more remote.)

2. Independent film corroboration of the original Dinsdale film.

3. Multiple reproducible sonar contacts with large objects moving about in the depths of Loch Ness.

4. Unidentified animate sounds recorded in the depths of Loch Ness.

5. Considerable collateral data on the limnology of Loch Ness (including the recorded animate sounds, known flora and fauna, and interesting physical characteristics of the lake, all of which ought to be helpful in making a reasonable judgment as to what might or might not be in Loch Ness).

6. Underwater still photography of various portions of the anatomy of large objects moving about in the depths of Loch Ness. (This came after my 1970 decision but played a key role in my analysis.)

The second class of material—prior to 1962—consisted of miscellaneous collections of eyewitness reports, still photographs, and film sequences, many available for study only with difficulty or, in some cases, not at all.

In the pages that follow, the evidence and what we believe it means is presented as fully as is possible on the printed page. Data continue to accumulate slowly, and we hope to resume our work at Loch Ness, keeping in mind that what is really needed in the final analysis is an actual specimen.

Part Two

THE EVIDENCE

The sum total of evidence collected over the years is extensive. It falls naturally into four categories: 1) visual observations, 2) still photographs, 3) motion picture film, 4) sonar contacts. Each of these classes of evidence is qualitatively different and is purposely treated here in order of increasing objectivity. I include not only the impressive and spectacular but also the less than satisfactory and that which does not agree with my own conclusions. From this evidence as a whole we will then derive the basic characteristics of the Loch Ness phenomena, analyze them, and hopefully thereby answer the two questions posed during our researches: 1) Are there large animals in the loch? 2) If so, what is their identity?

Some animals are sufficiently unusual that identification can easily and accurately be made on the basis of only 2 or 3 key characteristics. Others require many more identifying criteria. How many facts do we need before we can identify our "monster"? No one knows. We cannot say in advance exactly how many are *enough*. Our difficulty is compounded if perchance we are dealing with an unknown type of animal, one existing nowhere else except in the deep freshwater lakes we are investigating. Our task then is to collect as many characteristics from as much data as possible, hoping that at some point we will have enough crucial facts to answer our questions. We can remember the Sherlock Holmes dictum: "Eliminate the impossible, and whatever remains, however improbable, must be the truth."

VI
Eyewitness Observations

As noted earlier, evidence for any phenomena in man's experience always begins with observations of some kind, and the activity labeled "scientific research" is no exception. To be sure, a variety of devices and machines can extend man's own sensory range. But the fact remains that ultimately we must rely on a human sensory response—to a visual image produced by a machine, to a pointer on a dial, or to the direct observation of the phenomenon itself. So the Loch Ness problem must be subject to these same conditions.

Eyewitnesses exhibit the virtues and vices of subjectivity. Their personal involvement is an advantage: they were *there*; they *saw*. But on the other hand all the problems of bias and of the psychological state of an observer are also involved. Furthermore, when they talk or write about or draw what they saw, we have both the precision and the problems of communication. Words have different meanings for different persons. Take the word "hump." It appears again and again in descriptions of what was seen in Loch Ness, but it does not always mean exactly the same thing to each observer. Then there are other weaknesses inherent in human observation; for instance, people have great difficulty estimating accurately the speed of a moving object. Finally, there is the problem involved in viewing any large body of water: mirages. (See "Mirages on Loch Ness" in Appendix K.)

A personal experience illustrates the vagaries of observations. Over a period of a month or so, we received a number of reports of a multi-humped animal traveling at very high speeds. Because the different observers had been standing more or less in the same location, I went to investigate, choosing a clear, sunny day when the loch exhibited a perfectly flat, calm surface, since this was the sort of day on which all these observations occurred. I too saw a 3-humped, 40-mph monster! It turned out that the loch surface was a mirror and reflected 3 ducks flying low, casting 3 dark reflections on the water. The ducks themselves were almost invisible because they could be viewed only against the background of the opposite shore, which consisted of trees, rocks, and debris.

Nevertheless, even with their shortcomings, I regard eyewitness observations as very important indeed. They can certainly help us answer our two key questions: *Is* there something unusual in Loch Ness? If so, *what?*

Over the years there have been at least 10,000 known *reported* sightings at Loch Ness but less than a third of these *recorded*. By "reported" I simply mean that the observers told someone about what they saw. It may have been an interested scientist, an inquiring reporter, a sympathetic friend, a skeptical relative. But at least it was *some*one; the observer didn't keep it to himself or herself. The matter became in some manner, if only briefly and in a very limited way, "public." Almost 3,000 such reports have been recorded in some written or printed form: newspaper stories, books, articles, diaries, official reports. I have evaluated almost all of them and kept what I determined to be 251 valid observations. I discarded all reports of sightings that seemed clearly to be waves, birds, logs, and other such known objects. Those I kept seemed authentic and significant *or* had so little information that there was no basis for saying yes or no. No attempt was made to weigh the reliability of observers in terms of occupation, age, experience, or character; however, I did exclude three reports because the individuals showed overt signs of mental disorders. In most cases, of course, I was dependent upon others and their judgments; that is, I had no control, for example, over the way an interview had been conducted in the 1930s or over the criteria used in the 1950s for accepting or rejecting a report. Therefore, I have been very cautious in my judgments—perhaps overly cautious. So, if I have unwittingly *in*cluded a few erroneous observations, I have surely *ex*cluded many more reports that others would consider valid. At least I feel comfortably confident in erring in the direction of exclusion rather than inclusion, because none of the reports I have rejected contains any unique aspects that could result in serious loss of data.

Table 1 (See Appendix A.) details the 251 eyewitness observations. Here I summarize that data with a few comments and generalizations:

Time. Do the observations occur during any portion(s) of the day more than other portions? Illustration 1 plots the 122 sightings for which exact time of day is recorded. The distribution of frequency is logically related to the behavior of the observers (rather, presumably, than of the Loch Ness phenomena). That is, we would expect fewer persons to be watching the loch at night and during the midday or siesta period. Do the observations occur during any particular month(s) during the year? Yes, July and August (See Illus. 2.), again reflecting human behavior: more people watching the loch during the summer months. Have any years been more productive of sightings than other years? Illustration 3 plots the 62-year period 1907-1969. The 1934, 1960, and 1964-69 peaks can be accounted for, of course, because special expeditions were at Loch Ness for intensified observations and were collecting sighting reports from others. But why so many in 1933? In the spring of that year a large road-building project began at Loch Ness. The detonation of many explosives by the construction crew along the shore produced penetrating shock waves; also, tons of blasted rock tumbled into the loch and sank along the sides. These reverberations and rocks certainly disturbed the bottom- and side-dwelling animals. And with the hundreds of workers brought in for the construction project, there were simply more observers around to see any animal unwittingly prodded from its home. Furthermore, workmen felled many trees along the shore, thus creating a clearer view of the loch.

In summary, there is no significant evidence to suggest any pattern to the appearances. The phenomena seem to be present at a relatively constant level in relation to time of day or year or to a period of many years. This is perhaps not too surprising when we consider that the environmental conditions below the upper layer of the loch water are unchanging with time.

Location. Sightings occur in any part of the loch, but there seems a significant clustering in areas around river mouths. Does this represent animal behavior or human behavior (Whyte suggests that more people live in the river mouth areas and thus more observations are made there.)? In this case the human sightings appear to reflect the animal behavior. Observations from the submarine *Pisces* and subsequent sonar experiments showed a considerable concentration of animal life opposite river mouths. Further, as Burton correctly points out, not all river mouths, including some where there have been fre-

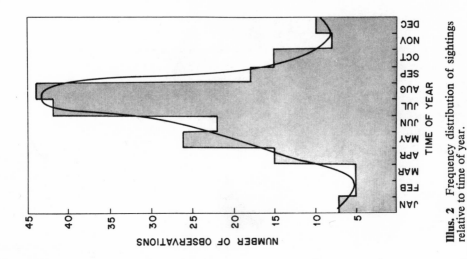

Illus. 2 Frequency distribution of sightings relative to time of year.

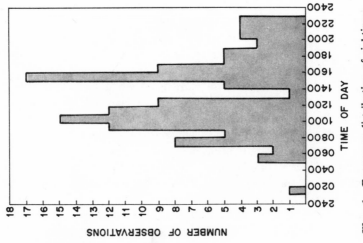

Illus. 1 Frequency distribution of sightings relative to time of day.

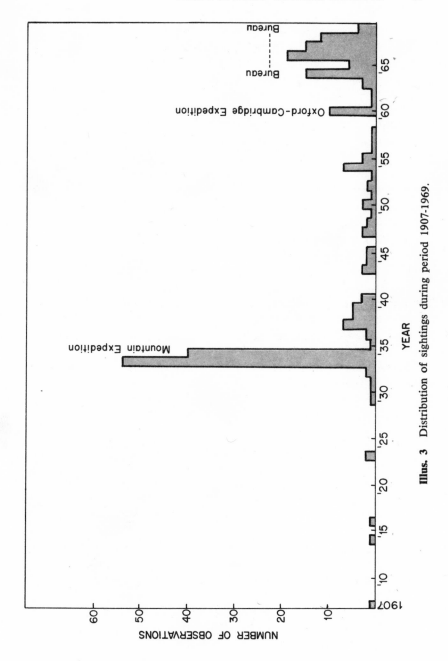

Illus. 3   Distribution of sightings during period 1907-1969.

quent sightings, have concentrations of houses; and where there are such concentrations, the houses are well back from the mouths, with views of the loch largely blocked by trees and foliage. Besides, most of the reported observations do not come from people near their own homes.

Duration. Most observations are brief, usually lasting a few minutes; only several of the 251 are as long as ½ hour or more. Clearly, the phenomena stay at the surface for only short periods. This is the sort of fact, for example, that must be taken into account when we come to narrow down our candidates in terms of known behavior and body characteristics. For instance, the question is asked: Do the animals surface to bask in the upper, warmer layer of the loch? The answer: Not likely; their surfacings are too brief.

Weather and loch surface conditions. Most observations are made on calm, sunny days. Do the phenomena come to the surface more frequently under these conditions or are observers more likely to be out looking on such nice days? I conclude the latter, especially taking into account that disturbances at the surface are much easier to detect when the surface is otherwise calm. The relatively rare sightings involving choppy waters are at fairly close ranges of a few hundred yards or less. (Cf. Observation 221.)

Range. The distance between the observer and the object is recorded in Table 1 under the heading "Range," but the helpful use of binoculars, telescopes, or other visual aids is indicated in the last column, "Remarks."

Tail, head-neck. Observers very often confuse the tail and the head-neck in their descriptions, so I list them together in Table 1. This confusion is understandable when we note that many observations are made at some distance or with the object motionless (i.e., there is no movement to establish a front-rear direction). Recognizing this confusion helps explain some otherwise puzzling descriptions. For example, "extremely long, thin neck" descriptions often in fact represent viewings of tails, not necks. (This is true especially if a tail is seen from above instead of the side, because our conclusions suggest that the animals' tails are laterally flattened. In the next chapter we will see that some "extremely long, thin neck" descriptions do not represent unusual phenomena at all but rather diving *birds* common to the loch; cf. P 2, Chapter VII.) This mixup of tail and head-neck can also explain the failure of some observers to see eyes on the "head." It may also help account for the "mane" presumably seen running along the neck right up to the head. Clearly, the flopping or falling over sideways (0 222) refers to a flattened tail; and the "curling" (0 231) and extreme flexibility must be observations of tails.

An analysis of the tail and head-neck descriptions in Table 1 suggests the following summary. The head is hardly differentiated from the neck, being approximately the same diameter. There is a definite neck, somewhat elongated, tapering slightly away from its base, ranging up to 5 ft. (1.5 meters) in length (with diameter ⅓ to ⅕ the head-neck length, representing probably 15-25% of the total length of the animal). In a few cases a frill-like structure is seen on or about the neck at a point where head and neck meet. In others a mane or fin begins at some distance—up to 4 ft. (1.2 meters) or so—from the head. Some describe the head as being flattened, with a wide mouth, which opens and closes almost rhythmically. Some see teeth, and one account (0 31) describes the mouth interior as red. Four observers (0 31, 0 101, 0 150, 0 193) refer to protrusions on the head. One, Mrs. Finlay, describes knobbed or enlarged tips. Burton suggests that she saw a row deer, with its ears laid back and thus not visible. While certainly possible, this explanation fails to account for the subsequent disappearance of the deer in the midst of considerable splashing —unless it just happened to expire at that very moment. When eyes are mentioned, they range from large to small, from round to oval to mere slits. Nothing like ears have ever been mentioned.

The head-neck appearance above the surface is usually almost vertical, like a telephone pole protruding from the water, though occasionally the angle made with the water is less. Sometimes the "head-neck" is almost parallel to the surface, but many of these observations undoubtedly refer to the tail.

Body. When an observer sees only a tail or a head-neck or a hump breaking the surface of the loch, it is impossible to determine accurately the overall length of the animal. But of course estimates *are* made. Some seem ridiculously large, so I am cautious and conservative and in my own mind halve the largest estimates of length and girth. In addition to the variation in size estimates made by observers, we must remember that the sightings are made of individual creatures which together comprise a population. (That is, there is not just a single Loch Ness animal.) Therefore, it is proper to define a size *range*. We are dealing with a population that ranges in overall length from 3-ft. (.9 meter) juveniles to 20-ft. (6 meters) adults (with an occasional specimen perhaps 25 ft; cf. Appendix I, Frequency Distribution #7: Length of Object). The body clearly tapers both front and rear. A small juvenile would measure about 6 in. (15 cm.) in maximum diameter; a 20-ft. animal would at its thickest portion have a diameter of about 4 ft. However, this diameter (12½-ft. circumference) is not exhibited by all large specimens. Some are much more sinuous. The animal sometimes shows a portion of its anatomy as a single convex portion (described as a "hump"), in some cases smooth, in others showing a "ridge." Sometimes it displays two or three portions of its anatomy, with or without water between each part; these are described as multiple humps. When great distances are reported between two humps, it is reasonable to assume that two animals are being observed. The creatures' shapes range from low-lying convex configurations to more triangular aspects, especially when viewed end-on, when a ridge-like structure can be observed at the apex. Sometimes the uppermost edge is described as smooth and continuous; in other cases serrations are indicated. That the dorsal contour can be quite variable is definitely established; however, some observers report that the convexities can move back and forth rapidly along the curve and give the impression of many humps. Many observers describe a structure that can best be identified as a continuous dorsal fin or fin-like structure, often referred to as a mane or even as a fin.

Another important question of the animal's external morphology concerns appendages. Most sightings do not mention any limbs, but some do. There is agreement by eyewitnesses that the appendages are short and ineffective for terrestrial locomotion, but here consensus ends, even among those who might be expected to provide a more complete description: observers who have seen the animals on land. (See Appendix A, Table 2, Episodes 7, 11, 12, 14, 16, 17.) Perhaps the best that can be made of the conflicting evidence is that there are appendages and they appear flipper-like, but the observers are hard pressed to find something in their experience to compare them to. My own conclusion leans toward a single pair of anterior appendages, but a case can also be made for two pair. It is even possible that both conditions are present in one species; if this were true, identification would be quickly reduced to a very few possibilities indeed.

Color and texture. The color of the animals is most frequently described as black to gray or dark-appearing. (Black of course is not a true color but rather the absence of light; so this impression is given whenever little or no light is reflected, or especially when an object is viewed in silhouette.) Actual colors reported range from blackish-brown to dark brown to brown to reddish brown to light brown to yellowish. Some observers report a greenish component. When a portion of the underside is viewed, it is always lighter in color. "Shiny" or "glistening," of course, refers simply to the reflectivity of a wet surface or perhaps mucous. A few persons use the word "slimy" to describe a smooth, scaleless surface texture. To some, the surface has a rough appearance. More rarely it is mottled; in one case, blistered (0 36). A very few times the idea of roughness is conveyed by the word "wrinkled."

Motion. Most observers agree about movements. A common description is a stationary or slowly moving object which suddenly dashes off and finally submerges. This describes a fish-predating behavior pattern, which is also consistent with reports of zigzag movements and very rapid changes of direction. Repeated surfacings over a short time span are also observed. Submergings are of two modes: a planing dive; a sinking or effortless submergence, indicating the presence of a hydrostatic organ. The animals' speed bursts are probably 15-17 mph (13-15 knots); the more usual "cruising" movements are 6-10 mph (5-9 knots). (Cf. independent measurements from film sequences and from sonar, Chapters VIII, IX.) The mode of propulsion is clearly an elongated, powerful, laterally flattened tail which moves from side to side. This movement and other lateral splashings (often interpreted as evidence for one or two pairs of appendages) are less violent, presumably, than the "considerable disturbance" frequently referred to by observers.

Special note should be made of unique descriptions, e.g., 0 85, in which the object appeared to swim on its side, and 0 161, in which the object rolled completely over.

Among the eyewitness observations, we must consider three reports establishing sightings in the sea loch, Loch Linnhe. (See Table 1, following 0 251.) While not particularly complete reports, they are of great importance because they seem to establish the presence of Loch Ness animals in salt water. Can the *fresh*water animals of Loch Ness tolerate the *salt* water of Loch Linnhe? Skeptics reasonably answer No, and maintain that this of course demonstrates the myth of the monster. That is, if animals keep popping up where zoologically they should not (Most animals do not live in fresh water *and* salt water.), it only proves they are figments of the observers' imaginations. Refutation to this comes from a surprising fact. Everyone has always *assumed* Loch Linnhe to be a simple sea loch, but until recently no one ever scientifically measured its salinity. I discovered previously unpublished data regarding the salt content at various locations and depths of Loch Linnhe (Appendix B) which indicate, contrary to expectations, that animals remaining in the upper 15 ft. (5 meters) of this sea loch encounter essentially *fresh*water conditions.

The data obtained from eyewitness observations strongly support the animal hypothesis, but they are insufficient to determine the type of animal. Even if sufficient, we would want to corroborate with other more objective data which do not depend so much on subjective evaluations. The next three chapters consider just such data and present new facts, all of which help lead us to a single unique solution.

VII
Still Photography

Actual photographs of any phenomena are far superior to verbal eyewitness descriptions. There is no need to attempt a reconstruction of what the witness saw—the very picture is before our eyes. A photograph is a permanent record which can be studied, compared, and measured. Further details may be present which escaped the observer and would never be known from a verbal or written report. But limitations apply whether the camera or the human eye is involved. In a few cases the camera may be technically superior, but in general the human eye is more flexible and capable of seeing more than a camera can record, even under the best conditions.

If we place our camera below the surface of the water, new possibilities occur—and new problems are encountered. Underwater photographs are much more useful than surface observations or photos in that they may reveal anatomy of aquatic animals which normally never otherwise appears.

However, several questions still arise when considering photographic evidence. Is the picture genuine? Can it be established that no conscious fraud or hoax is involved? Such questions usually cannot be answered with complete certainty. One can only examine the picture, and preferably the negative, for signs of fraud and, when possible, subject the material to scrutiny by independent experts. If a fraud is discovered, that is that; however, if none can be demonstrated, it does not *necessarily* follow that no fraud is involved—only that the picture *may* be genuine.

Frauds are mainly of two types. The first type, resulting from alteration of the negative, is practiced in a mild sense when magazines sharpen outlines, change shading, etc. However, when an objective mechanical process such as image intensification or variations in printing techniques are employed, thereby revealing more information, one would hardly suggest that this constitutes fraud. When negative tampering occurs, the negative is usually not made available for examination; only prints from it are presented. If a negative is available, however, it is necessary to remember that one can fabricate what appears to be a perfect original negative from an altered negative.

The second type of fraud is the *staged* photographic episode, i.e., the manipulation of events to be photographed in order to produce a desired result. In this case the evidence for fraud must be sought in the content of the picture itself. The negative obviously will be perfect.

Hundreds of still photographs have been made of Loch Ness surface disturbances, but disappointingly most can easily be identified as pictures of logs, birds, waves, etc. Of the many photos I have sought out to study and of the many brought to me for identification by tourists, scientists, and others, I have chosen 17 to deal with here. These are significant in terms of the evidence they present and/or in terms of sketching how I go about analyzing such pictures. Introducing my discussion of each photograph is a summary paragraph indicating the time/date the photo was taken, the photographer, some newspapers or books (a selective listing only) where it has been reproduced, and my evaluation of the photo. I evaluate in terms of four categories: positive evidence, unacceptable as evidence, inconclusive, identified as something else (e.g., bird, log, etc.).

P 1: November 12, 1933; photographed by Hugh Gray; published in Glasgow *Daily Record and Mail* (6.xii.33) and other papers; R. T. Gould, *The Loch Ness Monster*; C. Whyte, *More Than a Legend;* F. W. Holiday, *The Great Orm of Loch Ness.* [positive evidence]

P 1 *Courtesy Glasgow Daily Record.*

Gray was personally known to Constance Whyte and has been interviewed independently by Tim Dinsdale, F. W. Holiday, and many others. He has always lived at Foyers, a village on the east side of the loch about 12 miles from the northeast end and has been employed by the British Aluminum Company at Foyers since 1916. Whyte states that he had observed what he identified as the monster 6 times (up to 1955 when she interviewed him).

According to Gray, he customarily walked along the Foyers River and Loch Ness on Sundays after church. On the Sunday of November 12, he took his walk with his camera (type and lens not specified) along a path on the northeast some 30 ft. above a promontory built up by the river over a period of time. As he was looking down, there was an upheaval of water, with considerable disturbance, some 100 yards offshore, and a rounded back and tail appeared. Nothing that could be identified as a head became visible. The animal moved about vigorously, tossing up much spray. The object was observed for a few minutes; then it sank. Gray described the loch surface as a mill pond with the sun shining brightly. Five pictures were snapped. The film was left in a drawer until December 1, when Gray took it and another film to be developed in Inverness; only one of the five November 12 shots came out.

The *Daily Record and Mail* obtained the rights to this picture. According to Whyte, the negative was examined at the *Daily Record* office by M. C. Howard of Kodak, C. L. Clarke of the *Kodak* magazine, and two other individuals. No fault whatsoever was found with the negative. The picture was examined by a number of zoologists, who at first had no comments. They were pressed to make statements, and some finally did. A few are quoted by Whyte, Burton, and Holiday in their books.

In evaluating this photograph, it should be noted that Gray first estimated the length of what he observed at 40 ft.; but later, during an interview on December 6, 1933, he stated, "I cannot give any definite opinion on size except that it was very great," adding that the creature had dark grayish skin, glistening and smooth. He did say that the object rose about 3 ft. above the loch surface. Without the picture, Gray's verbal description is classic and corresponds to many of the descriptions in Chapter VI and Table 1.

I believe the picture is probably a genuine photograph of one of the aquatic animals in Loch Ness. However, objectively, nothing decisive can be derived from this picture. There is no apparent basis for determining which is front or back, and any such decisions must depend largely on what preconceptions one may have. Nevertheless, the two protuberances along the waterline may well represent appendages (fore and hind limbs), and the outline at the waterline appears to show a horizontal sinuous undulation. The importance of providing photographic evidence of these possibilities is not to be underestimated.

P 2: 0700-0730, April 1, 1934; photographed by R. Kenneth Wilson; published in London *Daily Mail* (21.iv.34) and other papers and periodicals; R. T. Gould, *The Loch Ness Monster*; C. Whyte, *More Than a Legend*; M. Burton, *The Elusive Monster*; F. W. Holiday, *The Great Orm of Loch Ness;* D. James, *Loch Ness Investigation*; E. M. Campbell, D. Solomon, *The Search for Morag*; T. Dinsdale, *Monster Hunt*. [identified as a bird]

P 2   *Courtesy Associated Newspapers Group Ltd.*

This is perhaps the best known of all Loch Ness photos, and I go against strong consensus in my interpretation of it.

R. K. Wilson, F.R.C.S., a London surgeon, is a man of excellent reputation. His character was vouched for by Eric Parker, editor of the *Field*, who knew Dr. Wilson and indicated he was a man of unquestioned character and veracity. According to the record, Wilson and a friend were at Loch Ness on a short vacation intending to have a look at some land he had leased for bird-shooting and also possibly to take some pictures of game birds. His camera is described as a quarterplate camera with a telephoto lens.

Wilson, after driving all night, stopped at the roadside 2 or 3 miles beyond Invermoriston toward Inverness, at a place about 100 feet above the loch. He climbed out of his car over a low retaining wall, advancing a few yards down the slope toward the loch. He first noticed a disturbance about 200 to 300 yards from shore. When he saw the head of an animal rise out of the water, he returned to his car for his camera, went back farther down the slope to see better, and made 4 shots of something moving through the water. The episode ended with the object's disappearing completely. Wilson continued on to Inverness, and a pharmacist, George Morrison, developed the plates immediately. Two shots were blank. The *Daily Mail* acquired the rights to one of the 2 good pictures. According to C. Whyte, Morrison kept a print of one negative plus the other negative, the better one, showing what has since become the classic head-neck photo.

As in the case of Hugh Gray's photo, a stir was created when the picture was first published. It was subsequently shown before the Linnean Society in London. Again, a variety of statements were issued by zoologists and laymen alike. Many of these are recorded by Gould and Whyte. Gould cites Dr. W. T. Calman as suggesting that this might represent a grebe or other diving bird; Dr. Wilson responded that it was too large to be anything of the kind.

Dinsdale devotes an entire chapter to an analysis of this photograph (but completely ignores the second, less well-known picture).

He makes much of what he interprets as a second, smaller ring of ripples. I find unconvincing his argument that these ripples, 14 ft. to the rear of the neck, are caused by movement of another portion of the same animal. Burton correctly points out that actually there are two more sets of concentric ripples extending from the left hand side of the original 8″ x 10″ print. The print as originally published, representing only a 1½″ x 1½″ square out of an 8″ x 10″ print, obviously cannot show all four rings.

This single photograph is by far the most famous and contributed much to the popular plesiosaur hypothesis. Every student of the Loch Ness phenomena, except Maurice Burton, has accepted this picture as depicting the head-neck of a large animal in Loch Ness. Burton rejects this theory in favor of the idea of its being the tail of a diving otter. I agree fully with Burton that the pictures taken by the London surgeon do *not* represent large animals in Loch Ness, but I reject Burton's otter notion. My conclusions are based on my own observations of diving birds (reported in Chapter I) in the general area where Wilson took his pictures. Since my first bird sighting there, I have seen three more such birds in that vicinity and dozens of additional birds on other parts of the loch. The birds always looked dark, usually showed little or no body, and produced circular ripples comparable to those in the photograph. It is certain that grebes, cormorants, loons, herons, gulls, and even semidomestic ducks and geese are responsible for many observations—and, in my opinion, for these photographs as well, though here I cannot be sure of the species.

P 3: June 10, 1934; photographed by a woman tourist; published in the *Scottish Daily Express* (11.vi.34); M. Burton, *The Elusive Monster* (sketch only). [inconclusive]

Little data are available about this picture. Burton states that it was taken near Fort Augustus and shows a long low hump, quiescent at the surface; he compares it to the Taylor film (F 4, Chapter VIII). In view of the paucity of data, nothing much can be said except that it agrees with many verbal descriptions. I can find no valid reason for rejecting it, and so it remains as supporting the general hypothesis of large animals in the lake.

P 4: July 13, 1934, and later; photographs by members of the Sir Edward Mountain Expedition; published in the *Field* (22.ix.45) and other papers; M. Burton, *The Elusive Monster*. [inconclusive]

P 4   *Courtesy Sir Brian Mountain.*

Some 21 pictures in all were made by expedition members, all of which I have examined. Most must be dismissed as no more than wave forms, some of which may or may not have anything to do with the presence of large aquatic animals in Loch Ness. In any case, they cannot be considered independent evidence for anything unusual in the loch. Of the 5 pictures described by Constance Whyte as "fairly good," 3 are correctly interpreted by Burton as wave effects, one as the wake of a boat which has passed, and the fifth as a single 12-ft. hump perhaps 100-150 yards from shore showing spray (Burton's interpretation). I agree that this latter picture is probably the only one to represent the monster proper, but again it contributes nothing more than general support.

P 5: August 24, 1934, photographed by F. C. Adams (photographed by Dr. James Lee, according to N. Witchell); published in the *Daily Mail* (25.viii.34); N. Witchell, *The Loch Ness Story;* P. Costello, *In Search of Lake Monsters.* [positive evidence]

Few data are available about this picture. Burton describes the picture as showing a dark object projecting up from a mass of foam and looking uncommonly like a trunk or a branch brought up from the depths by some underwater explosion. I disagree with this assessment as being too conjectural. The appearance of the object is very suggestive of an aquatic animal's appendage, and there is no reason to consider this picture identifiable with known objects. If we assume the object to be a flipper or fin it should be compared to the underwater photograph of an appendage obtained by R. Rines (P 16). While the

P 5   *Courtesy Associated Newspapers Group Ltd.*

overall configuration is similar, the tip of this object is more rounded. It may be, if there are four appendages, that the front and rear pairs differ somewhat in contour; or the observed difference may simply be within the normal range of variation.

P 6: 0630, July 14, 1951; photographed by Lachlan Stuart; published in the *Sunday Express* (15.vii.51); C. Whyte, *More Than a Legend*; M. Burton, *The Elusive Monster*; D. James, *Loch Ness Investigation;* E. M. Campbell, D. Solomon, *The Search for Morag.* [positive evidence]

Constance Whyte expresses the utmost confidence in Lachlan Stuart, whom she met and interviewed three days after the picture was taken. In addition, she saw the actual picture in proof on the same afternoon it was taken after it had been developed by John MacPherson of Drumcharrel, Cawdor, who stated it was normal in every respect. Stuart also was interviewed by Maurice Burton two months after the episode. Burton concludes that there could be no doubt the photograph is genuine.

Stuart, a woodsman employed by the Forestry Commission, lived with his family in a croft cottage located some 30 yards above the loch surface on the southwest side. Rising early to milk his cow, Stuart happened to look outside and saw what he thought to be a powered boat moving in the center of the loch. However, the object seemed to move too fast for a boat, and he noticed a long rounded hump, with a second hump trailing behind the first. At this point he shouted to three others, including his wife, picked up a box camera (type not specified), and rushed down to the loch shore. Meanwhile the object had approached to within 50 yards of Stuart. According to Burton, Stuart said he took only one picture because it was necessary to take the camera indoors after each picture to adjust the shutter release. He observed and photographed three humps. A head and neck in size and shape like a sheep's were observed dropping down into the water periodically. The object(s) turned with splashing and moved out toward the center of the loch, submerging at an estimated distance of 300 yards. According to Burton, the color of the object(s) was reported as uniformly blackish; there were no signs of hair, scales, eyes, ears, antennae, horns, or any other feature such as flippers. Details of the typical reactions and statements following publication of the photograph are presented in Whyte's book.

Stuart estimated each hump to be 5 ft. at the waterline, the first protruding about 2 ft., the second 4 ft., the third 3 ft., and the head-neck about 6 ft. He also observed a disturbance 15-20 ft. behind the last hump. About 8 ft. of water appeared between each hump. Stuart believed that the humps were not undulations, but a friend of his who also saw the humps thought they might have been. Burton concludes that Stuart's estimate of size, distance, and maximum speed of 10 mph were about right.

It is clear from the account that the observers believed the head-neck and three humps belonged to one animal because these objects moved together and submerged together. However, this conclusion need not be drawn, as should be apparent to anyone who has watched underwater photography of schools of fish or a group of porpoises. It is remarkable how such groups move in concert, executing rapid turns and complicated maneuvers as though they were one unit.

If we accept Stuart's size estimates and the idea that a single animal was observed, we arrive at an overall length of 52-57 ft., a clearly unacceptable figure. Are the figures wrong, or were 3 separate animals involved? If we assume 3 separate animals, sizes become quite consistent with 20-ft. animals. Is there any objective evidence to support this assumption? Yes. First, we know from independent evidence (the Birmingham sonar contacts, Chapter IX) that the large Loch Ness animals do on occasion travel in groups. Second, suggestive evidence,

P 6   *Courtesy London Daily Express.*

if not proof, of the presence of three separate animals is contained in the photograph itself. It is clear that the bases of each of the 3 humps do not project along the same straight line. Clearly the center hump is closer to the observer than the one to the right, and the base of the left object is at an angle to the center one. Now, it is true that an elongated body could flex horizontally into an undulation that would project 3 humps positioned similarly to those in the photo. However, those portions of the anatomy visible above the surface would, in such a situation, curve in conformity to the flexure of the body beneath the surface. This is not the case in the photo; that is, the 3 projections, when studied carefully, do not exhibit this curvature. And it is implausible to postulate that the animal is flexing underwater *only between* the humps. Certainly, the interpretation that there are three animals involved makes more sense than that only one is responsible for all of the parts showing, and it makes more likely the conclusion that the photograph is genuine. This picture is of considerable importance because each of the depicted humps is very similar to the single hump filmed by Tim Dinsdale (F 5), discussed in the next chapter. This similarity lends further support to the interpretation that the three humps represent three animals. Together with Dinsdale's film we have direct photographic evidence as to the probable shape of the central back region of the animal.

P 7: July 29, 1955; photographed by P. A. MacNab; published in C. Whyte, *More Than a Legend*; T. Dinsdale, *Loch Ness Monster*; D. James, *Loch Ness Investigation*; E. M. Campbell, D. Solomon, *The Search for Morag.* [unacceptable as evidence]

P 7 *Courtesy P. A. MacNab.*

This photograph presents such a puzzle that I have reserved until later my analysis and discussion. See Appendix C. Suffice it to say here that the problem arises because there are two versions of the same shot or there are two different though almost identical shots and/or there are two versions of the photographer's story of taking the picture(s). I have not been able to unravel the mystery.

P 8: Autumn 1958; photographed by H. L. Cockrell; published in *Weekly Scotsman* (16.x.58); M. Burton, *The Elusive Monster*; T. Dinsdale, *Loch Ness Monster.* [identified as small log]

Cockrell, who wrote a series of Loch Ness articles for the *Weekly Scotsman* and has corresponded with Tim Dinsdale, is a professional trout farmer. A serious student of the monster, in 1958 he embarked on a specific attempt to photograph the animal at night. To do this, he employed a kayak and an ingenious device consisting of a waterproof camera with a flash attached to his head and triggered by means of his mouth. Two unsuccessful night hunts led to a third which was also unsuccessful until dawn. At first light, the breeze had dropped

P 8   *Courtesy Camera Press.*

and the loch was very calm. Cockrell noticed something to his left about 50 yards away. The object appeared to be swimming very steadily and converging on him. According to Dinsdale, Cockrell said it looked like a very large flat head that was wide and 4 or 5 ft. long. He also noticed a thin line 3 ft. astern of this. He took two pictures, but then a slight squall came up. After it was over, he closed in on the object and found a 4-ft. stick, one inch thick.

Later, when he viewed what he had photographed, he had second thoughts and wondered whether he perhaps had photographed "Nessie" after all. His final answer to this question, reported by Dinsdale, is: "I just don't know."

What is one to make of such a bizarre episode? I am quite content to accept Cockrell's first assessment that he photographed a stick or small log and assume that a combination of fatigue from three nights of activity on Loch Ness and a tremendous psychological bias of belief and expectation produced the recorded experience.

P 9: 0600-0630, May 27, 1960; photographed by Peter O'Connor; published in *Weekly Scotsman* (16.vi.60); T. Dinsdale, *Loch Ness Monster*. [unacceptable as evidence]

P 9

Dinsdale has met with O'Connor and regards him as a straightforward, completely sincere person.

Both Burton and Dinsdale give an account of the circumstances surrounding the taking of the picture. Dinsdale's account, much more complete, is an extract from a letter written by O'Connor. While camping near Foyers on the shore of Loch Ness, O'Connor was awakened by the need to urinate, got up, and walked some 100 yards from camp. At this point he noticed the "Loch Ness monster" gliding around a headland at the speed of a fast walking pace. He waded out into the water, waist deep, and snapped a picture with flash, turned to shout at his companion back at camp, and then snapped a second picture without flash. He estimates he was within 25 yards of the animal. He states that it had small sheep-like features set on very strong neck muscles which kept rippling. He judges the head was about 10 in. long, neck 6-7 in. in diameter, increasing in diameter, about 2-3 ft. visible. He saw no eyes but indicates that its facial structure suggests it had them, but that its "lids" were shut. The "hump" or body was smooth, grayish-black, about 16 ft. long at the waterline, with about 3½ ft. of water separating neck and body. His friend at the camp observed something black for a moment as the object submerged with considerable disturbance.

Burton severely criticizes this picture and account, implying that it is not genuine. He states that there are many discrepancies and inconsistencies in the remarks attributed to O'Connor.

Some of the discrepancies can be disposed of easily. For example, whether or not the picture was taken with flash. It clearly was, and the confusion arose because O'Connor took a second picture without flash, which did not come out. Other points, however, offer some difficulty. As Burton points out, the highlights in the picture suggest it was taken from a height of about 12 ft., when in fact O'Connor was waist deep in water, in which case the camera at eye level would be only 2 ft. above the water. Others who examined the picture have stated that the estimated size and degree of lighting are incompatible with a camera-to-object distance of 25 yards and the equipment and film used. (The camera was a Brownie Flash 20, aperture set at f 14, 1/50th second shutter speed; film, Ilford H.P.3; flash bulb, Philips Photoflux P.F.5.)

My opinion is ambivalent. If the negative were made available for expert analysis, one might be able to arrive at some definite conclusion. As things stand, my judgment is that this particular picture probably has nothing to do with the animals in Loch Ness.

P 10:   1100-1130, June 22, 1960; photographed by Jane Burton; published in M. Burton, *The Elusive Monster*. [inconclusive]

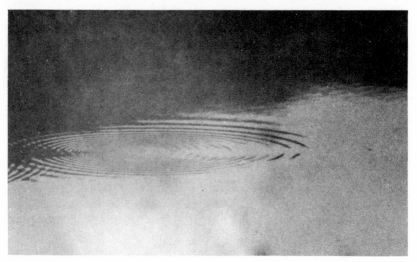

P 10   *Courtesy Jane Burton.*

Maurice Burton is a well known zoologist and writer, and there can certainly be no question as to the authenticity of his two pictures. The circumstances associated with the taking of these pictures were as follows: About ½ mile from where Burton and his children were standing on the loch shore, they observed a series of transverse ripples starting to appear and to form a V with slightly concave sides. They could see nothing of the cause of this disturbance, which was traveling toward them. Some of the ripples were slightly out of line, and Burton suggests they might have been caused by a long neck moving to one side or the other. After a while, the direction changed abruptly, and a small dark object appeared at the surface to the right of the last transverse ripples. The object appeared and reappeared briefly several times, leaving a set of concentric ripples each time it appeared. While Burton's attention was distracted, his son observed two humps instead of the single oval-shaped object: the front hump was estimated at 1 ft., the second 2 ft. at the waterline, with about 1 ft. of clear water between. The size of the single, oval object also was estimated to be about 2 ft. long. The object was traveling at about 11 mph.

Burton states that the photographs were submitted for expert examination, that they prove something was traveling under the surface in an undulating manner, and that each of the transverse ripples represents a point at which the moving body approached but did not break the surface. It could also represent a body traveling steadily but raising and lowering a head on a long neck, he said. He concluded it could not have been an otter because the speed and the pattern of movement were not typical for an otter. However, Burton later changed his mind and decided the object was an otter.

Ordinarily I would dismiss this observation as being caused by one or more diving birds, but since no bird finally surfaced to fly away, this explanation fails. In view of these considerations, I feel compelled to retain these pictures as possibly showing a relatively small specimen of our Loch Ness animals but providing no further descriptive information.

P 11: 1615, August 7, 1960; photographed by R. H. Lowrie; published in T. Dinsdale, *Monster Hunt*; N. Witchell, *The Loch Ness Story*. [inconclusive]

This disturbance, which was photographed from the yacht *Finola*, was independently observed by Mr. and Mrs. Torquil MacLeod. The

P 11

Lowries normally took the yacht *Finola* to the ancient Priory at Fort Augustus on Sunday mornings and returned to the northeast end of the loch in the afternoon. On this particular Sunday, the loch was smooth as glass. At 4:15 P.M. the Lowrie family observed a strange object that came abeam at about 7-12 mph. (The craft was moving at 6 mph.) It looked like two ducks, sometimes submerging; a neck-like protrusion broke the surface. The object passed on the right, moving away from the boat and producing a considerable disturbance. What little could be seen of the object at the surface was described as green and brown. Pictures were taken during the episode, which lasted over 10 minutes.

The wake in the photograph looks exactly like that photographed on June 13, 1967 (F 15, Chapter VIII). Apparently it was far too substantial to have been a bird or an otter, and since there is no reasonable basis to declare this independently witnessed episode or picture a fraud, it must remain as another possible sighting of one of the Loch Ness animals swimming at the surface.

P 12: 0815, May 21, 1964; photographed by Peter Hodge; not published. [inconclusive]

This episode involved Hodge, his wife, Pauline, Roland Eams, and four other observers. Peter and Pauline Hodge are personal acquaintances of mine, and I regard them as the most reliable observers and witnesses one could ask for.

The episode began when Hodge was standing in Fraser's Field, some 150 ft. from the water's edge and about 50 ft. above the loch surface. The loch was flat calm, and visibility was excellent. Peter heard a great splash, turned, and saw a pillar-like object protrude about 2 ft. out of the water. It disappeared, then reappeared again a little farther out. Looking like a black dot, it moved across the loch at 3-5 mph. Hodge states that it left a considerable primary wash with an even bigger secondary wash 15 ft. behind.

In the middle of the loch the object turned, and Pauline noticed that there was splashing from one of the washes. The object presented a black silhouette. The wash continued for a while before disappearing altogether. Pauline Hodge exposed a 4-ft. segment of 8mm movie film just after the object turned at a distance of ¾ mile; Peter Hodge made 3 still photographs with a 35mm camera with a 4X Tameron lens. He estimated the still pictures were made at about 250 yards, but examination of the negatives suggests the distance was much greater (perhaps ¼ mile, according to F. W. Holiday). The washes are clearly visible, but nothing else is except for some trees at the water's edge. (It should be added that the 8mm film added nothing more since the range was far too great. See Appendix D, F 12.)

These pictures clearly are not frauds. Moreover, since there were a number of observers, and since, according to all the observers, the episode ended with a final submergence rather than with something flapping away in the sky, the object could not have been a bird. It is also unlikely to have been an otter, because the behavior described is not at all typical of this animal.

Still, while there can be no question of the genuineness of the photographic material, it must remain uncertain as to exactly what kinds of animal or animals were observed.

P 13: August 20, 1966; photographed by Patrick W. Sanderman; not published. [inconclusive]

This picture shows a V-wash moving directly away from the observer. The loch was flat calm, but the photograph merely depicts another one of the enigmatic wakes—a fishing bird, an otter, etc.

P 13

P 14: 1130-1135, July 15, 1967; photographed by Peter Dobbie; not published. [inconclusive]

Dobbie, a service manager, and his wife, a druggist's assistant, saw a disturbance in Urquhart Bay at a distance of a few hundred yards. The weather was sunny and clear with a slight ripple on the loch surface. Mrs. Dobbie reported seeing a smooth black tail rise out of the water momentarily while her husband was getting a camera. The object, described as large, smooth, and black, moved away and finally was lost from view behind some cottages. It was described as coming up and going down several times. While this episode is typical in many ways and no negative information regarding the observers is known, the picture by itself is simply inconclusive.

P 15: 1430, July 27, 1972; Frank Searle; published in the *Daily Record* (1.ix.72). [identified as log]

Searle, who is extremely interested in Loch Ness, has spent three years on the shores of Loch Ness, observing and hoping for an opportunity for photography. July 27, 1972, was a bright day, with good visibility. A light west wind rippled the loch surface. At 2:30 P.M. he observed two humps moving slowly from right to left at a range of about 80 yards. They appeared to surface and submerge in unison. He observed the object for about 12 seconds, snapping two photographs during that time.

A detailed analysis of the Searle photograph convinces me that the object in the picture is not animate. I judge it to be a crooked log or the section of a tree floating in the water. Searle has produced several additional photographs which he claims represent the Loch Ness animals, but having examined them, I believe they too have no connection with large animals in the loch.

(Unfortunately, Searle refused permission for his photo[s] to be used in this book.)

P 16: 0140-0210, August 8, 1972; photographed by Robert H. Rines; published in *The Photographic Journal* (official organ of the Royal Photographic Society) (April 1973), *Nature* (both photos) (11.xii.75), and in the popular press, including *Time* magazine (November 20, 1972). [positive evidence]

These are the most significant photographs to date of our Loch Ness animal. The credentials of those responsible for the photos are impeccable. Rines (of the Academy of Applied Science, MIT), in cooperation with LNIB, set up underwater sonar-camera apparatus whereby sonar contact with a large, moving object would trigger the strobe-camera unit into action, photographing every 55 seconds as long as the object was within range. The result was spectacular pictures of what seems clearly to be an appendage of Nessie; at least it does not match any known aquatic animals in the loch. H. Lyman of the New England Aquarium states: "Does not appear mammalian. General shape and form of flipper does not fit anything known today." Even so, this shape is a very good hydrodynamic design for an aquatic appendage, and many similar configurations can be found among aquatic animals, including mammals. I conclude that these photos very likely show the pectoral limb of one of the large animals in Loch Ness.

(See Appendix C for details about the circumstances surrounding the taking of these pictures and for comparisons of this appendage with those of other aquatic animals.)

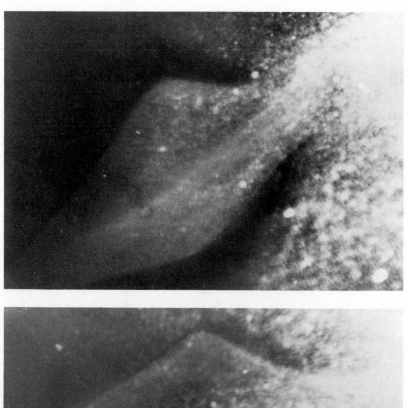

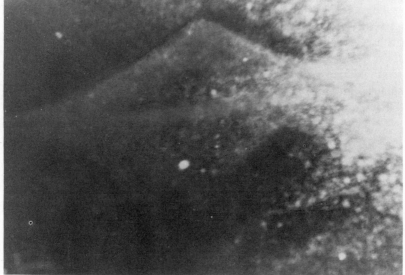

P 16 *Courtesy R. H. Rines* (© Academy of Applied Science).

P 17: 0430, June 20, 1975; photographed by Robert H. Rines; published in *Nature* (11.xii.75) and in the popular press. [positive evidence]

A second series of photographs was obtained by Rines in 1975 with equipment similar to that used in 1972 but with improved arrangement of the apparatus. For example, as noted earlier, the range of an underwater camera in Loch Ness is very short, due to reflection and scatter of light (because of the peat-saturated water); in 1975 the light source was placed off to the side of the camera and aimed at an angle toward the area to be photographed. This provided better illumination, thus increasing the range to 20-25 ft. In addition to the main equipment at 80 ft. below the surface, a backup camera and a light source were deployed at 35-ft. depth. The main camera rig, triggered by sonar contacts, took a number of pictures, but no discernible images appeared when they were developed; apparently the shots were obscured

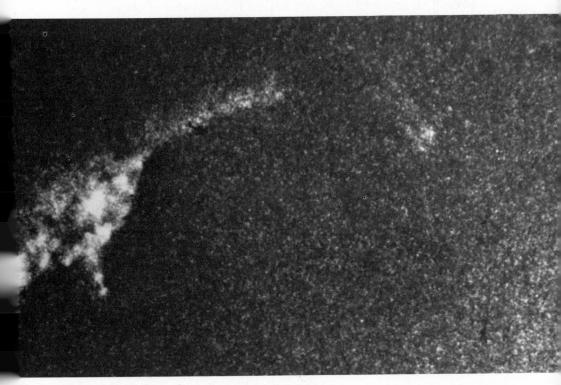

P 17 *Courtesy R. H. Rines* (© Academy of Applied Science).

by silt, possibly stirred up by animal(s) swimming close to the bottom.

The backup camera also took several pictures, but it had no simultaneous sonar record; instead, it shot automatically every 55 seconds. The best shot of this series is reproduced here; the others are hard to interpret or include inanimate objects, such as the bottom of Rines' service boat. (See Appendix C.) The photo above is best interpreted as part of the body including two appendages and the head-neck (7 ft. in length) of one of our animals. Unfortunately the dorsal surface of the animal is not clearly delineated, so that the diameter of the neck cannot be estimated with any degree of certainty. Nevertheless, this photo corroborates the general configuration developed from the other evidence: at least two anterior appendages, as well as the elongated head-neck.

Of the 17 photographs analyzed, I accept only 5 as positive evidence. This may seem a meager harvest for 4 decades of attempts to provide photographic evidence at Loch Ness—and it *is*. Certainly, above-surface still photography has not made a major contribution to solving our problems. However, it has, along with the underwater pictures, given us important information. The rather convex contour of the animal's back is graphically corroborated by the Stuart photograph (P 6), and the Gray photograph (P 1) offers evidence for sinusoidal flexure. The shape of appendages now ranges from probable (P 5) to highly likely (P 16). The appendage shape does not tell us all we would like to know, but it does establish that the animals are highly adapted to an aquatic environment. This conclusion is consistent with the clumsy, ineffectual mode of locomotion on land reported by eyewitness observers. The Gray photograph (P 1) is again relevant here: the pair of lateral protrusions shown tend to support the idea that at least some of the animals possess 4 limbs.

VIII
Motion Pictures

Motion picture film sequences as a source of information are superior to still photographs for several reasons. Films are qualitatively different because a new dimension is added. This dimension, subjectively experienced as time, extends our recorded perception of an object or event to include variation through time or, as applied especially to living creatures, behavior. In a few specific cases we could identify an animal from its behavior alone. That is, certain physiological characteristics can be deduced from an animal's activity. For example, data on the submergence of an aquatic animal might permit us to infer the presence or absence of a hydrostatic organ. So by making and by studying the films of the Loch Ness animals, we hope to add a few more pieces toward solving the identification puzzle.

An additional consideration of some importance is that motion picture film sequences are more difficult to fake than still photographs, partly because of the problems involved in attempting to produce a "doctored" film sequence and partly because the possibility of staging an episode by means of mechanical devices is too difficult and costly a project. Certainly the films obtained by the LNIB and analyzed by JARIC (the British RAF's Joint Air Reconnaissance Intelligence Centre) are beyond the possibility of fraud. Further, in my judgment, the remaining non-Bureau films discussed here (except where noted) are genuine and unstaged. Generally, films supported by adequate mensuration data are convincing and offer evidence far more objective than any of the other types of evidence presented so far.

However, even when the film has impeccable credentials, the question of interpretation remains. In the previous chapter I detailed briefly for each of the 17 still photographs analyzed the thinking and evaluation that went into my interpretation. This illustrated adequately, I feel, the process by which I arrive at a judgment and the ambiguous results often obtained from seemingly objective evidence;

therefore, in this chapter I deal with only a few of the total films. The remainder *are* similarly treated, but to smooth the reading here I have put their descriptions and analyses in an appendix.

I know of only 22 film sequences. There are undoubtedly more, and some of them might be significant, but for one reason or another they have not come to public attention. Three of the films discussed below have in a partial and peculiar way come to public attention: their existence is announced but not demonstrated. Obviously these films cannot be evaluated because they cannot be seen. I have included them nevertheless simply as an indication of the bizarre attitudes occasionally encountered. Naturally, in such situations the most extreme skepticism is justified.

As with the still photographs, I introduce each film with a paragraph summarizing when taken, by whom, where available for viewing (e.g., published stills), and my evaluation (in brackets).

F 1, F 2: Middle 1930s; made by Dr. McRae. Trustees of the films: Alastair Dallas, Tolbooth House, Kirkcudbright; Colonel Sir Donald Cameron, Lochiel, now deceased; and a third unnamed individual. [unacceptable as evidence]

F 1: This film allegedly has been held in a secret trust and has never been properly examined, though F. W. Holiday (on the basis of an interview with Alastair Dallas) reported on the film in his book, *The Great Orm of Loch Ness.* Supposedly, a London physician named McRae filmed the monster for several minutes at a range of 100 yards. According to Dallas, one of the trustees, the film shows three humps and head-neck held low over the water. The head is described as conical, with two horn-like organs and a bristly mane running down the neck. The mane appears stiff yet flexible, fibrous rather than hairy. Slits identified as eyes are visible but indistinct. The animal rolled over in the water, showing a thick, fleshy forward flipper. A flux or play of head-neck musculature was observed.

F 2: The second film was taken at Loch Duich. Here an animal is lying along the shore and is writhing its neck over seaweed. It has a longer neck and a more tufted mane.

McRae reportedly resorted to this secret trust device because of the ridicule that was heaped on anyone taking the Loch Ness monster matter seriously. Further, the trust was to prevent the film from falling into unworthy hands, presumably those interested in commercial exploitation.

The problem is complicated by the fact that Holiday's account (summarized above) is, according to Alan Wilkins, disputed by Dallas himself. Wilkins recently interviewed Dallas and reports basic discrepancies: there is no trust; there is only one film (F 2), not two, and Dallas does not know where it is.

If indeed such film(s) exists, it should be placed in the hands of a responsible non-profit organization for analysis and study.

F 3: (See Appendix D.)

F 4: (See Appendix D.)

F 5: (See Appendix D.)

F 6: 1200, May 29, 1938; made by G. E. Taylor. Still No. 1 published in M. Burton, *The Elusive Monster*. [positive evidence]

This important film, consisting of two segments (the second portion filmed 45 minutes after the first) has been exlusively in the hands of Maurice Burton.

Taylor, a South African, was touring the highlands of Scotland. While at Loch Ness, opposite Foyers, he noticed a dark stationary object about 200 yards from the opposite shore of the Loch. The object is described as dark, large (6 ft. at the waterline), rounded, and tapering down to the neck, which was raised and lowered periodically. This region was estimated to be 1-½ feet long, being raised above the water 6 in. Taylor obtained some 3 minutes of 16mm color film, the first segment about 1,000 frames, the second about 1,500 frames. The reason for the 2 segments, according to Taylor's diary, lies in the fact that after obtaining the first portion, he continued on his way and soon related his experience to an elderly Scottish lady. She insisted on seeing the scene, so they returned and found the creature had moved to within 150 yards of the opposite shore. It was still clearly visible; therefore, he filmed a further sequence. It was a sunny day. The loch surface was covered with wind-borne waves and some white caps. In the second sequence the object appears light chestnut or straw color, probably due to a change in illumination with the changing angle of the sun. The second sequence shows more movement than the first. Most significantly, during the first segment after the 80th second the object submerges completely just after assuming a single-humped aspect. Fifteen frames later a darkened area is observed beneath the water. In the next 9 frames the shadow intensifies, and again a single hump appears.

Burton stresses that the object seen resembles an animal but is not an animal. One of his grounds for rejecting the animal explanation is that the movements and behavior are unlike those of any known animal. This is not in fact the case, however; the observed behavior at the surface is quite compatible with fish predation. But aside from this, it is absurd (especially in light of all the Loch Ness data familiar to Burton) to decide a priori that an *unknown* moving object is not an animal merely because its behavior does not correspond to the behavior of a *known* animal. Further, Burton's conclusion that he finds it difficult to believe that any aquatic animal would be at the surface for over 1-½ minutes without raising its head to look around can be countered with the statement that an animal waiting for a fish to approach would hardly be expected to look for its prey above the surface of the loch.

Burton next cites a variable back contour—humps—as an argument against the object's being animate. As will become clear later, at least two kinds of animals most adequately explain this feature. Further, the humps are certainly not explained more adequately by assuming an *in*animate floating object. Indeed, all of Burton's arguments can be disposed of.

The fundamental problem, of course, is the unavailability of the film. Burton has shown the film to a few persons and has reported their responses; he has also described the film in his book. Because Burton has proved himself in other circumstances to be a careful and accurate reporter, I believe we can accept his description as reliable. Nevertheless, his refusal to allow independent analysis of the film forces skepticism upon us all. My own experience is instructive. In July of 1968 I was on a BBC television show with Burton. Afterward we talked about the Taylor film, and he agreed to let me view the film later. In August I wrote Burton, asking him to set up a screening for me the week of September 20, when I would again be in London. No response. In September I tried repeatedly to reach him by phone, but I was always told he was unavailable. Perhaps it made some sense in the 1930s for Dr. McRae to withhold his films from the public and thus escape the risk of ridicule. But those times are gone. The 1970s provide a different atmosphere for judging such evidence. The monster is now known worldwide. It behooves anyone with Loch Ness data to make his or her evidence as public as the mystery itself is public.

F 7: 0900, April 23, 1960; made by Tim Dinsdale; stills published in T. Dinsdale, *Loch Ness Monster*. [positive evidence]

This 4-minute film sequence is the most famous of all available photography. It is, you will recall, the piece of evidence that ˙persuaded me to join the Loch Ness search.

The film, about 50 ft. long, was made in black and white with a 16mm Bolex cine camera with telephoto lens from an elevation of 300 ft. above the loch, beginning at a range of 1,300 yards (estimated). Filming ended when the object was at distance of 1,800 yds.

Dinsdale was on the sixth and last day of his solitary surveillance of Loch Ness when he observed an object on the surface about two-thirds the way across the loch from Foyers near the northeast shore. He examined the motionless object carefully through 7X binoculars, noting a mahogany color, with a dark blotch on the left side. Putting down the binoculars, he began to film as the object moved away, eventually partially submerging and swinging around sharply to the left. At this point he realized that not much unused film footage remained, so he stopped filming in case the object should change to a more advantageous direction and surface more fully. Later he filmed a boat following the same track as the earlier object. This film of a craft of known size/speed proved very valuable later for size/speed measurements when the film was submitted to JARIC for analysis.

The 1966 JARIC analysis is important as an independent and expert study, free of either pro or con monster bias. JARIC concluded that the object was most probably an animate object inititally projecting 3.0 to 3.7 ft. out of the water and moving at speeds up to 10 mph. The length at the waterline was at least 5.5 ft. (actually more because the object was not filmed at right angles to its long axis; the view in the film is neither purely a side or rear view but some intermediate aspect). JARIC's estimate of the boat length was 13.3 ft., speed 6.5 mph. The actual length was 15 ft., moving at 7 mph, showing that JARIC's estimates were conservatively accurate.

The Dinsdale film is a most important item of authentic data, agreeing with many eyewitness observations and with at least one still photograph, P 6. The great distance at which the film was made makes the film grainy and disappointing as far as detail is concerned; nevertheless, it provides objective information as to size, speed, and propulsive behavior.

F 8: (See Appendix D.)	**F 12:** (See Appendix D.)
F 9: (See Appendix D.)	**F 13:** (See Appendix D.)
F 10: (See Appendix D.)	**F 14:** (See Appendix D.)
F 11: (See Appendix D.)	

F 15: 1140, June 13, 1967; made by Richard Raynor, Loch Ness Expedition, 1967. Three stills from film shown in illustration below. [positive evidence]

Three stills from the Raynor film:

Raynor, while on Loch Ness expedition camera watch opposite Dores at the north end of the loch, obtained a short 35mm black and white sequence at a range of about 2,000 yards, 50 ft. above the loch, using a Newman Sinclair cine with 17″ lens. The film shows a wake with an object periodically appearing at the head of the disturbance. During the filming episode, the tourist vessel *Scott II*, which makes a daily run from Dores to Urquhart Bay, passed and was recorded on film. The known size, speed, and path of this vessel adds considerably to the confidence with which one can accept JARIC's size and speed estimates of the unknown object. JARIC indicated that the mean speed of the object was not less than 5 mph and a possible length for the part of the object that breaks the surface is in the order of 7 ft. This particular sequence appears to qualify as an authentic film of a large animal in Loch Ness and provides corroboration for the Dinsdale film.

F 16: (See Appendix D.) **F 20:** (See Appendix D.)
F 17: (See Appendix D.) **F 21:** (See Appendix D.)
F 18: (See Appendix D.) **F 22:** (See Appendix D.)
F 19: (See Appendix D.)

In summary, the films provide independent, objective evidence for the existence of unknown animate objects in Loch Ness. About these animals we learn something of speed, mode of movement, size, and configuration. The maximum swimming speed established by the films is about 10 mph. The mode of progression and movement as seen in F 7 and F 15, particularly the repetitive up-and-down movement, is extremely interesting and is best interpreted as related to fish predation just below the surface of the loch. (See Chapter XIV for further discussion of this point). Size measurements deduced from the films are consistent with aquatic animals 20-25 ft. in length showing only a portion of their body at the surface. The back contour seen in films confirms not only many eyewitness observations but certain still photographs as well.

All things considered, continued photographic surveillance of the loch is likely to produce not much more data than summarized above. It is as if, analogously speaking, we knew very little about sharks and tried to increase our information about them by repeatedly filming the dorsal fin as it breaks the surface at a considerable distance. At Loch Ness we seem to be dealing with a deep-dwelling aquatic animal that only occasionally shows a small portion of its anatomy at the surface. A photographer is going to have to be spectacularly lucky if we learn significantly more about our monster from surface films or photos.

IX
Sonar

Of all the evidence presented here, I regard the sonar data as the most important. First, because sonar provides an objective, permanent record of contact and tracking of objects that can later be analyzed and studied; second, because this experimental approach makes the Loch Ness phenomena data reproducible—i.e., the large number of positive results obtained make it clear that anyone with reasonably sophisticated sonar equipment can expect to contact a target of interest if enough time is spent in searching. The results tabulated in Table 3 (Appendix E) have been obtained by a number of different and unrelated investigators using a wide variety of sonar equipment. This independent kind of corroboration is the sort of evidence near and dear to the scientific mind and comprises a most important part of the scientific method.

Early in our research we realized that the Loch Ness phenomena spent very little time at the surface. As indicated in Chapter VI, most observations can be related to *known* objects, both animate and inanimate, so that genuine surface observations of the *un*known animals are rare indeed. And Chapters VII and VIII showed the small contributions made by surface photographs and films. Therefore, it became obvious that to obtain information we would have to probe the depths of Loch Ness. The most apparent approaches were underwater photography and observation. However, the extremely poor visibility in the waters of the loch and the tremendous volume of water involved severely limited these approaches. Sonic energy beams, in contrast, are not affected appreciably by suspensions of particles that limit visibility.

In its simplest form, information about the universe around us is derived from our surroundings through our sensory organs or through machines that are extensions of our sensory organs. Sonar is one such

Illus. 1
Hugh Braithwaite
and assistants
lower into Loch Ness
the University of Birmingham
multi-element
fixed sonar transducer,
or sound energy transmitter.
Stuart Markson photo.
Courtesy LNIB/World Book.

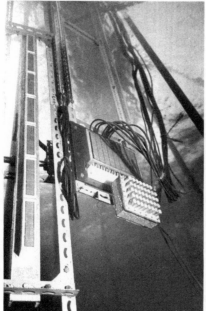

Illus. 2
Birmingham transducer
mounted in place
10 ft. below the loch surface.
Every 10 seconds a pulse of energy
at a frequency of 50 KHz (50,000
cycles/sec) with duration of
1.5 thousandths of a second was
sent out in the loch.
The beam of energy consisted of a
12° cone, essentially providing a
sound curtain through which objects
had to pass if they were moving
along the length of Loch Ness.
Robert Love photo.
Courtesy LNIB/World Book.

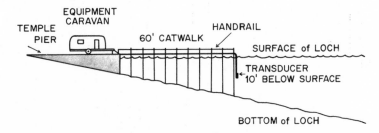

Illus. 3   Sonar transducer location
Birmingham sonar experiments

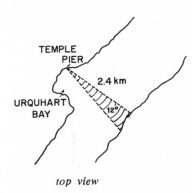

top view

Illus. 4
Diagramatic representation
of the Birmingham
fixed sonar screen experiments.
A = position of transducer;
B = sonar beam (a 12° cone of
sound energy).

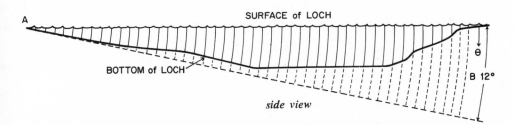

side view

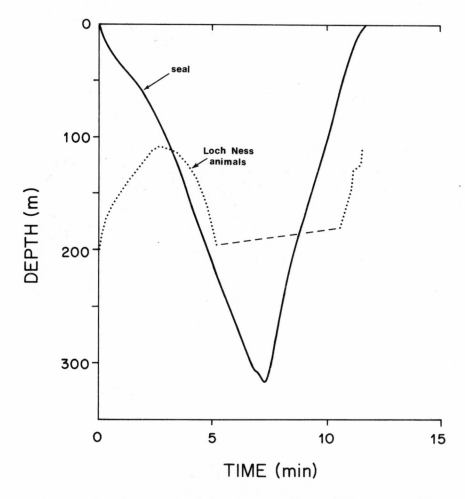

Illus. 5 Comparison of diving profiles of Loch Ness animals and the Weddel seal (*Leptomychotes weddelli;* seal profile redrawn from Kooyman, p. 75). The 6-minute dash line represents the time when the sonar lost the Loch Ness animals, presumably at the bottom of the loch. The rates of dive (indicated by slope of the up-down portions of the curves) of the Loch Ness animals and the seal are quite comparable, although the difference in diving distance is of course 3 times greater for the seal. However, we must note that the seal had a considerably deeper body of water in which to dive; the 200-meter (650-foot) depth of the Loch Ness animals puts them at or near the bottom of the loch. This data supports the hypothesis of benthic (bottom-dwelling), non-air-breathing forms in Loch Ness. That is, the profiles clearly show air-breathing seals diving from and returning to the surface, while the Loch Ness animals rise from and return to the bottom of the loch.

Illus. 6 Research vessel, *Rangitea,* with transducer assembly mounted on prow. Assembly consisted of 12-ft. shaft with transducer on one end and on the other cable connections to main console, rotating mechanism, and electronic equipment for maintaining stabilization of transducer. This latter feature is of considerable importance at Loch Ness, where waves of up to 8 ft. are sometimes encountered. Although sonar traverses were not made under these extreme conditions, the stabilizing feature is capable of pointing the transducer at a constant angle even when its supporting boat is moved through 20° of roll and pitch due to wave action. *Robert Love photo. Courtesy LNIB/World Book Encyclopedia.*

Illus. 7
Transducer for Honeywell Scanner 11-F, used by Robert E. Love in his 1969 mobile sonar search. This high definition pulse-ranging system has maximum range of 3,600 ft. *Stuart Markson photo. Courtesy LNIB/World Book.*

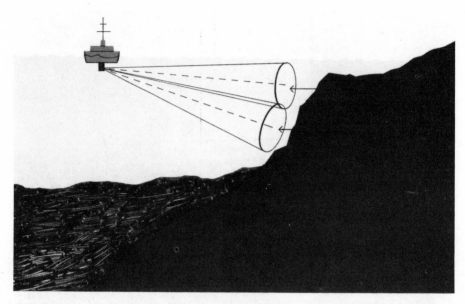

Illus. 8   The sonar beam consisted of a 100 KHz cone of energy 15° wide; gear was so arranged that a scan automatically was made at a beam depression of 8° below horizontal (Hi-Beam) followed by a scan at a depression angle of 20° (Lo-Beam). *Courtesy World Book Encyclopedia.*

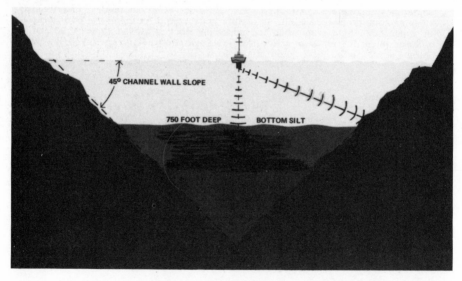

45° CHANNEL WALL SLOPE

750 FOOT DEEP   BOTTOM SILT

Illus. 9   Operation on the 2,400-ft. range permitted scrutiny out to the channel walls on both sides along most of the length of Loch Ness. *Courtesy World Book Encyclopedia*

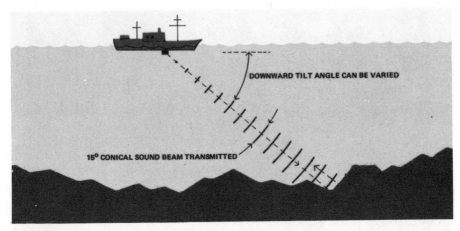

Illus. 10

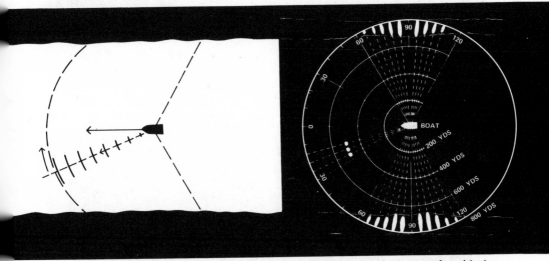

Illus. 11   Target information is displayed on a 10-in. circular cathode ray tube with the center representing the boat position. The system provides automatic scan of the beam clockwise from a bearing 100° left of the boat to a bearing 100° right of the boat. An overall sector of 200° is thus searched out to a distance of 2,400 feet. The beam then automatically reverts to its 100° left bearing; the 200° scan is then repeated. Actually, the beam of energy is transmitted continuously during these 40-second long, 200° scans. Every 5° a pulse of energy is sent (interval between pulses, 1 second) so that the screen display appears as above. The elongated bright spots to the left and right represent channel wall returns while the three dots represent contact with a single, large object. For relatively large objects three or more dots appear on the screen, representing consecutive intersections of the 15° beam with the object during successive pulses directed 5° apart. *Courtesy World Book Encyclopedia.*

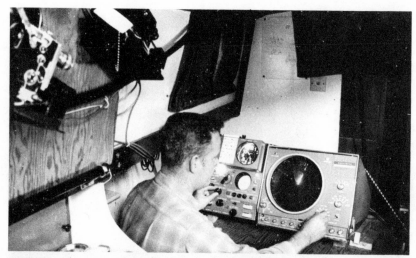

Illus. 12 Bob Love at control console aboard *Rangitea*. Gear could also switch from the normal 200° search scan to a narrow-sector scan mode to provide more frequent "looks" at an area of particular interest. Two Bolex 16mm cameras (upper left) make permanent record of displays and data in a series of single-frame photographs. Drive pulses for these cameras were backlighted for photo-recording. Individual intensity control for each display and automatic compensation for various operating modes provided balanced exposure of film. A full 200° sector scan was recorded on each film frame by time exposure before the film was advanced to the next frame at the start of the next scan. *Stuart Markson photo. Courtesy LNIB/World Book Encyclopedia.*

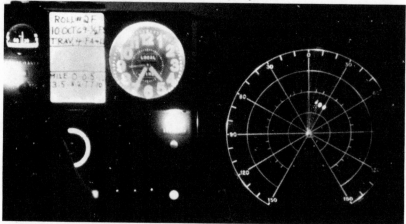

Illus. 13 Photograph of sonar oscilloscope screen showing contact (three dots) with large moving object during 1969 mobile sonar search. (Cf. Illus. 11.) *Robert Love photo. Courtesy LNIB/World Book Encyclopedia.*

machine. Sonar, like radar, employs a short pulse of directed energy, which is transmitted to and reflected back from an object within its path. Unlike radar, which uses radio waves transmitted through the atmosphere, sonar employs sound pulses directed through the water. The sound reflected from an object in the beam is simply an echo, and a sonar system is analogous to a drill sergeant calling cadence through a megaphone in a military compound. If, after each call, the sergeant reverses the megaphone, holds it to his ear, and listens to the echo from the compound wall, he could determine the distance to the wall by measuring the time required for the echo to return. Since the speed at which sound travels in air is constant, he could then point the megaphone toward a more distant wall and, in like manner, determine its distance.

Modern sonar systems utilize similar techniques of directing repeated sound pulses through water and measuring the time before an echo returns. (Sonar technology was developed primarily during World War II and used to detect enemy submarines; since then it has been employed in depth-finding operations and by commercial fishing vessels in locating shoals of fish.) Electronic circuits amplify the echos many times, compute the time, and display automatically on a visual screen or a paper recording chart the direction and range of the reflecting target. The strength of the echos depends upon the rigidity of the reflecting target. (The drill sergeant would not expect to hear as loud an echo from a paper screen as from a concrete wall. Sonar echos underwater also depend upon the nature of the reflecting material.) Metal objects which are heavier than water provide strong echos, as do objects such as air bubbles that are much lighter than water. It is this last property that permits sonar detection of certain aquatic creatures—for example, fish which contain swim bladders within their bodies.

The earliest account we have of possible sonar evidence relating to our Loch Ness monster is from 1954. To the surprise of the crew, the echo-sounding device being used as a depth-finder on a commercial boat passing through the loch turned up on its chart something strange—a large moving form between the boat and the bottom of the loch, at a depth of 480 ft. The object was never identified, and we must rate the matter "inconclusive." However, the public attention surrounding the incident did prompt other boat crews to report unusual chart records during the next two decades; a number of such hard-to-explain items were recorded, but "inconclusive" was again the upshot in each case. During the early 1960s three university expeditions installed sonar gear at Loch Ness. Results: virtually nothing.

It was not until 1968, 1969, and 1970 (Cf. Chapters II, IV, V.), when better equipment integrated into a more systematic program was employed that significant and positive results were obtained. Both stationary shore-based units and mobile boat-mounted units were used. The University of Birmingham experiments administered by Professor D. G. Tucker are examples of the former. (See Illus. 1-4.) Their results clearly show that a number of large (6 meters [20-ft.] long), animate objects are swimming in Loch Ness at up to 17 mph and diving at rates up to 5 mph. The acute angles of descent and ascent, plus the speed and size involved, rule out any of the fish with closed swim bladders which are known to inhabit the loch. The pattern of their movements suggests non-air-breathing animals with homes along the bottom and sides of the loch, rather than air-breathing types which only occasionally penetrate the deeper portions of the lake. (See Illus. 5.) The data further support what has been suspected from sighting reports and photographs—that the animals sometimes swim in groups, not just as individuals; e.g., one small shoal of 5-8 animals was tracked for almost ¼ hour.

Subsequent fixed-mode experiments using different sonar equipment have produced similar results and confirmed the Tucker-Birmingham conclusions. Also, a number of mobile sonar searches (See Illus. 6-13.), again using various types of equipment (including a submarine-mounted unit), have resulted in unambiguous corroborative evidence about the animals' presence, size, and movements.[1] These additional data reinforce, for instance, the conclusion that the animals are bottom and side dwellers, suggesting that they move into mid-water almost as infrequently as they are observed at or near the surface. One particular sonar contact provided an intriguing display—very interesting but open to differing interpretations: the record suggests either periodic physical features such as humps or an elongated animal flexing sinuously as it passes through the sonar beam. (I prefer the latter.)[2]

---

[1] See Appendix E for more technical details of the operation of the various sonar experiments.

[2] See Chapter XIV, note 5 for more information on this point.

Part Three

THE ANALYSIS

We can now ask: What does the evidence mean? Is there a single rational explanation for the sum total of the data consistent with established scientific principles? I submit that a small population of relatively large freshwater animals is the most adequate explanation for the Loch Ness phenomena and that essentially all of the characteristics ascribed to the Loch Ness "monster" can be referred to a single species of animal. The following chapters examine the Loch Ness environment and the body characteristics and behavior characteristics of our Loch Ness animal, comparing this data to all the possible species that might fit and thereby zeroing in on the most probable candidates. I narrow the candidates to two or possibly three, but certainly *one* kind of animal can account for all the data. My preferred hypothesis is a life form thought extinct for 250 million years.

X
The Candidates

We now consider briefly certain forms of mammals, reptiles, amphibians, fish, and invertebrates as candidates for the animals believed to inhabit Loch Ness and certain other freshwater lakes. Those candidates with particular promise of accounting for the Loch Ness evidence are discussed at greater length in subsequent chapters. More scientific detail on a few points only touched upon here can be found in Appendix F.

Mammals. Of these we need only consider the aquatic orders: Mustelidae (otters), Pinnipedia (seals, sea lions, walruses), Cetacea (whales, dolphins, porpoises), Sirenia (dugongs, manatees, Steller's sea cow).

Illus. 1 Manatee.
(Note short head-neck region.)
Courtesy World Book Encyclopedia.

During the past four decades, the otter has from time to time been presented as an explanation of the Loch Ness monster. (Cf. discussions in the books by Rupert T. Gould [1934] and Maurice Burton [1961].) However, this was prior to the accumulation of sonar data, which now rule out otters as realistic possibilities. Suffice it to conclude that no known otter dives to 700 ft. and then behaves as if it could take its oxygen from the surrounding medium. No, otters simply are not sufficiently aquatic. Let us not overlook the fact that there

135

are otters in Loch Ness and that a good number of monster sightings reported by tourists *do* result from the observations of otters. But the otter is not our mysterious beastie.

Pinnipeds offer a more attractive repertoire of characteristics. For instance, the diving capabilities of certain species could account for the diving profiles deduced from sonar data. And the elephant seal would be adequately large to account for a conservatively sized Loch Ness monster. Further, the temperature of the loch would be comfortable for pinnipeds. Nonetheless, this theory can be faulted on many grounds; one of the most serious objections is that all pinnipeds bring forth their young on land or on ice floes. An occasional birth in the water may occur, but survivals in these cases are indeed rare. If the Loch Ness animals were some form of seal, for example, there would be no problem to be solved at Loch Ness; land sightings would be frequent.

The only things to recommend the Cetacea suggestion are adequate size and skin texture. Whales, dolphins, and porpoises have no amphibious capability whatsoever, and their necks are not elongated. Not even archaic forms such as zeugolodon, though more serpentine in shape, had elongated head-neck regions. We must eliminate the Cetacea as candidates.

Sirenians are the most likely mammalian contenders, and the most suitable species among them is *Rhytina stelleri* (Steller's sea cow).

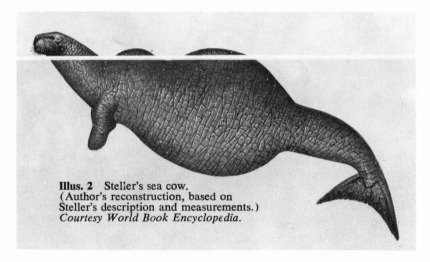

Illus. 2   Steller's sea cow.
(Author's reconstruction, based on
Steller's description and measurements.)
Courtesy World Book Encyclopedia.

(See also Appendix F for table of Sirenia classification and for discussion of the discovery and measurements of *R. stelleri.*) Georg Wilhelm Steller first saw this unusual animal in 1741 off Bering Island (55° N latitude in the Bering Sea). *R. stelleri* is thought to be extinct since 1768, since it was sought as an excellent supply of fresh meat by sailors in the Northern Pacific. However, an occasional report of a sighting still crops up, the most recent in 1961.

Reptiles. In 1965, when I first met David James and began thinking about the Loch Ness problem, I quickly dismissed reptiles from Loch Ness consideration. Further study has not changed my mind. The chief zoological difficulty is the low temperature of the loch, ranging on a warm, sunny summer day from 42° F at the bottom to 58° F at the surface. Since our animals in question spend most of their time at the bottom or around the sides of the loch, they are at home in temperatures only 10° above freezing. Reptiles are *not* at home in such temperatures. The suggestion has been made that perhaps a particular species has developed a special adaptation to this low temperature; this is a logical thought and is exactly what the stem reptiles (Synapsida) did by becoming mammals. As a matter of fact, the Leatherback or Green Turtle (Dermochelys; see Appendix F.) currently exhibits temperature adaptation significant enough to warrant our keeping an open mind on reptiles as a possible explanation for the Loch Ness phenomena.

The most popular theory suggests that the loch monster is a form of plesiosaur. (See Plesiosauroidea classification, Table 5, Appendix F.) Several features fit the facts: long neck, flippers, hump, fish diet,

Illus. 3 Plesiosaur *(Crypotocleidus oxoniensis).* (As it may have appeared in the Upper Jurassic seas. Cf. Chapter XIII, Illus. 2.) *Courtesy World Book.*

20-ft. length; furthermore, some forms believed to swim at considerable speeds and to give birth to live young in the water. One major
problem with this reptile proposal is that the plesiosaur has been extinct for 65 million years. Their fossil record stops at the end of the
Cretaceous period. Until 1938 this simple fact would have completely
ruled out plesiosaurs. However, since then the scientific world has
been twice startled and scientists have had caution forced upon their
absolute judgments. The coelacanth, a primitive fish believed extinct
for 70 million years, was discovered off the coast of Africa; and neo-
pilina, a small primitive mollusk believed extinct for 300 million
years, turned up alive in 1957. Therefore, this gives the reasonable-
ness of precedent to the claim that plesiosaurs, presumed extinct,
might exist, perhaps in an evolved form, in Loch Ness.

Amphibians. Closely related to reptiles and up until recent time included in this group are the amphibia. (See classification table, Appendix F.) These include the well-known frogs and toads, newts and
salamanders. To account for a tail and at least one pair of appendages
in our loch animal, we need consider only the order Urodela among
living amphibians (Illus. 4). We must also examine extinct fossil
forms, for we cannot be sure that a primitive form has not persisted
beyond its supposed end in the geological record.

Illus. 4 Common newt
(Triturus vulgaris;
maximum length: 7″)

The age of amphibians was the Carboniferous period, which ended approximately 270 million years ago. However, amphibians still were present in great abundance during the Permian and even to the end of the Triassic 150 million years ago. While the amphibia had to a large extent become semiterrestrial in the Carboniferous, later many species returned to the water. Many show a tendency toward eel-like forms while others may well be described as half-fish, half-lizard. Of the extinct orders the Embolomeri (Table 6, Appendix F) probably come closest to our Loch Ness morphology. Some Embolomeri were primitively aquatic, others were terrestrial, and still others became readapted to lake life. Typical genera are Palaeogyrinus and Eogyrinus (Illus. 5). Eogyrinus was about 15 ft. long with a short head-neck region. Palaeogyrinus and Eogyrinus were aquatic animals with very weak, definitely reduced appendages. It has even been suggested that these appendages may have been more flipper-like, resembling fins. It is also possible that some of the descendants of the lake-dwelling forms, after returning to the water, developed a larger, more agile head-neck region as an adaptation for efficiently predating fish. Later most of the amphibians were removed to a large extent both from land and water by their own descendants, the reptiles. However, in some large, cold lake environments such as Loch Ness, inhospitable to reptiles, some of these large aquatic amphibians might have survived. It may turn out to be significant that a great many of these fossil remains have been found in the Coal Measures of Scotland. (See Watson [1923].)

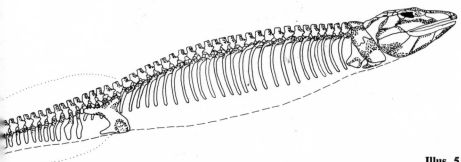

Illus. 5
Eogyrinus attheyi skeleton.
(Author's reconstruction, after Watson [1926], based on fossil remains of Ichthyostega and other Embolomerous Labbyrinthodonts.)

Fish. To many, the idea that a species of large fish inhabits Loch Ness and accounts for the monster sightings seems most reasonable. The varieties suggested have been many: salmon, sunfish, ray, shark, oar fish, sturgeon, catfish, eel. Most proposals have been made with little regard for zoological facts, but the idea of large eels is an outstanding exception.

While the eel hypothesis has been put forward by numerous students of the Loch Ness phenomena, including Burton and me, the credit for this idea must be given to local inhabitants at the loch. In talking with many local people, I collected a healthy number of accounts in which the animal is identified as an unusually large eel—and in some cases also a thick-bodied eel. One peculiarity I noted was that *un*qualified identifications of large eels were extremely rare. That is, the references usually include the qualifying adjectives "hair" or "horse." If a discrete attempt is made to pin down more definitely what is meant by horse or hair eel, one often finds that the observer himself does not know precisely what he or she means. The general impression is that the "eel" was somehow, in addition to size, peculiar in some way as compared to the garden variety of small eel. In a few cases this peculiarity was identified with a mane, frill, or fin; or, in some instances, the witness implied when pressed that *eel* was the best identification he could make, but he could not explain why the term "hair eel" or "horse eel" was used (except perhaps that these terms are an integral part of the vocabulary of the region). In the following chapters additional attention will be given to eels and a detailed comparison made between their characteristics and the Loch Ness phenomena data.

Other fish suggestions are so inadequate in accounting for the Loch Ness evidence that I will not consider them here, except to mention in passing the shark theory. The extremely rare and primitive shark, *Chlamydoselachus anguineus*, is found primarily in Japanese waters, although some have been captured off California and in the Atlantic from Norway to Portugal. These light brown sharks have a monster-like appearance, looking more like a snake than a fish (Illus. 6). They rarely exceed 6 ft. in length, but B. Heuvelmans reports the capture of an animal about 25 ft. long and 10 in. in diameter which fits the description of *C. anguineus* fairly well. However, sharks are marine animals, saltwater fish. But there is one known exception, the bull shark, *Carcharhinus leucas*. Pregnant females frequent river mouths where the brackish water seems to be preferable. At least in one case this species has adapted completely to fresh water: the fresh-water Lake Nicaragua shark has been identified as a bull shark, which at some time in the distant past entered this lake, probably when it was part of the sea.

Illus. 6 Frilled shark *(Chlamydoselachus anguineus). C. S. Wellek drawing.*

While sharks belong to the class Elasmobranchii, having cartilaginous skeletons, eels, in spite of their snake-like appearance, are true bony fish of the class Osteichthyes. (See Table 7 for classification, Appendix F.)

Invertebrates. Animals without backbones may well seem incompatible with many of the characteristics we have deduced about the Loch Ness monster. Though they may not be first-rate candidates, invertebrates as explanation of the mystery is not entirely improbable. Certainly, historically, when much less evidence was available, this theory seemed more plausible, especially in accounting for the large size and the variable back contour so often reported by eyewitnesses. In 1933, William Beebe, the famous American naturalist, first speculated that perhaps giant squids inhabited the loch. Others since have taken up the idea that giant mollusks, though not necessarily squids, may indeed be the answer. Its chief proponent recently has been F. W. Holiday (1962, 1968). He now suggests that the monster is a giant form of *Tullimonstrum gregarium* (Illus. 7), an aquatic, worm-like creature found only in fossil remains, the largest known specimen being 14 in. long. In 1967, when I was actively studying mollusks, a

Illus. 7
Tullimonstrum gregarium.
(Fossils found in great abundance in strip mines south of Chicago.)
Courtesy World Book Encyclopedia.

group capable of explaining the Loch Ness phenomena seemed to be gastropods (Illus. 8, 9), that very large class of animals represented by such forms as snails, slugs, and periwinkles. I soon concluded that

Illus. 8
Unusual sea slug (*Melibe leonia;* maximum length: 4";
this nudibranch shows a remarkably well differentiated head-neck region.)
Courtesy World Book Encyclopedia.

Illus. 9
Carnivorous sea slug (*Navanax inermis;*
maximum length of this tectibranch: 7")
Courtesy World Book Encyclopedia.

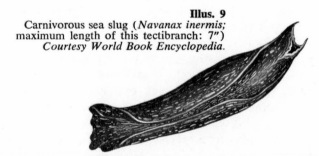

none of the known species of the vast group of mollusks (Table 8, Appendix F) can account for the loch data. However, a transitional form related to the Opisthobranchia (subclass of aquatic gastropods) but possessing the large size and cartilaginous skeletal elements of certain cephalopods *might* begin to account for the data. Notwithstanding their lack of promise, I do give some consideration to invertebrates in the following chapters.

XI
Morphology

This chapter compares the Loch Ness animal characteristics (those falling together loosely under the heading "morphology") with the most probable candidates sketched in the previous chapter. Included here are size and body shape, back contour ("humps"), appendages, head-neck, integument, "horns" and "mane," eyes. Each body characteristic is analyzed in terms of (and in the same sequence as) the categories from Chapter X: mammals, reptiles, amphibians, fish, invertebrates.

Size and body shape. The size of the creature in Loch Ness has been much debated, particularly in view of the many claims for 50-60-ft. monsters. Actually, the best valid estimates for the largest Loch Ness animals are 20-25 ft. (6-7 meters). In fact, Maurice Burton remarks on the recurring estimates by observers of measurements in the neighborhood of 20 ft. The claims of much greater length have been rejected in light of our experience at the loch: eyewitness observations, still photography, film sequences, and, most importantly, sonar returns. Wave motion, for instance, accounts for quite a few mistaken identities—and thus mistaken size estimates. We found that a great number of the many-humped (more than three) reports result from the observation of wave forms produced by the passing of ships through the loch. Because of the long and narrow shape of this lake, long spectacular trains of waves resembling black humps are produced, often up to ½ mile or more in length. These persist for quite a while after the ship creating them has passed, so that the untrained observer does indeed see something unusual to him. Occasionally a shore-reflected bow wave interacts with an incoming stern wave, producing quite unusual hump-like waves, which when observed by believing tourists usually result in a sighting report.

Among mammals, manatees and dugongs normally reach maximum lengths of 10-12 ft., insufficient to account for a 20-ft. Loch

Ness animal. However, giantism does occur—e.g., Steller's sea cow, up to 35 ft.

With respect to reptiles, there are animals large enough to qualify for our Loch Ness data—e.g., *Plesiosaurus aconybeari* (17 ft.) or Muraenosaurus (20 ft.).

In considering amphibians, size is a more serious problem, perhaps *the* most serious problem with the amphibian hypothesis. Most living amphibians are small, the largest being the giant salamanders (Megalobatrachus) of Japan and China, reaching 5½ ft. in length and weighing up to 100 lbs. The hypothesis fares better when incorporating fossil forms, since larger sizes are indeed recorded among the extinct animals—e.g., labyrinthodonta: Eogyrinus (15 ft. length), *Icthyerpeton bradyleyae* (discovered in Jarrow Coal Measures of Kilkenny, Ireland), *Parocyclotosaurus davidi* (11 ft. with 3-ft.-long skull), Mastodonsaurus (16 ft. with 4-ft. skull); however, these latter three giants were mostly head, thus making their morphology unconforming to the Loch Ness data.

One must bear in mind that when estimating size from fragmentary skeletons, considerable error (either plus or minus) may creep into the reconstruction. Further, unless a large number of specimens are available, which is rarely the case with fossil remains, one cannot know whether the specimen is an average one, or is larger or smaller than the average for the species. When Watson made his reconstruction of Eogyrinus, he had 26 presacral vertebrae; the more forward ones showed no evidence of being near the skull, so he conservatively allowed 32, but this is not necessarily correct. In view of these considerations, I submit that some of these animals or related ones may well have been 20 ft. or more in length. Clearly the amphibia never achieved the gigantic proportions of the reptiles (e.g., Elasmosaurus, 47 ft., although over 20 ft. was due to very elongated neck). Therefore, if the Loch Ness animals turn out to be 20-25 ft. amphibians, a great shock will be felt throughout the world of zoology.

As I indicated in the previous chapter, among fish the eel furnishes the most promising hypothesis for explaining the Loch Ness mystery. It certainly has the serpentine body shape so often reported of the loch monster. But what about size? Can eels grow long enough to account for a 20-ft. animal? and bulky enough to match the data that point to a body thickened centrally along the axis? Yes, evidence suggests the possibility of large, thick-bodied eels in Loch Ness.

The maximum size of the common European eel, *A. anguilla*, is usually set at 5-6 ft. in length and about 2 ft. in circumference. The same is true for *A. dieffenbachii*. And there are reports of 8-10-ft. *A. marmorata* eels in South Africa. Also, conger eels and moray eels 9-10 ft. in length have been found. These maximum sizes have been established on the basis of actual specimens captured and measured (Illus. 1, 2). Speculations about much larger eels are based upon

Illus. 1   Conger eel in London market: 160 lbs., 9′ lgth., 30″ circumference. *(Illustrated London News,* September 17, 1904.)

Illus. 2
New Zealand eels,
Anguilla dieffenbachii
(from Schmidt)

some evidence but remain hypothetical. One such speculation goes back to January 1930 when a Danish expedition discovered giant leptocephali, the larva form of eels and a few other fish orders. Off the coast of South Africa, they caught a 6-ft.-long leptocephalus. The larva of the common eel is only 2-3 *inches* before it metamorphoses into an elver. Assuming the 1930 find was an eel larva, some writers suggested that an adult eel developing from a giant 6-ft. larva could indeed be enormous—15-100 ft. in length would not be unreasonable. This theory has persisted for over four decades and has been used to explain the Loch Ness phenomena. However, more recently these giant leptocephali have been identified as the larva of notocanthiform fish.[1] Therefore, while there may be giant eels in the sea (and in Loch Ness), we cannot base such speculation on these giant larvae.

Hypotheses about large, thick-bodied eels in Loch Ness must root in different evidence, such as growth patterns of fish in general and such as specific data about Loch Ness eels collected at the loch itself. First, the growth patterns. How is it that such a wide range of sizes can exist in certain fish, even within a particular species? For example, sturgeon (*Huso huso*) inhabiting the Volga River and the Black and Caspian Seas reach lengths of 28 ft. and weights of 2,860 lbs. The answer lies in the growth pattern of fish, which is quite different from mammals. Growth and size are the result of a complicated interaction of genetic and hormonal characteristics with a variety of environmental factors such as, among others, temperature, food supply, light, population density, available space. Fish, including eels, are cold-blooded, and for most growth is a continuous process with fluctuating rates in some cases. Generally the specific growth rate drops off with increasing age, but still continues at a level greater than zero. Disease, starvation, and predation cause the death of some fish, but the others are potentially immortal. Of course, our knowledge of this subject is far from complete, so we

---

[1] Cf. D. G. Smith; J. G. Nielsen and V. Larsen. The Notocanthiformes (See Heteromi, Table 7, Appendix F.) are little known deep sea fish (the spiny eels). While not actually eels, their closest relatives, according to A. S. Romer, are the true eels, Apodes. It is not known which species develops from these leptocephali, or for that matter whether the adult is known. It may still be possible that these larvae grow into rather large eel-like notocanthiform fish.

must recognize it is possible that individuals of some species might "die of old age," whatever that may mean, but it is certainly not the rule in fish, as it is in mammals. Further, since the structural limitations imposed on land animals are not present in the water, the potential size of aquatic animals is much greater.

Freshwater eels appear to fit the pattern of continued growth and indefinite lifespan.[2] Sexual maturation and size are related. The normal pattern is that when eels become sexually mature, they return to the sea to spawn. (If for some reason the return is blocked, the eel loses minerals and dies.) However, there are, both in captivity and in nature, numerous examples of an abnormal pattern: some individual eels do not undergo the changes of sexual maturity, following which they continue to grow, thus reaching unusually large size.[3]

The specific study of eels at Loch Ness paid particular attention to size distribution in the loch. On the basis of capturing and measuring a random sampling of eels in Loch Ness, a statistically significant skewing toward greater weights occurred. That is, the size distribution is somewhat favorable toward the hypothesis that the eel population of the loch includes a few rather large specimens. (See Appendix G.)

Even if eels do reach 20-ft. lengths, the overall and narrow snake-like configuration customarily associated with eels would not correspond with the central body thickening of the Loch Ness animals, would it? The answer is that as eels increase in length, the body tends to become bulkier. This was shown to be true in our special Loch Ness eel study (Appendix G) and is demonstrated in photographs of large eels. (Cf. Illus 2, especially the eel on right.) In summary, the size and body shape of giant eels can, presumably, account for the Loch Ness data.

Among invertebrates, there is difficulty in accounting for size. No

---

[2] M. E. Brown lists the maximum observed age for *A. anguilla* as 55 years, although there are other claims of eels having been kept as long as 80 years. V. D. Vladykov reports a Swedish specimen caught in 1863 at the age of 3 and kept in captivity until 1948, finally dying at the age of 88 years in the Museum of Hälsingborg.

[3] E.g., David Graham writes with regard to the New Zealand eels that in certain rivers, lakes, or lagoons, where some obstruction prevents return to the sea, large eels which have passed the age of reproduction are occasionally found and remain in such places.

known gastropod, for instance, is large enough; the largest, *Aplysia gigantea*, is only 2 ft. long and weighs 15 lbs. Other mollusks such as the giant clam (*Tridacna gigas*, 5-6 ft., 600 lbs.) fall far short of our 20-ft./2,500-lb. Loch Ness animal. Among the cephalopods, the giant squids and octopuses are quite large enough,[4] but other characteristics prevent their being considered as tenable contenders.

Back contour. The back is, of course, that part of the Loch Ness animal we assume is being seen and photographed most. On the one hand, dorsal contour descriptions exhibit little uniformity in terms of the number of humps seen, although almost half of the eyewitness observations refer to humps of some sort. Of 38 sightings picked at random, 8 descriptions list one hump, 19 list two, 9 list three, 12 list more than three humps. Of course, all of the latter 12 may not be true sightings of the animal; some undoubtedly refer to wave trains. On the other hand, one uniformity among the eyewitness descriptions is reference to the back looking like an upturned boat or like an elephant's back, usually 1-2 ft. out of the water and 3-10 ft. in length. The "upturned boat" phrase occurs again and again. In brief, sifting down the observations to a valid summary, a large percentage of back contours are rounded and solid; fewer but a significant number display more triangular shapes; occasionally a multi-humped and somewhat variable dorsal contour is produced. Clearly, a viable hypothesis must account satisfactorily for these features.

Among mammals, it is known that manatees, when in deep water, often float with the body arched, the rounded back close to or breaking the surface, with head, limbs, and tail hanging downward. Because of the commonly observed "upturned boat" aspect, it is interesting to note Stejneger's report of Steller's 18th-century sighting of the sea cow: "Here and there he observed a huge blackish back like

---

[4] Squids larger than 100 ft. in length probably exist. The largest suckers on the tentacles of a 55-ft.-long squid are 4-5 in. in diameter. Much larger sucker marks have been observed on the skin of captured whales, leading one to infer the existence of much larger squids. It might be objected that because the giant squids are atypical (in that they possess certain internal supportive structural elements—cartilaginous plates and pen—which are uniquely responsible for their large size), it is therefore invalid to cite them as proof that giant mollusks are possible. However, it now appears that giant octopuses, possessing none of these internal structures, also exist. Based on recent research, there is evidence of a 4-5-ton giant octopus with a body 21 ft. long and measuring 200 ft. from the tip of one tentacle to the tip of the opposite tentacle. (See Wood and Gennaro.)

an overturned boat moving slowly about and every few minutes a snout in front of it emerged for a moment and drew breath with a noise like a horse's snort." *R. stelleri* (Chapter X, Illus. 2) apparently had a hump at the shoulder similar to some cattle, buffalo, or members of the extinct proboscidian genus mammuthus. Single offspring are the rule for sirenia, which carry the young on their back; a combination of individuals, some with young, might account for the multi-humped, variable back contour. However, no combination (two males, male and female, females with juveniles on backs, etc.) would explain changing contours clearly seen as relating to a single animal. Finally, the more triangular shape of back contours is hard to explain.

Plesiosaur anatomy does not reconcile at all well with triangular or variable back contours. Almost in desperation some have postulated auxiliary lungs or air sacs to account for these observations.[5] Even if we could suggest some reasonable function for such organs, they would have to lie above the vertebral column in the fashion of a camel's hump, since flexure of the vertebrae to an extent sufficient to match the described contours would otherwise not be possible. While we must infer many plesiosaur characteristics, the one we know with certainty is the vertebral skeletal structure, and there is nothing in the skeletal remains that gives the slightest support to the inflatable organ idea. (See Illus. 3.) However, if the vertical rhomboidal tail flap reconstruction by W. Dames is correct, a 2-humped aspect would be possible and could account for a triangular "back" (tail) contour and considerable water intervening between protruding tail and back. (See Chapter XIV, Illus. 2.)

Illus. 3 Hypothetical (but unlikely) plesiosaur, showing modifications necessary to account for descriptions of multi-humped Loch Ness animals. *Courtesy World Book Encyclopedia.*

---

[5] Inflatable air sacs do, of course, occur in some living reptiles, notably the chameleon, but these serve different functions.

In contrast to the mammals and reptiles, the morphology of aquatic urodeles goes further toward explaining the dorsal aspect than any so far considered. Let us examine the series of drawings of amphibian *Triton cristatus* in Illus. 4. A continuous dorsal and ventral fin-like structure of considerable variability is present. This structure is present in many other salamanders and newts and in practically all of the larval forms. The tendency to arch the back clearly gives the upturned boat effect with or without a ridge (Illus. 4a) depending on whether we are observing a female (Illus. 4a) or a male (Illus. 4e). In many forms even the more conspicuous crests (Illus. 4f) collapse under certain conditions, giving the impression of a ridge when viewed end-on. A two-humped aspect is easily obtained when the back region and part of the tail structure protrude from the water. The edge of the dorsal crest may be smooth and continuous or ragged and broken, even with jagged breaks triangular in silhouette. In addition, portions of these structures may fall over, giving an almost endless variety of variable dorsal contours. In my judgment, these characteristics can account for the relevant observational data most adequately.

The perplexing multiplicities of dorsal contours of the Loch Ness animals can also be accounted for quite adequately by an eel-like body configuration. It is true that the great majority of teleost fish possess a laterally flattened body which can only be flexed from side to side, which results in carangiform swimming (Illus. 5). The eel, however, having a very elongated body with a rounded cross section, can also flex vertically. Anguilliform swimming, as practiced by eels, still involves sinusoidal flexure from left to right as in other fish, which when viewed at a distance will appear to have a vertical component, looking like a series of humps. (See Chapter XIV for discussion of the geometry involved in this aspect.) Further, eels occasionally swim on their sides, and when doing so at the surface, the series of undulations appear to an observer as vertical by virture of the fact the animal is on its side. This motion can easily produce a violent splashing of water at the surface and a series of humps above the waterline. M. Burton and I have independently observed eels swimming on their sides (London Zoo and Shedd Aquarium); he concludes about such a display at the surface: "A really large eel carrying out such a manoeuvre would give the picture of the sea-serpent." (Cf. 1934 eyewitness observation at Loch Ness: Table 1, Appendix A,

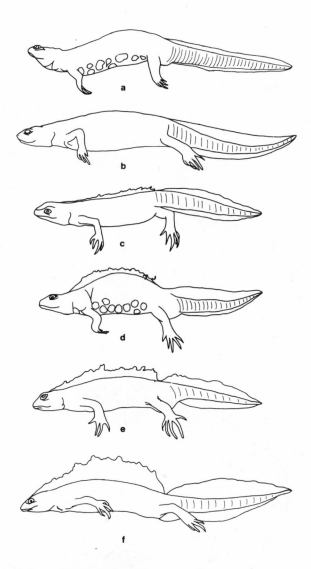

Illus. 4 *Triton cristatus,* showing wide variation in the dorsal development of the males and the marked sexual dimorphism between the sexes: a, b, subspecies karelinii, females; c, d, e, f, males in mating garb. (redrawn from Camerano)

0 85.) In my viewing at the Chicago aquarium, I noted a further point of great interest: one conger eel remained for ½ hour with a vertical flexure about midway between the beginning of the dorsal fin and the tip of the snout. This vertical flexure corresponded to an angle of about 120°; it would, if carried out at the surface, sharpen up the overturned boat aspect even more than shown already in Illus. 6. The

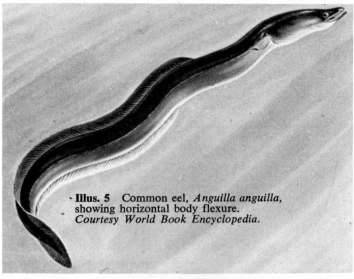

Illus. 5 Common eel, *Anguilla anguilla*, showing horizontal body flexure. *Courtesy World Book Encyclopedia.*

Illus. 6 *A. anguilla,* showing anterior dorsal surface breaking water giving appearance of an overturned boat. *Courtesy World Book Encyclopedia.*

fact that the dorsal fin begins at some distance from the head of the animal permits the display of a smooth convex surface. If the flexure occurs further to the rear, a ridge or even a partial ridge-like aspect would be displayed if the dorsal fin had collapsed more or less completely. That this occurs can be seen in Illus. 7, showing an eel moving over land; the dorsal fin is lying flat against the back, clearly appearing as a ridge.

A more triangular two- or three-humped appearance can occur when portions of the continuous soft-rayed dorsal fin collapse while breaking the surface (Illus. 8).

Illus. 7 *A. anguilla,* moving over land.
(Ernst Zollinger photo, from Bertin)

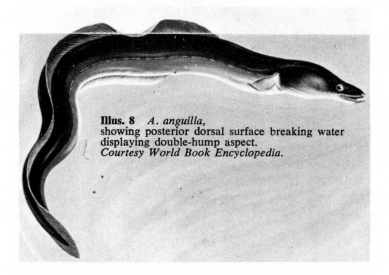

Illus. 8 *A. anguilla,*
showing posterior dorsal surface breaking water
displaying double-hump aspect.
Courtesy World Book Encyclopedia.

Returning to the question of vertical flexure in teleosts, it is pertinent to consider briefly the order Synbranchii (Table 7, Appendix F). These eel-like fish of uncertain relationships demonstrate the considerable increase in freedom of flexure which occurs when a rounded, elongated form is developed. Of particular interest is the freshwater, land-going synbranchid, *Amphipnous cuchia* of the family Amphipnoidae. These air-breathing fish, found in Bengal and Burma, have rudimentary gills associated with breathing sacs developed from the gill cavity. The animals are able to leave the water completely, and they regularly rise to the surface to breathe. They can flex both vertically and horizontally with ease, and when on land are often observed in a typical cobra-like pose, with the front portion of the body raised vertically, head tilted forward, and the posterior tail region curled around horizontally (Illus. 9). Clearly, an elongated eel-like configuration represents a most suitable basis for interpreting the Loch Ness observations.

Illus. 9   *Amphipnous cuchia,*
showing simultaneous vertical and horizontal flexure.
(from New York Zoological Society photo)
C. S. Wellek drawing.

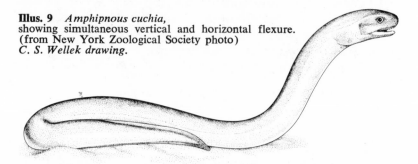

To explain variable number of observed humps and the change from one to two or even three or more, the body flexure and muscular contraction of invertebrates such as gastropods would also seem adequate. One can surmise that such changes might be important for locomotion, respiration, or some other function, such as changes in specific gravity. If, for example, one were to postulate that a mantle cavity as found in some gastropods were involved in one or more of these functions, a change in external back contour might be a necessary consequence. Another consideration could be that a rudimentary shell might be present, as is the case in many gastropods, which could provide an angular hump-like aspect.

Appendages. Appendages are important diagnostic tools as we try to determine what kinds of animals we may be dealing with. Evidence for flippers or paddle action comes primarily from eyewitness reports and from two photographs (Chapter VII, P 5, P 16, especially the latter). The few land sightings are most relevant among the eyewitness accounts (Table 2, Appendix A). From this evidence one concludes there are a pair of front appendages. The overall evidence is much more ambiguous about whether the Loch Ness animals have two or four appendages.[6] At least some of the data suggest that only a front pair is present. This assessment was supported by my own interviews with observers in Ireland.

In sirenia, the anterior modification of the forelimbs into flippers or paddles would adequately explain the observations at Loch Ness and in Ireland of a single pair of flipper-like appendages. In *R. stelleri* the paddles were relatively smaller and would correspond even more closely with some of the eyewitness descriptions.

Without exception, all of the Synaptosaurian reptiles had four paddle-like appendages of almost equal size, although the front pair was usually slightly longer. In all cases there were five digits with some extra bones in each digit. The single pair of anterior appendages inferred from the classification data (Table 5, Appendix F) and the impressions of a single pair of pectoral limbs gathered from my interview data in Ireland cannot be reconciled with two pairs of substantial paddles. If the posterior plesiosaur paddles were much smaller, as in marine turtles, one could perhaps make a case for an observer's missing the second pair because they were relatively inconspicuous. Or if one prefers to interpret the Loch Ness data as indicating four appendages, the problem vanishes, of course.

A consideration of amphibians provides a new and interesting possibility in dealing with the uncertainty of whether the Loch Ness animals have two or four appendages. Among amphibians, *both* forms

---

[6] Mrs. MacLennan (Table 2, E 12) claimed to have seen four short, thick, clumsy, hoof-like limbs; however, when she initially reported her observation, she did not mention any appendages, and only "remembered" them over 25 years later when M. Burton pressed her about the animal's limbs. Therefore, I can attach little weight to her reference to appendages. Mr. Grant (Table 2, E 14) was definite about a strong pair of front flippers but very vague (both verbally and in his drawings) about rear appendages.

may be present at the same time. Most aquatic urodeles have four limbs, but there are species such as *Siren locertina* which have only an anterior pair. There are even forms with no appendages at all, or have them so reduced as to be unnoticeable. This variability is so extreme that in certain single species, specimens may occur with four limbs *or* four limbs with one pair reduced to a rudimentary state or even absent altogether. Therefore, if the Loch Ness animals are a species of large urodele, observers reporting one pair of limbs and those reporting two pairs of limbs may both be correct.

The adaptation of the form of the limb to different modes of existence is very great in amphibians. Some aquatic forms have webbed digits on shortened, stubby limbs suitable for their life in the water but most inadequate for moving about on land. Most living forms have four digits on the front pair of limbs and five on the rear pair. There are also at least three families that have only four digits on the hind limbs. As noted, the most primitive amphibians, such as Eogyrinus, may have had more paddle-like appendages; unfortunately, with the exception of a single femur, limb bones have not been preserved. Thus, our knowledge of primitive amphibians rests on inference. (See Appendix C, P 16, Rines photo, Illus. 7) From the foregoing it is clear that the nature and variability of urodele limbs account most adequately for the appendage observations at Loch Ness.

All species of freshwater eels possess a pair of pectoral fins; pelvic fins are completely absent. Thus we have a correspondence with the Loch Ness animals if we assume a single pair of anterior limbs. However, if hind limbs must also be accounted for, we are in serious trouble. Further, there are no other species, including all the known marine varieties, that have a pair of pelvic fins in addition to pectoral fins. As a matter of fact, the morays have neither. If we examine the fossil record of eels (unfortunately very fragmentary) the situation is much the same. Of the few families of eels represented, most are relatively close to living forms. However, one fossil genus, Anguillavus of the Upper Cretaceous, is of great interest because the pelvic fins were still present (Illus. 10). No fossils exist bridging the gap between this primitive form and the teleosts in general. This one example, however, establishes that two pairs of fins may be expected in primitive eels, which might explain the possible presence of four appendages in the Loch Ness animals, if eels that had retained this archaic feature were involved.

Illus. 10 Reconstruction of Anguillavus,
based on descriptions of fossils *A. quadripinnis* and *A. bathshebae* by Hay
and *A. hackberryensis* by Martin. Whether Anguillavus possessed a row of
lateral scutes as shown is uncertain; this feature is found only in
A. quadripinnis, and Regan holds that since there is no trace of a
dorsal fin in this specimen, it is a representative of another genus
and probably not an eel at all. *C. S. Wellek drawing.*

Most mollusks do not have appendages which lend themselves to
identification as the one or two pair required by the data from Loch
Ness. However, there are a number of families of sea slugs which
have developed rounded rowing parapodia or appendages. An example is Lobiger, which has two or three pairs of prolonged, lateral, oar-
like appendages. In some forms the parapodia are modified into wing-
like structures. Typical is the carnivorous pteropod, *Clione limocina,*
a gymnosomate which has converted parapodial wings into two-way
sculling organs. These kinds of organs could account for the reported
appendages of the Loch Ness animals.

Head-neck. In reports from Loch Ness and Loch Morar, many
descriptions, on the one hand, use such phrases as "horse-like,"
"about the size of a cow's head," "sheep-like," "head and face the
size of a large dog," and "giraffe-like." On the other hand, one finds
equally compelling and just as numerous descriptions such as "eel-
like" and "serpent-like." A few observers report a vertical flattening.
The head-neck is generally estimated 2-7 ft. in length, tapering slightly
from 4-12 inches in diameter. It repeatedly is described as pole-like,
with no differentiation at the head-neck juncture.

Steller's sea cow description is pertinent: "The skull is not too different in its general shape from a horse's skull; when it is still covered
with flesh and hide it resembles a buffalo's head." The head of *R.
stelleri* was smaller than other sirenians. This conformation would
conform much more to the Loch Ness descriptions than would the

shape of the head and neck of manatees and dugongs. The fact that these sirenians all have very short necks, of course, rules out these forms as we know them. However, since the cervical vertebrae in these animals are not fused (with one exception of two vertebrae in manatees), it would be possible to suppose that a relatively long-necked, small-headed form of sirenian (Illus. 11) could have evolved, developing a longer neck as an adaptation to fish predation.[7]

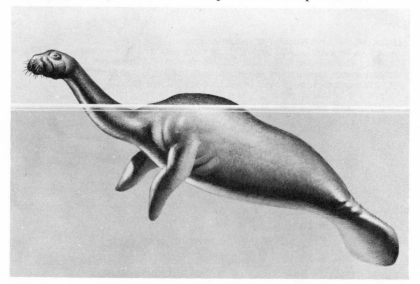

Illus. 11   Hypothetical (but unlikely) sirenian, showing anatomical changes necessary to account for descriptions of the animals reported in Loch Ness. *Courtesy World Book Encyclopedia.*

---

[7] Although, as noted, no complete specimen including soft parts of *R. stelleri* has survived, Steller's measurements of the head-neck region of a 24.7-ft.-long individual are relevant here. He records the length of the head and neck of this specimen as 52 in. (4.3 ft.). Applying the same ratio (52/296) to a 35-ft. specimen gives a head-neck length of 6.2 ft. Little or no skeletal change would consequently be required to account for the 2-7-ft. head-neck attributed to the animals in Loch Ness. The relative thickness, musculature, and soft tissue would, however, have to be reduced even in the case of Rhytina, as Steller recorded a neck circumference of 82 in. (26 in. in diameter) compared to the 4-12 in. reported from Loch Ness. What zoologists think of this possibility can be summarized by Dr. Bertram's short comment, made to me during a luncheon in London: "They [the sirenians] don't like to have their necks stretched."

The occasional behavior of sirenians in standing out of the water, more or less vertically, could account for some of the observations of a vertical pole-like head and neck which have been reported at Loch Ness.

Evidence from fossil remains leaves no doubt that the head-neck region of Plesiosaurus, including a relatively enlarged trunk region, would be more than adequate to account for the Loch Ness descriptions. However, if we examine the relevant skeletal material more closely, we find there are difficulties. Again and again we hear observers state that they could detect little or nothing which differentiated the head from the neck region. While it must be recognized that much uncertainty accompanies restoration of soft parts of fossils when only skeletal material is available, I submit that no paleontologist or comparative anatomist would reconstruct the plesiosaur head-neck region without a definite narrowing at the point where the skull is joined to the first cervical vertebrae. However, in certain living reptiles, such as legless lizards (Pygopodidae), head and neck are relatively continuous.

Upon examination of the head-neck region of living and extinct amphibia, one is struck by the abundance of relatively large heads with short necks. However, this general condition is not without exception. In many salamandrids a tendency toward a more snake- or eel-like configuration is present, resulting in heads only slightly differentiated from the neck with some elongation of the neck region. Such tendencies are exhibited by the Crested Newt (*Triturus cristatus*) and the Common Newt (*T. vulgaris*). Still more pronounced is the neck elongation in the Bespectacled Salamander (*Salamandrina terdigitata*) and in the genus Batrachoseps. A fair number of species approach the approximate proportion of 20% of the animal's length consisting of head-neck.

Extinct orders of amphibians also show a more or less short head-neck region. Watson reconstructed Eogyrinus in that manner. However, it should be borne in mind that according to Watson the placement of the shoulder girdle in the reconstruction depends on the assumption that the post-temporal bone of Eogyrinus was a size corresponding to that of a closely allied form, Pholiderpeton. He further states that the presence of a quite distinct neck in Embolomeri is confirmed by the skeleton of Cricotus and that of Pholidogaster, in both of which there is a *considerable length* of vertebral column lying in

advance of the shoulder-girdle. It seems clear from this that no anatomical feature in the skeletal structure of these primitive amphibians
would have prevented the subsequent evolution of a longer agile neck
adapted to predating fish.

The combined head-neck region as used in these discussions refers
to the region that would be so identified by the average nonprofes-
sional observer. In the case of eels, this would be the entire region
ahead of the pectoral fins. This region measured 7-21% in the case of
some 129 specimens taken from Loch Ness. (See Appendix G.) A
trend toward a relative increase with increasing length was noted.
This proportion agrees rather well with conservative estimates of the
corresponding region of the Loch Ness animals (especially if the
bias toward an excessively long neck introduced by inclusion of bird
observations and tail descriptions is eliminated).

The observation that the head is continuous, with little or no differentiation from the neck, is admirably accounted for by the eel configuration. The pole-like aspect so often described is exactly what one
observes when eels poke their heads out of the water. And maybe
even their tails. We have already referred to Burton's interesting description of eel behavior relative to "humps." One additional description of this may be relevant to reports in which the tail of the Loch
Ness animal is mistaken for an extremely long head-neck region. During his aquarium observation, Burton noticed one 2½-ft. conger rise
from the bottom and tilt its body until it was suspended in midwater,
head down. It then glided to the surface until its tail protruded vertically 9 in. above the water, in which position it swam gently along.
A 20-ft. eel carrying out this maneuver would present an aspect which
could be interpreted as a slender 6-ft. long neck, especially if viewed
on edge; it might also look pole-like at a distance.[8]

Of all the groups of mollusks, the gastropods are the best choice
when attempting to account for Loch Ness head and neck descriptions, because a distinct head-neck region is present in the majority.
This is in marked contrast to the Bivalvia and Placophora which have
no distinct head. Among the Opisthobranchia (sea slugs), a fair number of species possess an elongated head-neck region, reduced markedly in diameter relative to the trunk. This is particularly pronounced
in the free-swimming orders, such as the Sacoglossa and Pteropoda,

---

[8] See Chapter XIV for discussion of the incompatibility of an extremely long
neck and a long, powerful tail in aquatic animals.

specific examples being *Elysia viridis* and *Clione limacina*. While those forms which are shell-less approach the confiration exhibited by the animals in Loch Ness, they are all less than 2 ft. in length, a great many being very small indeed. While one cannot rule out gigantism absolutely, it seems certain that the physiology and structure found in these small animals would not permit viable scaled-up versions 20 ft. long with head-neck regions in proportion. However, if special evolutionary changes in physiology and structure occurred, a self-supporting mobile head-neck representing 20-25% of the body length might be possible. In this connection we should recall the extremely powerful muscular tentacles of the cephalopods (squids and octopuses).[9]

---

[9] The evolutionary "program" of the Opisthobranchia has been outlined by Morton and Yonge in *Physiology of Mollusca*. The following is a brief summary, oversimpled but still indicating what the major trends are. There are, of course, many examples of individual exceptions which make the group as a whole extremely interesting. There has been a gradual development of a smooth slug-like body with a reduction or even complete loss of a shell in many forms. Almost full bilateral symmetry is achieved in the more advanced forms. Morton and Yonge list five evolutionary stages as follows:

"1. With animal still displaying torsion and with visceral connectives still crossed (chiastoneury), with spacious pallial cavity and gills, and fully spiral shell, sometimes with an operculum.

"2. With parapodia enlarging and mantle beginning to enclose the fragile shell with reduced or inviolate spire; pallial cavity reduced and to the right, the spiral visceropallium already dominated by the bi-lateral head-foot.

"3. With complete enclosure of visceral mass and vestigial shell plate within a slug-like contour, mantle cavity still a small recess on the right, or the mantle skirt projecting over fully exposed gill.

"4. With a shell-less, externally symmetrical form; mantle cavity lost and with sensory, respiratory, and protective functions devolving upon the naked upper surface.

"5. With external prominence of the visceral mass reasserted by the extension of the digestive gland into club-like cerata.

"Imposed upon this main plan and cropping up adventitiously through each Opisthobranch line we find the habit of temporary or permanent swimming, either by parapodia or by the action of the whole body; in pelagic pteropods, swimming and equilibrating adaptations take command of the whole structural plan."

A careful consideration of these stages of development shows that many of the observed trends favor the development of animals approaching the general configuration attributed to the Loch Ness animals.

Integument. The surface texture and color of an animal may or may not be useful in identification. For example, if hair is observed, one can be sure we are dealing with a mammal; if hair is absent, we may still be dealing with a mammal, as several almost hairless species exist—e.g., elephant, walrus, porpoise. The Loch Ness creatures are described most commonly as black, greyish black, blackish brown, reddish brown, and "black like the skin of an elephant." Olive green or greenish-black have also been reported. Some few have indicated that the body color is lighter or even whitish on the underside. The surface is repeatedly described as tough looking, sometimes rough, like the skin of an elephant, bare not hairy, and in some cases wrinkled. No scales are present. Dinsdale and some few others report dappling; Dinsdale described a dark blotch on the left flank of the hump he filmed. It cannot be determined with certainty whether a true color is being described or whether reference is being made to effects of lighting, shade, shadow, or reflectivity, depending on the angle of observation and lighting conditions in general. We must remember that any portion of an object seen in silhouette or any portion shaded will appear dark or blackish.

Rhytina had a tough, leathery skin, dark brown like the skin of an elephant, practically hairless and wrinkled when undergoing extended periods of semistarvation. Manatees have dark grey skin running to bluish black with a tinge of olive green above and yellowish below. It is obvious that the color and texture of the sirenia accord remarkably well with the descriptions attributed to the phenomena in the loch.

Most people, when thinking of reptiles, picture the familiar snakes and lizard and think of scales. While in fact most reptiles have scales of one sort or another, a few living forms do present a smooth, scaleless appearance. In the case of plesiosaurs, the only traces of skin available suggest that the skin was smooth, with no dermal armour. Thus, consensus is that these reptiles were completely smooth and may well have had an appearance compatible with Loch Ness descriptions of a hairless, scaleless skin. We know nothing whatsoever about the coloration of these primitive reptiles, so all we can say is that the wide range of skin color found in living reptiles more than encompasses the black or black-brown to greenish shades reported at Loch Ness. Some species are variegated and have elaborate color patterns, while other forms, such as the chameleons, can actually change color.

The skin of the amphibians also corresponds rather well with the Loch Ness descriptions. The color variation and range in all groups of amphibia is very wide indeed. Black, black-brown to brown, and greenish tones are not uncommon, although bright and bizarre color patterns are also found, especially as exhibited by certain males during the mating period. A wide range of spectacular mottled, spotted, and striped patterns, in addition to drab uniform coloration is exhibited by many species. A lighter underside is also present in many terrestrial and aquatic forms. Some amphibians change color under varying conditions, rivaling the chameleons in this respect. Generally higher temperatures, drying, or increased light produce a lightening.

In aquatic and many terrestrial amphibians the skin is smooth and scaleless, the exceptions being the worm-like caecilians which do not concern us directly. Two kinds of glands are found: one type excreting mucous, the other excreting substances of varying toxicity. The slimy mucous retards drying, and in the case of aquatic forms may contribute to more efficient swimming by reducing friction. The more terrestrial forms may have a much rougher and dryer skin surface. Again, both in some terrestrial and aquatic species considerable rugosity (wrinkling) or skin folding may be present. In many urodeles transverse creases are found along the trunk and tail, particularly in regions of flexure. A number of these special features of the skin of amphibia would account remarkably well for certain rarely reported features of the animals in Loch Ness (discussed in more detail below).

The color range and skin texture of eels is completely consistent with the observations reported from Loch Ness. Olive green to olive brown, dark brown to black, and various other shades of medium to light brown are the colors observed in freshwater eels. The undersides range from yellowish milky white to white. The color range exhibited by eels caught in Loch Ness was very wide, ranging from essentially black to very light brown, with at least two specimens showing excessive mottling. The various species of moray eels show even greater varieties of color and patterns, even including stripes and speckled patterns.

The skin of many marine species of eels is smooth, having no scales. Freshwater eels do have scales, but they appear smooth because the scales are deeply embedded in the skin and are invisible for all practical purposes. Mucous is secreted, forming a slippery layer over the skin. The mucous serves a number of functions, among which may be the reduction of friction during swimming, an aid in osmostic regulation by the skin, prevention of drying in air, and as an aid to the coagulation and precipitation of mud held in suspension in the water.

The body surface of opisthobranchs varies from smooth to warty or papillate. Coloration includes almost every color of the visible spectrum. Colors ranging from extravagantly bright and vivid shades to drab brown or black are found throughout the group. The epidermis consists of a single layer, in many cases containing two types of gland cells, one of which produces a mucous secretion. Certain parts of the body may have cells specialized for certain functions, such as, among others, producing special secretions, color changes, shell secretion, light and tactile sensitivity. These features of the molluscan skin are adequate to account for the integument descriptions of the Loch Ness animals.

"Horns" and "mane." Many have dismissed these features as pure fantasy; others, failing to account for them, have rejected the whole idea of large animals in Loch Ness. But "horns" and "mane" *are* reported (in only about 5% of valid sightings), and my personal experience is that observers reporting these features are no less reliable than those who have not observed them. Therefore, I can find no justification for eliminating "horns" and "mane" from consideration.

Neither horns nor mane can be accounted for by the anatomical features of known sirenia. One could perhaps postulate a mane present in only one sex as a result of sexual dimorphism, or nostrils evolved into tube-like structures to facilitate a surreptitious intake of air at the surface. However, there is no evidence from the fossil record or elsewhere that such evolutionary trends or potentials were present in the sirenia. We must always remember that so far as the fossil record is concerned, we know nothing directly about soft parts, and can only infer the probable configuration of the animal from skeletal material.

Relative to plesiosaurs, nothing much can be said about these features, again because very little soft-parts evidence is available. Protrusions enclosing the nares (nostrils) are certainly possible.

Various living reptiles exhibit dorsal ridges, in some cases spectacularly, so we cannot rule out these reptiles. However, in no case is positive evidence for horn-like structures extant.

The dorsal crests and continuous fin-like structures in the aquatic urodeles account most adequately for the reports of a mane; nothing more need be added to the earlier discussion of these features under "Back contour."

However, the characteristics of horns or protuberances reported by some observers is not so easily explained. Few urodeles exhibit structures that might account for these observations.[10]

Possibly the structures that come closest to resembling the Loch Ness descriptions are found in the male of the species *Manculus quadridigitatus*. In this form the nasolabial grooves at the front and to the sides of the upper jaw are extended into a pair of short cirri. In the apoda the nasolachrymal duct is strongly developed, lying in a long, drawn-out "palpus" having the role of an extended nostril. Such structures, if present in modern descendants of embolomerous amphibians, could account for the recorded "horn" descriptions.

The continuous soft-rayed dorsal fin of eels, beginning at various distances from the head (depending on species) and ending ventrally at the anus, can well account for the observations of a mane. Whether or not it would be observed depends on which part of the dorsal surface was viewed above water.

The descriptions of horns correspond very well with the external nares of eels. Eels have two pair of openings located on the upper portion of the head. The front pair, the anterior nares, are generally ciliated tubes which project to varying degrees. In some species they hang down; in others they stick up like stalks. In most species the posterior pair do not protrude, although there are a few examples where they also have the form of conspicuously protruding tubes. These nares are olfactory, giving the eel the ability to detect the presence of only a few molecules of a chemical substance. Water enters through the front pair, passing through the olfactory organs and exiting through the rear pair. These nostrils may take on a variety of shapes, ranging from simple tubes to hour-glass and leaf-shaped forms. The Hawaiian dragon eel has long, tube-like nostrils that begin just above the eye. The correspondence between the known charac-

---

[10] Certain frogs have a long pair of tentacle-like tactile organs, hardly, however, resembling the descriptions from Loch Ness. In *Xenopus calcaratus*, an aquatic African frog, the nasolachrymal duct is terminated at the apex by a marked protuberance below the eye. According to Schmalhausen the broad aperture of this duct stands as evidence of a secondary restoration of its function as the posterior nostril of fishes.

teristics of eels with this part of the Loch Ness data is obviously re-markable.

At this point, one might be tempted to conclude that the Loch Ness animals are giant, thick-bodied eels. To do this, however, would be premature, since we must keep in mind that convergent evolution, i.e., adaptation to similar environment and food supply, may produce almost identical shapes and forms in unrelated animals.

In gastropods a great variety of tentacles and body protuberances occur within the group. A sensory function is associated with the various types of tentacles, whereas respiration, digestion, and other functions are associated with the other protuberances, when present. Of most interest are the one or two pairs of cephalic tentacles widely distributed within the group. When only a single pair is present, it is considered to be the rhinophores, or olfactory organs. The diversity in form of these organs most adequately accounts for the observations at Loch Ness relative to horns or antenna. Many of the other kinds of structures, such as external gills or cerata, could account for an observation mentioning a frill or even a mane.

Eyes. Most descriptions of the Loch Ness phenomena make no reference to eyes, but when mentioned are in some cases described as small, in some cases as slit-like, and in others large. This leaves us in a rather unsatisfactory situation relative to identifying an animal. Further, we do not know to what extent the observer is describing or inferring eyes because he thinks an animal ought to have eyes.

The sight of sirenians is very poor. Present are small, rounded eyes with nicitating membranes and imperfectly formed eyelids, capable, however, of contracting. Steller says that the eyes of Rhytina, in spite of its size, are not larger than sheep's eyes and are without eyelids. The smallness of the sirenian eyes would account adequately for fail-ure of observers to see eyes, since most observations are made at some distance. Further, many animals were viewed in silhouette; that is, with the object between the observer and the source of light, eyes or surface detail would be obscured regardless of size. Contrac-tion of the eye could perhaps account for slit-like descriptions and might be a normal reaction for an animal surfacing abruptly from dark waters. On the other hand, it is hard to accommodate descrip-tions of large eyes, unless some other anatomical feature were present which might be mistaken for eyes. Such features might be a special circular coloration or perhaps ear structures. In the case of all sirenians, however, the ears are so small and hidden as to be invisible.

The eyesight of the Synaptosauria was undoubtedly good, especially in the fish predating types. (Cf. *Prehistoric Sea Monsters* by J. Augusta and Z. Burian.) In living reptiles the eye presents many specializations, some having movable eyelids, others not. Some forms have completely lost nicitating membranes, having a spectacle instead of eyelids. If plesiosaurs had eyelids, their eyes might, on occasion, appear narrow and slit-like, as reported by some Loch Ness observers. While the external eye anatomical features were probably well differentiated, they were quite small, especially in the small-headed forms, the only ones which need concern us. Without proper lighting and with views in silhouette, many observers may miss this feature. On the other hand, reports of very large eyes are just as incompatible with these reptiles as with sirenia. We may note that the teeth were conical, set wide apart, long and very conspicuous, so that one would scarcely expect such a feature to have escaped all observers.

The eye development in many aquatic urodeles could account for the perplexing range of Loch Ness descriptions: small eyes, large eyes, no eyes, slit-like eyes. During the larval phase of development, the eyes are generally large and lidless, although there is an enormous variation in size within the class as a whole. In some forms the eyes are first reduced in size during development and the eyelids only develop at metamorphosis except in those species that are neotenous. There is additional variation in that the lids are reduced in some aquatic forms and even absent in some cases. The upper eyelid is incapable of independent motion, which is also the case in some urodeles with regard to the lower eyelid. In others, however, muscles are attached and in some a completely functioning nicitating membrane is present. This can be drawn up over the cornea so that under certain conditions such an eye will appear slit-like. Thus we see that a given species of urodele could during its life span exhibit eye conditions as described at Loch Ness.

The eyes of eels range from slightly oval to round in shape. In contrast to most other teleosts, eels are an exception in that they show considerable pupil movement and are able to contract the iris in response to increased light. In fact, there is evidence that this response may be direct and automatic, without central nervous system involvement. While in some sharks, all of which have contractile irises, the pupil contracts to form a horizontal or vertical slit, similar information for many kinds of eels is lacking. In a number of ways, the eel eye is more like marine teleosts and sharks, i.e., predominance of the eye pigment Rhodopsin instead of Porphyropsin. Rhodopsin is the exclusive eye pigment in the case of sharks. Whether the eyes of a large eel, contracting the iris in response to the bright light at the surface, might give a slit-like appearance cannot be answered definitely. At close quarters the eyes of the ordinary small eels from Loch Ness do not appear slit-like. As freshwater eels grow and mature, the relative eye size increases until at the time of metamorphosis to a sexually mature adult, the eye size has doubled and the retinal pigments have been replaced by those suitable for a marine existence. The pigments of *A. anguilla* in fresh water are purple, while on reaching maturity they become golden colored. Thus the variation observed in eye size might be accounted for.

While extremely advanced eye structures resembling vertebrate eyes are found in some mollusks such as the cephalopods, in the sea slugs the eyes are more rudimentary. In some the eyes are located on the tips of the tentacles, but in a great many a pair of eyes are located on the head. The various forms of eyes found in the mollusca as a whole are adequate to account for the Loch Ness data; however, if we restrict our consideration to sea slugs, such is not the case.

XII
Environment

Regardless of how well the anatomical features of a particular kind of animal correspond with the Loch Ness data, the animal must also be able to exist in the environment provided. This chapter, then, analyzes the Loch Ness environment in terms of temperature, freshwater conditions, and food supply, briefly examining the compatibility with this environment of the most probable candidates sketched in Chapter X; the same categories (and their sequence) from that chapter are retained here: mammals, reptiles, amphibians, fish, invertebrates.

Temperature. The temperature of the loch is relatively constant below the thermocline at approximately 42° F, never freezing at the surface. (See Appendix K.) This low temperature of the water severely restricts the kinds of animals that might be expected to be found there. The latitude of Loch Ness is 56° N, which normally would be almost subarctic if located more centrally in a large continental land mass, but the tremendous heat capacity of the North Atlantic and the warm Gulf Stream combine to reduce the extremes of heat and cold at that latitude of Scotland, producing warm winters and cool summers.

Living forms of sirenia are restricted to tropical waters, but the presence of Rhytina around Bering and Copper Islands (55° N) indicates a possible former normal range of latitude for this species, say, from 50° N to 60° N. The observation of these creatures among the ice floes indicates they were quite at home even in freezing or close-to-freezing water. Since the sirenians are mammals, they are homoiothermic, and in the case of Rhytina adapted to cold, maintaining a high metabolic level under arctic or at least subarctic conditions. And there is no reason why forms related to Rhytina should not be at home in the 42° F waters of Loch Ness.

The low temperature of the loch almost rules out a reptile hypothesis. However, an endothermic characteristic *may* have been present in plesiosaurs, so we leave this loophole. (See Chapter X for elaboration of this point.)

In contrast to reptiles, amphibia have adapted to a very wide range or temperatures. Thus, species are found in tropical regions and in permafrost regions of Siberia. This is true in spite of the fact that amphibians, like reptiles, are cold-blooded. Many aquatic urodeles are found in cold mountain streams and lakes, at temperatures quite comparable to those found in Loch Ness. Stability of the temperature is a prime requisite which would make the constant year-through temperature in Loch Ness a most suitable environment for large aquatic amphibians.

No question as to the suitability of the temperature of Loch Ness for eels can be raised since small eels are actually thriving in the lake, as evidenced by the 129 specimens trapped in 1970 and 1971. The constant low temperature, however, can be expected to have several consequences of interest. Experiments with *A. japonica* by Kuha Itsuo in 1936 established that as the temperature is reduced, the feeding velocity decreases. If the temperature drops low enough, hibernation ensues, although under natural conditions not all members of a population will actually hibernate. Since the temperature in Loch Ness below the thermocline is constant throughout the year, such behavior would not be expected. However, the low temperature, coupled with a low feeding velocity, might contribute toward very slow maturation and toward large size. (Cf. Appendix G.) That the Loch Ness environment has profound effects on the growth of the eels living therein is supported by the finding that the otoliths or ear stones of these eels are ambiguous, not showing clearly the annular zones or rings, which are normally observed in eels living under less constant conditions.

The temperature which mollusks can tolerate almost represents the extremes for multi-cellular organisms (32°-115°F). It is of interest to note that certain Lake Geneva pulmonates live at a depth of 200 meters (650 ft.) but surface regularly only when water temperature at the surface is relatively high and the lake is calm, without wind. Many freshwater and marine mollusks would be perfectly comfortable at the temperatures encountered in Loch Ness.

Freshwater conditions. Loch Ness is fresh water so that any animals, large or small, must be completely at home under these conditions. However, reliable sightings have also been reported in Loch
Linnhe, which is, as commonly designated, a sea loch with typical
marine conditions. The *assumption* of Loch Linnhe as a saltwater es-
tuary has only recently been put to *empirical* test. The results are surprising. Normal marine salinity is 33 parts per thousand. A salinity
of only 16 parts per thousand extends along most of the length of
Loch Linnhe, and the top 5 meters (15 ft.) of water is practically
fresh, with salt concentrations as low as *one* part per thousand. (See
Appendix B.) These semifreshwater conditions result from the 700
million gallons per day of fresh water entering from sources near the
upper end of the loch. Studies by Adams and coworkers show the
presence of a great variety of freshwater plankton, establishing un-
equivocally that the environment is suitable for freshwater life forms.
It is of great interest to compare the salinity at the northeast outlet
of Loch Ness, the Inverness and Beauly Firths, where *no* sightings
have been reported. Studies by Craig and Adams show that salinity
is much higher, rarely dropping much below 20-24 parts per thousand.

This evidence leads us to conclude that our loch animals are at
home in fresh water and brackish conditions of low salinity.

Dugongs, with rare exception, do not enter rivers, but will survive
in fresh water and have been kept in captivity at Mandapam Camp
in South India for nearly a decade. Manatees, like dugongs, are restricted to inshore waters, but also freely enter lagoons and the fresh
waters of estuaries and rivers, reaching to hundreds of miles from the
sea. The fact that *Trichechus inunguis* is landlocked in the Amazon
and Orinoco river systems proves that sirenians can exist exclusively
in fresh water, if necessary, and provides a parallel with Loch Ness
and its phenomena. The question has often been raised as to why the
Loch Ness (and similar) phenomena should be confined to freshwater lakes, semilandlocked, but connected at least on occasion to the
sea by rivers and streams. One of many logical explanations is that
these environmental cul-de-sacs provide suitable barriers against deci-
mation by predation. Sirenians, under marine conditions, are attacked
by sharks and if sick or hurt are also prey to parrot fish. Thus, a
northern variety might have sought refuge in freshwater lakes such

as Loch Ness and the southern species in a South American river system.

No problem is presented with the fresh water of Loch Ness relative to plesiosaurs. While many forms have been found under marine conditions, some also have been discovered under conditions from which we can infer a freshwater environment, particularly estuaries and rivers. One can speculate that these reptiles moved up rivers and perhaps into lakes pursuing fish and perhaps escaping predators that were more rigorously confined to salt water. One might raise the question why these reptiles should now be found only in freshwater lakes when the fossil record clearly indicates that in their heyday they were mainly, if not exclusively, marine. Those who accept the possibility of "sea serpents" would reply that indeed they are not confined to fresh water, especially in view of sighting reports similar to Loch Ness in the open sea. In this connection we must remember that a relationship between "sea serpent" observations and the animals reported in Loch Ness is at most tenuous.

We have already discussed briefly the fact that amphibia are for all practical purposes confined to fresh water (Chapter X). The fresh water of Loch Ness is most suitable for them, as would be the fresh water conditions in Loch Morar and in the lakes of Ireland where observations have been made. Further, the recent salinity analyses of Loch Linnhe help us account for the sightings there; that is, the extremely low salt content in the upper layer of that loch would permit freshwater amphibians to use the lake as a feeding area when necessary. With regard to the observations in the River Ness, it must be remembered that the animals were actually observed in the fresh water of the river, and it does not necessarily follow that they actually continued downstream and entered the sea. In any case, no observations have been reported from the Inverness Firth and it is tempting, as indicated, to relate this fact to the higher salt concentrations there. Since I cannot find a valid basis for rejecting the three observations reported in Loch Linnhe, it seems necessary to postulate that at least a transient exposure to brackish water would have to be tolerated by our amphibians. Of course, if these observations are in error (certainly a possibility), we have only the observations in the River Ness to explain, which are hardly as compelling.

Anguillidae are catadromous fish; that is, they are oceanic fish that leave the sea to pass their period of growth in fresh water. Those that mature sexually return to the sea to spawn. This fact and the known presence of eels in Loch Ness eliminate the need for further discussion regarding the appropriateness of the freshwater environment of the loch.[1]

Quite a variety of freshwater mollusks are known, including gastropods. However, the known opisthobranchs or sea slugs are almost exclusively marine; cephalopods (octopuses and squids), without exception, are marine. While most sea slugs are confined to waters of normal salinity, some typically inhabit brackish waters; one species, *Embletonia pallido*, tolerates extremely dilute sea water. The fact that very few sea slugs have adapted to fresh water raises some difficulties, although the great variety of freshwater pulmonates, a closely related group of gastropods, demonstrates that adaptation is not only possible but can be highly successful.[2]

---

[1] Further, the reported observations of Loch Ness animals in the saltwater lake Loch Linnhe are also completely compatible. Adult freshwater eels in addition to larvae are regularly observed in the sea and in estuaries. These observations include cases, especially in New Zealand, outside of the periods when sexually mature eels are returning to the sea to spawn. Males are in general more prone to remain in brackish water, leading some authorities to believe that males never enter fresh water. This extreme view, however, has been contradicted by the identification of sexually mature males in fresh water. In any case, there can be no doubt that large, freshwater eels would be expected to be observed in salt water as well as in fresh water.

[2] The problem for marine mollusks is mainly one of osmotic adaptation to the much lower salt concentrations in fresh water. In brackish water few maintain their body fluids hyperosmotically. They simply adjust their body fluids to the lower salinity. Successful freshwater gastropods, such as the pulmonates, maintain low hyperosmotic ionic concentrations, and active uptake of ions is the rule. Most importantly, the osmotic and ionic regulation in mollusks is such that successful acclimitization to fresh water can be achieved by gradual dilution of the environmental sea water over a 5-8-month period. This has been demonstrated by Beudant in the laboratory with such marine mollusks as Patella, Nucella, Cordium, Ostrea, and Mytilus. What can be done in the laboratory in a few months may have occurred in nature over a much longer period.

The decreased surface area per unit volume of tissue mass in the case of larger organisms would make the problem of maintaining the internal fluids at suitable ionic concentrations less acute. The relatively decreased surface area (See table below.) through which ionic losses could occur would mean that a smaller fraction of metabolic energy would be necessary for homeostasis. It would appear that a large freshwater gastropod is a physiological possibility; nevertheless, it is curious that not a single example

Food supply. Zoologists concerned with the Loch Ness creatures often ask: "But what would they eat?" Obviously no single animal could survive over the hundreds of years during which sightings have been reported, so the animals must be present in sufficient numbers to assure reproduction and to withstand attrition from disease and other natural causes. Such a group of large aquatic animals must consume a substantial amount of food. How much food is required for a particular kind of animal depends not only on its size but also on its metabolic rate and energy requirements for maintaining its activities. An aquatic mammal, for instance, consumes per day food equal to 1-10% of its own body weight. This requirement is the highest (except for birds), since mammals in Loch Ness would be maintaining a body temperature above that of the loch.

Many life forms in lakes such as Loch Ness ultimately depend on the sea for subsistence. Loch Ness, a freshwater lake, is connected to the sea via the River Ness, Loch Linnhe, and the two sections of the Caledonian Canal. A similar situation obtains in the Irish lakes and in Loch Morar, from whence also come reports of unusual aquatic animals.

Loch Ness is lean in its content of freshwater plankton. The peat-stained water of the loch severely limits light penetration; consequently, plant life grows only in a few shallow areas, being insufficient to support even a small group of large herbivores. The bottom silt is essentially inorganic material, lacking insect and other life forms

---

of freshwater cephalopod is known.

Relationship of Size to Surface-Mass Ratio

Length L	Distance through thickest section D	Surface area S	Mass M	Ratio of surface to mass S/M
2 ft.	½ ft.	2 sq. ft.	.006 tons	330
20 ft.	6 ft.	195 sq. ft.	6 tons	33
40 ft.	6 ft.	372 sq. ft.	12 tons	31

Calculations have been made for an idealized conical configuration.

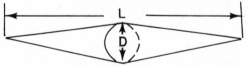

Since for a given species of animal, volume is directly proportional to mass, S/V ratios have similar relationships.

that might otherwise play a significant role in the food chain. In summary, there *is* a food chain in Loch Ness, but aquatic vegetation and microscopic and other smaller life forms are found in lower concentrations—lower than in more hospitable lakes such as Lake Windermere in England, a typical lake often subjected to detailed biological studies.[3]

What, then, can provide an adequate food supply for our Loch Ness monsters? The answer is fish. The loch contains an abundance of trout, pike, sticklebacks, char, eels, and salmon. And among these the salmon is a key source of food for our colony of creatures. A 2,500-lb. mammal would eat 25-250 lbs. of salmon per day. Are there enough salmon to provide for such voracious appetites? Yes.

Appendix H details a census of salmon and their population dynamics in and around Loch Ness. Suffice it here to summarize a few of those pertinent facts before we consider how our candidates relate to the loch's food supply. The spawning migration of the Atlantic salmon (*S. salar*) is a well-known odyssey. Eggs spawned in streams during the fall hatch out in the spring. The yolk sacs attached to the newly hatched fish are gradually absorbed. Then called fry, they feed on aquatic insects and crustaceans in the streams. Having reached a length of 3-4 in., the males become sexually mature, and the fish are now referred to as parr. With increasing food requirements, they move slowly downstream into the larger rivers and lakes where they reach a length of about 8 in. at an age of 2 years. They then undergo bodily changes preparing them for life in the sea. Now known as smolts, they spend a few days in brackish estuaries adapting to the salt water environment, then swim freely to the sea where they will feed for the next few years.

After 2 years at sea, most have reached a length of about 2 ft. and weigh about 10 lbs. They then begin a return migration to their parent stream where they will eventually spawn. Upon reentering fresh water, they cease feeding and develop the reproductive resources required for their parental roles. In the fall, when biological and environmental conditions are right, the salmon enter the mouths of the streams from which they were hatched some 4 years before. As they

---

[3] Even with lower concentrations, Loch Ness still provides a good quantity of life forms simply because of its vast volume of water: 263 billion cu. ft. See Appendix J. See also, for a careful biological study of Loch Morar, Campbell and Solomon, Chapter 7.

move upstream the males and females pair off as mates. When they reach the spawning grounds, the female digs a nest in the gravel with her tail fin. She lays a portion of her eggs which are immediately fertilized by the male. Moving a few feet upstream she cuts another nest, allowing the gravel from the second nest to be carried downstream and cover the eggs in the nest below. More eggs are laid and fertilized in the second nest, and the process is repeated several more times until all the eggs have been deposited. Weakened and depleted, the fish migrate back to sea to feed and regain their strength. The Atlantic salmon, unlike its Pacific cousin, does not die after its first migration, and the adults may return to spawn in the same stream 2 or 3 more times. Thus, lakes such as Loch Ness are somewhat like cul-de-sacs whose food supply is constantly replenished from the sea.

In brief, Loch Ness may well contain, prior to their spawning, *13 million adult salmon* with a total weight of *65,000 tons.* (Appendix H.) The periodic nature of this food supply would present no difficulty, because many aquatic carnivors feed heartily during annual cycles when food is plentiful and fast during lean periods. However, fish predators in Loch Ness do not have to wait a year. In addition to the *in*ward migration of adult salmon coming for the spawning season, there is the *out*ward migration of those spawned—that is, the 2-year-old juveniles making their way to the sea. Thus, the migratory cycle produces within Loch Ness another and even greater food source, one not periodic but constant in its supply. Feeding in Loch Ness and its tributaries at any given time there may also be about *19 billion juvenile salmon* with a total weight of *68,000 tons.*

How many of our large, unidentified predators could such a food supply support? (Remember, salmon are not the only fish in Loch Ness.) There could easily be a population of 150-200 in the loch.

Factors favorable to successful migration are cumulative in their effect. A reproductive environment combining the many beneficial influences we have discussed must develop as a very prolific system. The homing mechanism is self-perpetuating in number and in kind, with each stock genetically tailored to spawn in its parental area. And Loch Ness, with its constant replenishment from the sea, provides a sustaining reservoir for a highly efficient natural feeding network which, in its own right, represents an enormous food resource.[4]

---

[4] Could Loch Ness support a small population of large animals even if no migratory food were available? This question has been explored by A. W.

In the process of natural selection and dispersion, it would seem strange indeed if some species of predatory animal had not succeeded in exploiting such a veritable Garden of Eden.

The herbivorous nature of the known sirenia is a characteristic that does not fit the almost certain fish-eating nature of the Loch Ness creatures. The anatomical features of sirenians, including fossil forms, are specialized for feeding on vegetation. Tusks are present in dugongs, but not in Rhytina or manatees. There is one possible exception: Dr. Bertram told me that one of the fossil dugongs may have been a mollusk-eater, similar to walruses in their eating habits. Like sirenians, walruses spend a great deal of time along coasts, sinking to the bottom to feed by raking up clams and mussels instead of vegetation. Of course, examples of striking adaptations to an atypical food supply within a group, resulting in extensive morphological changes, are common enough in the animal world.

The Plesiosauridae were superbly adapted for predating the fish of the Cretaceous seas. We need not rely only on inference for our knowledge of the diet of these reptiles: in some fossil remains the remnants of the animals' last meals are preserved, consisting in one case of a pterodactyl, a fish, and a cephalopod, and in others of fish alone. Since these remains are found within the body cavity of the fossil, there can be no doubt that these animals were actually ingested. There is some uncertainty regarding the degree of flexibility of the neck. Some restorations show extreme swan-like flexures; however, these extremes are probably not realistic. Perhaps a fast side-

---

Sheldon and S. P. Kerr of the Bedford Institute of Oceanography and by W. Scheider and P. Wallis in two papers published in the journal *Limnology and Oceanography*. Both groups calculated a possible population density of monsters in Loch Ness based on estimated standing stocks of living organisms. Sheldon and Kerr calculated the range of the total mass of monsters as between 3,135 and 15,675 kg (3½-17¼ tons). Therefore, depending on the standing stock and average size (Sheldon and Kerr used 100 kg [220 lbs.] as minimum weight of a monster), the number of monsters in the loch could be as many as 156. Scheider and Wallis used an alternate method of calculating but arrived at similar biomass estimates: 14.3 cubic meters of monsters (= 15,725 kg [17⅓ tons] if one cubic meter represents 1,100 kg [1-1/5 tons]). They suggest that the total population of our animals in Loch Ness might range, depending upon weight, between 10 large monsters and 157 small monsters.

ways motion was utilized to grasp a fish straying too close to a motionless plesiosaur. The whole structure of the paddle mechanism also suggests that fast turns were in order for this reptile. In any case, since the fish population in Loch Ness is the only adequate supply of food, the fish-eating plesiosaurs would be quite happy in this lake.

Amphibians are generally carnivorous, although not exclusively so in the larval stages. In some species the adults will eat almost anything that moves. Many aquatic forms eat fish, as most certainly did the large aquatic primitive types found in the fossil deposits of Scotland and Ireland. Some living types do not limit their feeding to consuming live animals, but will also eat carrion and other organic debris. Cannibalism is also observed in some species. In general, they require much less food than mammals and can go for long periods of time without food altogether. It is true that when engaged in physical activity, such as swimming, considerable energy requirements must be met. However, energy need not be expended to maintain a constant high body temperature. It is clear from these considerations that the fish population of Loch Ness would be a suitable supply for these animals.

Eels are omnivorous, eating almost anything. By and large, carnivorous feeding predominates in nature and includes most animals available to the eel. Relative size limits the prey which are vulnerable to the eel.[5] Eels may also be cannibalistic but probably only under conditions of extremely limited food supply. There can be no doubt that the fish population of Loch Ness would be an excellent food supply for large eels.

Large animals in Loch Ness must be carnivorous, piscivorous to be more specific. The fastest moving mollusks, the squids and the pteropods, are also carnivorous. Meat-eating species are not confined to these groups alone, but are present in every class. Fish-eating forms are well represented among many groups, so that food supply of fish in Loch Ness would be perfectly suitable for large, carnivorous gastropods.

---

[5] D. Cairns examined the stomach contents of New Zealand eels and found that those over 30 in. long had a predominantly fish diet, particularly trout, while eels 16-30 in. preyed on trout only occasionally. At Loch Ness an eel was caught using trout as bait; see photograph in T. Coulson and J. Gibbinson. In the case of lakes such as Loch Ness, even small eels feed on juvenile salmon: D. Solomon found that the stomach contents of an eel from Loch Morar included a small salmon.

XIII
Behavior

If we had little or no otherwise descriptive data on an animal but had complete information about its behavior, a definite identification could in most instances be made. Unfortunately, our knowledge of the behavior of the Loch Ness phenomena is far from complete, but we do know enough to make some significant comparisons. This chapter, then, compares the Loch Ness animal characteristics (those falling loosely under "behavior") with the most probable candidates sketched in Chapter X. Included here are surfacing, amphibious behavior and respiration, locomotion, submergence, basking, reproduction, sensitivity to sound, production of sound. Each behavioral characteristic is analyzed in terms of (and in the same sequence as) the categories from Chapter X: mammals, reptiles, amphibians, fish, invertebrates.

Surfacing. The rarity of acceptable sightings at Loch Ness is proverbial. This suggests that either the creatures are extremely clandestine when at the surface or are non-air breathers and spend most of their time in the depths of the loch.

With regard to the Sirenia: "In the wild, animals are exceedingly difficult of observation, often verging on the impossible, unless there is a superabundance of time available. This is because they are shy and surreptitious in nature, and normally live totally submerged in the water and only put their nostrils above the surface to breathe." (Bertram and Bertram) These breathing episodes ordinarily occur at least once every half hour and therefore could account for the appearance of the so-called blobs observed on occasion in Loch Ness. Burton reported one such observation and I myself have observed this phenomenon. (See Chapter I.)

Plesiosaurs were reptiles and required air just as mammals do. Therefore, since these animals had to take in oxygen from the atmosphere, we may inquire whether this process may have been incon-

179

spicuous and elusive. If we examine the skull of typical plesiosaurs, we find that the nares or nostril openings are found not in a forward position but back about halfway between the eye sockets and the tip of the snout. This anatomical feature may mean that they could lie just beneath the surface, essentially invisible from above yet able to breathe regularly.

The fact that the Loch Ness creatures are rarely at the surface is of concern mostly when considering air-breathing animals, such as reptiles and mammals. In the case of urodeles, many species of which are completely adapted to taking air from the water or coming to the surface rarely under special conditions of oxygen depletion, no problem exists with regard to the rarity of surface observations. This is particularly true of those forms living in well aerated cold mountain streams or lakes. Loch Ness is well oxygenated even at the greatest depths (Appendix K) so that frequent excursions to the surface for taking in air would not be necessary.

All eels have completely functional gills and need not surface to breathe, so if eels are the Loch Ness monsters, it is not surprising they are so rarely observed at the surface.

Gastropods include both completely aquatic forms having gills and completely terrestrial forms breathing air by means of a lung. Since air breathing is not a requirement of many gastropods, the animals might remain below the surface much of the time, for the most part escaping detection by man.

Amphibious behavior and respiration. We now come to one of the most curious and interesting characteristics associated with the Loch Ness phenomena—the rare *land* sightings (possibly 18 in 436 years). Such observations of the creatures completely or partly out of the water are extremely important, because they indicate that a limited amphibious capability must be present and because they give the best opportunity for obtaining descriptive detail concerning parts of the body never seen when in the water. Unfortunately, the recorded observations (Table 2, Appendix A) were not made at sufficiently close range or for long enough periods to help as much as we might like. The descriptions of the mode of progression on land refer to clumsy and awkward movement, consistent with creatures predominantly adapted to an aquatic environment. These alleged land sightings at first appear to contradict our conclusion that the animals are non-air-breathing bottom dwellers; however, if there are animals possessing both abilities, the problem vanishes.

No sirenians either living or extinct could exist at the bottom of Loch Ness for long periods of time (as required by our sonar data). Observations on land would be compatible with sirenians as air breathers but cannot be reconciled with their inability to leave the water. They are occasionally found stranded by the tide, but there is no evidence that manatees or dugongs can or do leave the water under their own volition. This undoubtedly holds also for Rhytina, since Steller states at the beginning of his report that the sea cow confines itself to the sea.[1]

Plesiosaurs most certainly were able to come out of the water onto the shore. Their powerful paddles were probably used to move on land in a manner similar to seals. The ribs between the two pairs of limbs meet to form a dense plastron which probably served as a solid support for the trunk of the animal. But if they are inhabiting Loch Ness, one wonders why these air-breathing reptiles should venture so rarely on land and what purpose such excursions might serve. What about the deep-diving profiles obtained during the Birmingham sonar experiments of 1968? Since we know nothing of the diving capability of the plesiosaurs, we can only guess that some of these species might have developed considerable facility in rapid depth changes. But plesiosaurs generally lived in shallow, warm seas and estuaries. Even as air-breathing animals with this habitat background, some species might exhibit the kind of underwater behavior deduced from the sonar data.

Amphibia possess a number of respiratory mechanisms, all of which are not available to all species at all stages of development. The available means of respiration include gills in larval forms and lungs in adults. Larvae also possess buccopharyngeal and cutaneous respiration as do many adults. As has already been noted, some aquatic urodeles (those found in cold, fast-running, well-oxygenated mountain streams) may have rudimentary lungs or none at all. The situation is further complicated by the presence in urodeles of neoteny —the failure of larval forms to go through the metamorphosis result-

---

[1] Later in his report Steller mentions a male that for two days in succession came to its female lying dead on the beach, as if to inform himself of her condition. In view of Steller's earlier remark, we must interpret this later observation to mean that the animal approached the beach but remained in shallow water.

ing in fully developed adults.[2] All of these considerations are important in determining whether a particular form of amphibian can possess a combination of characteristics consistent with those apparently possessed by the animals in Loch Ness. If a urodele is our animal, then it is likely an adult with some degree of neoteny present: neotenous because it must be an aquatic form able to remain submerged for very long (or indefinite) periods and able to breathe in air long enough to account for the head-neck observations and for the more rare excursions on land. It would possess certain clearly adult characteristics—e.g., eyelids, pigmented skin, and especially a lung functioning as a hydrostatic organ and at least partially as a respiratory organ, with buccopharyngeal and cutaneous respiration also playing a part.[3] The few reports of frills could easily refer to the external larval gills; that is, these observations would have been of subadult individuals which had not yet lost these structures. While we have concerned ourselves here specifically with urodeles, it is reasonable to assume our conclusions can apply with equal validity if we postulate a more primitive amphibian—e.g., some descendant of the embolomers.

The two major respiratory organs of eels are the gills and the skin.

---

[2] Some species are definitely neotenous in that they do not undergo metamorphosis under any conditions. In some, only certain characteristics are developed while others remain in the larval stage. Still other species show transformation under some circumstances in nature (or in the laboratory) but not in others. Finally, some forms eventually undergo metamorphosis but require a very long time to achieve the fully adult stage. Sexual maturity and reproduction can and does occur in all of these various conditions. While the mechanisms of neoteny are not completely understood, it is clear that the endocrine glands, particularly the thyroid and the anterior pituitary, play a central role. Secondarily, a variety of environmental conditions also have a great effect. For example, the salamander, *Ambystoma tigrinum,* is neotenous in cold lakes but not in warm lakes.

[3] Cutaneous respiration is of considerable importance in all aquatic amphibia but becomes progressively less efficient as the animal increases in size with reduced surface-to-mass ratios, thereby putting a greater burden on other modes of respiration. That is, the surface (S) available for diffusion divided by the volume (V) of the animal indicates the size limits for creatures that live submerged by means of cutaneous respiration. The precise mathematical relationship is $S = {}_X V^{2/3}$ where X is a species constant. The tremendous difference, for example, in the S/V ratio between an animal 2 ft. long and 20 ft. long is shown in the table in note 2, Chapter XII.

Eels need not surface to obtain oxygen although they are also able to breathe in air to a limited extent. The behavior of eels moving overland for distances up to 20 miles is well known.[4] Clearly the eels' amphibious and aquatic abilities can easily account for the Loch Ness data. We must remember, however, that the same problem of size and cutaneous respiration holds for eels as for amphibians. (Cf. note #3 above.) That is, very large eels probably would have a much lower capability for obtaining oxygen in air. In some fish with open swim bladders, the air in this structure acts as a reservoir and may aid in respiration in air. In other fish, even the gills may make a contribution, although in eels this does not seem to be of significance, since the gills are covered and structurally overlapped, thus preventing free circulation of air over their surface. Frills (or frill-like structures) appear to have no identifiable counterpart in adult eels; however, in some larvae such a structure is transiently present: this jugular organ (or patch of jugular villi) appears very frill-like at the stage shown in Illus. 1e. If neoteny (or partial neoteny) occasionally occurs, this structure might persist longer or even indefinitely.

To recapitulate: To account for 20-ft. size, active tempo of life, speeds of 10 mph or more, infrequency of surfacing, deep and rapid diving, we probably must find animals capable of extracting adequate oxygen from the water rather than from the atmosphere.

Non-gilled mollusks will not do, for oxygen would have to be obtained solely by diffusion through the skin surfaces. (Cf. note #3

---

[4] See Chapter XI, Illus. 7 for picture of eel moving on the ground. This kind of activity is not confined only to elvers or young eels entering fresh water from the sea, or to sexually mature adults returning to the sea to sqawn. Eels living in freshwater lakes or streams move overland to other nearby bodies of fresh water when necessary. These excursions usually are made at night and over wet grass, although they are by no means confined to these conditions. Apparently eels will come out on land for other reasons: D. H. Graham relates that while living in the bush section of the Bay of Plenty in New Zealand, his three children came running to tell him that they had found some addled duck eggs, and, on throwing a few of them into the creek, eels had come out of the water for more eggs. He thought this story far-fetched, but went to investigate. The children had a good supply of rotten eggs, so he threw a bad egg on the surface of the water hole and a large eel came from under the bank to swallow the egg whole. He then threw an egg onto a stony patch of the creek, and again an eel came out of the water to eat the egg. He then threw a series of eggs (each further out of the water) onto the stones, and still the eels came after them.

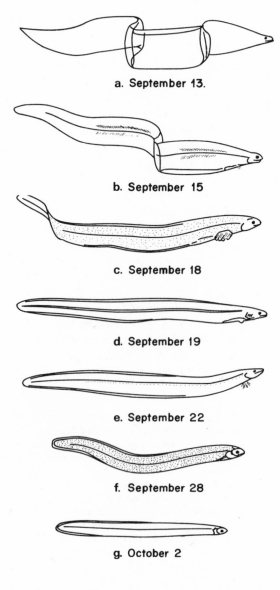

a. September 13.

b. September 15

c. September 18

d. September 19

e. September 22

f. September 28

g. October 2

Illus. 1   Metamorphosis of a *Conger leptocephalus,* showing transient frill-like jugular organ (e). (redrawn from Dean)

above.) Some form of gilled mollusk would suffice, and we have such: gills in the shape of external frilled structures called ctenidia or similar internal gills in the mantle cavity. However, how account for some degree of amphibious capability?—i.e., surfacings and limited activity out of the water. Some forms, such as the sea slug group Onchidiacea, have a pulmonary sac which permits respiration equally well in air or under water. In general many kinds of mollusks would be able to meet this requirement, but the presence of a large inverte-brate on land is hardly a possibility from a structural point of view. While clumsy, ineffective movements of primarily aquatic mollusks is possible for smaller animals, large mollusks such as the giant squid are completely helpless on land. To account for this aspect one would have to postulate considerable development of supportive structures, even beyond the rather well developed internal cartilaginous skeleton of cuttlefish such as *Sepia cultrata*.

Locomotion. The best information as to speed and mode of propulsion comes from the 1960 Dinsdale film, the 1967 Bureau film, the sonar tracking by Professor Tucker (the University of Birmingham experiments), and Bob Love's sonar data: measured speeds of 10 mph or more at the surface with diving rates up to 5 mph.[5] These speeds and the mode of propulsion observed rule out inefficient swimming based only on paddling with pectoral and/or pelvic fins or flippers.

Aquatic mammals and most fish use the carangiform method (or ostraciform if the tail is short and the body relatively stiff). This consists of moving a flattened tail or tail fin from side to side or, in the case of aquatic mammals, up and down. In the case of sirenians the pectoral flippers are used for additional power and changes of direction. From what we know of living sirenians and from Steller's description of Rhytina, we would hardly expect these animals to win any races. However, manatees, normally slow and quiescent, have been reported to be capable of bursts of speed when being attacked by sharks and can swim quite fast at the surface, although very little

---

[5] Eyewitness estimates of speed at the surface go much higher, but the highest of these cannot be taken seriously. In tests we made, asking a variety of individuals to judge the speed of craft whose exact speed was known to us alone, we obtained estimates ranging from right on the mark to 5-fold too high. There were no low guesses and the more inexperienced, casual observers were almost always high in their judgments.

is known of their speed underwater. The anatomical features of these animals have at least the potential to provide fast swimming as an adaptation for preying on fast-swimming fish. The horizontally flattened tail of dugongs and manatees is admirably suited for propulsion, as was also the case with Rhytina.

That plesiosaurs were good swimmers can be inferred with some certainty from the structure of the shoulder and hip bones. The lower bones of these regions were large and wide, so that very powerful muscles could be attached for pulling the four flexible paddles.[6] Undoubtedly the smooth skin of these reptiles contributed to their speed, but could plesiosaurs achieve speeds of 10-17 mph as suggested by the Birmingham sonar trackings? In my judgment, 10 mph is possible, but hardly 17 mph, utilizing only ostraciform swimming. However, in earlier references, one specimen (in the Berlin Museum) appears to have been provided with a rhomboidal (diamond-shaped) tail flap of skin in a vertical plane. If this is correct, the tail may have been used not only as a rudder but also possibly as a propulsive organ. Most later studies and reconstructions of plesiosaurs have ignored this feature, and it has been assumed that these animals were paddlers only. The resemblance of the Berlin reconstructed tail flap (Illus. 2)[7] to the Rines "flipper" picture (P 16, Chapter VII) is remarkable indeed. Perhaps the object in Rines' photograph could actually be a tail and not an appendage at all.

Illus. 2   Restoration of *Plesiosaurus guilelmi-imperatoris,* showing rhomboidal tail configuration.

[6] Some paleontologists quite incorrectly liken the plesiosaur to marine turtles in their swimming ability even though marine turtles employ only the front paddles for the propulsive force, having much reduced rear paddles used mainly in steering.

The primitive aquatic amphibians were most certainly powerful swimmers, capable of capturing fish. This characteristic and particularly the laterally flattened tail have already been mentioned in connection with Eogyrinus and Paleogyrinus. While many present-day urodeles present similar anatomical features, including a continuous dorsal and ventral structure equivalent to a fin, none appears to be able to produce swimming performances up to that observed in Loch Ness. The epaxial (top back) muscle mass in urodeles is arranged as in fish, but with little of the folding characteristic of fast-swimming fish. However, the evidence from Loch Ness suggests only that bursts of speed of short duration occur, not greatly prolonged periods of high-speed swimming.[8] The clumsy, inefficient mode of progression described in the land sightings (Chapter VI) is in accord with what one might expect from either a urodele or a more primitive descendant of the fossil Embolomerous amphibians primarily adapted to aquatic existence. In my opinion it is also among the latter forms that one might expect to find swimming ability adequate to account for the observations at Loch Ness.

The maximum swimming speeds in teleosts range roughly from 2 to 30 mph, with perhaps a few exceptions (tuna) falling outside of the maximum; however, very fast dashes for a few seconds are possible. Sustained cruising speeds of 10 mph for large fish is no mean feat (although short of the 28-mph dashes of the barracuda). Eels are capable of such speeds and substantially greater speeds for short periods. They epitomize the anguilliform method of swimming which is basically a series of sinuous horizontal undulations, with the main propulsive force being generated by the side-to-side motion of the extremely powerful tail. The maximum speed that can be attained depends on the maximum frequency and amplitude with which the tail can oscilate. The eel tail is so powerful that if it can hook itself against pegs or a rock, a force of twenty times the body weight of the eels can be exerted. This fact is important in connection with the

---

[7] W. Dames in *Abhandlungen der Königlichen Preussischen Akademie der Wissenschaft* (1895), pp. 1ff; *Encyclopaedia Britannica* (11th ed.), p. 836.

[8] The giant Japanese salamander (Megalobatrachus) and the hellbender (Cryptobranchus) are quite sluggish while lying on the bottom of cold mountain streams, but are capable of springing up very quickly to capture a passing fish.

description of the inefficient, clumsy progression noted in some of the land sightings where progression over a relatively smooth road was noted. Eels move rather well over a rough surface, but have great difficulty on a smooth surface. This can easily be demonstrated by watching an eel move over a pegged board and then over one which is smooth.

The speed requirement rules out all but the fastest mollusks. As noted, it is unlikely that a single pair of anterior flippers or paddles would be adequate without some other propulsive aid such as a flattened tail. In the mollusca, propulsion by means of siphon jets has been developed by several groups. Some of the cephalopods, especially the "flying" squids, are capable of such great speed that they build up enough momentum to leap out of the water 15 ft. or more. They are swift predators, swooping down on a school of fish with great efficiency. As far as sea slugs are concerned, at least two families of opisthobranchs, the Dolabellinae and Notarchinae, have developed a form of jet propulsion. Of direct concern to us are the fastest gastropod swimmers, the pteropods, already mentioned as possessing a pair of paddle-like, two-way sculling organs. These shell-less animals with tapered cylindrical bodies, highly streamlined, can attain considerable speed, and having a center of gravity toward mid-body, are able to maneuver freely. While these tiny animals reach high speeds relative to their size, it is unlikely that any enlarged version 20-ft. long could achieve similar performance.

Submergence. Considerations with regard to submergence and diving severely restrict what kinds of animals can be involved in the Loch Ness problem. From our sonar results (Chapter IX), we know that our animal candidates must be capable of changing depth at 5 mph.

Some observers report submergence in a manner normally expected: a forward motion, head-neck followed by the body and tail. Dinsdale believes that this occurs only when the animals are suddenly frightened. It is alleged that more commonly they appear to sink vertically from sight, almost without a ripple. Whether this interpretation is correct or not, it should be pointed out that an elongated aquatic animal may indeed appear to sink vertically when in fact it is diving.[9]

The skeleton of the sirenia is indeed massive, and the bones have a high density (especially the skull and ribs), which add to the specific gravity of these animals, being an aid to easy submergence. This condition, known as pachyostosis, is also present in some other aquatic vertebrates, and might contribute to the fact that no dead carcasses have been reported in the water of Loch Ness and other similar lakes. This consideration is by no means necessary, however, to explain the absence of floating carcasses in cold, deep lakes where scavengers and predators are feeding. Because of the low temperature and slightly acid conditions of the water, gas production by putrefying bacteria proceeds slowly. Any gas produced tends to diffuse and escape before a carcass acquires appreciable buoyancy. Thus dead animals are rarely, if ever, seen floating under these conditions. Instead, they sink and decay or are eaten.

Little or nothing is known about maximum speed or diving capabilities of the sirenia. The living forms, and also Rhytina, are found normally in shallow water, so that in the absence of positive evidence to the contrary, it seems reasonable to assume that rapid and deep diving abilities are not developed.

Anything said relative to the diving ability of plesiosaurs can only be speculative. From study of the skeletal remains, there is no doubt that these reptiles were good swimmers, but there is nothing to suggest special or unusual mode of submergence when at the surface.[10]

---

[9] This is especially true if the animal is relatively uniform in noticeable features of its anatomy over a substantial portion of its length—features which act as visual indicators of forward motion. One may notice only the continuous lowering of the observable countour, without being aware that a fixed point on the body is also moving forward and disappearing from sight before the whole animal has submerged.

[10] We noted the suggestion of inflatable air sacs to account for a variable back contour. This idea also has been invoked as a means of submergence; i.e., these hypothetical air sacs might be hydrostatic organs which, when deflated, permit the animal to submerge vertically because of an increase in specific gravity. Burton has pointed out that the red-throated diver (*Gavia stellata,* a loon found on Loch Ness) can ride at varying heights at the surface according to whether it is alarmed or not, and it does so by the inflation and deflation of air sacs. This situation, in which a bird becomes more inconspicuous by sinking lower into the water is hardly analogous, since in this case a particular function is apparent. Why should an aquatic animal, found mostly in the depths, have developed air sacs to ride at the surface, continually changing its back contour and buoyancy and then submerging vertically? What possible function could be involved? The animals must be fishers and, as already noted, may occasionally be at the surface feeding on salmon. For

The anatomy of many aquatic urodeles is quite consistent with the ability of the Loch Ness animals to submerge by sinking. The forms inhabiting deeper lakes have lungs which act largely as hydrostatic organs, very much like the swim bladder in fish. In addition, many have a Y-shaped cartilage attached to the pubis, which in conjunction with the attached muscles controls the shape of the lungs. This permits the animal to force air forward into the lung by contracting the appropriate muscle, making the front end of the animal more buoyant; the reverse occurs upon relaxation. The sinking factor of these animals is probably quite similar to freshwater fish, particularly eels (Anguilla) with values around 1001 to 1003.[11]

Since the animals in Loch Ness have been observed by sonar to change depth 300-400 ft. at 5 mph, we must further inquire whether these urodeles, or primitive forms with a similar anatomy, could be expected to possess this capability. Many aquatic urodeles (except those which have completely lost their lungs or have them reduced to mere rudiments) have lungs which are functional to varying degrees.

---

this purpose great speed or an agile head-neck (or both) is important. It is hard to imagine how hydrostatic organs permitting vertical submergence could play a part. This does not, however, rule out other adaptations for submergence as found, for example, in some seals.

[11] The percentage volume of the hydrostatically functional lung ranges probably 7-9%. The sinking factor for both freshwater and marine fish is defined as the density of the animal divided by the density of the environment. Since the average density of living tissues is more or less fixed, and fresh water is less dense than salt water, freshwater fish require a large swim bladder to provide the same relative density (i.e., sinking factor) as compared to saltwater forms. (The freshwater eel [*A. anguilla*] has a swim bladder volume 7% of its entire volume; the marine eel [*Conger conger*] has a swim bladder volume 4.7% of its total volume.) This value is of importance in determining diving ability and of great interest to us in the analysis of sonar contacts, especially in interpreting their meaning relative to possible size and nature of the targets. (Cf. Chapter XIV.)

The ability to sink vertically as a consequence of hydrostatic organs can be observed rather well by stationing oneself at the eel tanks in a public aquarium. Here, if sufficiently patient, one sees eels occasionally swimming up toward the surface, suddenly relaxing, and sinking vertically. To the extent that some aquatic urodeles have similar anatomical features, identical behavior may be expected. Of course, none of these features precludes a more active form of submergence by urodeles involving not only the lungs but the use of the laterally flattened tail and other appendages.

This means that they are open sacs similar to the open swim bladder in eels, rather than the completely closed swim bladders of many other teleost fish. Fish with open swim bladders can generally change depth much more readily than those with closed hydrostatic organs. It therefore seems reasonable to conclude that large aquatic amphibians with similar anatomical features should also be able to perform depth changes of the order observed.

As noted, one only has to watch eels in an aquarium to see how they are able to sink below the surface by using the swim bladder as a hydrostatic organ. The swim bladder of eels is not closed but open to the outside via the pneumatic duct. In contrast to other physostomes (fish with open swim bladders), eels also have functional gas glands which secrete gas into the swim bladder. While some of the other physostomes can secrete gas into the swim bladder, they do so very slowly compared to physoclists (fish with closed swim bladders) Eels can gulp air, but also rapidly secrete gas into the swim bladder. Eels consequently can change depth rapidly and are not limited as are fish with closed swim bladders. This was clearly demonstrated in 1970, when our expedition trapped some eels at a depth of 600 ft. and raised them very rapidly; they were perfectly viable, showed no discomfort, and remained in the holding tanks without any sign of ill effects. It would appear that the anatomical and physiological characteristics of eels are compatible with the underwater behavior of the Loch Ness animals.

Aquatic animals denser than the liquid surrounding them have a continuous task when they wish to remain afloat. Many mechanisms for bringing the specific gravity of the animal close to that of the liquid environment have evolved. Some of the most ingenious developments are found among the mollusks. In the case of the cuttlefish, Sepia, buoyancy is changed much as in a submarine. The cuttlebone consists of a number of thin chambers containing both liquid and gas. Liquid is pumped out to reduce density and pumped in to increase density, thus producing submergence. This structure is somewhat bulkier than the fish swim bladder but has the great advantage of being relatively independent of depth. This kind of diving mechanism is perfectly compatible with the rapid depth changes at Loch Ness.

Basking. The more prolonged sightings (up to 40 minutes) of the upturned-boat aspect—virtually motionless on flat, calm, sunny days —has been (not unreasonably) interpreted as basking behavior.

Whether this is really the case cannot be determined. What looks to us like basking may well be something else. In most observations at Lock Ness, the "basking" animal suddenly dashes off at speed from its floating position and then submerges. Such behavior matches exactly that of aquatic predators who remain motionless, waiting to attack a fish that swims nearby. Why should this occur at the surface? The food supply is often in the layer of water close to the surface.

Sirenians do indeed engage in basking. Along the shores of the Indian, Malayan, and Australian Seas, dugongs may occasionally be seen basking at the surface of the water. Steller stated that when the sea cows want to take a rest, they turn on their backs in a quiet place in a bay and allow themselves to drift on the water like logs.

Many kinds of reptiles bask. But what about plesiosaurs? We simply do not know. However, plesiosaurs may be assumed to present such a pose while waiting quietly for an opportunity to prey on a fish. A portion of the reptile's dorsal surface might be visible under these conditions, with subsequent fast motion or even submergence.

I know of no amphibians that bask, but of course there are fish-predating amphibians that wait quietly for their prey.

D. Cairns' description of the large (c. 3 ft.) New Zealand eels predating fish is most suggestive. He has watched them stalk trout (1-2 lbs.) until with "a quick twist" the eel swoops under the fish and clasps it in its jaws. "If the trout is small it is killed by the crushing of the jaws and swallowed whole. If it is a large trout it may be bitten and shaken vigorously until it is in halves." Cairns comments on the "great commotion" often seen in the water as a trout is torn to pieces. Sometimes an eel lies in wait "with the back exposed," and "makes his capture by a quick dart."

Many kinds of aquatic mollusks may remain quiescent at the surface for periods of time, involving a variety of behavioral aspects. In the case of gastropods, such as certain freshwater pulmonates, which have a lung or lung-like organ, we have already noted that they may rise to the surface and remain there as long as calm conditions are present. In the case of some pteropods, Meisenheimer relates that they often float for hours with parapodia fully extended. Some species remain at depth but surface at night. It would appear that the relatively wide range of molluscan behavior could encompass the related observations at Loch Ness.

Reproduction. All animals reproduce at some time during their life cycle. Many kinds of animals spend parts of their life cycle in different environments. As mentioned earlier, certain species of salmon live most of their life in the sea but return to fresh water to spawn. In the case of the Loch Ness animals, it is not absolutely clear whether they reproduce in the loch or elsewhere. If in the loch, they must be independent of laying eggs on land or giving birth on shore, since such activities would certainly have been observed. If they reproduce elsewhere, this may or may not be the case.

Sirenians would have no difficulty at Loch Ness, because like Cetaceans, they give birth to their young in the water.

Most reptiles lay eggs on land. However, some lizards and snakes are ovoviviparous, producing eggs that are incubated and hatched within the parent's body, but without formation of a placenta. In the case of the ovoviviparous sea snakes, the Hydrophinae, a complete adaptation to aquatic life has been achieved, and the young are brought forth in the water. Clearly, then, plesiosaurs could also have developed this ability. Whether they actually did so we do not know, but most authorities agree that their behavior was probably more like marine turtles, laying eggs on the shore. Plesiosaurs engaging in such activity could scarcely escape detection.

Reiteration: If reproduction occurs in Loch Ness, it must occur in the water. While most amphibians, both aquatic and terrestrial, lay their eggs in water, many also deposit eggs on land; and some are ovoviviparous, bringing forth their young alive. The aquatic reproductive capabilities of amphibians are in accord with the requirements for reproduction in Loch Ness.

Under the heading of reproduction it seems appropriate to call attention to the wide range of sexual dimorphism in many amphibians, including the urodeles. The great differences in secondary sexual characteristics between males and females may well account for some of the variety of observations at Loch Ness. These sexual differences are so varied and large in number that only a few particularly relevant ones will be cited. Many of these characteristics are present permanently while others appear transiently during the mating period. They include color changes, appearances of dorsal crests, swellings on a variety of areas of the body, and changes in some digits of the limbs. In some salamanders the skin of the male is much smoother than that of the female, and differences in average size of the entire animal or of specific features may also be the rule.

All freshwater eels without exception return to the sea to reproduce. This is not, however, true for all teleosts, as many undergo the complete life cycle in fresh water. A. Frake has raised the question of whether a species of eel might adapt to reproducing in fresh water. While this cannot be ruled out as impossible, in the absence of any positive evidence, it must remain only a speculation. In any case, we do know that elvers (young eels) enter Loch Ness in great numbers and follow the normal eel life cycle,[12] which is compatible with the known data about the loch animals.

Reproduction in sea slugs, the mollusks that concern us most, is very complicated. In the majority of animals, there are individual males and females that retain their sex throughout their lifetime. There are, however, throughout the animal kingdom examples where each individual is both male and female. Many variations of such a hermaphroditic condition exist. Sea slugs are hermaphroditic, with the exception of only two species. Most are simultaneous hermaphrodites, that is, they have functional male and female organs, although some are male when young, becoming female when they grow larger with age. These animals do not fertilize themselves but crosscopulate with reciprocal insemination. In many, a behavioral courtship occurs, where one individual trails another, making tentacular contacts. Copulation may be prolonged, lasting hours. Little or no sexual dimorphism is present within the group, so that male-female differences cannot be invoked as contributing to the diversity of characteristics observed at Loch Ness. The aquatic species all reproduce completely in the water, beginning with egg deposition and the subsequent de-

---

[12] When European (*A. anguilla*) and North American (*A. rostrate*) eels mature sexually, they are known as silver eels because of their nearly black dorsal surface (somewhat bronzed, with a purple sheen) and a silvery white belly. Many other physical and physiological changes occur, some of which, such as the enlarged eyes and eye pigment changes, have already been noted. The animals return to the sea by any route possible, even over land, eventually arriving in the general area of the Sargasso Sea (between 22° and 30° latitude and 48° and 65° longitude). Spawning may occur in warm, saline water at a depth of 400 to 700 meters (1,300 to 2,300 ft.) but over very much deeper water. The eggs are pelagic, developing into transparent leaf-like larvae. These larvae, undergoing a number of metamorphoses, are carried north by currents to North American and European coasts. After the last change, the small eel-like forms called elvers enter freshwater rivers and lakes where they may live for many years.

velopment of two larval stages. Eggs may be fixed to objects or float freely. In a few, the ova develop in the body of the parent, including subsequent larval stages. The free-swimming larval stages, the trochophore and the veliger, are usually very different from the adult and do not lend themselves readily to identification with any aspect of the Loch Ness phenomenon; however, the basic requirement of reproduction entirely in the water is met easily.

Sensitivity to sound. Can the Loch Ness monster hear? The popular conclusion is definitely Yes. As one writer typically assures us: "Nessie is very sensitive to noise." Actually, we just do not know for sure. There are a dozen or more recorded accounts that suggest the loch animals do react immediately to sound—to a shouted exclamation, to a motorboat engine, to the slam of a car door. One must wonder, however, if the creatures of the deep have not gotten used to the noise of boats *frequently* passing through the loch; that is, surely the sounds of outboards, diesels, and propellors must have become a familiar part of the animals' underwater world. Nevertheless, a careful examination of the accounts tells us that the animals do seem to respond to certain sudden changes in their environment. Perhaps hearing apparatus *is* present—or at least some sort of sensitivity to vibrations in the air or water.

Although, as stated, ears are almost invisible in sirenia, their hearing is extremely acute when on the surface or below water. In Guyana the sensitivity of manatees to sound, particularly to the human voice, has been observed; and off the coasts of Australia, many dugong hunters describe how silently they had to approach the animals with oars well muffled. They are also disturbed by power boats. (Cf. Bertram and Bertram.)

There has been much discussion with regard to hearing in reptiles, particularly in snakes, where there is practically no middle ear region. Opinion now greatly favors the contention that snakes do not hear airborne sounds but are very sensitive to earthborne vibrations. On the other hand, many other reptiles do communicate by sound. Many naturalists can attest to hearing the roar or bellow of the male crocodile from as far as a mile away. Since the Synaptosauria are not at all closely related to the Ophidia (snakes), we have no reason to postulate a lack of sensitivity to sound. The sensitivity to airborne sounds, explosive detonations, and other disturbances attributed to the Loch Ness creatures, therefore, present no difficulties.

The most primitive amphibians such as Eogyrinus undoubtedly possessed an ear apparatus very much like fish. As these aquatic animals gradually developed into land-living forms, the ear underwent remarkable changes. The important function of the inner ear, as an organ of equilibrium, was retained, but developments also occurred converting the ear into a true hearing organ. The most advanced forms are the toads and to a lesser degree frogs. While there can be no doubt that hearing plays an important role in the life of these animals, the situation in the group of interest to us, the urodeles, is not nearly so clear. Hearing ability has been claimed for some salamanders, but experiments in the laboratory have failed to clearly demonstrate hearing in the usual sense. However, in the aquatic urodeles, lower frequencies stimulate lateral-line organs which are present just as in fish. While we have to conclude that a true sense of hearing has not been adequately demonstrated in urodeles, this does not mean they are deaf. Studies of their auditory apparatus suggest that larvae receive vibrations through the lower jaw while lying on the bottom of ponds, while in the adults vibrations are transmitted via the forelimbs. Schmalhausen, one of the world's leading authorities on the origin of terrestrial vertebrates, believes it is quite clear that the ancestors of the urodele amphibia had actual apparatus for sensing sound transmission from the air. He concludes that besides the tympanic-stapedial system of hearing in air of the frogs and toads, all amphibia hear by means of a dermal-venous system of reception and transmission of sound vibrations in a watery environment. In view of this and the fact that a great deal about the amphibian hearing apparatus still remains obscure, the most we can conclude is that sensitivity to underwater sound, particularly lower frequencies, is undoubtedly present, while in air we cannot rule out some form of sensitivity to aireborne vibrations.

In contrast to amphibians, the evidence for hearing among teleosts is very impressive; there is no doubt of the well-defined biological significance of sound perception and production. Hearing has been reliably demonstrated in eels. For the common eel, the frequency range of hearing is 36-650 cycles per second. The inner ear, as in other vertebrates, appears to be the chief organ of hearing, although a variety of structural mechanisms may be involved. The lateral-line organs, primarily organs for sensing water movement, disturbance, and currents, may respond to sound although it appears that sound vibration is not an appropriate stimulus for these organs. There are many reliable instances of eels in captivity being taught to come at the call of a whistle, or even by a human voice, so that the data from Loch Ness regarding this point are adequately accounted for.

Little is known about molluscan sensitivity to sounds although several of the sensory organs may be capable of reacting to sound. A few studies of hearing in mollusks are available. Hubbard concluded from experiments under laboratory conditions that the octopus' behavior was not modified by the presence of sound waves. However, Maturana and Sperling found that when the supporting table was gently tapped while penetrating the octopus' statocyst nerve with an electrode, structural elements were found which responded with a series of 4 or 5 bursts of impulses for each tapping. It appears that these elements in the nerve were highly sensitive to low frequency vibrations transmitted through the ground but not to airborne sounds. The general consensus is that the molluscan receptors sensitive to mechanical stimuli of various frequencies include statocysts, tactile receptors, and propioceptors. However, no sensitivity to airborne sounds seem to exist.

Production of sound. There is no good evidence that our Loch Ness animals normally make sounds above water which humans can hear. Only three reports occur, and they are not substantial. The 6th-century St. Columba story has the "fearsome beastie" approaching with a loud roar, but this sound reference may well be mere historical embellishment. More recently, Clem Skelton heard a swishing sound, not unlike the intake or exhalation of breath, but this was at night when his outboard motor failed in the middle of the loch. Alfred Cruickshank (Table 2, E 7) heard a bark sound, but his description of the animal suggests that it was not our Loch Ness creature.

Despite their name, sirenians seem in fact to be almost voiceless. The swishing or hissing noise described by one of our observers, if correct, might be accounted for by the breathing of an aquatic mammal. Any visitor to a zoo where marine mammals are kept has heard this characteristic sound when near to such surfacing animals. However, manatees are remarkably silent when taking air, whereas Steller described the air intake of Rhytina as similar to a horse's snort.

Living reptiles cover the entire spectrum of sound-producing capability, ranging from completely silent species to species which produce very loud calls. Certainly the extremely rare report of a swishing or hissing sound could be accounted for by a noise a reptile might make. We know nothing about whether plesiosaurs made sounds and therefore can say no more in this regard, although we have no reason to exclude them on grounds related to the possible presence or absence of a sound-producing ability.

Among amphibians the ability to produce sounds ranges from the vociferous chorus of frogs in the spring to the completely mute species of salamanders. Nothing can directly be known about extinct fossil forms, but must be inferred from skeletal remains and the capabilities of living amphibia. About the most that can be said is that the report of a hissing or swishing and the bark reported by Mr. Cruickshank do not seem cogent reasons for rejecting the amphibian hypothesis. It is not inconceivable that air intake or release by an amphibian with a lung might produce such a sound. Even a sound resembling a bark is perhaps not impossible.

Eels are capable of making a variety of sounds. Underwater studies with *A. rostrata* have demonstrated that weak clicks and long-continued, low-clucking sounds, resembling the "put-put" of an outboard are produced. Spontaneous and underwater clicking was recorded only during nighttime activity of groups. Rasps and single dull thuds or thumps 25-1200 Hz were induced by mild shock. In air, squeaks were produced on capture. A hissing or swishing noise has been reported when a Green Moray was impaled on a skin diver's fishing harpoon; the eel, after being harpooned, moved off with its head above water making this sound. D. H. Graham reports some interesting sounds produced by freshly captured conger eels. He says that this eel, "as in the case with some other fish, after being caught and also while lying in the cockpit of a launch or a trawl, does make grunting and gurgling noises, or '*bark*' as the fishermen say. This is produced by the expulsion of air from the air-bladder through a narrow tube, known as the pneumatic duct. This *bark* is more evident as the fish is being taken out of the water, rather than later in the cockpit. The *bark* of the Conger Eel is considerably louder than the monotonous sound of a Seahorse, and not as loud as the pig-like grunt of a Gurnard." (Italics added.) Certainly eels could account very well for alleged sounds made by the Loch Ness animals.

Mollusks as a group are not capable of producing sounds for communication or other purposes. There have been only unsubstantiated reports that certain species of squids can produce sounds. However, it is conceivable that if the animals possessed a mantle cavity filled with air, as is the case with many freshwater pulmonates, contraction or changes of shape of such a cavity might expel air vigorously enough to produce a swishing noise.

Finally, we must recall our hydrophone experiments (Chapter V) and remember that our underwater acoustic monitoring data strongly suggests the presence in the loch of "multiple, animate, sound-producing sources capable of a varied repertoire."

XIV
Conclusions

The evidence has been presented, compared, and analyzed. As noted earlier, I conclude that a population of moderate-sized, piscivorous aquatic animals is inhabiting Loch Ness. These animals are moderate in size relative to animal life in general but large when compared to the known freshwater fauna. This seems to be the most adequate and reasonable interpretation of the data, even perhaps a conservative assessment—conservative in the sense that it is a single, simple hypothesis in accord with established physical and zoological scientific principles. It is in marked contrast to some of the tortuous attempts to explain parts of the data by unique, far-fetched coincidences and circumstances; these efforts have generally avoided the idea of an animal explanation at all costs, straining not only the data but also one's credulity.[1]

The realization that surface observations are rather rare has developed gradually over the years. The number of recorded reports during the 30-year period following 1933 was roughly 3,000. This figure, taken at face value, would mean that about 100 observations were made annually. From this it is clear why it was reasonable to expect photographic surveillance of the loch surface to produce evidence rapidly. However, as noted, a more careful examination of the reports tells us that a large proportion of these observations, perhaps 90%, can be identified as errors, mistakes, misinterpretations, and, in a few

---

[1] Maurice Burton has proposed that vegetation mats might account for the Loch Ness phenomena. While such mats are found in lochs with shallow, clear areas of water where vegetation material can grow luxuriantly, these conditions do not exist at Loch Ness: the sides shelve steeply so that water vegetation is extremely sparse. Vegetation mats simply cannot form in Loch Ness. The most that occurs is occasionally during the winter ice forms in a few shallow spots at the southern end; this ice may include some vegetation, and if the water level changes so as to break portions loose, a floating piece of ice entrapping vegetation has a very transient existence.

cases, conscious frauds.[2] As we have seen, many natural phenomena at the lake are confused with the Loch Ness animal—ducks, fishing birds, otters, wakes from some of these animals, small fishing boats, floating logs or other debris, waves, unusual light effects on the water, and so forth. Making allowances for the unique situation in 1933-1934 and the special activities of groups or individuals collecting data, an average of 10 valid sightings per year is probably a solid figure representing observations over the past decades. Even this lower figure supports the view that a stable population of animals well adapted to existing conditions in Loch Ness is present, and is inconsistent with the suggestion that a single animal inadvertently strayed into the loch in 1933. The data now available, such as observations at the surface of more than one animal, simultaneous observations at different locations around the loch, multiple sonar contacts, and basic zoological requirements, all make the idea of a *single* animal absurd.

What about the behavior of the animals beneath the surface? Let us summarize our findings from the previous chapters. The diving behavior, as observed via sonar, supports the view that the animals can respire underwater, as seemed likely when the relative rarity of surface appearances became evident. The rapid depth changes of 5 mph

---

Also, it has been suggested that earth tremors or earthquakes might release quantities of gas from the floor of Loch Ness: these gas bubbles, when bursting at the surface, would appear as one or more humps. There are earth tremors in the area, not at all surprising since Loch Ness is a wrench-cleft with the northeastern shore slowly slipping north and the southwestern shore slowly moving south. (James Barron in his *The Northern Highlands in the Nineteenth Century* records 7 earth tremors of some consequence: 1816, 1817, 1818, 1839 [two], 1841, 1846; more have likely occurred since 1850, but data for the modern period is less readily available.) Nevertheless, there is *no* evidence that these disturbances ever release gas bubbles from the loch floor.

[2] Perpetrators of Loch Ness frauds are rarely malicious; they are simply practical jokers. When caught, they readily admit their chicanery, regarding the matter as amusing tricks designed to test the expertise or gullibility of the investigators. While such fun frauds have done no harm to life or property, they have been exaggerated by critics and the media, thus exacting another sort of harm: discredit has been cast on the serious investigator and his activities at the loch, making it extremely difficult to acquire research funds and to involve other competent professionals.

recorded on sonar is inconsistent with closed swim bladders but not with the open type found in eels. The mode of submergence suggests the presence of a hydrostatic organ, which might be an open swim bladder, a lung functioning as such, or another means of changing specific gravity as found in some mollusks.

The ability to move horizontally at the surface and underwater at speeds of 10 mph or more (as established by observation, film, and sonar) requires powerful tail propulsion, again consistent with the eyewitness observations of such tail configurations and action. The adaptation for such efficient propulsion in water is more or less incompatible with efficient progression over land. Thus the awkward movements observed when the animals were moving over land are to be expected. The observed degree of amphibious activity of the Loch Ness animals is very limited and does not correspond with the two groups of aquatic mammals considered here: the pinnipeds are too land-dependent, while the sirenians never come out on land at all. Anguilla, on the other hand, fit this aspect rather well; and aquatic urodeles certainly have the potential, especially possible aquatic descendents of forms such as Eogyrinus. Reptiles such as plesiosaurs probably came out on the land to a degree quite sufficient to satisfy the evidence from Loch Ness.

Closely related to the amphibious behavior is the matter of reproduction. If reproduction occurs in Loch Ness itself (this is by no means required), it must occur in the water. Since plesiosaurs may have been ovoviviparous, although more probably viviparous, only the pinnipeds can be excluded on this basis. However, if gastropods were involved, it would be surprising indeed that no trochophore larvae have ever been reported. All the observations which might conceivably be of juveniles described animals which are more or less smaller versions of the adult, consistent with the eel, plesiosaur, and amphibian hypotheses.

The food supply in Loch Ness of various kinds of fish, particularly salmon, is more than adequate. The behavior and distribution of fish life around river mouths and in the upper water layers may be directly related to the relatively more frequent observations around river mouths and to surface sightings per se. That is, the question of why one should observe well adapted aquatic fish predators at the surface at all can be explained by the hydrodynamics of swimming objects. The relationship of the resistance an object encounters in the water relative to depth is shown in Illus. 1. The unshaded area within the curve represents fixed resistance of the object related to its shape, surface, etc. The shaded area indicates how resistance increases as a swimming object approaches the surface. The maximum resistance

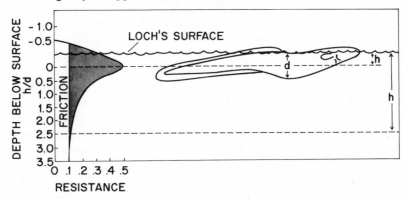

Illus. 1 Relationship of total resistance to submersion depth encountered by a swimming animal.

is encountered when the distance of the object below the surface is equal to ½ of its diameter. One can, therefore, imagine a fish predator about 2 ft. below the surface chasing a salmon and losing ground. However, if such a predator permits a portion of its anatomy to break the surface, drag resistance decreases sharply, permitting a surge of speed if the propulsive effort is maintained. (The same considerations apply of course to the salmon, but since they are much smaller in diameter they do not encounter much resistance at 2-3 ft. below the surface.) The behavior described as basking can also be related to these relationships: The description of a quiescent hump suddenly moving off at speed could be explained very well as a predator waiting motionless until a fish approaches, then with part of its anatomy projecting above the surface dashing off after its prey and submerging when successfully apprehending its quarry.

Such activity requires a substantial source of metabolic energy, at least in the short run. Considering the low temperature of the water, reptiles are more or less excluded, although the other animals considered might be able to carry out such activities. The freshwater environment, on the other hand, is compatible with all the animals considered, including reptiles. The question of whether or not the animals are also at home in salt water cannot be answered with certainty. Only the amphibians would have difficulty in this regard.

In the course of the preceding chapters, we have built up a fairly extensive physical description of our animals. We have conservatively estimated that their length ranges up to 20 ft., with an occasional specimen perhaps 25 ft. Some central body thickening, with a maximum circumference of about 40-60% of length (5 ft. diameter for a 25-ft.-long specimen) appears to be the rule.[3] Reduced surface-to-mass ratio for a thickened body configuration may also play a role in reducing the heat losses in the 42° F environment of Loch Ness.

Using the eel data acquired at Loch Ness as representative, we can calculate that a 20 ft. specimen will have a weight of 2,500 lbs. This is a minimal value since any increase in circumference will increase the weight greatly. Because of similar density of animal tissue throughout the animal kingdom, this estimate is valid for eels *and* other animals (as long as the overall length and general shape is as described). The sonar data provide a similar and independent size estimate based on the comparison of target strength at known distances.[4]

---

[3] The possible reasons for the evolution of a bulkier body in aquatic animals are many. An example perhaps relevant in our context is the case of the Hydrophidae or sea snakes. In these aquatic reptiles the tail is laterally flattened and the head small and not very well differentiated from the rest of the body. The head and neck are narrow, joining the body by a slow progressive thickening. In some species the body may be 5 times as thick as the head and neck. This body provides sufficient resistance to allow the narrow and flexible head-neck, by quickly straightening out a horizontal curve, to make a sudden forward lunge for the fish on which it exclusively feeds. The animals in Loch Ness, however, appear to rely more on sudden and rapid spurts of swimming speed in predating fish, rather than this snap-neck lunge of the sea snake or the snatching method of the plesiosaur.

[4] In Chapter IX we deduced an equivalent air volume for the object contacted at Foyers in the range 4-13 cu. ft. with a large but unknown part of this value probably due to gas contained in a lung or swim bladder. The calculated value of 23 cu. ft. for Steller's sea cow is far too large in comparison, which is probably also the case for other aquatic mammals. For plesiosaurs and gastropods, no estimate is possible since required information is not available. The relative lung or swim bladder volume in anguilla and aquatic urodeles must be about .07, which would give us a calculated value of 2.8-3 cu. ft. for a 2,500 lb. specimen, in good agreement with the sonar values. Part of the return must, of course, be due to tissue and bone, so that the gas volume figure should always be somewhat less than the total equivalent value.

The contour displayed with all its variations has been most perplexing to students of the Loch Ness phenomena. First there is the convex, rounded single hump, smooth or showing a ridge. It is well established that two portions of a single animal also may be observed. The rhomboidal tail of some plesiosaurs combined with a convex back would account remarkably well for two humps (Illus. 2).

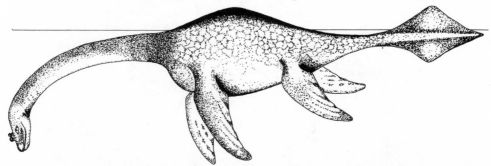

Illus. 2 *Plesiosaurus guilelmi-imperatoris,* showing 2-humped aspect. (redrawn from reconstruction by Dames; see above Illus. 2, Chapter XIII)

Less frequently, three portions are observed. The third portion may be identified as head-neck or even three parts of the dorsal surface. As established in Chapter XI, both anguilla (with a continuous soft-rayed dorsal fin beginning well back from the head) and aquatic urodeles (with an equivalent dorsal crest and continuous fin-like structure on the tail) account very well for these features. Observations of a changing contour—i.e., hump appearing to move back and forth rapidly, a larger number of smaller humps, serrated contour, or mane—are all consistent with a continuous soft-rayed fin or dorsal crest.[5] (See Illus. 3.)

---

[5] It should be noted that horizontal undulation either of the entire body of an elongated animal and/or the continuous fin or crest will always appear humped to an observer in any position, except when the eye is exactly at the same vertical height as the object viewed. For an object in the water, this would mean that the eye must be essentially at water level, which is rarely the case. This condition is, however, approached by an observer in a boat at a great distance from the object. The human eye can distinguish two separate objects at any given distance if the included angle formed by the two objects is of the order of 30 seconds of an arc. At a distance of a mile, this means that the objects must be at least 1 ft. apart. Depth perception is another matter, since triangulation based on stereoscopic vision ceases beyond a distance of 20-25 ft., so that an eel-like animal displaying horizontal undula-

Illus. 3   American eels, showing horizontal flexure of body and continuous soft-rayed fin displaying irregular contour; note also eel predation of small fish and amphibian. (from Walden)

tions will appear to have vertical humps, especially when little or no light is reflected to the observer from the near side, showing only a silhouette. For a given degree of horizontal flexure, the apparent amplitude (height of humps relative to the troughs) will increase as the elevation of the observer is increased, the maximum appearing when the observer is directly above the object. These relationships are clarified in Illus. 4. While there can be no doubt that actual vertical variations in the dorsal contour also occur, the appearance of a flexing dorsal fin or crest, viewed as described, adequately accounts for the mane and for a moving hump (O 163, Chapter VI).

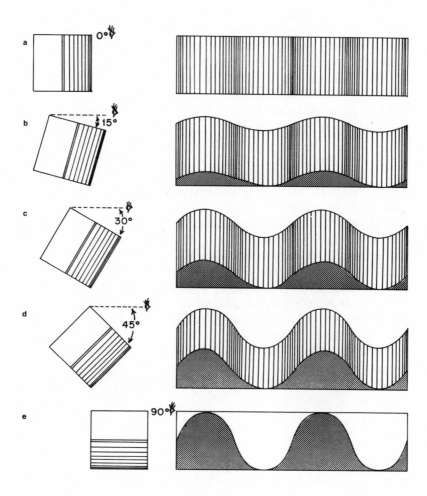

Illus. 4 Appearance in silhouette of a metal strip bent into a horizontal sinusoidal flexure, illustrating varying vertical contours when observed from different elevations:

a. Appearance of the object when eye is at same level as object.

b, c, d. Appearance when line of vision is 15°, 30°, 45° above object.

e. Appearance of object when viewed from directly above.

The aspect shown in *a* corresponds to an observation at distance from a boat, showing little or no humping, while *b, c, d* correspond to views from the shore of Loch Ness at different heights above the loch surface. The aspect depicted by *e* could only be observed from an aerial view.

The more triangular aspect sometimes described, filmed by Dinsdale (F 7), and depicted in the Lachlan Stuart photograph (P 6) is accounted for especially well by the rhomboidal tail of the Berlin plesiosaur (Illus. 2) or by the tendency of some aquatic urodeles to flex the back rather sharply. Of course, the crest or fin may also contribute to the acuteness of the apparent flexure.

Independent evidence of "humps" or horizontal or vertical undulation has also been provided by the sonar trace obtained by R. H. Rines in 1972. As indicated in Chapter IX, attributing the sonar trace to sinusoidal undulations, rather than physical protuberances, seems to me more consistent with the data. Regardless of which interpretation is accepted, the results are important corroboration of visual descriptions.

Since limbs are not employed either for efficient terrestrial locomotion or as major propulsive organs, they must function as a steering and swimming adjunct. While this use would favor the front pair of limbs, with the rear pair either reduced or completely absent, we cannot on the basis of the evidence settle this point. As was noted earlier, confusion of the head-neck and tail could contribute to the belief that there are rear appendages. This fact hardly helps to explain the inconsistencies in the land observations. In any case, all of the data bearing on this point are consistent with and establish the presence of a front pair of appendages. Only certain aquatic urodeles would be compatible with a *variation* in the number of appendages. To suggest that eels might show an occasional atavism by developing a pair of pelvic fins is an extreme speculation indeed. However, see Illus. 8, Chapter XI. The disagreement indicated in Table 2 (Appendix A) is not confined to this aspect alone but extends to the descriptions of the extremities of the limbs. The flipper or fin-like descriptions do have some independent support from still photograph P 5 and the underwater photograph P 16 (Chapter VII). Therefore, until more extensive evidence is obtained, the best assumption is that the limbs are flipper-like.

If we reject the surgeon's photograph (P 2), the only evidence relating to the head and neck is derived from eyewitness observations and from P 17 (Chapter VII). The references to excessively long, thin necks have been rejected as resulting from observations of birds and mistaking the tail for the head-neck. The remaining reports, many more than half, are descriptions ranging from moderately long to short. These descriptions more or less agree that the head is differentiated very little, if at all, from the neck. These descriptions are compatible with zoological principles, whereas the combination of an exceedingly long tail with a very long neck are not. The presence of a long, powerful, laterally flattened tail is firmly established not only by observation but is required to account for the speeds (at least 10 mph) established by observation, sonar, and film sequences.[6]

Descriptions of eyes are absent from many accounts, most probably because the observation was from too great a distance. Eyes, of course, will not be noted when the tail is mistaken for the head-neck. The reports describing eyes ranging from small to large correspond reasonably well with the developmental changes undergone either by urodeles or anguilla. The rare slit-like description is more readily accounted for by urodeles.

Even more rare are descriptions of horns or antenna. The external nares of anguilla account remarkably well for the "horns" described in O 106, Chapter VI. The external cirri and palpi in certain amphibians could also account for such observations. The configuration and

---

[6] In this context, it is of value to note that convergent evolution has produced the same kinds of adaptations in most of the aquatic animals which have similar requirements, regardless of whether they are fish, amphibians, reptiles, or mammals. As a rule, those animals having a powerful propelling tail have a short neck, acquired either by the loss of neck vertebrae or, as in mammals, the shortening and coalescence of the normal number of seven. (There are few exceptions to this rule of a short neck associated with a long tail. One such exception is the reptile known as Prognasaurus [Mesosaurus] found in the Paleozoic.) The reciprocal neck-tail length relationship is well illustrated by the plesiosaurs and related forms. Here the longest necks are found in species with the shortest tails, and vice versa, with moderately long necks associated with only moderately long tails. A further relationship is found between the kinds of limbs and the presence or absence of a powerful propulsive tail. As the tail develops as a propulsive organ, the limbs lose some of their propelling function and become merely organs of equilibration and control. In general, the hind ones have a much less important use as guiding organs, so that eventually many forms have lost them altogether. Further, those animals that propel themselves by the aid of the tail in the water generally have broad, short limbs. It should be noted that there is agreement on this latter point in spite of the confusion as to the nature of the Loch Ness animal limbs.

placement of these protuberances is such that they might easily be missed at greater distances and when viewed from certain angles. Of course, if these structures are retractable, they would not always be visible. The gastropods also can account readily for the data since many forms have retractable antenna. With the other kinds of animals considered, there are varying degrees of difficulty in accounting for these observations.

No structures identifiable as ears have ever been reported. The alleged sensitivity to sound is really not solidly supported by evidence. If such sensitivity does indeed exist, anguilla, reptiles, and mammals clearly have such sensitivity; some difficulty is encountered with urodeles, while gastropods apparently would not respond to air-borne sound. The questionable swish and bark described by only two observers might be produced by large anguilla and pinnipeds and less probably by urodeles or sirenia but hardly by gastropods. We do not know what kinds of sounds, if any, plesiosaurs produced, but hissing would certainly have been possible.

All the kinds of animals considered might possess a smooth, scaleless skin of suitable color; the correspondence with the known colors of anguilla and certain urodeles is excellent. The observations agree that the underbelly is light color, and that the upper portion of the animals is dark, ranging from dark olive green through shades of brown to black. The changes in skin color undergone during the life cycle of anguilla, as well as the ability to change color in many urodeles, account adequately for the range of color encountered. If plesiosaurs moulted periodically, as snakes do, they might on occasion present a blistered appearance. Urodeles may change markedly during mating periods and some actually moult, so that the single report describing a blister-like appearance might be a reference to such a moult. There are indications that mucous may be present on the skin which, while generally appearing smooth, may appear under certain conditions with a more textured roughness. Remembering that eels and urodeles secrete mucous and that eels do have embedded scales which in a large specimen might appear textured at close range with proper lighting, both rough and smooth appearing skin would be accounted for.

A few observations remain, which are relatively obscure but may be of significance and should be recorded. Several people have reported that the animal continually opened and closed its mouth and that the throat region appeared to vibrate and pulse. Gulping air to fill a swim bladder or to ventilate gills or help in respiration in some other way might be possible explanations. The continuous movements of the floor of the mouth associated with buccopharyngeal respiration in some amphibians is particularly suggestive.

Occasional references to flattening of the head would favor urodeles rather than anguilla. The side-to-side tossing of the head, as described occasionally, would be consistent with either anguilla or urodeles while disposing of a fish. One reference to a pouch-like structure located ventrally where the neck joined the body could be accounted for by the cloacal swelling of male urodeles, if the observer had confused the tail with the head-neck. The report of a frill-like structure at the head-neck juncture might refer to external gills, which would be compatible with the larval characteristics of urodeles, neotenous or otherwise, and perhaps some gastropods. While such rare and unconfirmed observations are interesting, further speculation would hardly be of value.

Finally a few words with regard to the asymmetrical distribution of the Loch Ness phenomena are in order. In the very beginning of this book it was pointed out that sighting reports are confined to the northern hemisphere, roughly between 50° and 60° N latitude. Do any of our major categories of animal types provide an explanation for such a distribution? Mollusks, eels, reptiles, and seals certainly provide no special insight. On the other hand, the limited distribution of *Rhytina stelleri* in the region of Copper and Bering Islands is interesting; the reason for this restricted distribution is unknown, and there is no evidence that the distribution was much wider in times past or whether it included the southern hemisphere.

The amphibian hypothesis, however, is most suggestive and accounts rather well for the asymmetry of the geological distribution. Schmalhausen reconstructs the story of amphibian-reptile competition approximately as follows: When insectivorous reptiles appeared on the geological horizon, amphibians were in great measure forced to revert to the water to feed. The further development of predatory reptiles resulted in an almost complete reversion of the amphibians to the water. However, competition between the two groups did not end there, for some reptiles also entered a secondary aquatic life. Thus the early amphibians, or stegocephalians, were quickly replaced by reptiles. On land the extermination took place predominantly during the Permian, in the water during the Triassic.

In *low* temperature areas reptiles did *not* predominate. In a low environmental temperature the activity of both reptiles and amphibians is reduced, but the reptiles are affected much more. The major reasons for this differential susceptibility are as follows: Reptiles expend considerable muscular energy in respiratory movements, whereas in aquatic amphibia this is not the case because of gill respiration in the neotenous forms and oropharnygeal and dermal modes of respiration in adults; little or no energy is expended in these amphibian methods of taking oxygen. Lack of sufficient food affects reptiles more since their requirements are higher by virtue of their prey-seeking activity; in contrast the amphibians generally lie in wait for their prey. Most reptiles lay eggs on land, so a cold climate including periods of freezing temperatures would destroy eggs; amphibians avoid this problem by continuing, as did their fish ancestors, to deposit their eggs in water. As a result, reptiles not only could not hold their own in colder climates but actually gave way to the amphibians, particularly urodeles. One therefore finds most urodeles in northerly mountainous areas, regions inhospitable to reptiles but suitable for amphibian adaptation. Urodele amphibians did not become abundant in the southern hemisphere since the smaller overgrown waters in which they usually bred were occupied by the dipnoan fishes.

An attempt to summarize the preceding material in a semiquantitative fashion is shown below. It must be admitted at the outset that such a procedure is subject to serious criticism. The 32 characteristics listed in the table are, first of all, not of equal importance; yet they are scored as if they were, as either compatible or incompatible with the candidates ($+$ or $-$). Secondly, each case is not necessarily clear-cut; in many instances varying degrees of correspondence exist so that in judging such cases an element of arbitrariness or subjective bias must play some role. Another problem is encountered because equal groups of animals are not compared. For example, gastropods include many more species than any of the other groups. Further, zoological classification itself is not precise in that the designation of one group at the level of an "order" or "genus" is not exactly equal to such a designation in another group. In spite of these difficulties, the comparison following is useful in making a judgment as to what the most probable identity of the Loch Ness animals is.

Comparison of Animal Characteristics with the Loch Ness Phenomena

Loch Ness animal character	Pinnepedia	Sirenia	Plesiosauria	Urodela Embolomeri	Anguilliformes	Gastropoda
Size	+	+	+	+	−	−
Thickened body	+	+	+	+	+	+
Humps (dorsal surface)	−	−	+	+	+	+
Anterior limbs only	+	+	−	+	+	+
Anterior plus posterior limbs	−	−	+	+	−	−
Head-neck configuration	−	−	+	−	−	−
No head-neck differentiation	+	+	−	+	+	+
Skin texture	+	+	+	+	+	+
Skin color	+	+	+	+	+	+
Horns or antenna	−	−	−	+	+	+
Mane	−	−	+	+	+	+
Frill	−	−	−	+	−	+
Eye, small to large	−	−	−	+	+	−
Eye, slit-like	+	−	+	+	−	−
Sensitivity to sound in water	+	+	+	+	+	−
Sensitivity to sound in air	+	+	+	+	+	−
Animal sounds, swish or hiss	+	+	+	−	+	−
Animal sounds, bark	+	−	−	−	+	−
Low water temperature	+	+	−	+	+	+
Fresh water	+	+	+	+	+	+
Salt water	+	+	+	−	+	+
Piscivorous	+	−	+	+	+	+
Difficulty of observation	−	+	+	+	+	+
Amphibious behavior	+	−	+	+	+	+
Respiration in water	−	−	−	+	+	+
Powerful, laterally flattened tail	−	−	−	+	+	−
Locomotion, speed	+	−	+	+	+	−
Diving, submergence	+	−	+	+	+	+
"Basking" or other applicable behavior	−	+	+	+	+	+
Reproduction in water	−	+	+	+	+	+
Pulsing throat region	−	−	−	+	−	−
Dorsal-ventral head flattening	−	−	+	+	−	−
Ratio characteristics accounted for	18/32	15/32	22/32	28/32	25/32	19/32
Percent	56	47	69	88	78	59

female

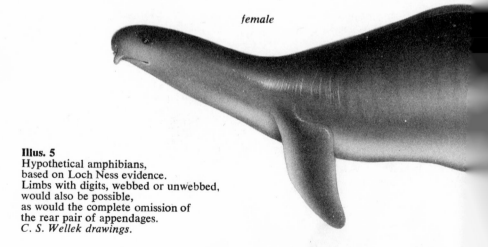

Illus. 5
Hypothetical amphibians,
based on Loch Ness evidence.
Limbs with digits, webbed or unwebbed,
would also be possible,
as would the complete omission of
the rear pair of appendages.
C. S. Wellek drawings.

male

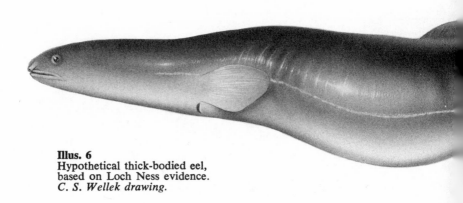

Illus. 6
Hypothetical thick-bodied eel,
based on Loch Ness evidence.
C. S. Wellek drawing.

Illus. 5, 6 represent my conception of what suitable "Loch Ness monster" eels or amphibians might look like. While these artistic renderings of course reflect hypothetical animals, they incorporate the data from the plus-minus comparison table above relating to the physical descriptions and they embody all other available evidence; further, they contain no contradictory or incompatible zoological features.

To those who are conservatively inclined, the eel idea will no doubt be more appealing. The evidence has led me to believe that the best possible candidate is a giant aquatic amphibian, probably some evolutionary descendant of an embolomer. Be that as it may, we must recognize that whatever the identity of the animals in Loch Ness, they exist—independent of man's prejudices or beliefs.

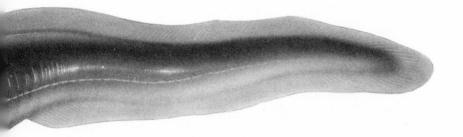

Epilogue

Prompted largely by interest and controversy surrounding the 1975 underwater photographs by Robert Rines, a presentation to both Houses of Parliament was arranged for December 10, 1975 in the House of Commons. Scientists, LNIB officers, and others delivered papers and showed slides and film. Among those on the program, David James spoke on conservation. Robert Rines and associates talked about their photography. Tim Dinsdale showed and discussed his film. (Cf. Chapter VIII, F 7.) R. H. Lowrie discussed his 1960 photograph and sighting. (Cf. Chapter VII, P 11.) G. R. Zug, curator, Division of Reptiles and Amphibians, Smithsonian Institution; C. McGowan, Department of Vertebrate Palaeontology, Royal Ontario Museum, Canada; and I made zoological presentations.

Dr. McGowan has said:

> Having assessed the photographic and sonar evidence collected in 1972 and 1975 . . . and having considered other data pertinent to the Loch Ness phenomenon, I have arrived at the following . . . I am satisfied that there is a sufficient weight of evidence to support that there is an unexplained phenomenon of considerable interest in Loch Ness; the evidence suggests the presence of large aquatic animals. . . . The Loch Ness phenomenon should be the subject of a consolidated interdisciplinary research effort.

Dr. Zug has said:

> [Of] the data gathered in 1972[:] . . . Sonar experts interpret . . . the larger objects as animate objects in the 20-30 foot size range. I concur with this interpretation and further suggest these are fish and the recently described *Nessiteras rhombopteryx,* previously known as the Loch Ness monsters. . . . The most distinct image is of a rhomboidal shape attached by a narrow base to a larger object. I interpret this as a flipper-like appendage protruding from the side of a robust body.
>
> The 1975 . . . images of objects . . . possess symmetrical profiles which indicate that they are animate objects or parts thereof.

218

I would suggest that one of the images is a portion of a body and neck and another a head.

I believe these data indicate the presence of large animals in Loch Ness, but are insufficient to identify them. This new evidence on the existence of a population of large animals in Loch Ness should serve to encourage research on the natural history of Loch Ness and its plant and animal inhabitants and remove the stigma of crackpot from any scientist or group of scientists who wish to investigate the biological and limnological phenomena in Loch Ness.

The name mentioned by Zug, *Nessiteras rhombopteryx,* was given to the animal by Robert Rines and Sir Peter Scott in their paper published in the scientific journal *Nature* (December 11, 1975 issue).[1] The generic term Nessiteras combines the name of the loch with the Greek word *teras,* meaning marvel or strange creature. The specific name rhombopteryx is a combination of the Greek *rhombos,* a diamond shape, and the Greek *pteryx,* meaning fin or wing. Translated, then, we have the Ness monster with diamond-shaped fin. The Rines-Scott name wisely avoids the risk of implying any zoological affinities, inasmuch as no actual type specimen is in hand; that is, we are dealing with unknown animals, possibly new to zoology. However, the naming of an animal based on a single feature (photograph of appendage) is an equally risky business, although permitted by the International Code of Zoological Nomenclature. Rines and Scott give as the overriding reason for labeling these animals at this time "the urgency of comprehensive conservation measures." Schedule 1 of the British Conservation of Wild Creatures and Wild Plants Act of 1975 provides protection for any animal whose survival is threatened. However, to be included under this Act or other forms of protective legislation requires that the protected species have a proper scientific name. "Better safe than sorry," argue Rines and Scott, recognizing that their name has little to do with zoological appropriateness.

In any case, for better or for worse, we will now be able to refer

---

[1] Unfortunately, Zug's hope that the "stigma of crackpot" would now evaporate was premature. Nicholas Fairbairn, M.P., found in the name *Nessiteras rhombopteryx* an anagram, "Monster hoax by Sir Peter S," which was given wide publicity. Rines countered with his anagram, "Yes, both pix are monsters. R." But, of course, the saner approach typically got buried.

to the animals in Loch Ness by a scientific binomial designation, which at least in some quarters will lend credence to the belief in the existence of these creatures.[2]

The isolation of a specimen is, of course, our ultimate goal. Scientists are always asking new questions, probing for additional facts, and seeking to learn more. Among the scientists' key questions and basic data is their aim for a better understanding of man, his origin, his relationship to the animal kingdom, and the animals' origin. Every time a new species or a new variety of animal is discovered, more light is thrown on these questions. This book should have made clear that photographs of the Loch Ness creatures, however good the pictures are, are insufficient; for the final analysis, the actual animal must be examined, preferably in a normal, viable state.

Responsible zoological scientists seek this end, not at any cost but by methods that will not endanger the ecology or the species. Many concerned environmentalists and conservationists have erroneously assumed that it will be necessary to kill a specimen for study purposes. Certainly death for the animal is *not* necessary, nor is permanent incarceration in a zoo or an aquarium. We aim only at temporary isolation of this unique life form without any injury or harm to the ecology or the animals themselves. Many techniques have been suggested for Nessie's capture, but we are convinced that the safest and most efficient is a deep-water trap designed by Bob Love. (See Appendix L for details and illustration of trap design.)

A live animal will settle the Loch Ness question once and for all.

---

[2] It is possible, of course, that the name *Nessiteras rhombopteryx* may not finally be accepted as the official label for the animals. For example, perhaps it could even be preempted by *Nessiesaurus o'connori,* a name given earlier to the animals by Peter O'Connor and published in 1961 in Tim Dinsdale's book *Loch Ness Monster.* O'Connor refers to "the Water Reptile Nessiesaurus O'Connori, which is (it is understood) the name the Northern Naturalists Organisation gave to the creature shown in the photograph on June 10th, 1960." (Cf. above Chapter VII, P 9.)

APPENDICES

APPENDIX A
(See Chapter VI.)

TABLE 1

Eyewitness Observations, Surface Sightings

Special Note to Reader: *For each sighting there are 13 columns of data, 8 on one page and 5 on the following facing page. Therefore, to read fully Observation No. 12, for example, read across this page at Obsv. No. 12 and then drop down to the facing page below to continue reading across at Obsv. No. 12 there. (Table 1 runs for 38 pages.)*

Obsv. No.	Date	Time	Observer	Observation Duration	Weather	Surface Condition	Range
1	565 A.D.	—	St. Columba Lugne Mocumin others	—	—	—	—
2	1871 or 1872 October	1200	D. Mackenzie	—	Sunny	Very calm	—
3	1885 (?) Summer	—	Roderick Matheson	—	—	—	—
4	1888	Early morning	Alexander Macdonald	—	—	—	—
5	1895	—	Salmon angler Forester, Hotel keeper Fishing Ghillies	—	—	—	—
6	1903, Dec.	—	F. Fraser two others	—	—	Calm	250 yds.
7	Prior to 1908	—	John Mcleod	—	—	—	—
8	1914, July	—	Mrs. William Miller	—	—	—	—
9	1916 (?)	—	James Cameron	—	—	—	—
10	1923, May 10	0730	William Miller James McGillvray	8-10 mins.	Sunny	Quite calm	1 mile
11	1929, Aug.	0930	Mrs. Cumming D. McGillvray	10 mins.	Sunny	Very calm	300 yds.
12	1930, July 14	0730 (0815) ?	Ian J. Milne	3½ mins.	Sunny	Calm	300 yds.?
13	Before 1933	—	Inverness anglers	—	—	—	—

This page is a continuation of the page above. See Special Note to Reader, previous page.

	Tail Head-Neck	Body	Color	Motion	Remarks
1		Some sort of animal killed a follower of St. Columba in the River Ness. Observed again when Lugne Mocumin swam in the river.			Original ms. in library of Schaffhausen, Switzerland; copy in Benedictine Abbey, Ft. Augustus, Scotland.
2	—	Log-like, then upturned boat.	—	Slow, then moved off at speed.	—
3		Described as the biggest eel I ever saw in my life, neck like a horse with a mane.			Reported in *Glasgow Herald*, 19.xii.33.
4	Called it a salamander.	—	—	Strange creature disporting itself.	*Northern Chronicle*, 12.viii.33.
5		Observers stated that a horrible great beastie appeared in Loch Ness.			Reported by Duke of Portland in 1933.
6		Hump like upturned boat	—	Could not get closer by rowing toward it.	—
7	Long tapering tail, eel-like head.	30-40 ft. creature lying in the water, flush with surface.	—	Motionless, then moved off.	—
8		Similar to her husband's observation May 10, 1923.			—
9		Stated that an "enormous animal" had suddenly come to the surface close to his boat while fishing.			—
10	—	10-12 ft. hump like upturned boat.	Dark	Stationary, moved off in arc, submerged.	—
11	—	Hump size of horse's body.	Black or dark	Motionless, sank with a splash.	Viewed with telescope.
12	—	2 or 3 shallow humps undulating along back.	Dark	Splash, moved in an arc at 16-17 mph, submerged.	Like an enormous conger eel.
13		While crossing loch encountered unknown creature of great bulk.			—

Table 1 continued on following pages.

Obsv. No.	Date	Time	Observer	Observation Duration	Weather	Surface Condition	Range
14	Early 1930s	—	D. A. C.	2 mins.	—	—	—
15	1932, Feb. 7	1600	James Cameron	Some mins.	Sunny	Quite calm	—
16	1932, Feb.	—	Miss K. MacDonald	—	—	—	—
17	1933 (?)	1145	Mrs. Kirton P. F. Grant	Quite a while	—	Flat calm	—
18	1933, Apr. 14	1500	Mr. & Mrs. Mackay	—	Sunny	Flat calm	100 yds.
19	1933, Apr. 28	—	Businessman and wife	1 min.	—	—	—
20	1933, May 3	—	Man and wife	1 min.	—	—	¾ mi.
21	1933, May 11	1700 to 1800	Alexander Shaw Alister Shaw	5-6 mins.	Overcast, showers	Calm	500 yds.
22	1933, May 11	—	Mr. A. S. Whitefield	5 mins.	—	—	—
23	1933, May 27	—	Mr. & Mrs. J. Simpson	10 mins.	Sunny	Slight ripple	450 yds.
24	1933, May 27	—	Miss N. S.	10 mins.	—	—	45 yds.
25	1933, May 27	—	Mr. S.	10 mins.	—	—	—
26	1933 May or June	—	Mr., Mrs., & Miss H. McLennan	—	—	—	—
27	1933, June	—	Mr. A. Ross	—	—	—	—
28	1933, July 15	—	Mr. J. Simpson	10 mins.	Sunny	Flat calm	700 yds.

See Special Note to Reader, p. 224.

	Head-Neck	Body	Color	Motion	Remarks
14	Horse-like, long.	—	—	Cruising 20-30 mph.	—
15	—	Hump like upturned boat.	Dark	Little or none; sank.	—
16	Short neck, toothed jaws.	6-8 ft. overall, described as crocodile.	—	Making its way up river.	Observed in the River Ness.
17	—	6 ft. by 1 ft. hump.	Black	Disturbance, moved about, great speed, disappeared and reappeared 100 yds. away.	Grant observed from another position.
18	—	20 ft. overall; 2 humps, one larger.	Blue-black.	Commotion, wake, then humps; turned in arc and sank.	—
19	—	1 hump like a whale.	—	Upheaval in loch.	—
20	—	—	—	Upheaval in water, rolling and plunging; submerged.	—
21	—	8 ft. hump like a log.	Dark	Wake, then hump moving faster than a rowing boat.	—
22	—	8 ft. hump.	—	Wake, then hump appeared; disturbance behind; disappeared.	—
23	—	2 humps like upturned boats.	—	Splash, moved off rapidly; lost sight.	—
24	—	30 ft. overall; 2 humps: one smaller, other longer tapering off.	—	Motionless; sank; observed V-shaped wash.	—
25	—	1 hump.	—	Motionless; sank.	—
26	3 ft. tapering head not differentiated from neck.	30 ft. overall, 2 humps.	Dark	Motionless, then moving.	Hair or wool on back of neck.
27		Described as giant eel 25 ft. long, 5 ft. maximum diameter, tail used powerfully when swimming.		When in motion, back curved into a series of humps.	Observed about 15 times.
28	—	1 hump.	Dark	Motionless, submerged.	—

Obsv. No.	Date	Time	Observer	Observation Duration	Weather	Surface Condition	Range
29	1933, Aug. 5	1400	Miss N. Smith	—	Sunny	Flat calm	1,000 yds.
30	1933, Aug. 5	1500	Miss P. Keyes R. A. R. Meiklem Mrs. Meiklem	Several periods during 1½ hrs.	Sunny	Flat calm	740 yds.
31	1933, Aug. 11	0700	Mr. A. H. Palmer	30 mins.	Very fine	Calm	100 yds.
32	1933, Aug.	1430	Mr. G. McQueen	Some mins.	Very clear	Calm	500–600 yds.
33	1933, Aug.	—	Mr. R. Fullerton	—	Sunny	Calm	½ mi.
34	1933, Aug. 15	1730	Mr. John Cameron	4 mins.	Sunny	Calm	150–300 yds.
35	1933, Aug.	—	A. J. G. and 3 bus passengers	—	—	—	—
36	1933, Aug. 16	1100	Mrs. E. Garden Scott	Few secs.	Fine	—	800 yds.
37	1933 Aug. 25 or 26	0900	Mrs. B. McDonell Mrs. Sutherland	2 mins.	Sunny	Very calm	300 yds.
38	1933, Aug. 26	2115	Mr. W. D. H. Moir	15 mins.	Sunny (sun setting)	Very calm	170–200 yds.
39	1933, Aug.	—	Mr. J. C. other men	—	—	—	Close to shore
40	1933, Aug.	1800	Mrs. C. MacDonald	3 mins.	Sunny	Calm	500–600 yds.
41	1933, Aug. (end of)	2000	Mr. Hector Macphail	—	Overcast	Calm	100 yds.
42	1933, Sept.	1545	Mr. J. M. McSkimming	—	Sunny	Calm	2,000 yds.

See Special Note to Reader, p. 224.

	Tail Head-Neck	Body	Color	Motion	Remarks
29	——	1 hump size of rowing boat.	Dark	Moved circling, submerged.	——
30	——	1 hump (4-6 ft.) seen end-on with ridge (size of cart horse).	Dark brown, blackish grey, "granulated".	Moved back and forth, submerged.	Viewed 6 times; glasses.
31	Head set low in water, front view, mouth opening and closing.	Width of mouth 12-18 inches, opened 6 inches.	Red inside of mouth.	Disturbance, wake, saw head, moved off.	Described short antenna each side.
32	——	12 ft. by 4 ft. hump.	Dark	Moving slightly, ripples, sank.	——
33	——	1 elongated hump.	Dark	Moved zigzag, submerged.	——
34	——	15 ft. long; hump about 8 in. up, like floating telegraph pole.	Dark	Moving fast; V-shaped ripple.	Below surface long tail moving side to side.
35	Head-neck.		——	Moving fast.	
36	——	Hump like upturned boat.	Elephant gray; blackish ridges at top; rough looking.	Submerged.	Skin marked with blister-like areas.
37	——	Hump with disturbances 20 ft. behind.	Brownish-black.	Moving in an undulating way; submerged.	——
38	——	Long sloping hump 40 ft. by 5 ft.	Brown, lighter toward waterline.	Wash, then moving hump; submerged.	——
39	——	8-ft.-long hump.	Bright and shiny.	Turned and moved toward center of loch.	——
40	——	Like a great eel but much thicker; portion 3 ft. out of water.	Blackish-gray.	Moved toward shore, sank.	——
41	——	Long hump gradually appeared; total animal 18 ft. by 2 ft. diameter.	Brown, smooth.	Moved slowly, submerged.	——
42	——	Single 30 ft. hump.	Dark brown.	Moved shorewards.	Lost to sight behind point of land.

Obsv. No.	Date	Time	Observer	Observation Duration	Weather	Surface Condition	Range
43	1933, Sept. 22	1100	Miss J. S. Fraser Miss H. Howden Mrs. G. Fraser Mrs. W. E. Hobbes	10-15 mins.	Sunny	Calm	1,000 yds.
44	1933, Sept. 22	1400	Mr. D. W. Morrison others	4 mins.	Sunny	Calm	950 yds.
45	1933, Sept. 22	0930	Mr. A. C.	Several mins.	—	Dead calm	500-600 yds.
46	1933, Sept. 29	—	D. W. M. and others	5 mins.	Clear	—	½ mi.
47	1933, Sept. (end of)	1200	Mr. James Cameron	10 mins.	Fine	Calm	250 yds.
48	1933, Oct. 1	1010	Mr. B. A. Russel	12 mins.	Sunny	Flat calm	800-700 yds.
49	1933, Oct. 18	—	Mrs. G. Miss R. Miss C.	—	—	—	—
50	1933, Oct. 20	0730	Mr. R. McConnell Mr. D. Cameron Mr. D. McKenzie Mr. J. McMillan	—	Sunny	Calm	200-300 yds.
51	1933, Oct. 22	0900	Mrs. J. Simpson	—	Slight haze	Calm	800 yds.
52	1933, Oct. 22	1130	Mr. A. Gillies	2-3 mins.	Sunny	Very calm	2,000 yds.
53	1933, Oct. 22	1215	Mr. G. McQueen	15 mins.	Sunny	—	200 yds.
54	1933, Oct. 22	1245	Miss C. MacDonald	10 mins.	Sunny	Flat calm	¾ mi.
55	1933, Oct. 30	1500	Mr. F. MacLeod	—	Clear, no sun	Slight ripple	450 yds.

See Special Note to Reader, p. 224.

	Tail Head-Neck	Body	Color	Motion	Remarks
43	Almost vertical, large circular shining eye; frill.	Two humps behind head-neck.	Dark	Rise and fall splashing at end opposite to head, moved off, submerged.	—
44	Snake-like.	Multi-humped, about 7.	—	Moved at 15 mph; submerged.	—
45	5 ft. by 1 ft. head held 2 ft. above water.	Single hump, 30 ft. overall by 1½ ft.	Dark gray-black; rough looking.	Moved along, then sank.	Paddle action noted near front.
46	Vertical, serpent-like head & neck; same diameter.	Multi-humped, about 7.	—	Moved at 15 mph.	Head-neck observed intermittently.
47	—	3 humps; 14 ft. overall.	Brownish-black.	Moved slowly.	Looked like huge tadpole.
48	Head not much larger than neck, 5 ft.	—	Dark	Moved slowly, V-shaped ripple, submerged.	—
49	Seemed like long snake			Swam more or less under-water, dived eventually.	Watched it for ½ mi.
50	—	Single log-like hump 8 ft. by 2 ft.	Dark	Moved out from shore, submerged, reappeared, submerged.	—
51	Vertical, 2 ft.	Impression of two flippers.	—	Dived.	—
52	—	Single hump, 2 to 3 ft. out of water.	Blackish	Foam disturbance; submerged, reappeared.	20X binoculars used.
53	—	Single hump, 5-6 ft. by 2 ft.	Brown	V-shaped wash zigzag across loch.	—
54	—	Single hump, splashing either side toward front.	Dark	Moving slowly; V-shaped ripple.	—
55	—	Single hump; variation in part showing, 1 to 9 ft.	Black	6 mph, changed direction, sank.	—

Obsv. No.	Date	Time	Observer	Observation Duration	Weather	Surface Condition	Range
56	1933, Autumn	—	Henry Ardan O'Flynn and student McBride	—	—	—	—
57	1933, Nov. 10	1400	Mr. C. MacRae Mr. J. MacKinnon	—	Sunny, occasional showers	Flat calm	1 mi.
58	1933, Nov. 11	1130	Mr. John Cameron Mr. J. McSkimming Mr. William Grant	10 mins.	Sunny	Dead calm	800 yds.
59	1933, Nov. 14	1500	Dr. J. Kirton Mrs. Kirton	10 mins.	Clear	Calm	1¼ mi.
60	1933, Nov. 17	—	Mr. A. R. McF.	12 mins.	—	—	½ mi.
61	1933, Nov. 20	0900	Miss N. Simpson	10 mins.	Sunny	Calm	45 yds.
62	1933, Nov. 24	—	Rev. and Mrs. D. Temple Pier, piermaster	—	—	—	—
63	1933, Dec. 11	—	Mr. A. U. Mrs. E. Miss E. F. Miss C.	—	—	—	—
64	1933, Dec. 25	0800	Mr. A. Mack Mr. John Cameron Mr. D. McIntosh	—	Clear	—	30 yds.
65	1933, Dec. 26	1015	Dr. J. Kirton, son, and friend; truck driver and friend	2 mins.	Clear	—	½ mi.
66	1933, Dec. 27	1100	Mr. G. Jamieson	—	Clear	Flat calm	100 yds.
67	1933, Dec. 30	—	J. D.	—	—	—	—
68	1933, Dec. 30	—	Mr. W. U. Goodbody and 2 daughters	40 mins.	Overcast	Windy	400-700 yds.

See Special Note to Reader, p. 224.

	Tail Head-Neck	Body	Color	Motion	Remarks
56	—	Single rounded mass.	Black	Moving along, submerged.	Reported shots fired at object.
57	—	Single hump like unturned boat, 25 ft. by 1½ to 2 ft.	Reddish-brown	Splashing; sank and rose 2-3 times.	Viewed with 20X telescope.
58	—	Single hump looked triangular end-on; 5-8 ft. by 1 ft.; also 2-3 ft. long.	Dark	V-shaped wash; sank, rose, sank.	—
59	Possibly seen end-on in line with hump.	Single hump end-on, 3-4 ft. at waterline.	Dark brown to black.	Moving away.	—
60	Tapered 5 ft. head hardly wider than neck.	—	—	Moved along straight course, slowly sank as a whole.	Whole head-neck moved side to side as a unit.
61	—	One low hump and one small hump, 30 ft. overall.	Dark	Motionless, sank; V-shaped wash.	—
62	Tail thrashing about.	Not much body showing.	—	—	Viewed through binoculars.
63	—	30 ft. long; no clear view.	—	Lashing about.	—
64	Object 6 ft. in front of hump.	Hump 10 ft. by 3 ft.	Black, shiny	Motionless, moved around, submerged.	—
65	—	Hump 10 ft. like upturned boat.	Dark	Moving, submerged.	—
66	Thick, 3 ft. long; head not differentiated from neck.	Two humps 15-20 ft. overall by 2 ft. and 3 ft.	Grayish-black; rough, mottled.	Moved across loch; rapidly dived, car horn sounded.	—
67	—	Single long object.	Dark	—	—
68	—	2 humps, variable up to 8-9 ft.; 16 ft. overall.	Dark	Moved slowly, turned, made swirl at end.	—

Obsv. No.	Date	Time	Observer	Observation Duration	Weather	Surface Condition	Range
69	1934, Jan. (1st week)	—	Mrs. W. U. Goodbody	Short time	—	—	Long way off
70	1934, Early	—	Mrs. MacL.	—	—	—	—
71	1934, Jan. 10	—	J. H. F. M. A. H.	—	—	—	50 yds.
72	1934, Jan. 30	1825	Mr. Howard Carson	10 mins.	—	Flat calm	2,200 yds.
73	1934, Feb. 22	Evening	Mrs. J. MacDonald	—	—	Flat calm	—
74	1934, Feb. 25	1620	Mrs. M. MacLennan	—	Bright	Calm	¼ mi.
75	1934, Apr.	—	Miss W. D. F. G. R. three others	—	—	—	—
76	1934, Apr.	—	Sergeant-major J. H. others	20 mins.	—	—	—
77	1934, May 1	—	Miss K. MacDonald	10 mins.	Clear, sunny at times	Calm	30-40 yds.
78	1934, May	—	Mr. Alexander Campbell	—	—	—	30 yds.
79	1934, May 26	—	Brother Richard Horan James Fraser William Macintosh woman golfer	20 mins.	—	—	30 yds.
80	1934, June 24	—	Miss Fraser	—	—	—	—

See Special Note to Reader, p. 224.

	Tail / Head-Neck	Body	Color	Motion	Remarks
69	—	Single hump 4-5 ft. out of water; like upturned boat.	—	Moved off, churning one side.	—
70	4 ft. long, tapered head no thicker than neck.	—	—	Observed to shake vigorously.	Hair or wool on back of neck.
71	—	Single 12 ft. object with 1 or 2 slight humps.	Black	Moving slowly along near shore.	—
72	3 ft. long.	Two humps 2 ft. by 3 ft., 13 ft. overall including head-neck.	—	Wash; moving slowly, submerged.	Evidence of paddle action one side.
73	—	Large object.	—	Moving at high speed.	—
74	6 ft. round column, top small pointed.	—	Black	Turned from side to side, submerged, left wash.	—
75	Huge long neck, glimpse of powerful tail 20 ft. away.	—	—	Saw head-neck rise out of water.	—
76	Object sticking out.	Two parts, not exactly humps as they were fairly long. (30 ft.).	—	—	Viewed with long-range sighting instrument.
77	Head-neck held at angle to water.	Single hump which flattened out; varied 1-3 humps.	Brownish; drab.	Stationary, raised head-neck, splashing either side of humps.	—
78	6 ft. long turning side to side.	Single 30 ft. hump.	Darkish gray.	Shot out of calm water, sank, lowered neck.	—
79	3½ ft. long; held 45° to water level.	—	White stripe down front.	Moved slowly, turned, dived.	Head blunt like a seal.
80	—	Observed two separate objects.	—	Evidence of tail propulsion; objects were swimming together.	—

Obsv. No.	Date	Time	Observer	Observation Duration	Weather	Surface Condition	Range
81	1934, June 29	——	Farmer	——	——	——	——
82	1934, July 12	1030	Mr. William McKay	Few secs.	——	——	——
83	1934, July 12	——	Capt. F. E. B. H.	10 mins.	——	——	400 yds.
84	1934, July 12	1630	Mr. William McKay Mr. William Campbell	3 mins.	——	——	1–1½ mi.
85	1934, July 12	1240	Mr. R. J. Scott	——	——	——	300 yds.
86	1934, July 14	1210	Mr. R. J. Scott	Few mins.	——	——	——
87	1934, July 16	1015	Mr. J. Macintosh	1 min.	——	——	½ mi.
88	1934, July 17	0820	Mr. A. Ross	——	——	——	——
89	1934, July 18	——	Mr. W. McKay	——	——	——	¾ mi.
90	1934, July 19	1000	Mr. W. McKay	——	——	——	30 yds.
91	1934, July 24	1520	Mr. D. Ralph	——	——	——	——
92	1934, July 25	1200	Mr. W. Campbell	——	——	Choppy	400 yds.
93	1934, July 27	1020	Mr. P. Grant Mr. James Legge	2 mins.	——	Rough	400–500 yds.
94	1934, July 30	0950	Mr. William Campbell	——	——	——	25 yds.

See Special Note to Reader, p. 224.

	Tail Head-Neck	Body	Color	Motion	Remarks
81	—	Observed two separate objects ½ mile apart.	Black	One thrashing about moving at speed; second object motionless.	—
82	—	Single object.	Black	Slowly moving streak on the water; later object appeared, disappeared.	Viewed through glasses.
83	4 ft. flattened head	2 humps, 6 ft., about 8 ft. apart.	—	Moved off, first hump producing V-shaped wash.	—
84	—	2 humps 6 ft. apart.	—	Surfaced 5 times, then moved off.	—
85	Stretched out low in water; small head	Overall 18-24 ft. long, body 2 ft. out with 3 humps above.	Light brown, darker toward water, black.	Appeared to swim on its side, fin or mane where neck and body met.	—
86	—	Object protruded 8 in. out of the water.	—	Stationary, then submerged.	—
87	—	2 humps 3 ft. out of the water, 3½ ft. apart; 15 ft. overall.	Like an elephant.	Moved slowly.	Viewed through field glasses.
88	—	Single hump 20 ft. long by 2 ft.	—	Turned over and dived.	—
89	—	Single hump 15 ft. long by 1 ft.	—	Moved at walking pace, submerged.	—
90	Head-neck appeared like huge eel.	—	Black, underside white.	Splash, trough in water.	—
91	—	Hump 8 ft. by 1½ ft.	Black	Submerged, no wash.	—
92	1 ft. small head like a hedgehog.	Hump 12-14 ft. by 1 ft.	Dark brown to black.	—	Viewed with binoculars.
93	—	Hump 15 ft. long.	Dark	Moving slowly (50 yds.).	—
94	4 ft. by 1 ft. at water line.	Egg-shaped 3 ft. flipper each side.	—	Moved 20 yds. at walking pace, submerged.	—

Obsv. No.	Date	Time	Observer	Observation Duration	Weather	Surface Condition	Range
95	1934, July 30	0945	Mr. R. J. Scott Mr. Evan Strang	2-3 mins.	—	—	½ mi.
96	1934, July	—	Mr. E. F. and daughter	10 mins.	—	Dead calm	200 yds.
97	1934	—	Mr. I. M.	—	Clear	Calm	Looked down on it.
98	1934, Summer	—	J. C.; M. McS. W. G. McS.	—	—	—	½ mi.
99	1934, Aug. 7	1245	Capt. Fraser Mr. Russell Smith Mr. William McKay Mr. D. Ralph	Few secs.	—	Calm	150 yds.
100	1934, Aug. 8	1800	Sir Murdock Macdonald and son and one other observer	5 mins.	—	Flat calm	—
101	1934, Aug. 12	1045	Mr. P. Grant	5 mins.	—	—	120 yds.
102	1934, Aug. 30	—	Dom Cyril	—	—	—	600 yds.
103	1934, Aug.	—	Count B.	—	—	—	—
104	1934	—	Mr. H. F. Colonel W.	Watched until disappeared around headland	—	—	Few hundred yds.
105	1934	—	Mr. D. MacK. Mr. J. C.	—	—	—	—

See Special Note to Reader, p. 224.

	Head-Neck	Body	Color	Motion	Remarks
95	—	Hump 14 ft., three portions showing; 2nd appearance 4 ft.	Dark	Moving slowly, submerged, reappeared, submerged.	Viewed from different position by Strang.
96	—	Impression of a long tremendous bulk swirling about.	Dark	Disturbance.	—
97	Head-neck lifted out; shook itself; mane began 4 ft. from head.	Moving humps (up to 12) about 1 ft. out of the water; 30 ft. overall.	Dark	Broke surface, moved off.	—
98	Raised like a bird; rocking motion.	Single hump, surface varying in length; 6-8 ft. by 1 ft. Seen end-on, distinct apex.	Dark	V-shaped wash; turned, finally submerged.	—
99	—	Single object 10 ft. long by 1½ ft.	Black	Submerged, reappeared 20 yds. closer, submerged.	—
100	—	2 humps; 15 ft. overall.	Blackish-gray.	Moved slowly: about 100 yds. in 5 mins.	Viewed with binoculars.
101	40 ins. long head like goat, two stumps like broken off sheep horns.	Eyes appeared like mere slits.	Dark brown; lighter underneath; smooth.	Moved about 8 mph, submerged.	Skin markings like a lizard.
102	Straight neck.	Small object.	Dark	—	—
103	Saw kind of steam come out.	—	—	—	—
104	—	Saw a huge beast.	—	Moving.	—
105	Observed in water as 6 ft. black line.	Single hump.	Black	V-shaped wash; moved at fair pace, turned and submerged.	—

Obsv. No.	Date	Time	Observer	Observation Duration	Weather	Surface Condition	Range
106	1934	—	Mr. J. C.	—	—	—	120-300 yds.
107	1934, Late	—	Mrs. C. A. McG. Miss R. C.	—	—	—	—
108	1935, Summer	—	Mr. Hunter Gordon Mr. Denman	7½ mins.	Clear	—	—
109	1936, June	—	Mr. & Mrs. Y. H. Hallam	—	—	—	—
110	1936, Oct.	Afternoon	Mrs. Marjory Moir Mrs. Grant Shewglie 3 others	14 mins.	Drizzle	—	⅓ mi.
111	1937, Jan. 3	—	Mr. C. B. Farrel	—	—	—	—
112	1937, June	—	A. Smith Anthony Considine	—	—	—	—
113	1937, July 13	—	R. R. Gourlay R. R. Gourlay, Jr. and wife Mrs. S. J. Stevenson	5 mins.	—	—	300 yds.
114	1937, July 27	—	L. A. R.	—	—	—	—
115	1937, Aug.	—	Rev. William Graham	4 mins.	Clear, not sunny	—	300-400 yds.
116	1937	—	John McLean	3 mins.	—	—	—
117	1937	—	Sir David Hunter Blair 2 school boys	40 mins.	—	—	—

See Special Note to Reader, p. 224.

	Head-Neck	Body	Color	Motion	Remarks
106	——	Like a 15 ft. telegraph pole with tapered ends, 8 ins. above surface.	——	V-shaped ripple from head end.	Saw powerful tail moving from side to side.
107	——	Described boneless motion of the monster.	——	Rolling	——
108	——	Single hump like a boat.	——	Moved slowly along, submerged.	——
109	Observed a head.	2 humps 20 ft. overall.	——	Moving fast down river toward the sea.	Observed in the River Ness.
110	Long slender neck, small head.	3 humps 30 ft. overall, middle hump largest.	Dark gray	Head-neck dipped into water often, stationary, turned, shot off, returned head-neck only showing; wake.	——
111	——	——	——	——	Saw animal at Foyers; continued on to Fort Augustus 10 miles away, observed a second animal.
112	Distinct necks	3 creatures 3 ft. long. Like eels, but had four rudimentary limbs; front limbs flipper-like, rear limbs held close to body. Similar to lizards.	Dark gray	Swimming away from stern of boat.	——
113	Pillar-like, small head held erect.	——	——	Moved at great speed.	——
114	——	2 humps 5 ft. by 2 ft. Either side, a separate 3rd and 4th smaller hump.	Black	One small hump moved off; other two animals moved off together.	——
115	——	2 humps, water seen between humps. 30 ft. overall.	Like an elephant.	Moved fast, 35 mph; left wake; submerged.	——
116	Like a sheep's head, two small eyes oval-shaped.	Saw single hump, when head put down, then 2 humps and a 6 ft. tail.	Lower part lighter, a straw color.	Saw head-neck come up, hump.	Observed mouth open and close.
117	Tail	Single hump.	——	Gambolling about.	——

Obsv. No.	Date	Time	Observer	Observation Duration	Weather Wind	Surface Condition	Range
118	1938, Jan.	—	William Mackay	1 hr.	Wind	—	—
119	1938, June	—	J. MacL.	—		—	20 yds.
120	1938, Aug. 30	1650	Capt. William Brodie A. Rich Mr. Sprout Donald Campbell William Lamb P. Byrne	—	Slight breeze	Calm	—
121	1938, Summer	—	Mr. & Mrs. Robert Wotherspoon and friends	10 mins.	Fine	—	20 yds.
122	Late 1930s	—	A. C.	—	—	—	—
123	1939, June	—	Andy Cowan Martin	—	—	—	½ mi.
124	1939 (?)	—	Robert R. MacEwen (1st observation)	—	—	—	¼ mi.
125	1939 (?)	—	Robert R. MacEwen (2nd observation)	—	—	—	Few hundred yds.
126	1939 (?)	—	William Mackay and friend; 10 others (Graham Pointon and son)	30 mins.	—	—	½ mi.
127	1939	—	Mr. S. Hunter Gordon Mr. P. Dale Bussell	—	—	—	200-300 yds.
128	1940	—	J. MacD. 2 others	—	—	—	—
129	1940, May 5	—	Dom Cyril Brother Robert Murray Brother MacKay	—	—	Dead calm	—

See Special Note to Reader, p. 224.

	Head-Neck	Body	Color	Motion	Remarks
118	—	2 humps 3 ft. and 2 ft.; size varied.	Elephant gray.	Stationary; veered around, spray thrown up.	Observed through a telescope: hair or mane blown up by wind.
119	Small pointed head; opening, closing mouth; head-neck several ft. long.	2 humps and whole length of tail 6 ft. long (overall 18-20 ft.).	Dark glistening.	Dived head first, hump rose up more.	—
120	—	1 hump, then 2 humps; 7 humps later; overall 30-40 ft.	Dark	Dived, wash.	Seen from steam tug.
121	—	3 humps, one large, water between; flattened out and humps joined forming long back.	—	Stationary; rising, then fair speed and sinking.	Salmon jumped ahead of hump.
122	Head-neck emerged covered with some entangling substance.	—	—	—	—
123	Like head of a seal.	3 humps, 2 more prominent than the other.	—	Submerged.	
124	—	Single hump like an upturned boat. 12 ft. by 4 ft.	Dark	Up and down motion.	—
125	Like a thick periscope.	—	—	Moved along; disturbance.	—
126	Came up, appeared between humps.	2 humps.	—	Emerged.	Observed at end-on angle so head-neck appeared between humps.
127	—	2 humps, 4 to 5 ft.	Smooth	Moving 20 mph; humps broke surface every 200 yds.	—
128	—	Part rose well out of the water, tapered both ends.	—	Broke surface.	—
129	Pole-like, 4 ft. long.	—	—	Moved at moderate speed, submerged, wash.	—

Obsv. No.	Date	Time	Observer	Observation Duration	Weather	Surface Condition	Range
130	1940-45	—	James Cameron	—	—	—	—
131	Prior to 1943	—	C. B. Farrel	—	—	—	—
132	1943, Jan. 8	1100	S. Grant Mr. Scott	—	—	—	—
133	1943, May	0515	C. B. Farrel	—	—	—	250 yds.
134	1944, Apr.	—	Retired Naval officer and wife	Several mins.	—	—	up to 1 mi.
135	1944, Summer	—	J. MacF. B. and 3 children	10 mins.	—	—	up to ½ mi.
136	1945, May	—	Mrs. MacL. Mrs. MacK. Col. and Mrs. L.	2 mins.	—	—	—
137	1945, Summer	—	I. C.	—	—	—	¼ mi.
138	1947, Apr. 8 (?)	—	4 persons	2 mins.	—	—	—
139	1947, Apr.	—	Mr. J. W. Mackillop Norman Mackillop Kenneth Cottier John C. MacKay	4-5 mins.	Sunny	Flat calm	¾ mi.
140	1947, July	1700	Mr. & Mrs. Donald MacIver and daughter 2 cyclists	10 mins.	Sunny	Flat calm	—
141	1947, July	1700	Mrs. A. MacKinnon and friends Uncle of Mrs. MacKinnon Miss MacDougall	4-5 mins.	Sunny	Flat calm	20-30 yds.
142	1948, June 14	—	Mr. & Mrs. G. D. 6 others	—	—	Flat calm	200 yds.
143	1948, Dec.	—	Mrs. Ellice, son Sandy, daughter Jean truck driver	10 mins.	—	Calm	150 yds.

See Special Note to Reader, p. 224.

	Head-Neck	Body	Color	Motion	Remarks
130		Enormous animal suddenly came to the surface quite close to his boat while fishing.			—
131		Boat he noticed in loch suddenly vanished.			—
132		Observed a moving animal and a second object disturbing the water.			—
133	4 ft. long with curious fin, prominent eyes.	Single hump, overall size animal 25-30 ft.	Dark olive, signet brown.	Submerged.	Observed with 6X Zeiss glasses.
134		Like submarine, more visible below water.		Stationary, began to move, then dashed off, disappeared.	—
135	Long snaky tapering, rose vertically.	15 to 18 ft. of body showing.		Commotion, set off at great speed, turned and raced back, submerged, reappeared several times.	—
136		Large object lying at loch surface.		Stationary, swerved, moved off at great speed, wake.	Observed with field glasses.
137		Single object.	Dark	Moved slowly, then dashed away 100 yds., submerged, wake.	—
138		Long form.	Dark	Moving slowly, submerged.	—
139	Held high ahead of hump.	2 objects (one hump and a head?).	Blackish	Long wake, humps submerged.	—
140	Held high out of water.	Single object.		Moved at speed.	Observations 140 and 141 were of the same object but by different groups and from different locations.
141		5 humps.	Dark brown	Moved at great speed.	
142	Object with ripple.	2 objects separated 20 to 30 ft.		Came up lazily and moved slowly until hidden by trees.	Viewed with binoculars.
143	Stood out of the water.	2 huge humps.		Humps sank when head-neck emerged.	—

Obsv. No.	Date	Time	Observer	Observation Duration	Weather	Surface Condition	Range
144	1949	—	Warden Alltsaigh Youth Hostel	—	—	—	—
145	1950, Apr. 19	—	Lady Maud Baillie Angus Warr Jonathan Warr Lady Spring-Rice	—	—	Perfectly calm	—
146	1950, June	—	C. E. Dunton and son S. Hunter Gordon	10 mins.	Clear	Very calm	—
147	1950, Aug. 29	—	Motorist	—	—	—	—
148	1950, Aug. 29	—	Miss Elspeth McI.	—	—	—	Close inshore
149	1951	—	R. B. R. MacL.	—	—	—	200 yds.
150	1952 Aug. 20 or 18	—	Mrs. Harry Finlay	—	—	—	20 yds.
151	1952, Apr. 28	—	Wm. McD. A. McL.	—	—	—	—
152	1953, Dec. 10	—	K. T. A. M. J. P.	—	—	—	—
153	1954, Feb. 26	—	A. J. G.	5 mins.	—	—	100 yds.
154	1954, July 9	—	Miss M. MacD. Miss K. MacK.	—	—	—	Several hundred yds.
155	1954, July	0930	W. H. Davidson mother and sister Mrs. Cary	15 mins.	Sunny	Flat calm	—
156	1954, July 20	—	Miss E. McG.	10 mins.	—	—	—

See Special Note to Reader, p. 224.

	Head-Neck	Body	Color	Motion	Remarks
144	Like telegraph pole, 5 ft. long.	—	—	Moved toward observer; side to side swaying.	—
145	—	Single hump.	Black	Stationary, moved off at high speed, V-shaped wash. submerged.	—
146	—	2 humps, 30 ft. each hump.	Dark	Stationary; one moved off submerged, other remained submerged.	Viewed with telescope.
147	—	3 humps.	—	—	—
148	—	3 humps.	—	—	—
149	—	Single hump like a log.	—	Moved off at great speed.	Observers approached by boat to within 70 yds.
150	2-2½ ft. head same as neck about ½ ft., 2 knobbed horns.	2 or 3 humps (15 ft. overall).	Black	Splashing, moved off, disappeared amidst commotion.	—
151	2 ft. long by 8 ins; head same as neck, some taper	2 objects 15 ft. apart.	—	Moved at 25 mph, lost from sight behind trees.	—
152	Like a perpendicular pole.	Several humps.	—	Splashing 20 ft. from head-neck; submerged; surfaced.	—
153	—	First single hump 4 ft. by 3 ft.; second hump appeared; about 3 ft. between humps.	—	Moved off slowly, commotion before sinking.	—
154	Head.	3 humps.	—	Disturbance noted first.	—
155	3 ft. long.	Single hump 30 ft. by 3 ft.	Dark	V-shaped wake, 5-6 mph, submerged several times.	—
156	Long snake-like neck.	3 humps.	—	Stationary, moved off at speed, undulation.	—

Obsv. No.	Date	Time	Observer	Observation Duration	Weather	Surface Condition	Range
157	1954, Aug. 8	—	Miss C. McI. Miss M. I.	10 mins.	—	—	—
158	1954, Aug. 14	—	Mr. P. McM.	—	—	—	—
159	1954, Oct. 8	—	Bus load of people Miss C. Fraser Miss M. Brodie Alistair Irvine Langley Ludgate	10 mins.	—	—	—
160	1955, Apr.	—	Robin Ward Gordon Lowe	30 mins.	—	—	2 mi.
161	1955, July	—	Miss Christine Fraser and friend	—	—	—	—
162	1955, Oct.	—	Col. Patrick Grant	8 mins.	—	Flat calm	100-200 yds.
163	1956, July	0615	Mr. & Mrs. Alan Graham Oxford-Cambridge party	—	Sunny	Very calm	300 yds.
164	1957, June 16	—	Mr. D. Campbell	—	—	—	1 mi.
165	1958, Spring	—	Mr. & Mrs. Hugh Rowland 2 friends	—	—	—	½ mi.
166	1960, May 24	1605	Peter O'Connor Eno Macdonald William Scott	10 mins.	Sunny	—	—
167	1960, During June 27 to July 23	—	Oxford-Cambridge team (30 students)	—	—	—	—
168	1960, July 3	1000	Peter O'Connor	—	Sunny	Slight breeze	—
169	1960, July 10	1850	Bruce Ing (1st observation)	20 secs.	—	Calm	½ mi.
170	1960 July 14 (?)	0530	Bruce Ing (2nd observation)	—	—	—	—

See Special Note to Reader, p. 224.

	Head-Neck	Body	Color	Motion	Remarks
157	Head-neck mouth opening and shutting.	2 humps.	—	Moved around slowly.	—
158	—	2 humps; 35 ft. overall.	Elephant gray; not smooth.	Stationary, then moved off.	Viewed with telescope.
159	—	3 humps, long shape, connected, middle hump largest; overall 25 ft. by 1½ ft.	Brown, underside orange-brown.	Moving about, undulation. Middle hump appeared to move back and forth rapidly.	—
160	—	2 humps; 20 ft.	Dark	Commotion, moved at great speed; lost sight of behind trees, reappeared.	—
161	—	Large object.	Darkish brown; underside lighter.	V-shaped wash; rolled over.	—
162	—	Single hump like a log, 10-15 ft. long.	Black	Commotion, moved off at speed, submerged.	—
163	—	Single hump 4 ft. by 1½ ft.	—	Surfaced, stationary 4 mins, moved off at fair speed, wash, submerged.	—
164	—	Object like overturned boat; second similar object 150 yrds. away.	—	Moving along, one object turned behind other, both disappeared.	—
165	—	Fin-shaped object 4 ft. by 4 ft.	—	Stationary, moved off.	—
166	—	Single object like large upturned boat.	Dark brown	Stationary, submerged.	12x40 and 16x45 field glasses.
167	—	Observed two objects, one giving the impression of continuously changing shape on the surface.	—	—	—
168	One or two specks at head of a wake	—	Dark	2 separate and parallel wakes 4-8 mph.	Viewed with 12x40 glasses.
169	—	8-10 ft. by 1½-2 ft. hump.	—	Moved along, bow wave.	Used 9X binoculars.
170	—	8-10 ft. by 1½-2 ft. hump.	—	—	—

Obsv. No.	Date	Time	Observer	Observation Duration	Weather	Surface Condition	Range
171	1960, Aug. 7	1640	Husband and wife Smiths and crew of small yacht	—	—	—	1,600-2,100 yds.
172	1960, Aug. 13	1515	Rev. & Mrs. W. L. Dobb and son	Few secs.	—	—	—
173	1960, Oct. 23	—	Rev. W. L. Dobb and family others	Few secs.	—	—	—
174	1960 Nov. or Dec.	—	Boys and girls of Ft. Augustus Junior Secondary School (50 students)	10 mins.	Dull	Choppy	200-300 yds.
175	1960, Dec.	—	Robert Duff	15 mins.	—	—	½ mi.
176	1961 (?)	2230	Mr. McIntosh Mr. Cameron	—	—	Flat calm	15 yds.
177	1962 Aug. 24 (?)	0600	F. W. Holiday	—	Breeze	Small waves	Several hundred ft.
178	1963, June 4	—	Sylvia Mackintosh	15 mins.	Sunny	Calm	¼ mi.
179	1963, Aug.	1930	Alastair Grant Mr. Ayton	20-25 mins.	—	—	100 yds.
180	1963, Aug.	1000	Alastair Grant	—	—	—	—
181	1964, Jan. 11	—	Alec Campbell	2½ mins.	Perfect	—	¾ mi.
182	1964, Mar.	—	William Fraser	—	—	—	—
183	1964, Mar. 25	—	Alexander Russell J. Mackenzie Donald Gaw	Several mins.	—	—	—
184	1964, May 6	—	5 Clansman Hotel employees	—	—	—	1 mi.
185	1964, May 17	—	Mr. & Mrs. Roland Eames and 2 daughters	—	—	—	400 yds.

See Special Note to Reader, p. 224.

	Tail Head-Neck	Body	Color	Motion	Remarks
171	—	Single hump 10 ft. by a few inches.	Greenish black	Wash; moved 9-10 mph; two pairs of splashes.	Used 7x50 binoculars.
172	—	Single hump, disappeared, then 2 humps.	Black	Wake; appeared and disappeared.	—
173	—	Single hump, then 2 humps.	—	Appeared and disappeared.	—
174	Head-neck and a tail.	1 to 3 humps.	Black to dark brown	Moving around; wash; submerged.	—
175	—	Large object.	Black	Moved about slowly, submerged; V wash.	—
176	5 ft. by 1 ft. wide head not set at angle to neck; mane.	Single hump.	Brownish black	Saw something cutting water; head-neck appeared vertically, sank, reappeared, sank, reappeared, submerged.	—
177	—	40-45 ft. object 3 ft. out; observed to taper either end below surface.	Blackish gray	Plunged under.	Observed with 10X binoculars.
178	Narrow at top, thicker toward body.	2 humps; part of body below surface; 30 ft. overall.	—	Sank, reappeared slowly, went down gracefully without a ripple.	—
179	3-4 ft. flat head; swan-like.	At least 4 humps; 35 to 40 ft. overall.	Black	Wash from front; submerged, reappeared momentarily.	Rowed after it in a boat.
180	—	Single hump.	—	Moved in different directions, disappeared.	—
181	—	Single hump, 15 ft. by 5 ft.	—	Moving 9-11 mph.	—
182	Pillar-like.	Single hump, 6-8 ft. by 1½ ft.	—	Surfaced, moved off, submerged.	—
183	—	Single hump 25 ft.	—	Cruising about.	—
184	—	Single object.	—	Disturbance; moving at speed.	—
185	—	Single 15 ft. hump.	Dark	Motionless.	—

Obsv. No.	Date	Time	Observer	Observation Duration	Weather	Surface Condition	Range
186	1964, May 18	—	Fred Pullen	—	—	—	2 mi.
187	1964, May 21	0815	Peter and Pauline Hodge	—	—	—	400 yds.
188	1964, July 17	—	Alec Campbell	—	—	—	—
189	1964, Aug. 9	—	Master James Dawson	5 mins.	—	—	200 yds.
190	1964, Aug. 19	—	John Thompson 3 others	—	—	—	—
191	1964, Aug. 30-Sept. 5	—	Local witnesses	—	—	—	—
192	1964, Sept. 6	—	Commander & Mrs. Quintin Riley	—	—	—	400 yds.
193	1964, Sept. 8	—	Mrs. Helen MacNaughton	—	—	—	230 yds.
194	1964, Oct. (early)	—	Mrs. Dallas Taxi driver	—	—	—	—
195	1964, Oct. (mid)	—	Woman	—	—	—	—
196	1965, Mar. 30	1920	Miss E. M. J. Keith Rothiennorman James T. Ballantyne	—	—	Flat calm	¼ -¾ mi.
197	1965, June	0730	Trawler crew of 6 men (including Simon Cameron and Alexander Younger)	4-5 mins.	—	—	—
198	1965, June	2230	F. W. Holiday William Fraser John Cameron	60 mins.	—	Calm	2½ mi.
199	1965, June 21	—	F. W. Holiday Mr. & Mrs. Eaves	—	—	—	—

See Special Note to Reader, p. 224.

	Tail Head-Neck	Body	Color	Motion	Remarks
186	—	Single 15 ft. hump.	—	Surfaced, submerged almost at once.	—
187	Pole-like object.	—	—	Moved off when car door slammed.	—
188	—	Single hump.	—	—	—
189	—	2 humps.	—	—	—
190	—	Observed single hump end-on 4 ft. by 4 ft.	Dark	Stationary; moved off at great speed; lost to view around point.	—
191	—	2 large humps.	—	—	—
192	—	1 dome-shaped hump.	—	—	—
193	6 ft. head-neck with marked protuberances at top; turned side to side.	—	—	—	Head-neck held at 45° angle to water.
194	Head-neck.	—	—	—	—
195	Head-neck.	—	—	—	—
196	4-6 ft. head like a python or conger eel.	Observed part of body.	Black	Commotion; wake; sank twice; moved at speed.	—
197	—	One hump like upturned boat; smaller hump 30 ft. away moved back and forth.	—	Turned, moved off.	—
198	—	Single hump like overturned whale boat; dark ridge at top; 10 ft. by 5-6 ft.	Yellowish brown	As moved faster, profile elongated; submerged several times.	Viewed with binoculars.
199	—	2 humps 4 ft. x 1 ft; impression of serrated edge.	Black	Surfaced, submerged quickly.	Observed with binoculars.

Obsv. No.	Date	Time	Observer	Observation Duration	Weather	Surface Condition	Range
200	1965, July 30	——	Hamish Ferguson George McGill	6 mins.	——	——	——
201	1965, Sept. 30	0700	Edward and Vivianne Elliott	7-8 mins.	Overcast	Slight ripple	½ mi.
202	1966, May 28	1430	Mr. & Mrs. Alastair Macdonald	——	——	Flat calm	——
203	1966, May 29	1005	Mr. & Mrs. Pommitz	10 mins.	——	Flat calm	¼ -½ mi.
204	1966, May 31	1115	Mae Macdonald Sylvia Paterson	——	——	Flat calm	——
205	1966, June 13	0945	B. M. Cameron and niece	——	——	Flat calm	——
206	1966, June 14	0730	F. S. Young	——	——	Flat calm	——
207	1966, June 14	0750	Mr. & Mrs. George B. Johnstone	——	——	Flat calm	——
208	1966, June 20	1030	Lena Holmgren	——	——	Flat calm	——
209	1966, June 29	1530	R. W. Swan	——	——	Flat calm	——
210	1966, July 7	2215	Mr. & Mrs. Robert Dickson Mr. & Mrs. Frank Clayton	3-5 mins.	——	Flat calm	——
211	1966, July 21	2011	Clem Lister Skelton A. D. Macdonald Christopher Aurial	6 mins.	——	Flat calm	——
212	1966, July 28	0800	Heather Cary and mother	——	Overcast	Ripple	——
213	1966, July 28	1610	H. S. Knapp 4 schoolgirls	——	Overcast	Ripple	——
214	1966, July 30	1600	Miss E. Lewis Miss C. Galliford Miss J. Gorton	——	Overcast	Calm	——
215	1966, Aug. 20	1030	Dr. J. Heathcote	Momentary	——	Flat calm	——
216	1966, Aug. 20	1550	Dr. J. Heathcote Felicity Heathcote Martin Henry	15 mins.	Light airs	——	——
217	1966, Sept. 5	0920	M. Pool	2 mins.	——	Choppy	——

See Special Note to Reader, p. 224.

	Head-Neck	Body	Color	Motion	Remarks
200	—	3 humps; 15 ft. overall; 4 triangular spikes along back.	Black, ridged skin.	Moved leisurely downstream.	Observed in River Ness.
201	Object protruding.	—	Dark gray	Saw wash 15 mins. earlier; sank slowly.	—
202	—	3 humps 25-30 ft. overall.	—	—	—
203	—	Single hump.	Shiny	Wake; moved in jerks.	—
204	—	3 humps.	—	Moving fast.	—
205	Small object at head of disturbance.	—	—	Moving at 17 mph.	—
206	—	Object in center of disturbance.	—	Appeared three times in center of disturbance.	—
207	—	Single object.	Dark	Moved at speed, leaving wash.	—
208	—	Single object.	Dark gray	Submerged when observer screamed.	—
209	—	Single hump 15-20 ft.	—	Gentle surface swimming.	—
210	—	7-8 ft. hump.	Black	Moving at 5-10 mph.	—
211	—	14 ft. hump.	—	Moving at 2 mph.	—
212	—	Single hump.	Black	Disturbance.	Observed with 40mm Ross telescope.
213	—	Double hump.	Brownish green	Moved slowly.	—
214	—	2 humps: 2 ft. and 3 ft. long.	Dark	Stationary, later vanished.	—
215	—	Like a large rock.	Gray	Linear wash.	—
216	—	Like a car inner tube.	Black	Repeatedly broke surface, disappeared when boat approached.	—
217	—	6-7 ft. by 4 ft. hump, like upturned boat.	—	Stationary, not bobbing; waves breaking against it.	—

Obsv. No.	Date	Time	Observer	Observation Duration	Weather	Surface Condition	Range
218	1966, Sept. 25	1800	Angela Veitch	——	Sun setting	Flat calm	——
219	1966, Sept. 28	1530	Mrs. N. Shulman	——		Glassy calm	——
220	1966	——	Frederick Gregory Mrs. E. Gregory Ian Gregory	——	Overcast	Flat calm	100-150 yds.
221	1967, Mar. 17	1500	John Cameron	——	Windy	Waves	35 yds.
222	1967, Mar.	1900	David Wathen	1½ mins.		Wave, calm areas	150-200 yds.
223	1967, Apr. 4	2030	Mrs. E. W. Cary Heather Cary Mary Morgan Michael Breaks	——		Ripple	300-400 yds.
224	1967, May 22	2140	Miss C. W. Atkin Mr. & Mrs. MacKintosh	5 mins.		Flat calm	35 yds.
225	1967, May 28	1010	Col. H. D. Pyman A. G. Taylor Jackie Higgins P. M. Christopherson	10 mins.	Excellent	Calm	2½ mi.
226	1967, June 13	1140	Richard H. Raymor	3½ mins.	Bright sun	Mirror flat	1 mi.
227	1967, July 15	1130	Peter Dobbie Mrs. Helen Dobbie and daughter		Sunny	Slight ripple	Few hundred yds.
228	1967, Aug. 6	1720	Peter Davies	——	Overcast	Choppy	——
229	1967, Aug. 7	0805	Norman Schofield	2 mins.	Bright	Calm	Less than 1 mi.
230	1967, Aug. 18	0555	David Field Eric Twelves	Short		Mirror flat	2 mi.
231	1967, Aug. 22	1205	Dennis Gartrell	2 secs.	Haze	Mirror flat	1,400 yds.
232	1967, Aug. 29	1845	Mr. H. C. Kewley Mrs. M. G. Kewley Charles Kewley Richard Francis Banyard	2 mins.		Flat calm	¼ mi.

See Special Note to Reader, p. 224.

	Tail Head-Neck	Body	Color	Motion	Remarks
218	—	10 ft. object.	—	Disturbance.	—
219	—	Single object.	Black	Surfaced and submerged.	—
220	—	2 humps each 15 ft. long.	Black, mottled, rough skin.	Objects submerged, wash parallel to car moving at 20 mph.	—
221	—	15 ft. of back with a mane or frill.	Brownish	Cleaving through waves.	Observed in wave trough.
222	15-20 ins. by 6 ins.; compared to seal or worm; no eyes observed.	—	Dark brown to gray.	Commotion, moved around in arc, submerged slowly, appeared to fall over sideways.	—
223	—	Single 10 ft. hump.	Black	Cruising along, submerged.	—
224	—	Object just below the surface; 40 ft. long.	Black	Cruising along, wash.	—
225	—	2 linked disturbances; momentary hump.	—	Cruising in arc.	Observed with 12x15 binoculars.
226	—	5-7 ft. by 9-12 in. hump, side to side thrashing to rear of object.	—	Wake moving at 6 mph, submerged.	Filmed; also 10x50 binoculars.
227	Tail came up and down.	Single, large object.	Black, smooth.	Moved off, lost to view behind cottages.	Impression of tail propulsion.
228	—	Single object 10 ft. by 3 ft.	—	Submerged with turbulence.	Field glasses used.
229	Small object.	Single hump, triangular 10 ft.; overall 20-30 ft.	Black	Small object submerged, reappeared with large hump, submerged.	10x50 glasses used.
230	—	6-8 ft. by 3-4 ft. hump.	—	Disappeared.	—
231	8 ft. long, flexible.	—	Black	Quickly rose up and curling, hit water with commotion.	—
232	—	Object 20-30 ft. in length, gave multiple hump impression.	Dark gray	Rose, submerged; resurfaced twice, turbulence.	8½x30 binoculars used.

Obsv. No.	Date	Time	Observer	Observation Duration	Weather	Surface Condition	Range
233	1967, Sept. 20	1545	Dennis Bland	Short	—	Glass-like	—
234	1967, Sept. 21	1510	A. E. Hayward Mr. Birnic Mr. Alexander Massie	—	Fine, no sun	Flat calm	½ mi.
235	1967, Sept. 26	1502	John Stroud	3 mins.	Rain	Calm	½ mi.
236	1968, Apr. 18	1730	Miss C. Sanders	—	Overcast	Flat calm	1 mi.
237	1968, Apr. 18	2102	Wallace V. Turl 9 others	—	Clear	Flat calm	—
238	1968, May 4	2100	Lindsay Irvine Sgt. Richard Young Arnold Barnett others	—	—	Flat calm	½ mi.
239	1968, May 5	2200	Philip Bull Howard Pratt	—	—	Flat calm	¾ mi.
240	1968, May 27	—	Mr. & Mrs. Kenneth Warren	—	—	Flat calm	½ mi.
241	1968, June 27	—	Sven Erik Lundberg Mrs. Lundberg Arne Lundberg	—	Sunny	Rather calm	½ mi.
242	1968, July 10	1120	Fred Deacon Mrs. Deacon	—	Fair	Smooth	100 yds.
243	1968, July 23	1000	Ronald Heal Mrs. Heal	7 mins.	Clear	Calm	1 mi.
244	1968, Aug. 26	0945	F. W. Holiday David Pickett Dorothy Pickett James MacKay 1 other	—	Sunny	Ripple	¾ mi.; J.M. from 100-200 yds.
245	1968, Sept. 4	1115	Mr. & Mrs. E. A. Grummet and son	30 mins.	Sunny	Very calm	⅔ mi.

See Special Note to Reader, p. 224.

	Tail Head-Neck	Body	Color	Motion	Remarks
233	—	Hump 9 ft. by 3 ft.	Rough texture; dark gray or blackish.	Small wave moving along, slowly submerged, wake.	9x40 glasses used.
234	—	20 ft. humped object.	Dark brown; roughish and flexible.	Wake, surfaced, submerged.	—
235	—	Long 20 ft. object.	—	Stationary, partially submerged.	Observer left scene while object still in view.
236	—	2 humps 15 ft. overall.	—	Sank slowly, vertically.	Used binoculars.
237	—	3 humps: 1st, 15-20 ft. by 1-1½ ft.; 2nd, 3-4 ft. by 9-12 ins.; 3rd, 2 ft.; distance between 1st-2nd, 15-20 ft.; between 2nd-3rd, 10-12 ft.	—	Humps rose together, sank below surface.	—
238	—	Long, log-shaped object, broke into two more bulky humps.	Dark	Moved off at speed.	Film made. (See F19, Chapter VIII.)
239	—	Single 10-12 ft. hump.	Grayish brown	Cruising fast; wash disappeared.	—
240	—	2 separate double-humped objects just below surface.	—	Cruising along, turned and moved in opposite direction.	Observed with binoculars.
241	—	Single object, like upside-down boat.	Green-black	Submerged.	—
242	—	Long body.	Blackish	Ripple; surfaced, traveled slowly, submerged.	—
243	—	Single 25 ft. by 2-3 ft. hump.	Dark brown	Moved along; lost from view around point.	Used telescope.
244	—	Long hump.	Black, shiny	Moving rapidly.	—
245	—	Spherical hump 3 ft. by 2 ft.	Black, smooth	Stationary, submerged twice, final submergence when boat appeared.	—

Obsv. No.	Date	Time	Observer	Observation Duration	Weather	Surface Condition	Range
246	1968, Sept. 19	1530	Cmdr. R. K. Silcock, Mrs. Silcock	5 mins.	Fine	Flat calm	——
247	1968, Nov. 6	0830	J. F. M. MacLeod	5 mins.	——	——	Less than 50 yds.
248	1969, Apr. 7	1045	Bruce Marshall, Bill Jobes	3 mins.	Sunny	Calm	¾-1 mi.
249	1969, July 26	1530	Mr. & Mrs. D. Clayton, Mr. & Mrs. Maurice Smith	5 mins.	Dull, light rain	Ripple	350-400 yds.
250	1969, Aug. 1	2030	R. A. Moyse, two sons and friend	15 secs.	Sunny	Flat calm	100 yds.
251	1969, Aug. 6	0920	Mr. & Mrs. Geoffrey Craven and 2 children	Few secs.	Fine	Ripple	60 yds.

Observations in Loch Linnhe (a "saltwater" loch)

Obsv. No.	Date	Time	Observer	Observation Duration	Weather	Surface Condition	Range
1	1954, June 21	——	Mr. Eric Robinson	2 mins.	——	Calm	——
2	1964, June 22	——	Mrs. Preston	——	——	——	25 yds.
3	1967, July 16	——	John Rankin Muir, William S. Muir, others	10 mins.	——	——	——

See Special Note to Reader, p. 224.

	Tail Head-Neck	Body	Color	Motion	Remarks
246	—	6-8 ft. hump.	Dark	Broke surface cruising along, submerged three times; V-shaped wash.	—
247	4 ft. long, held at 70° angle.	—	—	Slammed door; splash, ripples moved toward Loch Ness.	Observed in Bona narrows.
248	—	Single hump, then two humps; 20-24 ft. overall.	Gray; glistening, slimy.	Moved at great speed, disappeared; two reappeared, sank.	—
249	—	Single hump 6 ft. by 3 ft.	Black	Moved 6-7 mph, submerged, wake.	Observed independently by the Smiths.
250	—	3-humped object, 20-30 ft. by 12-14 inches.	Black	Moved at 3 mph, submerged, wash.	—
251	—	2-humped object, 25-30 ft. by 3-4 ft.	Black-gray, muddy black, silky black.	Disturbance, surfaced, submerged.	—

Observations in Loch Linnhe (a "saltwater" loch)

	Tail Head-Neck	Body	Color	Motion	Remarks
1	—	3 humps low in the water.	—	Moving 30-35 mph churning at rear.	—
2	Head-neck	—	—	—	—
3	Serpentine head-neck	2 or 3 humps.	—	Surfaced and submerged.	—

TABLE 2
Eyewitness Observations, Land Sightings

Episode No.	Date	Observer	Description	Remarks
1	Prior to 1527	Duncan Campbell	A terrible beast came out of the water on a midsummer morning, overthrew oaks with his tail, killed three men with his tail, then returned to the loch.	Not necessarily Loch Ness. Recorded in Hector Boece, *History of Scotland.*
2	1879	Group of children North shore near graveyard	Observed strange creature coming down hillside to loch. Color as an elephant, small head turning side to side on long neck. "Waddled" into water.	Related by a woman as a childhood memory to Edward Smith. This third-hand account agrees in general with other similar reports.
3	1880	E. H. Bright and cousin near Drumnadrochit	Observed "monster" emerge from wooded area and "waddle" to water on four legs. Left wash after entering water. Long neck, dark grey.	Description similar to main features of such reports.
4	1890s	Gypsy woman	No details.	Alleged episode too vague and indefinite to be of value.
5	1912	Five or six children including William MacGruer at Inchnacardoch Bay	Queer looking animal moved to the loch and vanished in the water. Compared to a camel but smaller: long neck, humped-back and fairly long legs, sandy pale yellow color.	Story reported by William MacGruer to the *Inverness Courier* 20 years after the fact as a childhood memory. Possibly another case of mistaken identity, even though allegedly observed from only a few yards distance.
6	1919	Mrs. Peter Cameron and two brothers	Small head like a camel, long neck, humped back and four limbs. Color like a camel.	Lurched down into the water.
7	1923, Apr. at night	Alfred Cruickshank	Body 10-12 ft. long; tail 10-12 ft. long. Maximum diameter of body 5-7 ft. Arched back. Khaki green color, lighter underbelly. Four legs, thick like an elephant's, with large webbed feet.	Gave out a bark like a dog. Observed within range of car headlights.
8	1930s	Alec Muir near Inverfarigaig	No details. A "monster" alleged to have crossed the road in front of car. Left visible trail and depressed area in moss where it must have been lying.	Information too limited to be of value.
9	1930s	School children at Drumnadrochit	Said they had seen a most peculiar and horrifying animal in the bushy swamp in	Picture of Plesiosaur was picked out as similar.

	Date	Observer	Description	Remarks
10	1933	Mrs. Eleanor Price-Hughes	Alleged to have seen "monster" emerge from bushes and vanish into lake. Carried "something pink" in mouth.	In the opinion of Rupert T. Gould, this incident an outright hoax.
11	1933, July 22 1530-1600	Mr. and Mrs. G. Spicer	Length 6-8 ft, long neck, thick body, greyish color; saw near where neck joined body something flapping up and down. (They later decided it was tail bent around. It could equally well have been a portion of dorsal fin or crest.) Maximum diameter 4-5 ft. Observed 150-200 yds. away. Later changed length estimate to 25 ft. based on road width. Another estimate 10-12 ft.	Moved across road in a series of jerks.
12	1933, Aug. 1st week	Mrs. M. F. MacLennan (Mrs. T. McLennan)	Observed a dark grey mass on the beach estimated 20-25 ft. in length; back looked ridged, had several humps on it. November 1959 Maurice Burton (via letter) asked Mrs. MacLennan about limbs; she answered saying it had short, thick, clumsy legs with a kind of hoof very like a pig's but much larger.	She stated (in 1959) it did not stand up on its legs, but kept hind legs on ground, seal-like.
13	1933, Dec.	Mrs. Reid Inverfarigaig	Strange animal resting on slope of loch shore. Partially obscured by brachen fern. Hairy mane on neck, rest of body seemed hairy. Shaped like a hippopotamus, large round head, short thick legs, dark coloration.	Observer seems vague about details. At the distance of 100 yds. this sighting appears to involve mistaken identity, possibly a congenitally deformed specimen of the highland cattle common in the area. A dwarfed type with shortened limbs would fit the description.
14	1934, Jan. 4 or 5 0130	Mr. Arthur Grant	Small head and long neck, bulky body with two slight humps, long tail, rounded at end. Head like an eel with large eyes. Overall length 15-20 ft, tail 5-6 ft, neck 3½-4 ft. long, maximum diameter 4½ ft. Color black or dark brown. Four flippers; front flippers strong.	Loped across road like a sealion, arching back. Some sketches limbs vaguely indicated, others more definite. In 3 of 6 different drawings he showed suggestion of digits, although verbally he referred to flippers with no digits. One drawing showed dashed lines representing flipper-like appendages; 2 others represent both pairs by vague lines. Conclusion: Grant obtained no clear impression of the limbs.

Table 2 continued on following page.

TABLE 2 (continued)

Episode No.	Date	Observer	Description	Remarks
15	1934, Feb. at night	Patricia Harvey Jean MacDonald Inchnacardoch Bay	Observed an animal crossing a stream by moonlight, moving out of sight toward loch. Thick body at shoulder tapering toward tail, dark color, underside of neck white; 4 short legs. Height about 6 ft., length 8-10 ft. Moved with speed.	Observation made at 20 ft. at night; would appear to be misidentification of wild or domestic animals, such as deer or highland cattle.
16	1934, June 5 1630	Miss Margaret Munro	Using binoculars observed at 200-300 yds. an animal almost clear of the water for 25 mins. Giraffe-like neck, small head, dark grey body, and two very short forelegs or flippers clearly seen.	At end of episode lowered its head and entered the water.
17	1960, Feb. 28 1530-1545	Mr. Torquil MacLeod	Observed on opposite shore of loch grey black mass at a distance of 1700 yds. Used binoculars 7 x 50. Estimated animal 45 ft. in length. Observed one pair of paddles, thought he saw a third, square-ended flipper forward of the other pair, described one end like elephant's trunk. Finally flopped into the water.	Witness seems unclear as to whether he observed head-neck or tail end. He definitely saw a pair of appendages, and he believes they were at the rear; however, when his sketches are examined, it is obvious they could equally well be at the front of the animal. Later, as the animal changed its orientation prior to flopping into the water, he saw the third, square-ended flipper forward of the big rear paddles; he shows it in his drawings at about the same anatomical location that the Spicers observed something flopping up and down. In another context (David James' book, *Loch Ness Investigation*), MacLeod reverses his earlier position and says there were only "two very short forelegs or flippers clearly seen." This does seem to fit better with the overall impression of his drawings.
18	1963, June 6	Members of the Loch Ness Phenomena Investigation Bureau Ltd. camera team	A large dark object was filmed at the water's edge on a small beach 2½ miles from the Achnahannet main camera rig; slight movement seems to occur, but may be caused by wave action or halation. Size estimate by Joint Air Reconnaissance Intelligence Centre 7-17 ft.	Distance is so great nothing conclusive can be deduced from this possible land observation.

Eyewitness Observation, 1973

During the latter part of 1973 a most interesting sighting report was presented to me by Ron Mercer, a long-time member of LNIB and presently a resident of Drumnadrochit at Loch Ness. The report and accompanying sketch are reproduced here. Because this head-neck sighting appears to be a genuine close-range observation of a Loch Ness animal, I requested and received further verification and detail from Mr. Jenkyns himself. My comparison of his observations with eels and amphibians follows the report.

Sighting Report. The following is a record of an interview between Mr. Richard Jenkyns of Pointclair, Invermoriston, Inverness-shire and R. Mercer. All details have been checked and confirmed with Mr. Jenkyns.

Mr. Jenkyns is English and a retired farmer. Having taken his holidays in Loch Ness area for many years, he and his wife purchased Pointclair 4 years ago, and on retirement moved in early this year. The house is situated on Loch Ness about 12 yards above surface level.

On Saturday, 10th. November 1973, at about 11:45 A.M., he tried to start a tractor which had been stuck for some weeks on a piece of rough ground sloping down to the loch edge to a partially built jetty. It was a cold, slightly damp day, with a strong SW wind on the surface giving a heavy swell, with waves 2-2½ ft. Mr. Jenkyns used "Easystart," and as the tractor did not have a silencer, there was an explosive noise, so loud that Mrs. Jenkyns heard it in the house, some 50 yards away, despite all the windows being double glazed.

Immediately after the noise of the starter, Mr. Jenkyns heard a very loud splash, which he described as an impact splash, as if something very heavy had been thrown into the water. It was a single noise and was not followed by any further splashing. Being under the impression someone must have thrown a heavy object into the water, he got down from the tractor, walked round it, and had a good look along the shore line. He then went back to the tractor and 2 minutes after hearing the splash noticed in the water 5 yards off the end of the jetty a ring of concentric circles, showing despite the waves. While he was looking, a little to his left, i.e., NE of the end of the jetty, an animal emerged quietly and smoothly (the distance from the observer being about 45 yards) in a NE direction, parallel to the shore, then submerged "on its tail", i.e., straight down. Throughout, the object maintained a rigid pole-like posture and its motion through the water was very smooth, with no apparent sign of any jerky movement.

The head and neck were slate black, quite rigid and about 9 in. in diameter. He observed a slit mouth, what appeared to be some large scales on the top of the head but not the neck, and above the mouth an eye or possibly a vent. The eye was quite tiny in proportion to the mouth. When the object rose out of the water, it formed an angle of 80° to the water, but when it started to move and throughout the movement it formed a 60° angle. There was no sign of any fins, horns, or other appurtenances. The water at this point is estimated to be only 10-20 ft. deep.

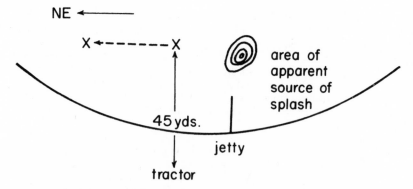

Illus. 1   (redrawn from Jenkyns' sketch)

Mr. Jenkyns refers to the "face" of the head (seen in profile) as being slightly rounded and used the expression "bull nose." If it was an eye he saw (not absolutely positive it was an eye as it was a comparatively small spot) then it was about half way along and above the mouth slit. In regard to diameter of head and neck, it was uniform, with no discernible degree of taper. The question of scales is difficult. He would not make a drawing and would only say he saw a small area on the upper side of the head which was different from the rest of the skin and he thought was a small patch of fish-type scales.

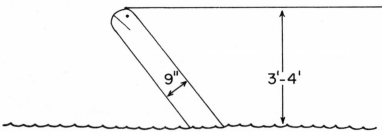

Illus. 2   (redrawn from Jenkyns' sketch)

Analysis. Clearly Mr. Jenkyns' observation was not one of the rather typical bird mistakes. Important features noted were:
1. No taper of head-neck region.
2. No differentiation between the head and the neck.
3. Possible eye—small.
4. Scales or scale-like patch on top of head.
5. Mouth extends well beyond the "eye."
6. Slate black color; no additional discernible features or skin texture.
7. "Bull nose" head contour.

In the case of the common eel there is some taper to the head that should be noticeable to an observer. In agreement, no demarcation between head and neck would be expected if an eel was observed. The eyes of the eel would appear larger and do not fit the description, nor is the scale-like spot or the extent of the mouth beyond the "eye" accounted for. It should be noted that some species of marine eels do have mouths extending far beyond the eye. The slate black color is, however, compatible with eels. The "bull nose" contour does not fit eel configuration. Two varieties of eels, termed broad-nosed and sharp-nosed, have been described by Bertin. Even the broad-nosed contour as viewed from the top does not correspond to Mr. Jenkyns' description. (See Illus. 3.)

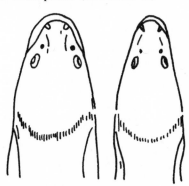

Illus. 3
Heads of a broad-nosed and of a sharp-nosed eel. (redrawn from Bertin)

A taperless head-neck region is found among a number of urodele amphibians, e.g., Batrachoseps. The lack of head-neck differentiation and a "bull-nose" head configuration is also common in the group. Generally the eyes are larger and protrude in amphibians. However, the amphibian hypothesis I present suggests a descendant of the extinct carboniferous embolomers which are known only from the fossil record. We must therefore infer possible characteristics from the primitive features found to persist in certain present-day amphibians. For this purpose the Gymnophiona or Caecilians are most instructive. These amphibians are mainly burrowing types, rarely exposed to strong light. (Cf. the dark condition in the depths of Loch Ness.) Most resemble large earth worms, for their bodies are usually provided with a series of transverse grooves. Within these folds some genera have patches of small *scales*. These are undoubtedly an inheritance from their *carboniferous* ancestors. Although the caecilians are highly modified for a burrowing life, they retain many very *primitive* characteristics. Among the distinctive features of these animals are a pair of *protrusible tentacles* found on the sides of the face between nostril and eye of all species. These organs, of course, would not be visible when retracted. The lidless eyes are usually indistinct and *small,* in some cases hidden under the bones of the skull. One genus, Typhlonectes, is *aquatic* and has developed a *flattened* tail. One species, *T. natans,* found in fresh water in Colombia, Venezuela, and Trinidad is an exceptionally skillful swimmer, often mistaken for *eels* by inexperienced observers. This genus gives birth to its *young alive* in the water.

The mouth slit extends well beyond the eye in many caecilians. The color range includes "slate black." Except for the limited patches of scales present in some species, it presents a typical amphibian smooth skin texture. This repertoire of features (especially those which are primitive), if present in varying degrees in embolomer descendants, accounts admirably for Mr. Jenkyns' observation.

APPENDIX B

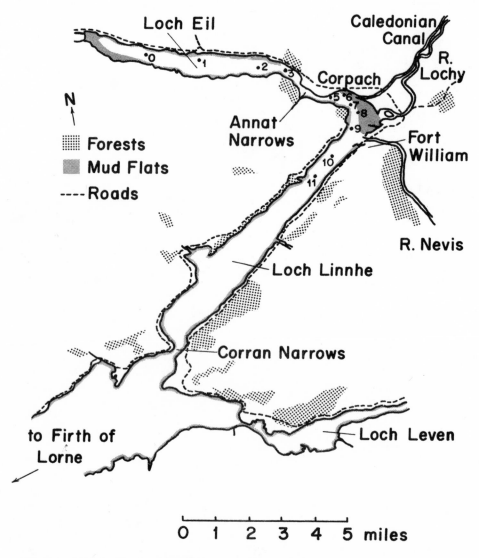

The map above depicts the general features of Loch Linnhe and Loch Eil.
The diagram to the right charts the salinity distribution along the axis of the two lochs.
(redrawn from R. Johnston)

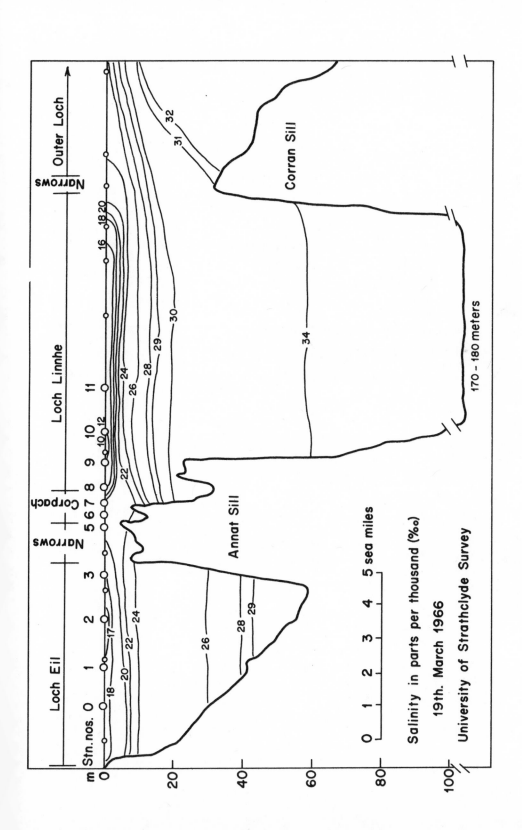

Salinity in parts per thousand (‰)

19th. March 1966

University of Strathclyde Survey

APPENDIX C
(See Chapter VII.)

Analysis of the MacNab Photograph

P 7. (See Chapter VII.) P. A. MacNab was a bank manager when he supplied Constance Whyte with a photograph and an explanatory letter. At present he is a professional guide. The camera used was stated to be an Exakta 127, single lens reflex 6" Dalmeyer lens, hand held, f8, 1/100 sec. According to MacNab, he was touring on vacation with his son when the episode occurred. Although his son was with him, he missed the sighting because he was looking at the car engine. MacNab was about to take a picture of the castle when he noticed a disturbance in the water. He changed lenses, fitting the 6" telephoto lens, and took a picture. He missed observing the actual surfacing, which presumably occurred while he was occupied in fitting his lens. He states that he was conscious of "something" big, undulating, and passing from left to right at 9-14 mph. He snapped his picture just before the object submerged. He also described what he saw as long and dark.

MacNab kindly provided me "the original" negative on loan. However, a full print made from this negative differs markedly from the version of the photograph published by Whyte in 1957. In the following discussion of the differences, I call the 1957 print the Whyte version (Illus. 1) and the negative supplied by MacNab the MacNab version (Illus. 2). Both versions are, of course, derived from MacNab.

Comparison of the two versions presents several inconsistencies. The Whyte version shows a large tree clump in the lower left foreground and much of the nearby beach, features that are not included in the MacNab version. This is most curious since it is certainly impossible for a print to contain more of a scene than was included in the negative from which it was made. In explanation MacNab has said that while he cannot clearly remember now, he thinks that he took another photograph of the scene with a Brownie fixed-focus camera and that maybe the Whyte print was made from the Brownie negative. While it is not impossible, it seems unlikely that a photographer equipped with a high-power telephoto lens and a quality camera would shift to a simple Brownie camera for a second photograph of such a remarkable object at this great range—though in fairness to MacNab, he said that the Exakta had a "doubtful shutter action."

There are other difficulties in addition to MacNab's 1961 statement that he snapped "just as the creature was sounding." The time interval required to change from one camera to another and take a second photograph would be at least 2 seconds, probably more. MacNab described the object as moving at a speed of 9-14 mph. On the surface, therefore, the object would have moved about 30 ft. in the 2 seconds before the second photo-

Illus. 1   Whyte version.

Illus. 2   MacNab version.

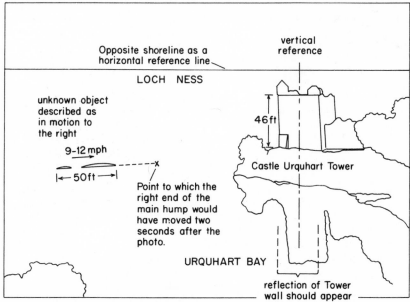

Illus. 3   Composite drawing made from two versions of the MacNab photograph.

graph, and the front of its main hump should appear at the position marked "X" in Illustration 3. Both versions, however, show the object the same distance from the tower, indicating exposure at a single instant in time.

Two other time-varying features occur in the natural scene. Several light areas along the shore in the foreground of the tower are formed by waves breaking over gently sloping pebble beaches, a pattern that is in constant change. The moving object was described as "undulating," a movement that would produce a varying display of humps and their associated wake. However, all of these features appear identical in detail in both versions of the photograph, again indicating exposure at the same instant in time.

A comparison of the alignment of the tower with details on the opposite shore indicates that both versions of the photograph were made from a single camera position about 900 ft. from the tower.

We are faced then with a quandary: Two differing versions of the same scene apparently had their origin at the same instant in time and the same point in space in the hands of the same photographer. This suggests the hypothesis that both versions have, in fact, evolved from a single original photograph, and that the differences were introduced during the *reproduction* of the two later versions. A careful study of the two versions lends weight to this hypothesis.

As seen in Illustration 3, the opposite shoreline of Loch Ness provides a convenient horizontal reference. The walls of the castle tower stand vertical, with their corners representing vertical lines. Vertical lines in a natural scene remain vertical regardless of the angle from which they are viewed. To satisfy the laws of optics, the reflections of the tower walls must also be vertical and lie on the horizontal surface of the water directly below the tower on shore. Telephoto lenses do not normally distort such a view, and the vertical angles should be preserved in a long-range photograph of this scene. The Whyte version confirms that this is so since the tower appears vertical and its reflection lies vertically below.

However, the tower in the MacNab version leans 4° to the left, and its reflection appears tilted off center in the water below. Since this is not possible in an original photograph of the scene, some other explanation must be sought. Might the two different versions have been produced by separate photographic reproductions of an original print? Would this possibility explain the inconsistencies we have noted? The answers are yes, but they raise still another question.

If the original print contained the tree clump and beach in the foreground, a rephotograph of the full print would also include these features, as the Whyte version does. With the print perpendicular to the camera, the vertical tower walls should also be preserved, as in the Whyte version. However, if the original print were rephotographed again with the camera slightly higher relative to the print, the foreground objects would be excluded from its field of view and be absent on the negative, as in the MacNab version. The effect of the leaning tower can be produced in such a rephotograph if the print is not perpendicular to the camera but tilted away at its top. From this perspective the tower and its reflection would appear to lean inward on the negative, as seen in the MacNab version. The object, if appearing on the original print, would appear in the same position relative to the tower in both rephotographs. This would also explain the identical details of the time-varying features of the two versions.

One question still remains: If the object did, indeed, appear in the water on the original negative exposed of the scene, why was it necessary to rephotograph the "original" print, with the resulting two different versions? MacNab has stated that his photographic ability is limited to shooting, developing, enlarging, and printing. Until these difficulties are resolved, I cannot accept this photograph as evidence for large animals in Loch Ness.

The Rines Photographs

P 16. (See Chapter VII.) This important sequence of underwater pictures is unique in that they are related to simultaneous sonar contacts. Briefly, the circumstances surrounding the taking of these photographs were as follows: During the early morning hours, a large intruding echo appeared on the Raytheon oscilloscope, remaining for some time in the vicinity of sonar transducer and strobe camera, which was flashing every 55 seconds. Tiny dots on the screen appeared as streaks as the fish swam away. The 16mm film cassette was later removed, flown to the United States, and developed by Eastman Kodak. (See Illus. 1-5.)

The *precise* distance of the photographed object from the camera lens cannot be determined. To be sure, the object must have been between the lens and the 15-ft. maximum range of the camera. Though some uncertainty about the size of the depicted appendage exists, an estimate of distance *can* be made, based on comparison of these pictures with others taken of known objects under the same conditions at known ranges. This is possible because the strobe light was so mounted relative to the camera that any very close-range objects of a foot or so in size are shadowed in darkness; objects within a few feet are very bright; and objects at extreme range take on the appearance shown in the photographs.

The appendage shown in the photo is different from those of all known aquatic animals in Loch Ness. However, compare the outline with the photo (P 5, Chapter VII) of the alleged appendage. Illustration 6 outlines the appendages of many kinds of aquatic animals. All of the outlines depicted are good to fair approximations of the configuration in this photograph, although none corresponds exactly. As discussed elsewhere, although the appendages of the giant primitive aquatic amphibian Eogyrinus are not preserved in the fossil record, the sum total of information about this form suggests an appendage which might be compatible with P 16. Cf. Illus. 7. Along the approximate center line of the appendage there is an impression of thickening, which if a true anatomical feature, is unusual. Whether or not this is the case cannot be established with certainty. We must remember that the contrast in this picture has been computer enhanced by the Jet Propulsion Laboratory at Pasadena, California. This is a perfectly legitimate technical procedure (Cf. NASA's computer enhancement of photos, e.g., of Mars taken from Mariner 9 spaceship), but caution must be exercised when interpreting internal detail of any photographs subjected to one or more special technical processes. Further, the exact configuration of the outline cannot be determined because the relative angle between the camera lens and the object is not known, nor is its size, as already noted. C. Wyckoff, Applied PhotoSciences, and A. Gillespie suggest the "flipper" appears to be 6-8 ft. long with a maximum width of 2-4 ft.; H. Edgerton says likely 6-8 ft. but no less than 4 ft. However, even the small sizes of the suggested range, 2 ft. by 6 ft., seem too large to me. But one can agree that the appendage appearing in the photograph appears much more substantial than the pectoral fins of the largest possible known fish in Loch Ness; it is indeed probably the pectoral limb of one of the large unknown aquatic animals in the loch.

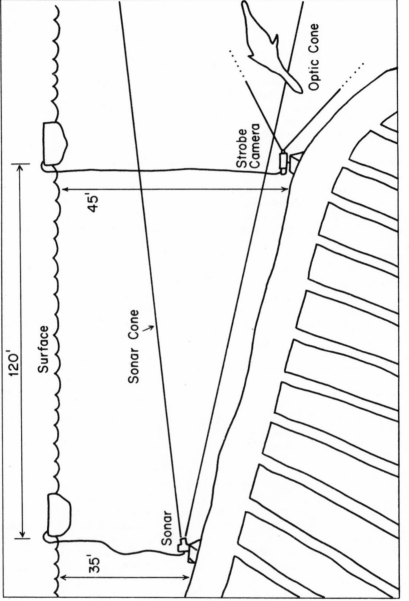

Illus. 1   Deployment of the Rines photo and sonar equipment in 1972. (from Willums)

Activities in sonar beam cone   Read-out on sonar chart

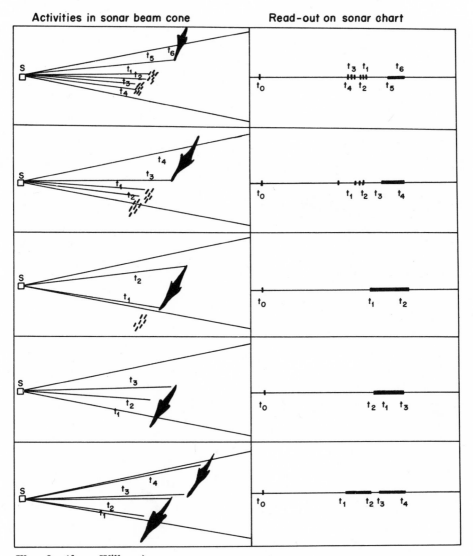

Illus. 2   (from Willums)

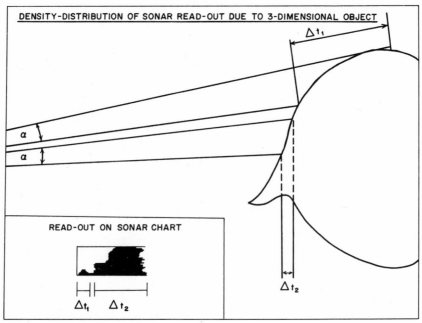

Illus. 3   (from Willums)

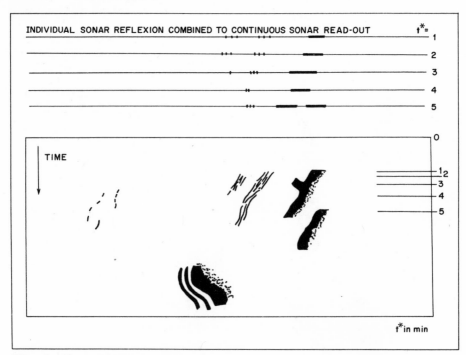

Illus. 4   (from Willums)

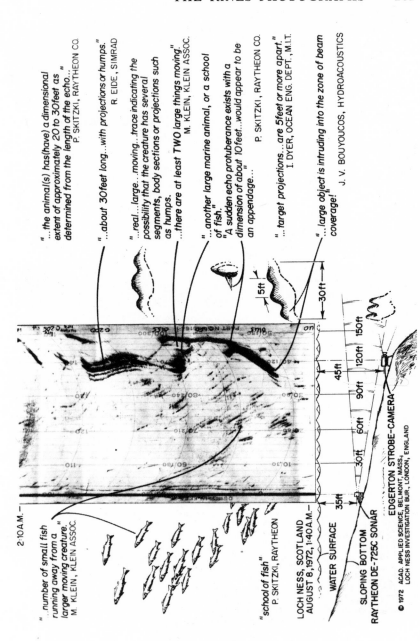

" ...the animal(s) has(have) a dimensional extent of approximately 20 to 30 feet as determined from the length of the echo... "
P. SKITZKI, RAYTHEON CO.

" ...about 30 feet long...with projections or humps. "
R. EIDE , SIMRAD

" ...real...large...moving...trace indicating the possibility that the creature has several segments, body sections or projections such as humps.
...there are at least TWO large things moving. "
M. KLEIN, KLEIN ASSOC.

" ...another large marine animal, or a school of fish.
"A sudden echo protuberance exists with a dimension of about 10 feet...would appear to be an appendage.... "
P. SKITZKI, RAYTHEON CO.

" ...target projections...are 5 feet or more apart. "
I. DYER, OCEAN ENG. DEPT., M.I.T.

" ...large object is intruding into the zone of beam coverage!"
J. V. BOUYOUCOS, HYDROACOUSTICS

2:10 A.M.

" ...number of small fish running away from a larger moving creature. "
M. KLEIN, KLEIN ASSOC.

"school of fish"
P. SKITZKI, RAYTHEON

LOCH NESS, SCOTLAND
AUGUST 8, 1972, 1:40 A.M.

WATER SURFACE

SLOPING BOTTOM
RAYTHEON DE-725C SONAR

EDGERTON STROBE-CAMERA

© 1972 ACAD. APPLIED SCIENCE, BELMONT, MASS.,
LOCH NESS INVESTIGATION BUR., LONDON, ENGLAND

35 ft   30 ft   60 ft   90 ft   120 ft   150 ft   45 ft

5 ft   30 ft

Illus. 5 1972 sonar chart and interpretation.

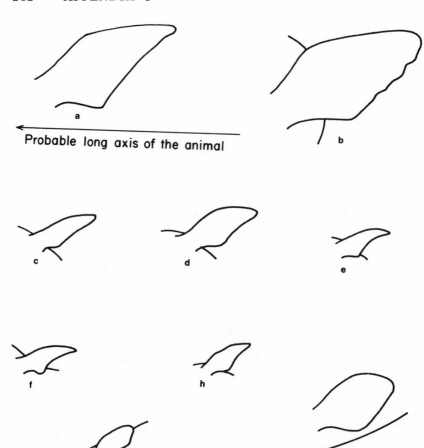

Illus. 6 Outlines of pectoral appendages (not to scale) oriented for comparison with Rines photographs (P 16, Chapter VII); the ventral portion of the body in the vicinity of each appendage is shown.

    a. Rines photograph, probably left pectoral appendage.
    b. Right forelimb of sea lion, Otariidae.
    c. Right pectoral fin of basking shark, *Cetorhinus maximum.*
    d. Right pectoral flipper of bottle-nosed dolphin, *Tursiops truncatus.*
    e. Right pectoral fin of dusky shark, *Carcharhinus obscurus.*
    f. Reconstruction of right pectoral paddle of ichthyosaur, Mixosaurus.
    g. Right pectoral flipper of sirenian, *Dugong dugong.*
    h. Right pectoral paddle of plesiosaur, Elasmosaurus.
    i. Left pectoral fin of freshwater eel, *Anguilla anguilla.*

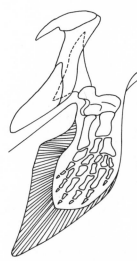

Illus. 7
Partially hypothetical reconstruction of the
pectoral flipper or fin of an Eogyrinus-like animal.
Outline based on the Rines photograph;
girdle supplied by Watson's Eogyrinus;
fin rays based on Watson's and Raven's reconstruction
of Eusthenopteron. If the animal adapted
secondarily to aquatic life, the fin rays would be
replaced by tissue and modified skeletal elements.
If the animal were very primitive, the number of
terminal digital bones would be fewer, representing
a condition much closer to Eusthenopteron.

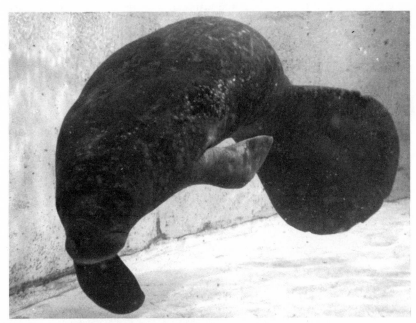

Illus. 8   Manatee, showing the shape of the appendages. *Courtesy Wometco Miami Seaquarium.*

P 17. (See Chapter VII.) Aside from the identity of the animal, one of the most important questions regarding this photograph is the animal's size. Unfortunately, as was also the case with P 16, a precise size estimate cannot be made. However, some estimate can be made based on comparison with other photographs taken of known objects under the same conditions at comparable ranges. For example, the same strobe-camera rig took a picture of an eel (Illus. 9) at a range of 20 ft. (estimation by Rines and Wyckoff). The eel is probably 18 in. long (the most common size encountered in Loch Ness as determined by our eel studies; see Appendix G). On the basis of degree and character of the lighting, Wyckoff estimates the range in P 17 to be 25 ft. Therefore, a comparison between the two photos permits an independent size determination of the animal in P 17: head-neck region about 7½ ft. in length.

Illustrations 10, 11, 12 show some of the photographs made by the same auxiliary camera some 8 hours after P 17 was taken. Illus. 10 is the bottom of the 20-ft. service boat, 35 ft. above the camera; that the boat was photographed has led to the speculation that the camera was oscillating wildly during this sequence. Depending upon the bias of the viewer, the other pictures have been interpreted in a variety of ways, from part of the Loch Ness animal to submerged logs, from a portion of a wrecked ship to a piece of the artificial monster lost by the Sherlock Holmes film crew. (Cf. Chapter IV.) I can say with certainty that the object appearing in Illus. 12 is not the artificial movie monster, of which we have a film sequence; nor is it part of an old ship. (In 1969 the submarine *Pisces* discovered a sunken ship; in 1970 we thoroughly explored it, identified it as a Zulu-style fishing vessel built in the 1870s, and took over 100 underwater photos of it.) George Zug of the Smithsonian has suggested that the object in Illus. 12 is not a log because of a number of points of bilateral symmetry, which suggest an animate object.

Illus. 9

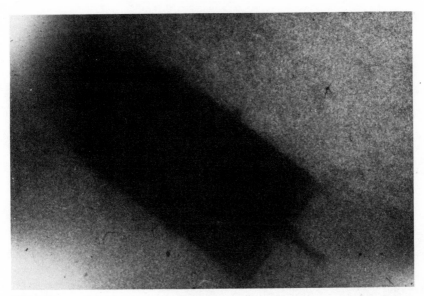

Illus. 10

Illus. 11

Illus. 12

Taking Photographs at Loch Ness

A summary of my evaluation of the 17 photographs analyzed in Chapter VII and in the previous portions of this appendix is as follows:

5 photos: P 1, P 5, P 6, P 16, P 17	Positive evidence
7 photos: P 3, P 4, P 10, P 11, P 12, P 13, P 14	Inconclusive
1 photo: P 2	Identified as a bird
2 photos: P 8, P 15	Identified as logs
2 photos: P 7, P 9	Unacceptable as evidence

I accept 29% of the photos as positive evidence and 41% as inconclusive (possibly genuine pictures but deficient as independent evidence).

In spite of the difficulties associated with underwater photography, not the least of which are poor visibility and severely limited camera range, further useful or even definitive data may be forthcoming from the application of this technique. Very sophisticated equipment and careful calibration and experimental design are paramount. Further efforts obviously should be designed to eliminate the uncertainties associated with the Academy of Science underwater photographs so that most, if not all, ambiguities can be eliminated.

As concluded in the text, above-surface still photography at Loch Ness has not been particularly helpful in exposing the mystery we are concerned with. And it is not likely to make a major contribution in the future. There are just too many difficulties confronting a photographer at the loch; further, there are the difficulties faced by a scientist trying to analyze photos poorly taken and furnished to him with little data. Notwithstanding the dim prospects for still photography at Loch Ness, photographers can greatly enhance the value of their photographs as evidence by following several simple steps:

1. Include in the scene a view of the shoreline on the opposite side of the loch. This usually occurs naturally in photographs taken near the water's surface.

2. Record the time and duration of the sighting.

3. Record carefully the height of the camera above the water. For low-angle photographs this height should be measured to within a few inches. If this is not possible with the equipment at hand, mark the position of the photographer and the water level (which can change several feet in a few days) for future measurements. In high-angle photographs the height is less critical in the analysis, but some attempt at actual measurement (rather than an estimate) should be made. If taken from a road, the distance from the nearest mile marker can be measured by automobile odometer to permit subsequent determination of elevation from Ordnance maps.

4. Record the location of the camera and the direction to the object. If a compass is not available, mark the location and note some landmark in line with the object for future measurements.

5. Record wind direction, wind speed, and weather conditions.

6. Record camera, lens, and exposure data including camera and film size, film speed, lens focal length, shutter speed, and lens aperture.

7. Record estimated range to the object and its size, along with a description of its behavior. An illusion of motion is often caused by moving cloud patterns and waves; this can be avoided by lining up some fixed landmark and checking motion relative to such a point of reference.

8. In printing the photograph an 8″ x 10″ enlargement should be made including the full frame of the negative and its borders. If the negative is enlarged more so that the borders of the negative lie outside the area of the print, landmarks and reference points which can aid in analysis may be cropped out of the print.

To a believer in the Loch Ness phenomena, it may seem unreasonable to subject a photograph to a detailed analysis. An open-minded investigator, however, will appreciate the importance of a critical examination of all possible data. A still photograph which documents an object with characteristics impossible to confuse with a log of reasonable size becomes, under analysis, all the more important as evidence of animate creatures in Loch Ness.

APPENDIX D
(See Chapter VIII.)

Motion Pictures   290

Motion Pictures

The analyses of films noted but not dealt with in Chapter VIII follow.

F 3: 1400, December 12, 1933 (December 22, according to Burton in *The Elusive Monster*); made by Malcolm Irvine, Stanley Clinton, and Scott Hay. Still #1 published in the London *Times* (1.iv.34) and elsewhere; M. Burton, *The Elusive Monster* and elsewhere. Still #2 published in Burton and in the popular press. [positive evidence]

The present whereabouts of this film (16mm, 2 minutes in length) is not known, but we do know that the first part was taken at a range of about 100 yards near Inverfarigaig and shows a dark, elongated, low-lying object. Initially, there is no movement. Later, more of the object protrudes with movement and evidence of some spray. As the object passed out of camera view it is alleged to have submerged. The length of the moving object was judged to be about 16 ft. This sequence corroborates eyewitness observations but not much more.

F 4: 0715, September 15, 1934; made by James Fraser and an assistant on Sir Edward Mountain's expedition. No stills published. [positive evidence]

The film, 10-20 ft. in length, was made at a distance of about ¾ mile with a cine Kodak and 6″ telephoto lens. It appears that the film has been lost, but when it was viewed by experts in 1934, the consensus was simply that some kind of animal was being observed.

F 5: 1530, 1936; made by Malcolm Irvine. Still #1 published in C. Whyte, *More Than a Legend*. Still #2 published in M. Burton, *The Elusive Monster* and elsewhere. [unacceptable as evidence]

Though this film, too, has been lost, it is known that the film showed an irregular dark object associated with considerable foam or turbulence, particularly toward the rear. The creature was moving fast (according to Irvine, at 30 knots [34 mph]). Although the object is mostly submerged, Whyte thought that appearances suggest front flipper action.

In my opinion the film and stills, if genuine, would support quite strongly the impression that a living creature is swimming rapidly along just below the surface. However, there is unsubstantiated suspicion that fraud may have been involved.

F 8: mid-afternoon, October 18, 1962; made by 7 members of the first David James expedition to Loch Ness. Two stills available, not published. [inconclusive]

The film, running just over ½ minute, is 35mm black and white made through a 6″ lens. There appears to be something dark swimming along that never quite breaks clear of the surface. The periodicity of the lightening and darkening is well within the period of waves in the loch, and this

290

might lead the casual observer to dismiss the phenomenon as a freak wave form. However, the isolation of this single phenomenon from an otherwise uniform loch surface makes this unlikely.

This film sequence was analyzed by JARIC in 1963. The height of the camera above the loch surface is a critical value required for calculations; JARIC put the height at 8½-11½ ft. (It was actually about 10 ft.) JARIC estimated the range between 450 and 600 ft. with a distance between humps of 2½-3½ ft. The overall length of this visible part of the object was 6-8 ft. Speed was estimated at a little over 2 mph. JARIC could say little about the nature of the object due to the absence of any detail in the photographs. They further expressed the view that it was not a wave effect but had some solidity, was dark in tone, and glistened.

While certain interpretation of this film is impossible, the probabilities seem to favor the presence of a swimming object rather than a single unusual wave phenomenon; but since no clearly defined object breaking the surface is recorded, this film sequence by itself is unconvincing.

F 9, F 10, F 11: June 6 and 13, 1963; made by 6 members of David James Loch Ness Expedition. Stills not published. [inconclusive or identified as birds]

A second expedition organized by David James spent 2 weeks at Loch Ness in 1963. Three pieces of 35mm black and white film were obtained by means of a Newman Sinclair cine camera with a 17" lens.

F 9: Examination of the first film resulted in the identification of the objects in the film as a group of mergansers.

F 10: The second film was also obtained on June 6. The observers reported that a dark cylindrical object emerged from the water and lay in the shallows on a beach 2¼ miles distant on the opposite side of the loch. The eyewitnesses observed a serpentine head and neck. The object was seen to move in the water both up- and down-wind before going onto or close to the beach. The total episode lasted approximately ½ hour. (See Appendix A, Table 2, E 18.)

This film was examined by JARIC. Their report states that the object appeared to move slightly, but that it was impossible to say if the movement was independent, caused by action of the waves, or simply due to halation. The film was viewed by an independent panel who agreed that insofar as was possible, considering the extreme distance involved, the shape observed in the film corresponded with the eyewitness descriptions but further definite conclusions were impossible to determine.

F 11: The third film obtained was photographically ruined by a thick heat haze. A large number of observers reported seeing a "dome" in the water in Borlum Bay and a trail or slick of material nearby. A panel (including Maurice Burton, chaired by Adrian Head) examined the film material and noted that distinct progression along the surface can be observed in the film. There was turbulence around the object and a streak behind it. The panel came to no definite conclusion but indicated that if the object were animate, it was a species unknown to any of them.

JARIC also looked at the film but concluded its poor quality and the absence of identifiable fixed points made it impossible to determine the dimensions of the dome-like object. They also suggested the "oil slick" had no particular significance, being fairly common in inland waterways.

F 12: 0815, May 21, 1964; made by Pauline Hodge. No published material. [inconclusive]

This episode has already been described in Chapter VII (P 12) since Pauline's husband, Peter Hodge, snapped some still pictures at the same time she exposed 8mm film with their personal camera. All that is depicted is a wash or wake at a range too great to merit analysis.

F 13: August 1, 1965; made by Elizabeth Hall, member of the 1965 Loch Ness Expedition. No published material. [inconclusive]

This film sequence was made with the main rig camera combination at the Achnahannet expedition site. (See Introduction, Illus. 1; cf. Illus. 2.) Approximately 9 seconds of film were exposed. It shows two wakes proceeding roughly parallel to one another. No solid objects are visible at the head of each wake. JARIC's analysis established that the objects (wakes) were 3,846 ft. from the camera and about 9 ft. from each other, one being about 7½ ft. ahead of the other. Speed was 1.09 mph. The wakes were converging slightly, beginning with a lateral separation of 70 ft. and closing to about 9 ft. The inshore wake was essentially straight, while the other deviated somewhat.

Unfortunately, as is the case with even the best analysis of wakes, a great deal of uncertainty cannot be eliminated. The real problem in this case is whether these wakes were produced by objects larger than otters, birds, or any of the known species of fish in the loch. Of course, if the objects had surfaced sufficiently to establish whether or not these known animals were involved, the problem would not exist. These wakes are substantial, having an average width over their length of 6 ft. or more, which might indicate sizable objects. For a given object a wake is wider, heavier, and longer the faster the object is moving. However, at any given speed, the smaller the object the larger the wake in proportion to its size. Since the wakes in the film were substantial but the speed was not, it follows that the objects were probably substantial. The most one can conclude, therefore, is that the wakes probably were not made by common loch animals. A comparison of the wake and hump filmed subsequently in 1967 (F 15), where a hump is visible periodically, tends to support this conclusion.

F 14: 1315, May 22, 1967; made by L. S. Durkin, Loch Ness Expedition, 1967. No published material. [identified as waves]

Durkin obtained a short (15 second) sequence of 16mm color film from a point south of Invermoriston. The film, as analyzed by JARIC, shows, at a range of 1,000 yards, 4 disturbed areas, 50-ft., 65-ft., 38-ft., and 45-ft. long, traveling at 6-7 mph. The raised portions are a maximum of 2 ft. above the water level. These phenomena are clearly identifiable as waves, the only question being as to what caused them. If all records are correct, no shipping had been in the area, and at the time of filming, an approaching vessel, the survey ship *Mara,* was still a mile away. However, it is likely that the waves were caused by this or another vessel, possibly not identified through some error on the part of one or more of the people involved in the recording of time, place, and circumstances.

F 16: 0800, August 22, 1967; made by Andrew Chapman, Gillian Christopher, Loch Ness Expedition, 1967. No published stills. [inconclusive]

Film was exposed several times over a 45-minute period in the same location and with the same equipment used to obtain the previous film (F 15). A long, shiny object appearing low in the water was observed. The filming had to be done almost directly into the sun, and in the first portion of the sequence nothing of significance can be seen. The second sequence, about 30 minutes later, shows a dark-toned, thin area on the surface of the loch, rather like a shadow. No range could be measured, but based on an estimated range of 800 yards, the shadow length was assessed at 90 ft. This entire episode is clearly of no use as evidence, and any speculation is pointless.

F 17: August 23, 1967; made by Christopher S. Hunter, Jeffrey W. Hunter, Loch Ness Expedition, 1967. No published stills. [identified as birds]

This short sequence of 35mm black and white film made from a point along the shore of Loch Ness, 2 miles north of Invermoriston, also was made under poor photographic conditions—extreme haze. A careful viewing of the film, coupled with the description of the observers, leaves no doubt that the objects observed were diving and fishing birds.

F 18: 1500, October 5, 1967; made by Clem Lister Skelton, resident technician, Loch Ness Expedition, 1967. No published material. [identified as birds]

Approximately 2 minutes of 35mm black and white film were exposed through a 20″ lens opposite Foyers at a range of 1,400-1,800 yards. Two light-colored objects were observed moving slowly; the objects are clearly seabirds, most probably large gulls.

F 19: 0900, May 4, 1968; made by Lindsay Irvine, Sgt. Richard Young, Arnold Barnett, and others. No published material. [inconclusive]

These men observed a long, dark, log-shaped object at a distance of about ½ mile, but the 8 mm camera equipment used was completely inadequate, leaving the whole episode inconclusive as a film record.

F 20: 1400, May 27, 1969; made by Harvey Barsky and a troup of Boy Scouts. No published material. [inconclusive]

The observers were located opposite Temple Pier on the southern shore. The object appeared low in the water, moving in a slow, erratic manner. Since a zoom lense was used, measurement from the film is impractical; moreover, although weather was clear and the loch calm, the distances involved are such that independent conclusions based on the film alone cannot be made. At most, the film is supportive of the verbal description and vice versa.

F 21: 1000, June 23, 1969; made by Alison Skelton, Peter Davies. No published material. [identified as birds]

From the Loch Ness Expedition site at Achnahannet, a V-shaped wash moving across the loch past Inverfarigaig was noted. Peter Davies exposed 35mm black and white film (36″ lens) with the main rig expedition camera. Careful examination of this film sequence permits identification of the object as a bird.

F 22: September 16, 1969; Ian Shield and Gerry Baker, Loch Ness Expedition, 1969. No published material. [identified as birds]

Examination of this 35mm black and white film established that the objects producing the wakes were birds.

In Chapter VIII and in this appendix, 22 film sequences have been considered, of which 2 must be excluded as evidence since their very existence is open to question. My evaluation of these films is summarized as follows:

5 films: F 1, F 2, F 4, F 5, F 15	Positive evidence
8 films: F 6, F 8, F 9, F 10, F 11, F 16, F 19, F 20	Inconclusive
5 films: F 7, F 17, F 18, F 21, F 22	Identified as birds
1 film: F 14	Identified as waves produced by passage of a ship
3 films: F 3, F 12, F 13	Unacceptable as evidence

I classify 23% of the films as positive evidence and 30% as known phenomena; 40% cannot be classified in either of these categories, mainly because of insufficient or technically inadequate data, poor film quality, extreme range, etc.

APPENDIX E
(See Chapter IX.)

TABLE 3
Sonar Contacts

Exp. No.	Date	Investigators	Type of Equipment	Type of Experiment	Significant Results
1	1954	Capt. Donald MacLean; mate, Peter Anderson	Messrs. Kelvin and Hughes, Marine Echo Sounder	Peterhead drifter *Rival III*; ordinary depth sounding	Inconclusive
2	1960-1972	Miscellaneous vessels passing through Loch Ness	Depth recorders of various manufacturers	Ordinary depth sounding	Inconclusive
3	1960 June-July	Dr. Peter F. Baker, Mark Westwood	Basdic Frequency 38 KHz	Preliminary survey	None
4	1961	Birmingham University Loch Ness Expedition	(no information)	Vertical echo sounding from surface	None
5	1962 July-Aug.	Oxford and Cambridge Loch Ness Expedition Dr. Peter F. Baker and team	Three Basdic Units (Sinrad of Oslo, Norway) Frequency 28 KHz	A. Single moving craft traverse B. Shore-based sonar gate C. Moving sonar curtain	Inconclusive (possibly none)
6	1968 April	Birmingham University, Prof. D. Gordon Tucker, Dr. Hugh Braithwaite, Dr. D. J. Creasy and team	Digital Sonar developed by Birmingham University Frequency 50 KHz	Fixed sonar screen, shore-based	Positive
7	1968 August	Same Birmingham team	Digital Sonar developed by Birmingham University Frequency 50 KHz	Fixed sonar screen, shore-based	Positive
8	1969	Same Birmingham team, except cooperation with Plessey Ltd. team	Digital Sonar developed by Birmingham University	Fixed sonar screen, shore-based	None

No.	Date	Team / Sponsor	Equipment	Mode	Results
9	1969 June-Aug.	Vickers, Ltd., R.W. Eastaugh and team	Western Marine Electronics SS100; Frequency 155 KHz	Mobile mode, sonar aboard *Pisces* submarine	Positive
10	1969 May	LNIB Ltd., Major Eustace Maxwell, David James, Lord Richard Percy, Dr. Ian Lyster	Marconi Depth Sounder Raytheon Model 729 Fathometer; Seascribe Depth Finder	Drifter *Penorva* mobile mode from surface craft	None
11	1969 Sept.	Independent Television (ITN) sponsorship. Plessey, Ltd. (in cooperation with Birmingham Tucker team)	Plessey Model 195; Frequency 10 KHz	Stationary vessel in middle of Loch; 5 kilowatts of audible sonic energy projected	None
12	1969 Sept.-Oct.	World Book Encyclopedia Griffis Foundation, LNIB Ltd., Robert Love & team, Capt. Don Boddington	Honeywell Scanar II Frequency 100 KHz	Mobile search mode made from surface vessel *Rangitea*	Positive
13	1970 Sept.	Birmingham University Prof. D. Gordon Tucker, Dr. Hugh Braithwaite Dr. D. J. Creasy & team	Digital Sonar developed by Birmingham University Frequency 50 KHz	Fixed sonar screen, shore-based	Positive results not published
14	1970 Aug.-Nov.	World Book Encyclopedia, Carl Byoir & Associates, LNIB Ltd., Robert Love & team, Capt. James Skinner	Honeywell II Frequency 100 KHz	Mobile search mode made from surface vessel *Rangitea*	Positive
15	1970 Sept.	Academy of Applied Science, Robert Rines, Martin Klein and team	Klein Associates, Model MK-300 Side Scan; Frequency 50 KHz	A. Fixed mode from shore base B. Towed mode from surface craft	Positive Positive
16	1972 Aug.	Academy of Applied Science, Robert Rines and team	Raytheon Depth Finder Model DE-725C Frequency 200 KHz	Fixed surface operation	Positive

Tucker-Birmingham Sonar Experiments, 1968

The University of Birmingham experiments (Table 3, S 6, S 7, and S 13) are excellent examples of a shore-based approach using a stationary sonar. The equipment employed by Prof. D. G. Tucker was termed "digital sonar" because it used echo-signal processing entirely digital in function. This means that the acoustic returns are fed to a digital computer, which sorts out the data and feeds it to an oscilloscope screen for visual display. A 16mm motion picture camera was synchronized with the energy pulse, so that the echo return from each pulse was photographed as recorded on the oscilloscope screen (Illus. 1). Fourteen reels of film

Illus. 1 Birmingham sonar oscilloscope screen with mounted camera and auxiliary equipment. *Stuart Markson photo. Courtesy LNIB/World Book.*

were exposed, equivalent to about 150 hours of surveillance. The resolution of this gear was very good in range, theoretically being able to distinguish objects or features separated by one meter. The target position accuracy in a vertical direction is much less than 2°, thus giving us excellent depth information. From left to right (azimuth) there is no information displayed; all that one can say is that if the object appears on the screen, it must be somewhere in the area enclosed in the 12° cone as seen from a bird's-eye view of the loch (top view, Illus. 4, Chapter IX).

Pre-trial runs made with this gear in the spring of 1968 produced some very interesting contacts. An object was observed rising from the bottom, almost vertically, while a second elongated object appeared some distance from the loch bottom. The overall length of this display was in the neighborhood of 50 ft. If allowance is made for an error of as much as 50%, the minimum possible size for the two objects, assuming they gave a display together of 25 ft., was 12½ ft. each—hardly the local salmon straying down to the bottom of the loch.

More interesting were the contacts obtained on August 28 and reported by Tucker and Hugh Braithwaite in the *New Scientist* (December 19, 1968). The film record of this 13-minute episode has been subjected to intensive analysis. Briefly, a large object (actually several objects, 5 to 8, designated A: Illus. 2, 3) is seen to rise from the bottom of the loch, moving out of the sonar beam at a distance of about 300 ft. from the bottom (horizontal dimension about 50 meters [164 ft.], vertical dimension 20 meters [66 ft.] or more). The track of these objects in azimuth (horizontal displacement) is unknown, so that the following velocity components are minimum values. The horizontal displacement along the axis of the sonar beam (range) is about 7.5 mph while the vertical displacement is about 1.1 mph. Tucker states in his paper, "This high speed component in the horizontal plane seems to rule out any possibility of the object being inanimate." There are no currents of sufficient magnitude to account for these speeds; moreover, the idea that currents could account for these movements is completely ruled out by the continued history of these objects. That a number of large, animate objects account for this display can be deduced from the echo structure, and my estimate of 5 to 8 individuals rests upon the hypothesis that Echo A consists of a number of objects equal to C as designated by Tucker (Illus. 2, 3). This object (C) appears in 3 frames but has a horizontal velocity component along the range axis of about 17 mph while diving at a rate of about 5 mph. My estimate for this single object is about 6 meters (20 ft.). (Echo B is omitted in the chart and the photo designation; Tucker identifies it as probably a single large fish or a small school swimming at constant depth.)

As noted, 16mm black and white film was used to record the 1968 Birmingham oscilloscope screen at 10-second intervals. From this film I made uniformly high quality glossy prints (130mm by 199mm) of each frame, including a sequence beyond that reported by Tucker and Braithwaite in *New Scientist*. I then scaled off both depth and range parameters and from these values constructed the diving profile presented in Chapter

Illus. 2 Two pictures from film of the Birmingham sonar oscilloscope screen. Frame #6 (top) shows Objects A moving toward fixed sonar reflection in midwater. Frame #17 (bottom) shows Objects A at edge of sonar beam and Object C diving rapidly toward bottom.

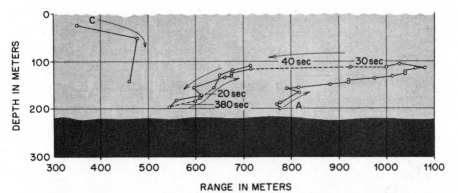

Illus. 3 Movements of large animals in Loch Ness plotted from Birmingham sonar data. The distance moved between each pair of white circles represents 10 seconds except when Objects A were out of the beam or at the bottom for 6 minutes. While not shown in the diagram, Objects A did again descend to the bottom before contact was finally lost.

IX, Illus. 5. The geometry and mathematics of these measurements are:

V = scale distance in mm from bottom edge of frame

H = scale distance in mm from left edge of frame

R = distance from transducer in mm = $H - 7$

D_B = distance from bottom of loch in mm = $V - 22$

D_S = distance from surface of loch in mm = $130 - 5 - V$

M = metric conversion of range (R),

distance from bottom of loch (D_B) and depth (D_S)

M for range = 185 mm = 2400 meters

1 mm = $\dfrac{2400}{185}$ = 12.973 meters

M for vertical distance = 103 mm = 200 meters

1 mm = $\dfrac{200}{103}$ = 1.941 meters

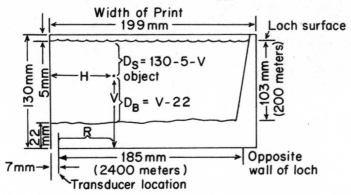

Object A
Minimum horizontal and vertical distance parameters

Frame No.	Time Seconds	V mm	H mm	D_B mm	D_S mm	M meters	R mm	M meters
1	0	22	67	0	103	200	60	778
2	10	28	66	6	97	188	59	765
3	20	31	67	9	94	182	60	778
4	30	40	70	18	85	165	63	817
5	40	45	68	23	80	155	61	792
6	50	45	70	23	80	155	63	817
7	60	49	75	27	76	147	68	883
8	70	51	79	29	74	144	72	921
9	80	52	79	30	73	141	72	921
10	90	55	82	33	70	136	75	974
11	100	57	85	35	68	132	78	1013
12	110	61	87	39	64	124	80	1038
13	120	63	87	41	62	120	80	1038
14	130	66	88	44	59	115	81	1052
15	140	66	90	44	59	115	83	1077
16	150	69	86	47	56	109	79	1026
17	160	68	85	46	57	111	77	999
20	190	68	78	46	57	111	71	921
24	230	65	62	43	60	116	55	714
25	240	60	59	38	65	126	52	675
26	250	57	59	35	68	132	52	675
27	260	57	58	35	68	132	51	662
28	270	49	58	27	76	147	51	662
29	280	45	53	23	80	155	46	596
30	290	37	54	15	88	171	47	610
31	300	31	50	9	94	182	43	558
32	310	24	49	2	101	196	42	545
70	690	32	53	10	93	181	46	596
71	700	36	54	14	89	173	47	610
73	720	46	56	23	79	153	49	636
74	730	58	57	36	67	130	50	649
75	740	61	59	39	64	124	52	675
76	750	69	62	47	56	109	55	714
				Object C				
16	150	111	34	89	14	24	27	350
17	160	99	44	77	26	50	37	478
18	170	52	43	30	73	140	36	466

Love Sonar Experiments, 1969

Robert E. Love's own summary of the mobile search follows:

Mobile search traverses with a sonar-equipped boat in 1969 produced new evidence that at least one large animate object resides in the depths of Loch Ness, Scotland.

Search traverses were run along the length of Loch Ness with the sonar beam scanning the volume of water to either side and ahead of the boat. The search course provided repeated scrutiny of the mid-water volume bounded on each side by the channel walls and permitted observation of the full depth of the loch ahead.

Approximately 56% of the total water volume in Loch Ness was displayed in clear areas of the sonar screen during each full 21-mile traverse. Assuming a single target creature moving at random anywhere in Loch Ness, the probability of sonar detection in the clear mid-water region is 56% in one traverse. Each successive traverse has the same detection probability but the likelihood of a randomly moving creature remaining outside the volume searched becomes increasingly remote. In the 160 miles of search traverses conducted the total statistical probability of detection reached 94%, high enough odds to be promising. The laws of probability dictate that an additional 160 miles of search traverses would be required for the same likelihood of a second contact.

Several sonar contacts were made with targets of possible interest. One of these occurred near Invermoriston during a nocturnal depth-sounding traverse. This weak target echo appeared at a depth of 510 ft. in water 585 ft deep. It remained in position for over 15 minutes while the search boat executed a crisscross pattern over several hundred yards to determine the expanse of the target. Such large distributed targets may be produced by groups of fish or eels above the bottom.

Seven other possible target contacts made during mid-water search traverses are assigned a low probability of significance due to the brevity of contact, reflections from stationary surfaces nearby, or their intermittent nature.

One target observed on 10 October 1969 was conclusively animate in nature. Initial contact was made one and one-quarter miles northeast of Foyers at a range of 1,440 ft. The target was tracked on sonar for 3 minutes 19 seconds during which time it moved 620 ft. along a looping path ahead of the boat. After moving parallel to the course of the approaching boat at 2.5 mph, the target slowed to 1.4 mph as it turned toward the boat, then accelerated to 4.0 mph as it turned and drew away from the intruding boat. (See Illus. 1.) At this point the boat, moving at 3.6 mph, had approached within 825 ft. and sonar contact was lost as tracking manipulation became more critical. The target was not re-encountered during 10 subsequent searches of this area.

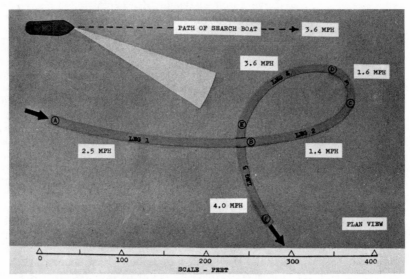

Illus. 1 Plot of movement of a target during Love sonar contact. (Scale refers only to path of animal.)

The physical width of the 15° conical sonar beam does not permit precise determination of the depth of this target. The bottom in the area is 690 ft. below the surface and is flat without projecting peaks or depressions. Upon initial contact, the target was at least 220 ft. deep. At closer tracking ranges the beam is narrower, and more precise depth limits can be calculated. Near the conclusion of the sonar contact the target was moving at a depth of between 210 and 540 ft., a minimum of 150 ft. above the bottom.

Exact size analysis of a target such as this is not possible from sonar data since little acoustic energy is reflected from tissue surfaces which probably have a density comparable to that of water. A large part of the echo observed on sonar from an animate creature is due to reflection from air volumes contained within the creature or, to a lesser extent, from its skeletal structure.

Sonar target strength does yield an approximation of the size of such contained air volumes. Calibration against a cylindrical test target 14 in. in diameter and 40 in. high at a range of 1,200 ft. showed target strengths comparable to the target tracked near Foyers. Another approach to determination of target size involves calculation of the maximum range at which targets of known geometry such as a spherical air volume can be detected by sonar in water of known chemical composition. Analysis of water samples taken from Loch Ness indicated a very low attenuation of sonar energy. Computations show that a spherical air volume with a diameter of 2-3 ft. would be required for sonar detection at the range of initial observation of the Foyers target.

These two approaches yield similar air volume. Air passages containing such large volumes point to known or unknown aquatic species of large proportions. This is all the more true since a volume of air inhaled at the surface would be greatly compressed as any creature containing it submerged. At a depth of 500 ft. a spherical air volume would be reduced to about 25% of its cross section when inhaled at the surface, with a corresponding reduction in its target strength as seen on sonar. Sonar tracking of this target at depth tends to imply that the creature is not a surface air breather but rather extracts its air from the water at the depth in which it functions.

The possibility that the Foyers target-returns resulted from a school of fish must be considered. A school of fish containing swim bladders whose total acoustic reflection could produce a target strength comparable to that of the Foyers target would be quite large. At the closer tracking ranges such a distributed target having a width of over 50 ft. could probably be distinguished from a single discrete target by its appearance on the sonar screen. While the "school of fish" argument cannot be conclusively ruled out, this is considered an unlikely explanation due to the discrete nature of the Foyers target as seen on the sonar screen.

Among other interesting knowledge collected during 1969, the sonar contact with an apparently animate object near Foyers stands out as the major discovery of the expedition. Added to the existing body of evidence, this sonar contact provides new scientific verification of the existence in Loch Ness of creatures commonly known by local residents as simply "the Animals."

With regard to the minimum equivalent air volume attributed to the Foyers target (sphere 2 ft. in diameter or about 4 cu. ft.), one can compare the air volume of about 1½ cu. ft. contained in the lungs of a 10-ft. pilot whale weighing 1,000 lbs. This suggests quite a substantial animal, possibly in the neighborhood of 20 ft. in length if one assumes the same circumference and reflectivity conditions.

Other Sonar Experiments, 1969-1972

Using the Honeywell equipment, sonar contacts similar to Love's were made in 1970 (Table 3, S 14) by Jeffrey Blonder, particularly on October 22 at 2:53 P.M. at a range of 300 yards and a depth of 130 ft. near Invermoriston.

The 1969 contact made from the *Pisces* submarine (Table 3, S 9) is best summarized in the words of its skipper, R. W. Eastaugh:

A sonar target was picked up whilst *Pisces* was hovering 50 ft. off the bottom. The target was picked up at a distance of 600 ft. *Pisces* homed on the target and when at a distance of 400 ft. the target rapidly disappeared from the screen. *Pisces* maintained its course and speed on the last heading, but no further contact was made. Nothing conclusive can be given upon this observation, nor have Vickers tried to do so—it is quoted here as an observation only. Depth of water: 520 ft. Main channel: 300 yards towards Inverness from Urquhart Castle. Observers: S. Boulton, T. Story, and B. Peach (ITN).

This appropriately conservative statement, taken in context with all of the other sonar data, is most significant as a further corroboration of the presence of large moving objects in Loch Ness.

The side-scan sonar experiments (Table 3, S 15) conducted by the Academy of Applied Science in 1970 using the Klein sonar were reported in detail in Tim Dinsdale's *Monster Hunt* and in a recent monograph, *Underwater Search at Loch Ness,* by the academy. Briefly, these experiments employed a transducer having a fan-shaped beam, wide in the vertical plane and narrow horizontally. When the sonar was mounted above the loch bottom, stationary targets were recorded on the chart as straight lines; moving targets appear as curved marks at varying ranges. Such moving targets, larger than comparable fish also recorded, were detected in Urquhart Bay. When the transducer was towed behind a vessel, its fan-shaped beams again detected numerous fish and at least one large target in midwater. Their conclusions are as follows:

1. There are large moving objects in the Loch.

2. There is abundant fish life in the Loch which could support a large creature.

3. There are large ridges or caves in the steep walls of the Loch which could conceivably harbor large creatures.

While the first two conclusions are in agreement with other experimental evidence, the third conclusion is more hypothetical. Side-scan sonar, with its high fan-shaped beam, is designed primarily as a search tool and provides range information without vertical resolution, other than the fact that a target is within the beam. When the beam is directed against a sloping surface, the recording chart can display strong echos at ranges where the slope is steep enough to reflect a substantial signal to the transducer, and no echos where the slope is so nearly horizontal that most of the energy bounces onward and is lost. Therefore, light and dark areas on a recording chart present the appearance of "ridges or caves" when, in reality, they represent only ranges at which sound energy is, or is not, reflected. There is no unambiguous interpretation of such recordings.

Some of the recordings made by the Academy using the Klein side-scan sonar along the shore of Loch Ness depict echos at ranges from 70 to 200 yards. The vertical beam width of some 20° depressed downward 10° defines the vertical limits of the bottom slope from which echos can be received. Thus the closest range of 70 yards at which the slope is recorded must lie within the lower beam limit and the most distant recorded range of 200 yards must lie within the upper beam limit. A line drawn between these two limiting points then defines the average bottom slope. The average slope in this case is 10°. While the channel walls do drop more precipitously at greater depths, the region depicted in such recordings is clearly one of gentle slope, hardly qualifying for the term "steep walls." Although "caves" could result in light areas on the recording, their extent (in one case, 200 ft. across) in such a gentle slope would certainly be described more correctly by the term "depression." In any event, it is hardly necessary to postulate caves as a refuge for creatures that have over 2 cubic miles of opaque water in which to carry on their activities.

Another very important sonar contact was made on August 8, 1972 by R. H. Rines of the Academy of Applied Science with a Raytheon DE-725C sonar unit (Table 3, S 16). The sonar unit was fixed at a depth of 35 ft. for continuous operation. There was general agreement by everyone examining the data (including P. Skitzki, Raytheon; R. Eide, Simrad; M. Klein, Klein Associates; I. Dyer, Ocean Engineering Department, M.I.T.; and J. V. Bouyouncos, Hydroacoustics) that at least one, perhaps two, large objects 20-30 ft. long had intruded into the sonar beam.

The trace further shows an echo protuberance with a dimension of about 10 ft. according to Skitzki. Whatever portion of anatomy of the animal was responsible for this trace, one can be sure it was not a 10-ft appendage. Most likely this echo represents a highly flexible laterally flattened tail or possibly the conjunction of two animals.

Summary

One can debate the fine structure of the sonar echoes, but the results cited coupled with the simultaneous underwater photography (Chapter VII) are extremely important as corroborative evidence that large animals exist in Loch Ness. These results also provide a basis for believing that a more refined and sophisticated effort along these lines may yield even more useful and detailed information.

However, all is not entirely favorable. As one would expect in the Loch Ness environment, negative and inconclusive results have also been recorded. There are a number of possible reasons for the failures. First, the equipment employed in early years (Table 3: S 1; part of S 2, S 3, S 4, and S 5; cf. the later S 10) was quite primitive compared to that used in subsequent years. Secondly, experience relating to use and interpretation has also vastly improved during the intervening period. Third, the frequencies used (28 to 38 KHz) are probably audible to some aquatic animals and may induce avoidance behavior.

In a similar way, the 1969 unsuccessful efforts (Table 3, S 8 and S 11) by the University of Birmingham, Plessey, and ITN also are explainable.

It had been hoped that operating the Plessey sonar from a boat, in conjunction with the Birmingham land-based fixed sonar, might result in better localization of possible interesting targets contacted within the two sound fields. However, the Plessey Model 195 Sonar was designed for long range use in the open sea, and its use in the confinement of Loch Ness produced an auditory shambles. The 10 KHz sound pulse is well within the hearing range of the human ear, and with an output of 5,000 watts the pulses transmitted into the water could be heard by human observers along the shore. These intense sound pulses were reflected and redirected throughout the length of the lake, rendering the target displays virtually useless. In addition, since these sounds are within the audible range of many sound-sensitive animals, they could well have driven the Loch Ness creatures out of the area and into hiding. In short, it is not hard to surmise why the Birmingham sonar operation from shore was unsuccessful.

We can summarize the information obtained from sonar experiments as follows:

1. Reproducible corroboration of the presence of large moving objects in the depths of Loch Ness.

2. Localization of these objects along the bottom and sides, and occasionally in midwater positions.

3. Speeds up to 17 mph horizontally and depth changes up to 5 mph; the rapid depth changes rule out large fish with closed swim bladders.

4. The overall patterns of movement suggest animals which are at home in the depths, rather than air-breathing types that only occasionally penetrate the deeper portions of the lake.

5. The objects appear as individuals but also in small groups.

6. Maximum size of objects in the neighborhood of 20 ft. (6 meters); asymmetrical, elongated in shape.

7. Detailed analysis of at least one sonar contact suggests features which may be interpreted either as sinusoidal flexure or periodic physical features such as "projections" or "humps."

APPENDIX F
(See Chapter X.)

TABLE 4
Classification of Living and Recent Sirenia

Class	Mammalia
Subclass	Theria
Infraclass	Eutheria (Placental mammals)
Super order	Paenungulata = Subungulata
Order	Sirenia (sea cows)
Family 1	Dugongidae
Genus 1	Dugong = Halicore
Genus 2	Rhytina = Hydrodramalis
Family 2	Manatidae = Trichechidae
Genus 1	Manatus = Trichechus

Important recent and living species
> *Dugong australis*
> *Rhytina stelleri* (gigas)
> *Trichechus senegalensis*
> *Trichechus manatus* { *T.m. latirostris* / *T.m. manatus*
> *Trichechus inunguis**

*This last species is landlocked in the Amazon and Orinoco Rivers system.

Rhytina stelleri

Rhytina stelleri or Steller's sea cow was discovered by Georg Wilhelm Steller during the second trans-Asiatic expedition (1741) led by Vitus Bering Svendsen (known to us as Bering) under commission from Peter the Great of Russia. While the expedition was returning from the coast of Alaska, their ship, *St. Peter,* approached what was thought to be Kamchatka. Instead, they were approaching two unknown islands, later to be named Bering Island and Copper Island, 150 miles east of Kamchatka. All things considered, the landing on Bering Island amounted to a shipwreck. Eventually, after many months, Steller and many of the crew did get off the island, although Bering died there. Steller, as the expedition naturalist, did his job very well, taking careful measurements of various animals, including the sea cow, recording all of his data in a journal. An English-language version of Bering's voyages, including parts of Steller's journal, has been published by the American Geographical Society. The

Illus. 1 Steller's sketch of the sea cow was lost in the 18th century, but L. Stejneger, naturalist and the translator for the AGS edition, reconstructed from Steller's measurements and account this drawing of what the animal might have looked like. (from Golder)

German version (published in 1753) of the portion of the journal dealing with the sea animals gives Steller's measurements from which I was able to calculate approximate ratios of lung to total body volume. This kind of information is extremely useful in interpreting sonar returns and estimating what kinds of echos may be significant. The calculations for this animal, *R. stelleri*, are as follows.

Range of size: up to 35 ft. in length
Calculations have been made for a 25-ft. specimen since Steller gives detailed measurements in *De bestis marinis.*

Length	25 ft.
Lung volume	46 cu. ft.
(23 cu. ft. per lobe)	
Trunk volume	144 cu. ft.
Head-neck volume	14 cu. ft.
Tail volume	12 cu. ft.
Total body volume	170 cu. ft.

Ratio of $\dfrac{\text{lung volume}}{\text{total body volume}} = .27$

Ratio of $\dfrac{\text{lung volume}}{\text{trunk volume}} = .32$

Assume 50% of lung volume to consist of tissue.

Ratio of $\dfrac{\text{lung gas volume}}{\text{total body volume}} = .13$

Ratio of $\dfrac{\text{lung gas volume}}{\text{trunk volume}} = .16$

If we assume 50% of the total lung volume to be represented by tissue, we arrive at ratios of 0.13 to 0.16. This is, as expected, higher than in man with a ratio of about 0.05, since these were aquatic animals especially adapted to remaining submerged for considerable periods of time. Steller estimated the maximum weight for a 25-ft. specimen at 200 poods (Russian weight units; 1 pood = 36.1 lbs.). Thus the estimated weight of one of these animals was about 8,000 pounds or 4 tons. If we assume a weight of 64 lbs./cu. ft., we can calculate that a 25-ft. specimen should weigh about 10,880 lbs; this is a not unreasonable figure, although somewhat greater than Steller's estimate. Either figure is certainly adequate to account for reasonable size estimates of the Loch Ness phenomena. No complete carcass of Steller's sea cow has survived although some parts are preserved in several museums.

Leatherback Turtle

It is just possible that the Leatherback Turtle might be functional at Loch Ness temperatures. These animals are observed regularly as far north as Nova Scotia and along the Canadian and New England coast, although they do not nest north of Florida. The water temperature at which they are observed to be active is as low as 53° F., and there has been speculation that leatherbacks may be endothermic (referring to the ability to conserve or lose heat generated within the body). Relative to this point, Dr. Wayne Frair and colleagues, working at Woods Hole, carried out some very instructive experiments with two specimens of leatherbacks. One was a male weighing 920 lbs., the other a female weighing 295 lbs. The male, which was studied first, was kept in fresh sea water at a temperature of 45.5° F for 24 hours. The investigators report that while the animal was in the tank, it swam vigorously for long periods at about 40 strokes per minute, raising its head for breathing 2-3 times per minute. When the deep body temperature of this animal was measured, it was found to be 77.9° F or about 32° F above that of its environment. Experiments with the second turtle, with respect to cooling and warming rates, established that this effect could not have resulted from warming during the time between removal from the low temperature environment and prior to temperature measurements. The authors suggest that the underlying mechanisms are probably heat production through muscular activity and heat retention aided by a large body mass. They conclude that the largest living turtle, the leatherback, is indeed capable of maintaining a considerable differential between its body temperature and the environment even when behavioral temperature regulation is not possible. They state: "This finding is relevant to speculations about the thermal existence of large extinct reptiles and the present distribution of Dermochelys." These experiments, which we have described in some detail, suggest that perhaps we should not rule out the possibility of aquatic reptiles solely on grounds of an incompatible temperature.

What about the other features of leatherback turtles relative to the Loch Ness animals? A leatherback turtle from a sideview is shown in Illus. 1.

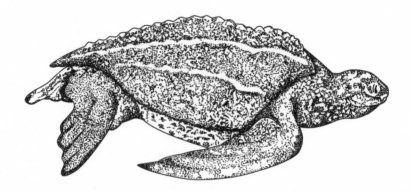

Illus. 1 Atlantic Leatherback Turtle (*Dermochelys coriacea coriacea*).

These turtles have been reported to reach lengths up to 10 ft. The highest recorded weight was reported in 1857 by the Swiss naturalist, Agassiz, who stated that he had seen specimens weighing over a ton.

The leatherback is further distinguished from other marine turtles within its range by the smooth, scaleless black skin of its back and the seven narrow ridges that extend down it, by the five longitudinal ridges on the plastron, and by the cusp on either side of the upper jaw. These turtles are strictly marine, although they have been reported to ascend the Plata River in Argentina to La Plata. Leatherbacks must come ashore to lay eggs in warm climates. They are believed to be omnivorous, feeding on jellyfish and some plant food. From this description it is readily apparent that while several features of these animals could account for some of the characteristics of the Loch Ness animals, many other characteristics remain unaccounted for. Specifically, the terrestrial egg-laying requirement of these turtles and their need for frequent breathing rule out this animal as a viable Loch Ness explanation. However, all that has been said about the low temperature adaptation of Dermochelys (leatherbacks) is applicable to a consideration of the Plesiosauria as a possible explanation for the Loch Ness phenomena.

TABLE 5
Classification and Check List of the Plesiosauroidea

Class	Reptilia
Subclass	Synaptosauria
Order	Sauropterygia
Suborder	Plesiosauria
Superfamily	a. Pistosauroidea
	b. Pliosauroidea
	c. Plesiosauroidea
Family I	Plesiosauridae
Genus	1. Archaeonectus
	2. Colymbosaurus
	3.* Cryptocleidus
	4. Eretmosaurus
	5. Microcleidus
	6. Muraenosaurus
	7. Picrocleidus
	8.* Plesiosaurus
	9. Tremamesacleis
	10. Macrocleidus
	11. Cimoliosaurus
Family II	Thaumatosauridae
Genus	1. Eurycleidus
	2. Seeleyosaurus
	3. Simolestes
	4. Sthenarosaurus
	5. Thaumatosaurus
Family III	Elasmosauridae
Genus	1. Alzadasaurus
	2. Aphrosaurus
	3. Brancasaurus
	4.* Elasmosaurus
	5. Fresnosaurus
	6. Hydralmosaurus
	7. Hydrotherosaurus
	8. Leuspondylus
	9. Mauisaurus
	10. Morenosaurus
	11. Ogmodirus
	12. Scanisaurus
	13. Styxosaurus
	14. Thalassomedon
	15. Woolungasaurus

*Of interest to us.

If we examine this relatively complete list of the Plesiosauria, we can clearly rule out a number of classifications because they do not have the correct body conformation. The two superfamilies, Pistosauroidea and Pliosauroidea, can be eliminated, particularly the latter whose members had short necks with gigantic heads, in some cases 8 ft. long. The best choices are to be found in the family Plesiosauridae, since most of the Thaumatosauridae and all of the Elasmosauridae had far too long a head-neck region. This trend reached its extreme in Elasmosaurus and is the record for a long neck, resulting not only from the elongation of individual cervical vertebrae, but also from increasing their number to the astonishing total of 76. The best known genus of the Plesiosauridae is Plesiosaurus, including at least a dozen species. Another good candidate for our purposes is *Cryptocleidus oxoniensis* which reached a size of 10 ft. or more. Except for a rather short tail, this species is about right in general body proportions. Perhaps the best choice of all is *Plesiosaurus aconybeari* which was at least 17 ft. long.

The Synaptosaurian reptiles are known only from fossil remains; consequently, we must keep in mind that many of the characteristics and habits of these animals are uncertain and have been inferred from the geological record, from the skeletal remains, and from what we know of living reptiles. Plesiosaur fossils are widely distributed (first remains discovered in 1821), being found in both hemispheres throughout the Mesozoic era, although most are found in the middle and upper portions of that era, in the Jurassic and Cretaceous period. In general, the range and combination of relative body proportions exhibited by the Plesiosauridae are more than adequate to account for the basic bodily features attributed to the Loch Ness animals.

TABLE 6
Classification of Living and Extinct Amphibia

Class	Amphibia
Subclass I	Apsidospondyli
Superorder 1	Labyrinthodontia
Order	1. Ichthyostegalia
	2. Rhachitomi
	3. Stereospondyli
	4.* Embolomeri
	5. Seymouriamorpha
Superorder 2	Salientia
Order	1. Eoanura
	2. Proanura
	3. Anura

Subclass II   Lepospondyli
Order
    1. Aistopoda
    2. Nectridia
    3. Microsauria
    4.* Urodela = Caudata
    5.* Apoda = Gymnophiona = Caecilia

*Orders of interest to us for one reason or another are asterisked.
While there is considerable difference of opinion regarding amphibia classification, I have followed A. J. Marshal, since his scheme seems both simpler and more natural to me.

TABLE 7
Classification of Living and Extinct Bony Fishes

Class	Osteichthyes
Subclass I	Crossopterygii
Order 1	Rhipidestia
Suborder	1. Osteolepidoti
	2. Coelacanthini
Order 2	Dipnoi
Subclass II	Actinopterygii
Superorder 1	Chondrostei
Order	1. Palaeoniscoidea
	2.* Acipenseroidei
	3. Polyterini
Superorder 2	Holostei
Order	1. Semionotoidea
	2. Pycnodontoidea
	3. Aspidorhynchoidea
	4. Amioidea
	5. Pholidophoroidea
Superorder 3	Teleostei
Order	1.* Isospondyli = Clupeiformes
	2. Haplomi = suborder Esocoidei
	3. Iniomi = Scopeliformes
	4. Giganturoidea = Giganturiformes
	5. Lyomeri = Saccopharyngiformes
	6. Ostariophysi = Cypriniformes
	7.* Apodes = Anguilliformes
	8.* Heteromi = Holosauriformes and Notocanthiformes
	9. Synentognathi = Beloniformes
	10. Salmopercae = Percopsiformes
	11. Microcyprini = Cyprinodontiformes

12.   Solenichthyes = Syngnathiformes
13.   Anacanthini = Gadiformes and
         Macruriformes
14.   Allotriognathi = Lampridiformes
15.   Berycomorphi = Beryciformes
16.   Zeomorphi = Zeiformes
17.   Percomorphi = Perciformes
18.   Gobiomorphi = suborder Gobiodei
19.   Scleroparei = suborder Cottoidei
20.   Thoracostei = Gasterosteiformes
21.   Hypostomides = Pegasiformes
22.   Heterosomata = Pleuronectiformes
23.   Discocephali = Echeniformes
24.   Plectognathi = Tetraodontiformes
25.   Malacichthyes = Icosteiformes
26.   Xenopterygii = suborder Gobiescocoidei
27.   Haplodoci = suborder Batrachoidei
28.   Pediculati = Lophiiformes
29.   Opisthomi = Mastacembeliformes
30.* Synbranchii = Synbranchiformes

*Orders of interest to us for one reason or another are asterisked.
In the last order the prefix "Syn" can be replaced by its equivalent "Sym."
Fish classification is according to Parker and Haswell.

The order Apodes or Anguilliformes contains 22 families, only one of which, the Anguillidae, spends time in fresh water. The two other well-known families are the Congridae (conger eels) and the Murenidae (moray eels). Two East Indies species, *Ophichthys boro* of the family Ophichthydae (snake eels) and *Murena polyuranodon* of the family Murenidae, also enter fresh water to feed.

TABLE 8
Classification of Mollusca

Phylum	Mollusca
Class I	Solenogastres
Class II	Placophora = Loricata
Class III	Gastropoda
Subclass 1	Prosobranchia
Subclass 2	*Opisthobranchia
Subclass 3	*Pulmonata
Class IV	Scaphopoda
Class V	Bivalvia = Pelecypoda
Class IV	*Cephalopoda = Siphonopoda

*Of interest to us.
Mollusca classification mainly according to Parker and Haswell.

APPENDIX G
(See Chapter XI.)

Eel Studies at Loch Ness

The summary in Chapter XI of eel sizes is based in part on these references. Jonathan Couch in his *History of the Fishes of the British Islands* (1868) records an *A. anguilla* specimen from the Hackney River weighing 26 lbs.; another taken in Medway, not far from Rochester: weight 34 lbs., length 6 ft., girth 25 in.; and one mentioned by a Mr. Daniel, taken in Kent: weight 40 lbs., length 5 ft. 9 in., girth 18 in.

A photograph of 5-6 ft. *A. dieffenbachii* appears in *Danish Eel Investigations During 25 Years 1905-1930* by J. Schmidt. (See above Chapter XI, Illus. 2.) There have been claims that this species reaches 9-ft. lengths. However, Dr. R. M. McDowall (Marine Department, Fisheries Research Division, Wellington, New Zealand) wrote to me that although their eels do grow to large size, they do not reach 9 ft., probably no more than 6 ft. The largest specimen heard of recently weighed 50 lbs. and was 5 ft. long. T. H. Potts writes of eels up to 96 lbs. in weight and states that a Dr. Hector recorded one 130 lbs. in weight from Lake Wakatipu. Mrs. J. L. B. Smith (widow of the late discoverer of the coelacanth and director of the J. L. B. Smith Institute of Ichthyology, Grahamstown, C.P. South Africa) informed me in a letter dated December 19, 1969 that *A. marmorata* weighing over 100 lbs. are found in the Eastern Province rivers. Length was not given, but calculations indicate that such eels must be 8-10 ft. long.

As far as conger eels are concerned, J. R. Norman, in his *Giant Fishes, Whales and Dolphins*, records a conger received in the London market weighing 128 lbs. A photograph was published in the *Illustrated London News* (September 17, 1904) showing a 9-ft. conger weighing 160 lbs., 30 in. in circumference. (See above Chapter XI, Illus. 1.)

To better deal with the hypothesis that large, thick-bodied eels are the Loch Ness phenomena, a project to capture and investigate obtainable eels in the loch was launched. This appendix reports on that study of some biometric, biochemical, and morphological characteristics of *A. anguilla* from Loch Ness. Increasing relative body circumference and skewness toward increasing size was observed. Weight estimate of a hypothetical 6-meter (20-ft.) eel was made. Variability in many characteristics was observed, with occasional specimens falling far outside of the mean for the species.

During the summer of 1970, under the supervision of Robert E. Love, director in the field of the LNIB underwater research, Mr. Jeffrey Blonder and Captain James Skinner collected a total of 80 eels of which some 69 were measured. Two further series of specimens were retained for study, the major portion being kept in holding tanks long enough to be measured and then returned to the loch in a viable condition. Specimens were taken by means of creels, hook and line, and "great lines" at depths ranging from 15 to 180 meters. The most effective bait was found to be smoked herring, although fresh herring, bacon, and worms were also successful.

Twenty-eight eel specimens were examined in detail, including morphology, dissection, internal anatomy, gut content, gonad examination, amino acid analysis of whole muscle tissue, and age determination by otolith examination.

Amino acid analyses were performed by automated ion exchange chromatography according to the general procedures of Spackman, Stein, and Moore. Protein samples were hydrolyzed in 6N HCl for 24 hrs. at 110°. Special precautions recommended for the preparation and hydrolysis of samples were observed (Crestfield, Moore, and Stein; More, Stein, Colowick, and Kaplan). Analyses were carried out on a BioCal BC-200 amino acid analyzer (BioCal Instrument Corp., Richmond, California). Five mg portions of muscle tissue were removed subcutaneously from a point 1 cm anterior to the dorsal fin insertion of the frozen specimens. For comparison, similar tissue samples were prepared from the carcass of a basking shark which was washed ashore at Scituate, Mass. prior to Nov. 15, 1970, on which date samples were collected and frozen for analysis by Robert H. Rines.

The morphology and anatomy of the specimens indicate that they are the normal common European eel, *A. anguilla*. This eel possessed four types of pigment distributed in two layers. In the course of sexual maturation, before migrating to the Sargasso Sea, considerable color change occurs in metamorphosis from the yellow to the silver eel. There were no migratory specimens in this small sample, but the color variation between individuals was pronounced, varying from uniformly black through shades of brown to beige. Two eels, beige-white in color, exhibited considerable mottling.

As was to be expected from eels taken in baited traps and with great lines, the majority of the stomachs were empty or contained small pieces of the bait itself. The stomach contents of specimen #M13 was of particular interest in that it contained a single 5 cm limb bone most probably from a small mammal or bird. Two other stomachs contained unidentifiable larvae and nymph remains. The effectiveness of kipper (smoked herring) as bait is interesting and, as many pieces were found in the eel stomachs after dissection, it is obvious that it was not just an attractant.

Size distribution and body shape, particularly maximum circumference relative to length, were of major interest. With regard to the possibility of large size, it is recognized that the only completely adequate evidence would be the isolation of an actual specimen for study. However, in view of the insufficiency of funds in 1970 for mounting an effort on this scale for this purpose, a biometric study of smaller specimens was carried out with the hope that some evidence bearing on relevant points might be forthcoming. A secondary purpose was to obtain direct evidence on which to base a reasonable estimate of the weight of a hypothetical eel so that tackle adequate for the isolation of a suitable specimen could be designed for use in the future.

The following measurements were made and the indicated products and ratios calculated:

$$\text{(a) } C^2l; \text{ (b) } \frac{C}{l} \, 100; \text{ (c) } \frac{[a-d]}{l}; \text{ (d) } \frac{[a+d]}{2l} \, 100; \text{ (e) } \frac{P}{l} \, 100$$

C: maximum circumference;
l: overall length;
a: pre-anal distance, tip of snout to anus;
d: pre-dorsal fin distance, tip of snout to base of dorsal fin insertion;
P: head-neck length, tip of snout to pectoral fin insertion;
w: weight.

In Fig. 1 a plot of the product of length and maximum circumference squared versus weight is shown. Since the product of the linear dimensions

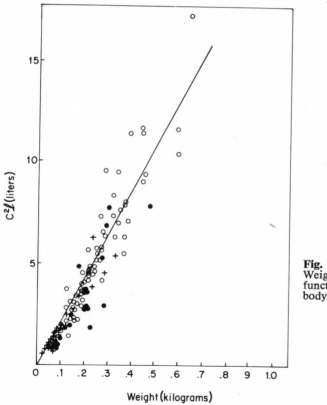

Fig. 1
Weight as a
function of
body dimensions.

is proportional to volume which is in turn proportional to weight, such a plot should be linear and pass through the origin, as is the case. The empirical equation for this data was found to have the following value: $w = .0464C^2l$ where w is in kilograms and the product C^2l in liters. W. E. Frost found that w/l^3 (weight divided by the cube of the length) was not constant for Windermere eels, which is what one would expect if the shape of the eel changes, i.e., gets more slender or bulkier with increasing length. In our equation this effect, if present, is compensated for by including maximum circumference.

The size of the eel in relation to its age must be a complicated, inter-related system involving a number of factors (Frost). If one considers the situation under natural conditions where the size variation is apparent even at the elver stage, one can assume that elvers arriving together at a river have traveled together with equal opportunity. Therefore, it seems likely that differences in size at this stage have primarily a genetic and not an environmental basis (Sinha and Jones). However, in view of the extensive hormonal influences which play so large a role in eels begin-ning with the earliest stages (Koch), it may be that slight variations in hormone levels of individuals of similar genetic constitution contribute to the size variation. The results shown in Figure 1 suggest that eels of the same length and habitat may also have considerable differences in weight. It has been suggested that differences in growth rate can be caused by variations in population density, food supply, temperature (Comfort; Liu and Walford), and living space; and it may be that any one or a combina-tion of these factors contribute to the variation in size of individual specimens.

The limitations which would be expected to contribute toward a slower maturation process, possibly resulting in some relatively large adults, are certainly present in Loch Ness, i.e., low population density, limited food supply, low temperature, and a vast volume of water.

In Fig. 2 the ratio $C/l \cdot 100$, representing relative body thickness, is plotted against length. If body proportions were constant for eels of all sizes, we would expect this plot to be a straight line parallel to the axis on which length is plotted. As can be seen, a very definite slope is ap-parent, indicating a tendency for larger eels to have a relatively greater maximum circumference. The empirical equation for this data is $C/l \cdot 100 = .137l + 12$ where circumference and length are in centimeters. In agree-ment with these findings at Loch Ness, Frost found that the yellow eels from the Windermere catchment area become bulkier and heavier in sub-stance or both as they grow in length. Clearly, this thickening trend cannot continue indefinitely with length, and one does not know how far the relationship is valid. However, a consideration of the large specimens of the freshwater eels of New Zealand and Australia (Schmidt [1927]), in conjunction with some measurements of large eels from Kent and other parts of the U.K. reported by Jonathan Couch suggest that the relationship is valid at least up to a length of about 2 meters. The calculated value of $C/l \cdot 100$ for 175 cm length is 36 which agrees well with calculations based

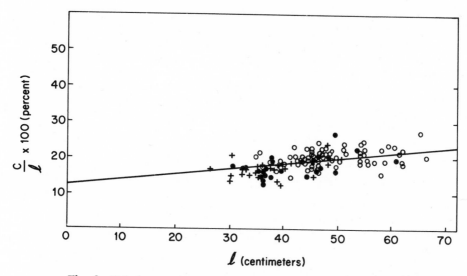

Fig. 2 Relative maximum body circumference as a function of overall body length.

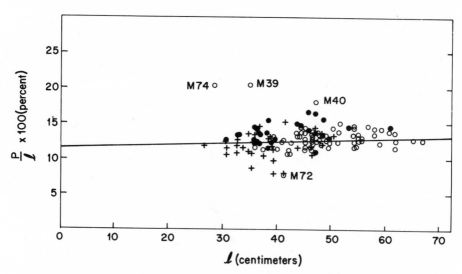

Fig. 3 Relative head-neck length in relation to overall body length.

on measurements reported by Couch and measurements taken from a photograph of two large specimens of New Zealand eels (See Chapter XI, Illus. 2.), giving values of 33 to 34 for eels 150 to 175 cm in length. Using the empirical equations derived from data shown in Figs. 1 and 2, an estimate of the probable weight of a 6-meter-long animal can be calculated. Taking the value of C/l conservatively as .34, the weight would be approximately 1,160 kilograms (2,558 lbs.).

In Fig. 3 the ratio $P/l \cdot 100$, representing relative head-neck length, is plotted relative to length, indicating a more constant relationship between overall length and head-neck length. A slight tendency toward longer head-neck regions with increasing size may be present, but one does not know if this slight slope is significant.

L. Bertin and others have divided freshwater eels into a long dorsal fin type and short dorsal fin type according to whether the value of $(a-d)/l \cdot 100$ (preanal − predorsal fin distance divided by length) is +7 to +17% or only −3 to +5%. All specimens examined were of the long dorsal fin type. In contrast to the extreme variability of this ratio, the most constant characteristic found was the average relative length of the eel body without dorsal or anal fins, represented by the ratio $(a+d)/2l \cdot 100$ (Fig. 4). Clearly, this characteristic is extremely constant over the range of sizes measured, and the individual points cluster tightly along a line parallel to the length axis.

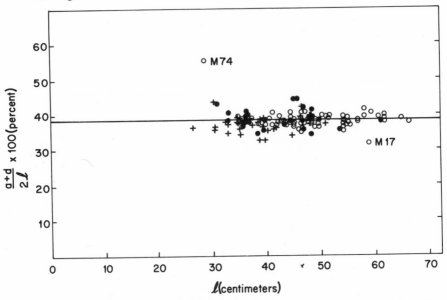

Fig. 4 Relative average length of body without anal or dorsal fins. ○, 1970 series; ●, 1971 series; +, 1971 series taken from the top Fort Augustus lock.

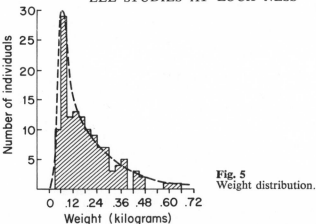

Fig. 5
Weight distribution.

Lastly, the size distribution relative to number of individuals is shown in Fig. 5. Clearly, our sample of eels cannot be representative of the total population because of the limitations of the tackle employed, i.e., size of traps and wire mesh, strength of materials, size of hooks, etc. In addition, the fact that a large but unknown number of elvers enter Loch Ness from the sea and an unknown number of adults leave makes it difficult to predict what the actual size distribution might be. For example, the influx of large numbers of small elvers may shift the observed mean toward a much smaller value. The data presented (Fig. 5) are skewed with the skewness extending toward greater weights. To determine if the skewness observed in the frequency distribution of the weight of Loch Ness eels was significant, a statistical analysis was carried out. The following measures of central tendency and the standard deviation were also calculated: arithmetic mean, 0.1857 kilograms; median, 0.151 kilograms; mode, 0.076 kilograms; standard deviation, 0.125 kilograms.

The most satisfactory measure of skewness employs the cubes of the deviations of the various values of a series from the arithmetic mean. This measure which is called β_1 was calculated to be 1.614 and compared to values found in a table given by Egon S. Pearson (p. 239). This table gives the upper 0.10 and 0.02 limits of β_1 when computed from random samples from normal population. The β_1 value for samples of 125 would be expected to equal or exceed 0.123 ten times out of 100 and to equal or exceed 0.258 two times out of 100; for samples of 150, β_1 would be expected to equal or exceed 0.103 ten times out of 100 and to equal or exceed 0.216 two times out of 100. It is clear that the observed value of $\beta_1 = 1.614$ is significant.

Symbols Used

    N: the number of items in a sample
    f: a frequency
    X: a value in a series; also, the mid-value of a class in a
         frequency distribution
    Σ: upper-case Greek sigma, meaning "take the sum of"

$\overline{X}$: the arithmetic mean
Med: the median
Mo: the mode
l_1 the lower limit of a class
Σ_1: when used in conjunction with f, $\Sigma_1 f$, the sum of the frequencies in the classes graphically to the left of l_1
i: the class interval
fmed: frequency of the class in which the median falls
Δ_1: upper-case Greek delta, the difference between the frequency of the modal class and the frequency of the class graphically to the left of the modal class
Δ_2: upper-case Greek delta; the difference between the frequency of the modal class and the frequency of the class graphically to the right of the modal class
s: the standard deviation of a sample
x: deviation of X from $\overline{X}$
β_1: lower-case Greek beta, a measure of skewness using the third powers of the x values
π_2, π_3: lower-case Greek pi, the second and third moments about $\overline{X}$

Calculation of the arithmetic mean, $\overline{X}$.

$$\overline{X} = \frac{\Sigma fX}{N} = \frac{23.955}{129} = 0.1857 \text{ kilograms}$$

Calculation of the median, Med.

$$\text{Med.} = l_1 + \frac{(N/2) - \Sigma_1 f}{\text{fmed}} i = 0.15 + \frac{(129/2) - 64}{12} 0.03$$
$$= 0.151 \text{ kilograms}$$

Calculation of the mode, Mo.

$$\text{Mo} = l_1 + \frac{\Delta_1}{\Delta_1 + \Delta_2} i = 0.06 + \frac{19}{19 + 17} 0.03 = 0.076 \text{ kilograms}$$

Calculation of the standard deviation, s.

$$s = \frac{\Sigma fx^2}{N} = \frac{2.01537}{129} = 0.125 \text{ kilograms}$$

Calculation of measure of skewness, β_1.

$$\pi_2 = \frac{\Sigma fx^2}{N} = \frac{2.01537}{129} = 0.01562$$

$$\pi_3 = \frac{\Sigma fx^3}{N} = \frac{0.32073}{129} = 0.00248$$

$$\beta_1 = \frac{(\pi_3)^2}{(\pi_2)^3} = \frac{(0.00248)^2}{(0.01562)^3} = 1.614$$

Data Employed for the Statistical Analysis of
the Frequency Distribution of the Weight of Loch Ness Eels

Class Weight in Kilograms	No. of Eels f	Mid-values of X	fX	Deviation x	x^2	fx^2	x^3	fx^3
.03–.06	10	0.045	0.450	−0.1407	0.019796	0.19796	−0.00278536	−0.02785
.06–.09	29	0.075	2.175	−0.1107	0.012254	0.35536	−0.00135657	−0.03934
.09–.12	12	0.105	1.260	−0.0807	0.006512	0.07814	−0.00052555	−0.00631
.12–.15	13	0.135	1.755	−0.0507	0.002570	0.03341	−0.00013032	−0.00169
.15–.18	12	0.165	1.980	−0.0207	0.000428	0.00514	−0.00000886	−0.00011
.18–.21	10	0.195	1.950	+0.0093	0.000086	0.00086	+0.00000080	+0.00001
.21–.24	9	0.225	2.025	+0.0393	0.001544	0.01389	+0.00006069	+0.00055
.24–.27	7	0.255	1.785	+0.0693	0.004802	0.03361	+0.00033281	+0.00233
.27–.30	7	0.285	1.995	+0.0993	0.009860	0.06902	+0.00097914	+0.00685
.30–.33	3	0.315	0.945	+0.1293	0.016718	0.05015	+0.00216170	+0.00648
.33–.36	4	0.345	1.380	+0.1593	0.025376	0.10150	+0.00404247	+0.01617
.36–.39	5	0.375	1.875	+0.1893	0.035834	0.17917	+0.00678346	+0.03392
.39–.42	0	0.405	0.000	+0.2193	0.048092	0.00000	+0.01054668	+0.00000
.42–.45	3	0.435	1.305	+0.2493	0.062150	0.18645	+0.01549411	+0.04648
.45–.48	2	0.465	0.930	+0.2793	0.078008	0.15601	+0.02178777	+0.04357
.48–.51	0	0.495	0.000	+0.3093	0.095666	0.00000	+0.02958964	+0.00000
.51–.54	0	0.525	0.000	+0.3393	0.115124	0.00000	+0.03906173	+0.00000
.54–.57	0	0.555	0.000	+0.3693	0.136382	0.00000	+0.05036605	+0.00000
.57–.60	1	0.585	0.585	+0.3993	0.159440	0.15944	+0.06366458	+0.06366
.60–.63	1	0.615	0.615	+0.4293	0.184298	0.18430	+0.07911934	+0.07912
.63–.66	1	0.645	0.645	+0.4593	0.210956	0.21096	+0.09689231	+0.09689
Total	129 N		23.955 Σfx			2.01537 Σfx^2		0.32073 Σfx^3

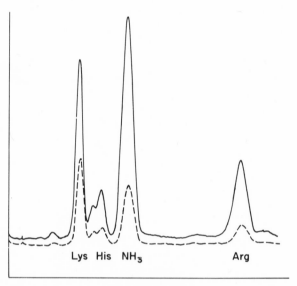

Fig. 6 Basic amino acid composition of eel muscle tissue.

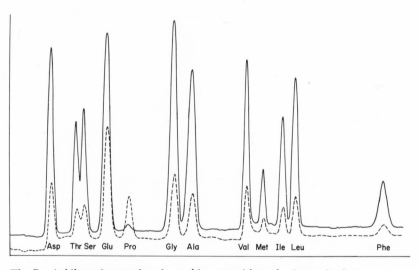

Fig. 7 Acidic and neutral amino acid composition of eel muscle tissue.

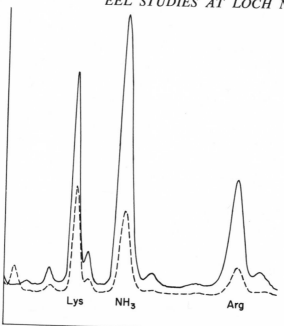

Fig. 8 Basic amino acid composition of basking shark muscle tissue.

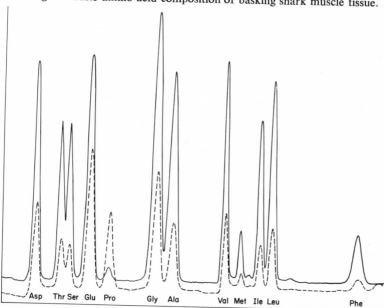

Fig. 9 Acidic and neutral amino acid composition of basking shark muscle tissue.

While one would hardly postulate extremely large specimens on the basis of the skewed characteristic observed, the size distribution found is somewhat more favorable to the hypothesis that the eel population of Loch Ness includes a few rather large specimens than if a more symmetrical distribution had been observed.

The extreme variability of the European eel is evident in Loch Ness. The extreme limits of this variability are represented by such specimens as M74 which has been indicated in the various figures. The numerical range of the values for ratios was as follows: $(a-d)/l \cdot 100$, 5.5 to 25.0, $\Delta \% = 19.5$; $P/l \cdot 100$, 7.3 to 20.6, $\Delta \% = 13.3$; $(a+d)/2l \cdot 100$, 31.0 to 44.4, $\Delta \% = 13.4$; $C/l \cdot 100$, 12.1 to 26.2, $\Delta \% = 14.1$. In the case of the last two ratios M74 has been omitted. The values of the four ratios for M74 were as follows: $(a-d)/l \cdot 100 = 15.9$; $P/l \cdot 100 = 20.5$; $(a+d)/2l \cdot 100 = 55.7$; $C/l \cdot 100 = 31.8$. Weight was 160 grams and length 28 cm, with a normal medium dark brown color. This specimen had an unsually thick body, a long head-neck region, was of great relative weight with over half of its body unfinned, and of the long dorsal fin type.

Amino acid analysis of whole muscle tissue was carried out, and the results are shown in Figs. 6 and 7. For comparison, analyses were also made of basking shark muscle tissue (Figs. 8 and 9). These analyses were carried out in the hope that they might, in conjunction with immunological and histological techniques, aid in the identification of tissue samples of unidentified animals when the whole specimen is not available. Whether amino acid analyses of whole tissues will be of value can only be determined after a large number of species have been analyzed and compared. Future research at Loch Ness will include such analyses of the animate life forms present in the lake. Clearly, differences and similarities can be observed when the analysis curves of the eel and shark are compared. No qualitative differences are apparent in the case of the acidic and neutral amino acids. However, more serine relative to threonine is present in the case of the eel analysis (Figs. 7 and 9). Some of the other amino acids also show less striking quantitative differences, i.e., relatively more proline in the basking shark analysis (Fig. 9) and more phenylalanine in the case of the eel results (Fig. 7). Differences in the basic amino acids are more pronounced in that histidine is absent, or present in very small amount, in the case of the basking shark (Fig. 8). An unidentified substance appears between the lysine and the histidine position in both analyses (Figs. 6 and 8). It is hoped that such comparisons may be of value in the event that a tissue sample of any possible unidentified animal from Loch Ness should come to hand.

APPENDIX H
(See Chapter XII.)

Salmon Studies at Loch Ness   332

Salmon Studies at Loch Ness

During October 1970, the Underwater Research team of the Loch Ness Investigation Bureau, led by Robert E. Love, observed dense shoals of salmon entering the mouth of the River Enrick where it flows into Urquhart Bay near the center of Loch Ness. Later in October of 1971 Robert H. Rines of the Academy of Applied Science took an interesting underwater photograph of this salmon migration (Illus. 2). The photograph shows 3 fish totally within the camera field. Schooling density and migratory population can be calculated from the photograph. This photo is, therefore, the basis for the census analysis that follows. The photograph (made with an automatic stroboscopic camera developed by Harold E. Edgerton of M.I.T.) was taken with the camera pointing upward and shows the light underbellies of the fish passing above. These salmon returning to spawn collect in lakes until they are ripe and conditions on the spawning grounds are suitable; then in response to natural cues they enter the river for the upstream run. It is useful, therefore, to visualize an "entry zone" in front of the river mouth, as shown in Illus. 1. Fish passing through the entry zone can be expected to become more densely packed as they converge into the river mouth. Therefore, the photograph taken in the center of the entry zone depicts the average schooling density of the fish out to a range of 60 ft.

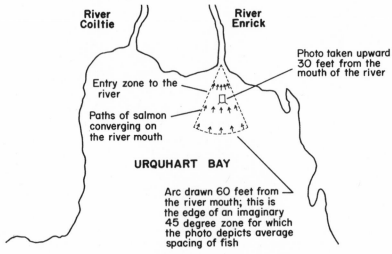

Illus. 1 Entry zone for salmon from Loch Ness converging on the mouth of a typical river during their spawning migration.

332

Illus. 2 Underwater photograph of school of salmon. Camera located at 35-ft. depth. *R. H. Rines photo.*

In 1970, salmon migrating through this same area averaged 22 in. in length; therefore, it is safe to assume that those depicted in the 1971 photograph are of equal size. Using this length to provide a dimensional scale, we can compute the area within the camera field of view at the range of the fish. This field of view is about 40 in. by 54 in., yielding an area of 15 sq. ft. Assuming that the migrating fish form a school one-fish-layer deep, the population density shown in the photograph is 3 fish per 15 sq. ft. or 0.2 fish per sq. ft.

As defined, the entry zone to the river has an area of about 1,400 sq. ft. Judging from the photograph, the number of fish in this zone is equal to the population density shown multiplied by the zone area, a total of about 300 fish. However, it is reasonable to suppose that the density is greatest near the center and decreases near the edges of the school. To allow for this uneven distribution we will reduce the number by one-half, concluding with the estimate that there were 150 fish within the entry zone at the time of the photograph.

Migrating salmon sustain swimming speeds of 3-5 body lengths per second for long periods of time. As a minimum, our average 22-in. fish can therefore sustain a swimming speed of 5.5 ft. per second. Allowing for relative water movement due to flow from the river we will reduce this figure somewhat and use an average migration speed through the entry zone of 4 ft. per second. By comparison, Chinook salmon in Alaska have been clocked at an average speed of 4.7 ft. per second for 29 days on their

1,500 mile migration up the Yukon River, suggesting that the estimated speed of 4 ft. per second is reasonable.

Any given salmon moving at 4 ft. per second will pass through the entry zone and reach the river mouth in 15 seconds. The salmon population in the entry zone is thus replaced by newly arriving fish every 15 seconds. At such a rate the number of fish entering the River Enrick can be calculated by dividing the entry zone population of 150 by the exchange time of 15 seconds, yielding an entry rate of 10 fish per second, or 36,000 fish per hour.

During the months before spawning begins, millions of salmon have moved into Loch Ness from the sea. Many physical and biological factors combine to trigger the spawning run upstream. Fall water temperature must drop to insure preservation of the eggs until spring. Spawning grounds must be flooded by adequate rainfall, but streams must not become too swift for fish to move upward against the current. Because of these factors the majority of salmon entering a river do so within a total period of only a few days. Such a period occurred during October 16-19, 1970 when salmon were observed entering the River Enrick from Urquhart Bay. At the peak of this period fish were literally leaping over one another in their efforts to enter the river mouth.

In such a 4-day period the entry rate is doubtless lower near the beginning and end of the run. As a conservative estimate we will assume that the photograph depicts the peak of activity and reduce the rate computed above by half, to an average of 18,000 fish per hour or about 430,000 fish per day. For such a 4-day spawning run the total number of salmon entering the River Enrick would be about 1,700,000.

This is a large number indeed, but the story does not end there. As shown in Illus. 3, Loch Ness is fed by a vast watershed containing seven major river systems, some larger and some smaller than the Enrick. Considering the River Enrick as typical of these 7 major rivers, the total number of fish entering the rivers would be 7 times the 1.7 million, or 11.9 million. In addition to the rivers there are some 30 smaller streams, allts, and burns up which salmon migrate after collecting in the lake below. Including these fish, it is possible that prior to their spawning Loch Ness might contain up to *13 million adult salmon.*

Adult salmon moving annually into Loch Ness constitute a huge resource, all imported from the feeding grounds at sea. At an average weight of 10 lbs. for a 4-year-old fish, their total weight would be 65,000 tons. Some are undoubtedly consumed by predators in the months during which they congregate in Loch Ness prior to spawning. Clearly, however, a significant percentage of the adults must survive to spawn if the migrations are to continue. And the migratory cycle produces within Loch Ness another and even greater food resource, one which is not periodic but constant in its quantity.

After returning from the sea, the salmon have stored about 10% of their body weight in fat, contained in orange globules beneath the skin. Prior to spawning the female converts this fat and muscle protein into

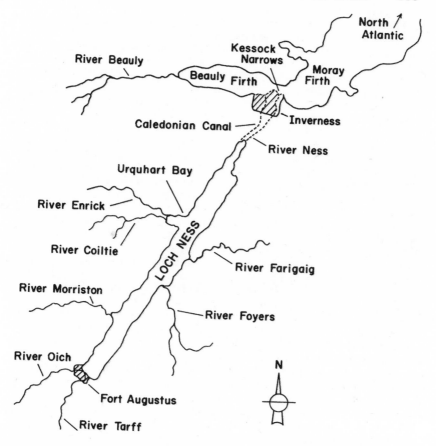

Illus. 3   The seven major river systems draining into Loch Ness.
(Dotted lines show the canal and river joining Loch Ness to the sea.)

eggs comprising 8% of her weight. Since each produces almost one pound of eggs, the eggs produced by 6.5 million females would total 2,600 tons a year. While the eggs themselves represent a sizable biomass, their main significance lies in their potential, when hatched, as a widely distributed food gathering system.

Each pair of mates lays and fertilizes about 6,000 eggs, of which 5,400 hatch out in the spring. These begin the growth cycle that will lead them to the sea about 2 years later. The total number of young produced by 6.5 million pairs of adults in the watershed is astronomical, but 90% are lost before they reach the sea. Based on the number hatched and this mortality rate, calculations indicate that about 19 billion juveniles could be feeding in Loch Ness and its tributaries at any given time.

These juvenile salmon range from tiny fry measuring only a fraction of an inch and able to survive on small insects, to the 7-in. parr feeding on the young of other fish. They are dispersed throughout the miles of rivers and streams, gathering their nourishment from this great area. As they move downstream many are lost, but those that remain grow larger, concentrating the food supply for larger animals. The incredible efficiency of this natural food collection system becomes apparent when one realizes that if 2,500 tons of eggs are laid annually then a juvenile population able to sustain the loss of 680,000 tons would result.

Death can come from disease, from adverse physical conditions, and from falling prey to other carnivores. Assuming that predation accounts for 10% of the total loss, about 500 of the progeny of each pair of adults are consumed by other animals. The surviving smolts depart for the sea weighing about 1.4 ounces. Based on a linear growth rate during the period of development to smolts, the average juvenile weighs one-half this, or 0.7 ounces. Thus the 500 offspring of each pair of mates which are lost to predation constitute a weight of about 20 lbs. For the possible 6.5 million adult pairs spawning into Loch Ness, the juveniles consumed by predatory animals would represent a food supply of *68,000 tons* a year.

Daily food requirements for a variety of aquatic predators range from 0.001-1% of their body weight compared to 1-5% for some mammals. Using the value of 1% per day, a predator will thus consume 365% of his body weight in food per year. Conversely, the body weight of the predators will be 1/3.65, or about 27% of the food they consume annually. Therefore, if 68,000 tons of juvenile salmon are consumed, the total weight of the predators is *18,600 tons.*

The exact quantity and size distribution of the predator population in Loch Ness is of course not known. By far the most numerous are trout, eels, char, and other small fish whose weight is of the order of a few pounds. But what about the numbers of large unidentified predators?

From the evidence of eyewitness observations and sonar contacts one can set the probable lower limit of their number in the neighborhood of 10 or so. While nothing precise can be said about the upper limit, it seems unlikely that more than a few hundred large individuals are present in the loch. While such a colony would doubtless contain members of intermediate size, we will confine our consideration to animals about 20 ft. in length and weighing around 2,500 lbs. (Chapter XIV and Appendix G)

We are faced then with a wide disparity between various known predators weighing a few pounds and unknown creatures weighing thousands of pounds. Let us make the assumption that only 1% of the food supply represented by juvenile salmon and consumed by predators is accounted for by the unknown animals. The total weight of such animals would be 1% of the 18,600 tons for all the predators, or 186 tons (372,000 lbs.). Dividing this by their individual weight we arrive at a remarkable conclusion. The juvenile salmon produced by 6.5 million adult pairs and constantly restocked by migrations into Loch Ness could support, in addition to many other predators, a population of *150* of the 2,500 lb.

aquatic creatures. If their food requirements are lower or adult salmon are also consumed in significant amounts, as seems likely, the number would be increased. In any event, a colony of this size would seem to represent a viable reproducing unit capable of assuring survival of the species.

But other questions can be raised. Could such large numbers of salmon actually inhabit the loch and its river systems? Why aren't they observed more frequently? Does Loch Ness possess any special advantages over other waterways? These questions lead to some revealing answers.

Upon first thought it would seem that the large number of salmon entering the River Enrick would result in the river becoming hopelessly clogged with fish. The reason that this is not the case lies in the proximity of the spawning groups to the river mouth and the resulting short time that each fish spends in the river. The main body of the river is about 15 miles long. It is fed along this length by numerous short tributaries. If we assume that the spawning run occurs when the average flow velocity of the river is about 40% of the maximum measured near its mouth in 1970 and that the average fish swims half way up the river before turning into a tributary, then spawns half way up the tribatary, we can compute the time required to reach the spawning area as about 7 hours.

Based on descriptions of the spawning behavior, the time spent in digging nests and in laying and fertilizing the eggs is probably around 1 hour. After spawning, the fish swim down the shallow tributaries until they reach swifter water, then face upstream and drift down with the current. The time calculated for this downstream trip to the loch is about 4 hours.

The average time spent by a given fish in the River Enrick is, therefore, about 12 hours. At this rate the population density will reach equilibrium 12 hours after the run begins and the river system will contain some 430,000 fish. Estimating the average width of the river as 25 ft. and that of its tributaries as 3 ft., one can calculate the average fish density as about 0.12 fish per sq. ft., or 8 sq. ft. per fish. This is about one-half the density shown in the schooling photograph, which was obviously acceptable to the fish.

It therefore seems reasonable that the River Enrick and its tributary system could support a spawning rate of this magnitude. In fact, migration into Alaska's Kvichak River of 9 million Sockeye salmon has been recorded in 9 days, a rate much higher than that for the Enrick. Although the Kvichak River is larger, salmon enter from the sea without the benefit of a collecting basin like Loch Ness.

Of the many factors affecting the success of salmon migrations into a river system, water temperature is among the most important. Measurements taken in 1970 provide a clue to the temperature mechanism operating near the River Enrick. Salmon prefer temperatures of 48-53° F. Studies in Oregon have shown that Pacific salmon succumb rapidly to disease and infection when kept in fresh water above 50° F. Through natural selection only fish which inhabit the colder waters have survived.

Such temperatures are present in Loch Ness in September within the thermocline at depths of about 150 ft., while surface temperatures are about 57° F. The numerous salmon moving into the loch are no doubt distributed in the thermocline, invisible to surface observers.

In early October the temperature of the Enrick has dropped to 51° F, flushing much of the warm water from Urquhart Bay, and the "preferred" temperature zone has risen to less than 70 ft. below the surface. Spawning migrations normally do not occur until river temperatures fall to 50° F. By mid-October the temperature of the Enrick has fallen below 50°, and increasing rainfall has created a preferred "cool zone" extending downward and inward from the river mouth to reach the thermocline in the bay, thus providing a passage for the salmon into the river. It was at such a time that the fish were observed in 1970 leaping over one another in their rush into the river.

In late October the flow of water from the Enrick had reached torrential proportions discharging up to 77,000 cu. ft. per minute into the bay, an amount which replaced 7% of the volume of the bay daily. Heavy rainfall at the end of October raised the level of the loch one foot in a 2-day period, lowering the surface temperature in Urquhart Bay to 49° F.

In addition to its protective effect on adult salmon, the lower water temperature serves to prevent hatching of the eggs until spring when abundant aquatic insects provide a food supply for the young. This "deep freeze" technique is so efficient that over 90% of the eggs survive to become fry.

Salmon enter Loch Ness from the sea in three ways. They run up the River Ness, passing over the low wiers. They have been observed gathered below boat locks in the Caledonia Canal and then moving upstream with boats as they are locked through the canal. In addition, two flow windows for excess water in each lock gate provide a passage area of 24 sq. ft. for migrating fish. For months before spawning, salmon move up the routes in Loch Ness. A few are observed, but their infrequent spacing and the dark water obscure the true number which have passed into the loch.

The Loch Ness waterway system enjoys unique geographical advantages in its ability to attract a large food resource. As shown in Illus. 3, effluent from the lock enters the sea at Kessock Narrows between the two large bays, Beauly Firth and Moray Firth. At this point the sea arm is about 3,000 ft. wide. During slack tides, the flow of fresh water carrying olfactory cues concentrates the odors within this small area. An average salmon in the middle of the narrows is only 1,500 ft. from the mouth of the River Ness. Swimming at normal cruising speed the fish can enter the river in about 5 minutes, well before a change in tidal current occurs.

However, salmon trying to enter the mouth of the Beauly River must swim the length of the tidal Beauly Firth, a distance of about 7 miles. During high tides, an additional volume of tidal water equal to about one-third of the residual volume enters the mouth of the Firth. Fish contained in this volume will thus be carried an average distance of one-sixth of the way into the Firth. They will still have over 5 miles to swim to the mouth of the Beauly River. At normal speed the fish will require about 1.5 hours to swim this distance and by this time the tide will be running strongly back toward the sea.

About 6 miles up the Beauly River lie the Dunwood Dam and Power Station. Fish counts there in 1967 showed that about 13,000 salmon ran up fish ladders during the season. Some fish entering the Beauly doubtless spawned in tributaries below the dam. However, the photographic evidence presented indicates that 36,000 salmon per hour enter the River Enrick from Loch Ness at the peak of the run. It is apparent that the spawning density varies widely from river system to river system. The numbers returning to spawn indicate the productivity of each system, culminating in the high population of offspring in Loch Ness.

The value of such a large deep lake with a stable thermocline system capable of collecting, over a period of months, large numbers of salmon and of maintaining optimum survival temperatures is obvious. Conditions are further enhanced by the bays which serve to confine, in a large area, the temperature mechanism for access to the spawning rivers.

Illus. 4 Salmon bearing predation marks have been reported from Loch Ness. (See Holiday, p. 170.) While none of these salmon has been photographed, an analagous documentation is seen in this photo of a trout scarred by a giant New Zealand eel. The eel scar is usually found on both sides of the body, formed by the small teeth which dislodge the scales of the trout and penetrate the flesh. The bite can be identified because although marked on both sides of the fish, only one side shows the impression of the vomerine band of teeth; this band of teeth is centrally located on the roof of the mouth, producing a unique impression. (from Cairns [Jan. 1942])

APPENDIX I

A Computer Analysis of Loch Ness Data
by Jan-Olaf Willums*

Frequency Distributions
Correlation of variables to the number of observations at Loch Ness
during the period 1962-1971 (10 years):

#1 Number of Observations—Months
#2 Number of Observations—Year
#3 Number of Observations—Duration of Observation
#4 Number of Observations—Air Temperature
#5 Number of Observations—Surface Condition of Loch
#6 Number of Observations—Moon Phase
#7 Number of Observations—Length of Object
#8 Number of Observations—Height of Object
#9 Number of Observations—Color of Object
#10 Number of Observations—Speed of Object
#11 Number of Observations—Concentration in River Mouths
and Active Bays
#12 Number of Observations—Active Fish Movement
#13 Number of Observations—Depth of Loch at Observation Point

Total number of observations: 258
Total number of variables: 24
Derived from computer output #CO 999, November 24, 1972
Computer program: DATATEX (Harvard); run on MIT IPC
Used release 3 of DATATEXT 360.

Frequency Distribution #1
No. Observations—Month

Jan	1	0.37%	Jul	44	16.36%
Feb	1	0.37%	Aug	69	25.65%
Mar	3	1.12%	Sep	36	13.38%
Apr	11	4.09%	Oct	7	2.60%
May	21	7.81%	Nov	2	0.74%
Jun	73	27.14%	Dec	1	0.37%

*Statistical distribution prepared by computer analysis of data compiled by
Holly Arnold, Richard Raynor, and David Wiseman for the Loch Ness Investigation Bureau. Sonar results from joint Academy of Applied Science and LNI
Experiments, August 1973, Loch Ness. Copyright © 1972, 1973 by Academy
of Applied Science, Loch Ness Investigation Bureau.

Frequency Distribution #2
No. Observations—Year

1962	7	2.60%	1967	40	14.87%
1963	40	14.87%	1968	26	9.67%
1964	12	4.46%	1969	29	10.78%
1965	17	6.32%	1970	26	9.67%
1966	42	15.61%	1971	30	11.15%

Mean: 66   Median: 67   SD: 5.6

Frequency Distribution #3
No. Observations—Duration of Observation

Less than 30 seconds: 61   25.21%
Less than 60 seconds: 79   32.64% (cumul.)
Mean: 935 sec.   Median: 67 sec.   SD: 5.6
87.19% of all observations are shorter than
(or equal to) 900 sec. = 15 min.

Frequency Distribution #4
No. Observations—Air Temperature (in Fahrenheit)

40-45 Degrees	2	0.80%	61-65 Degrees	77	31.08%
46-50 Degrees	9	2.01%	66-70 Degrees	43	17.27%
51-55 Degrees	20	9.64%	71-75 Degrees	12	4.83%
56-60 Degrees	68	27.31%	76-80 Degrees	18	7.23%

Mean: 62.53°   Median: 62°   SD: 7.146

Frequency Distribution #5
No. Observations—Surface Condition of Loch

Calm	160	63.75%	}
Ripples	50	19.92%	{ calm or only small ripples 83.67%
Waves	27	10.76%	
Strong waves	12	4.78%	

Frequency Distribution #6
No. Observations—Moon Phase

First	57	25.00%
Full	64	28.07%
Last	49	21.49%
New	51	22.37%
(No info.	5	2.19%)

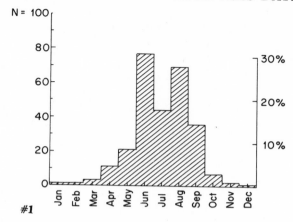

#1

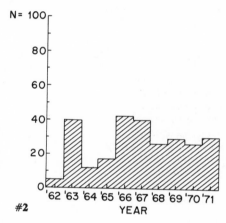

Distribution over First 60 Seconds

#3

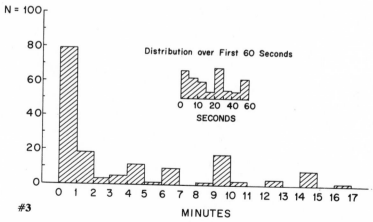

#2

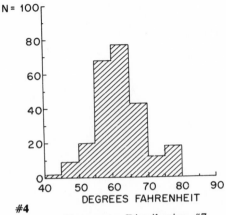

#4

Frequency Distribution #7
No. Observations—Length of Object

0 ft.*	16	9.20%	26-30 ft.	16	9.20%
1-5 ft.	25	14.36%	31-35 ft.	7	4.02%
6-10 ft.	26	14.94%	36-40 ft.	1	0.57%
11-15 ft.	32	18.39%	41-45 ft.	2	1.15%
16-20 ft.	23	13.21%	46-50 ft.	5	2.87%
21-25 ft.	14	8.05%	51-55 ft.	1	0.57%
			over 56 ft.	6	3.45%

*Body did not surface (only neck or waves).
Mean: 17.488 ft.   Median: 15 ft.   SD: 15.891

Frequency Distribution #8
No. Observations—Height of Object (visible above surface)

0 ft.*	32	14.10%	6 ft.	9	3.96%
1 ft.	53	23.35%	7 ft.	1	0.44%
2 ft	41	18.06%	8 ft.	3	1.32%
3 ft.	35	15.42%	9 ft.	2	0.88%
4 ft.	26	11.45%	10 ft.	5	2.20%
5 ft	16	7.05%	over 20 ft.	4	1.76%

*No neck visible.
Mean: 3.11 ft.   Median: 2 ft.   SD: 4.633

Frequency Distribution #9
No. Observations—Color of Object

Black	199	75.95%
Brown or other colors	25	9.54%
No indication*	38	14.50%

*Object did not surface or color was not strong enough to be identified.

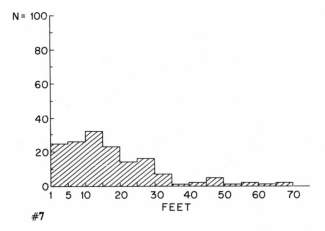

#7

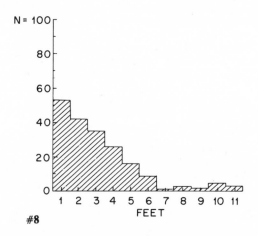

#8

Frequency Distribution #10
No. Observations—Speed of Object

0 mph*	61	35.88%	16-20 mph	12	7.06%
1-5 mph	39	22.94%	21-25 mph	5	2.94%
6-10 mph	34	20.00%	26-30 mph	7	4.12%
11-15 mph	9	6.30%	over 30 mph	3	1.77%

*Object did not move during observation.
Mean: 7.118 mph   Median: 4 mph   SD: 9.635

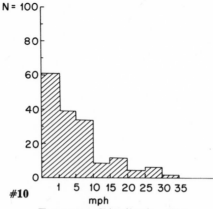

#10

Frequency Distribution #11
No. Observations—Concentration in River Mouths and Active Bays*

Fort Augustus Bay	12 observations
Invermoriston Bay	8 observations
Foyers Bay	23 observations
Inverfarigaig River	8 observations
Urquhart Bay	57 observations
Dores Bay	15 observations
Inverness outlet	13 observations
Total	136 observations

Percentage of observations in bays: 52.7%
*Active Bays = bays and regions with active water movement
(inflow or outflow of water).

Frequency Distribution #12
No. Observations—Active Fish Movement*

Fish observed close by	22	11.46%
No fish observed	169	88.02%
No information	1	0.52%

*Fish observed jumping out of water close by the observations site.

Frequency Distribution #13
No. Observations—Depth of Loch at Observation Point

50-100 ft.	40	15.66%		351-400 ft.	19	7.39%
101-150 ft.	20	7.78%		401-450 ft.	12	4.67%
151-200 ft.	56	21.79%		451-500 ft.	24	9.34%
201-250 ft.	18	7.00%		501-550 ft.	0	0.00%
251-300 ft.	30	11.67%		551-600 ft	9	3.50%
301-350 ft.	8	3.11%		601-650 ft.	6	2.33%
				651-700 ft.	15	5.84%

Mean: 308.408 ft.   Median: 250 ft.   SD: 176.861

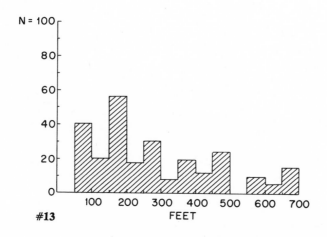

#13

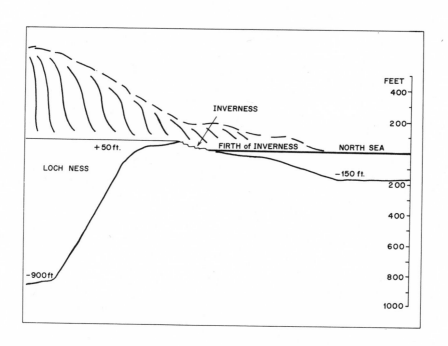

LOCH NESS   ROADS

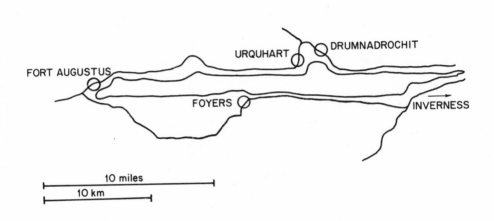

LOCH NESS   DISTRIBUTION OF SIGHTINGS

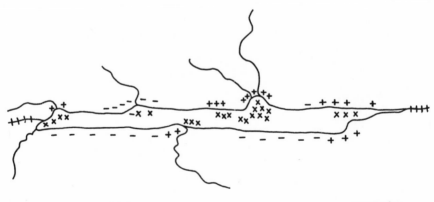

x Concentration of sightings

+ Good overview (road close to water, no trees)

– Bad or no view (trees or no road at all)

╫╫╫╫╫ Caledonian Canal

APPENDIX J

Birmingham University Loch Ness Expedition, 1961

The results of the expedition, as summarized in their Preliminary Report, are as follows:

Echosounding.

1. The presence of a scattering layer at 12-18 F (22-33 meters) was confirmed. The presence, horizontal extent, thickness, and depth varied from day to day, but it was normally found in the shallower waters of the bays (Foyers, Urquhart, Morriston). The layer at times extended upwards at night.

This layer did not necessarily coincide with any temperature discontinuity; on one occasion it was situated in the bottom of water at 10° lying on water at 8.5°, and both scattering layer and thermocline sloped slightly (deeper downwind). On at least 6 other occasions there was no correlation.

Vertical plankton hauls with a closing net gave no evidence of a greater concentration at the echo-layer depth.

The individual objects comprising this layer cannot be very large, because of the diffuse nature of the echo. The provisional identification is that they are small fish (less than 8 in.), possibly char.

2. Larger echos were obtained from objects in the top 20 F of the loch. By comparison with dead fish lowered on a weighted line, these echos came from single 2-lb. fish or from very tight small shoals.

3. Other non-biological echos were also obtained. In places, especially off the mouth of a river, echos were seen rising off the bottom at a rate of about 12-27 cm/sec. The size of the echos was such as would be given by less than 5 cc gas at normal pressure and certainly no sign of the bubbles could be seen against the small waves at the surface.

A deep layer (at 45-50 F) extending for approx. 1.5 miles and 0.25-0.5 miles wide was found in the deep part of the loch off Inverfarigaig. This layer had a smooth "hard" top and was probably quite narrow. It coincided with a temperature discontinuity of about 0.4° in 2 F (compare the thermal gradient of 0.1 per 10 F at similar depths elsewhere), and there are also indications from the oxygen analysis that there is a discontinuity. It is therefore possible that the layer is composed of detritus floating at the change in water density.

Oxygen. Oxygen concentrations ranged from 97% saturated at the surface to 85% at 128 F just above the bottom. The latter value is given as a percentage of the amount of O_2 which could have been dissolved in water of the appropriate temperature, but at the surface.

Salinity. Sodium ion concentrations ranged from 0.17-0.18 mM/L at all depths, and potassium ion 0.010-0.013 mM/L.

pH. pH varied between 6.0 and 6.5

350

Light penetration. The extinction coefficients for red and green light were 1.46/10 meters and 1.52/10 meters (log reduction of light intensity).

Plankton. A horizontal tow with a 97 m.p. net gave the following as an average of the better hauls (individuals per meter^3):

Copepods	1,500-1,900
Leptodora	0-19
Bythotrephes	6-60
Daphnia hyalina	6-30

Further analyses, including an estimate of total chlorophyll and the extent of vertical migration, have still to be made.

Hydrophone Watch. No fish or other animal noises were heard, at frequencies up to 60 KHz.

Bottom Dredging. Samples from the floor of the loch showed little life, and no evidence of rotting vegetation.

Large Animals. None seen.

Cambridge University Loch Ness Expedition, 1962

Aims of expedition.

1. To observe as much of the surface of the loch as possible, throughout daylight hours, for three weeks.

2. To search the loch by echosounder, using a very sensitive machine (BASDIC made by SIMRAD of Oslo). Three such sets were employed, the idea being to throw an unbroken current of ultrasound (38 KHz) across the loch. This was then moved from end to end (Fort Augustus-Dochfour) in the belief that any large object would either pass through the beam and be recorded or if disturbed by the ultrasound (which could be detected at 3 miles by the hydrophones on Col. Hasler's yacht *Jester*) would be driven before the advancing curtain and forced to the end of the loch where its discomfort should drive it to the surface.

3. To obtain further information on the freshwater biology of the loch.

Results.

1. No unidentified objects were seen within ½ mile of the observer. Two unidentified objects were seen for very short periods of time at distances between ½ and 2 miles. One of these was a light brown hump seen below Achnahannet from the southern shore of the loch; it was estimated to be 4 ft. in length. The other was seen from Foyers looking in the direction of Achnahannet. It was a "pole-like" object apparently moving through the water. Both were seen by competent observers under good conditions, but the period of observation was so short they scarcely had time to satisfy themselves that the object had no simple explanation.

2. No unexplained objects were detected by echosounding. The largest echos, obtained from shore-based echosounders pointed out into the loch,

were the type of echo given by a 20-lb salmon. However, echosounding cannot search effectively either the inshore waters—where shore echos interfere—or the layer of soft mud covering the bottom of the loch (see below) the presence of which had not previously been suspected.

3. A major undertaking was the sampling of the bottom by means of a dredge. This brought up from the deepest parts of the loch a very fluid, dark olive-green mud. This material appeared to cover the whole floor of the loch. It consists of the skeletons of microscopic plants—diatoms. The species present were the same as those found living in the surface waters of the loch. The depth of the fluid mud was estimated to be 10 ft. The living diatom population is *low*, 200/liter as compared with 5,000/liter in Lake Windermere. This is an indication of a lack of nutrients in Loch Ness. A low content of plant plankton results in a low content of animal plankton and a general scarcity of animal life. This seems to be the case in Loch Ness. The mud contains a few gas-(methane?) producing bacteria, but their numbers are very low.

The nature of the deep scattering layer, detected in 1960 and 1961, is still uncertain but may be caused by small fish.

Conclusions. The general impression from the plankton studies is that Loch Ness is a very poor loch (compared with Windermere). This is also borne out by the *relative* scarcity of fish (trout). It is doubtful if Loch Ness alone could support a colony of large animals. But because of the enormous watershed and consequent influx of eels, these creatures presumably constitute adequate food for a small population of predatory creatures. In this context, eels live close to the shore and as a result are not detected by echosounding. Anything preying on them would also be difficult to detect by echosounder, whereas a predator of the pelagic trout and salmon (and deep scattering layer creatures?) should be readily detected. Anything in the layer of mud at the bottom would evade detection.

APPENDIX K

TABLE 9
Chemical Sampling in Loch Ness, June 22, 1969*

Depth in meters	Temperature degrees centigrade	Salinity percent	Oxygen cubic centimeters per liter	BOD† milligrams oxygen per liter	Percent oxygen saturation	Phosphate parts per million	Nitrate parts per million	Nitrite parts per million	Silicate parts per million	pH
0	14.50	Nil	7.49	0.57	102.7	Nil	6.27	0.09	25.9	6.40
10	12.20	—	7.55	0.41	98.4	—	6.82	0.05	26.9	6.50
30	10.71	—	7.75	0.62	98.1	—	—	—	—	—
40	9.53	—	8.19	—	—	—	7.29	0.08	26.6	—
60	6.10	—	8.20	0.82	93.1	—	—	—	—	6.50
100	5.88	—	8.15	0.57	92.8	—	7.30	0.02	29.2	—
125	5.68	—	8.18	0.85	92.1	—	—	—	—	—
150	5.55	—	8.16	1.68	92.0	—	—	—	—	—
175	5.50	—	—	1.37	91.5	—	—	—	—	—
180	5.51	—	—	—	—	0.02	7.37	0.07	28.8	6.25
190	5.49	—	8.13	0.95	91.2	—	—	—	—	—
200	5.49	—	8.07	1.28	90.5	0.05	5.74	0.07	29.3	6.20
210	5.45	—	7.97	0.90	89.4	—	5.05	0.12	28.1	—
220	5.45	—	6.47	—	72.6	0.11	4.87	1.03	34.07	6.20

*Station was in the middle of the loch opposite Urquhart Castle, at a depth of 220 meters. Data in table from analyses by Department of Agriculture and Fisheries, Scotland. The following analyses of surface water were made under my direction by Clinical Laboratories, University of Chicago and Suburban Laboratories, Inc., Cicero, Illinois:
Mg .042 mM/L; Ca .011 mM/L; P < 5 mg/L; SO_4 3.0 PPM
Specific resistance: 21,500 Ohms
Specific conductance: 50.7 μmhos/cm
Dissolved mineral solids: 30.4 PPM.
†Biochemical oxygen demand

Bathymetrical Survey of the Freshwater Lochs of Scotland*

under direction of John Murray and Laurence Fullar

THE basin of the river Ness is one of the most important of Scottish river-basins, not so much on account of the area drained, which is small when compared with the areas drained by the Tay, Tweed, Clyde, and Spey, for instance, but because it includes within its boundaries the largest body of fresh water in Scotland (Loch Ness), as well as several other large lochs and numerous small ones. The basin extends from the mouth of the river Ness, at the junction of the inner Moray Firth with the Beauly Firth, in lat. 57° 30′ N. to lat. 57° N., south of Loch Quoich, and from long. 5° 30′ W., west of Loch Quoich, to long. 4° 10′ W., south-east of Inverness. The total area, as measured with the plani-meter on the 1-inch Ordnance Survey maps, is about 722 square miles, and of this by far the larger portion drains into Loch Ness, for the area draining into the river Ness, and into Loch Ashie which flows directly into the river Ness, is only about 36 square miles. With the exception of Loch Ashie, the superfluent waters from all the lochs within the basin find their way into Loch Ness, so that the total area draining into Loch Ness is about 686 square miles. The area drained by the tributary lochs, to be dealt with in subsequent papers, is about 354 square miles, leaving about 332 square miles draining directly into Loch Ness, independent of the other lochs.

The principal river-systems within the basin lie to the west of Loch Ness, viz. the Enrick, which flows through Glen Urquhart into Loch Ness at Urquhart Bay, where it is joined by the shorter river Coiltie; the Moriston, with its tributaries the Clunie and the Loyne, which flows through Glen Moriston into Loch Ness at Invermoriston; the Garry, with its tributaries the Quoich and the Kingie, which flows through Glen Garry into Loch Oich at Invergarry, and thence by the Oich into the head of Loch Ness at Fort Augustus. To the south of Loch Ness lies the Tarff, also entering Loch Ness near Fort Augustus; and to the east lie the Foyers, with its tributaries the Breinag and the Fechlin, which flows into Loch Ness at Foyers, and the Farigaig which

*Photo-reproduced from *The Geographical Journal* (of The Royal Geographical Society), vol. XXX, no. 1, July 1907, pp. 62-71, article subheaded "Part XIII.—Lochs of the Ness Basin. First Part." The reference to Plates I and II refers to maps in the original article, but these maps are not reprinted here.

355

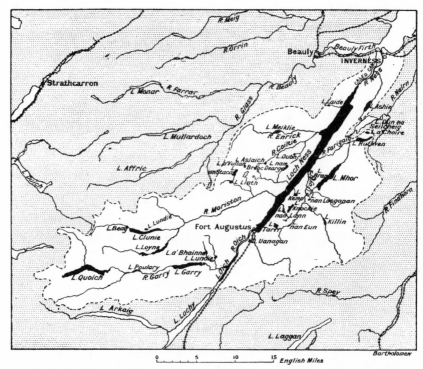

enters Loch Ness at Inverfarigaig.   Finally, to the north-east of Loch
Ness lies the Allt Mor (or Big Burn), draining Loch Ashie, which flows
into the river Ness 2 or 3 miles below Inverness, while the river Ness,
after issuing from Loch Dochfour, at the northern end of Loch Ness,
follows a winding course of about 6 miles, and pours its waters into the
Moray Firth.   Besides these, there are many shorter streams and burns
flowing directly into Loch Ness, or into the tributary rivers or lochs.

As will be seen from the summary table, the staff of the Lake Survey
sounded thirty-three lochs within the Ness basin, while a number of
small lochs could not be surveyed for lack of facilities.   These lochs
vary in size, from the little Loch nan Losganan, covering an area of
only 7 acres, and containing only a million cubic feet of water, to the
mighty Loch Ness covering an area exceeding 20 square miles, and
containing many thousands of millions of cubic feet of water.   None of
the other lochs in the basin can be compared with Loch Ness, neither as
regards area, volume, nor depth, but still a few of the lochs are of
considerable importance.   For instance, Loch Quoich is 7 miles in
length, while Loch Garry and Loch Mhor are nearly 5 miles in length,
and Loch Clunie and Loch Oich exceed 4 miles in length.   Loch Quoich,

again, covers an area of nearly 3 square miles, while Lochs Garry, Mhor, and Clunie exceed a square mile in area. Two of the lochs (Quoich and Garry) exceed 200 feet in depth, and three other lochs (Oich, Clunie, and nan Lann) exceed 100 feet in depth, while no fewer than twelve others include depths exceeding 50 feet.

The basin lies almost entirely in Inverness-shire, but a small portion of Ross-shire extends within the basin on its western border, the boundary-line running along the centre of West Loch Loyne and for a short distance along the centre of East Loch Loyne, and thence turning northward it crosses Loch Clunie in its central part; thus Lochs Loyne and Clunie lie partly in Ross-shire and partly in Inverness-shire, while the little Loch Beag, at the west end of Loch Clunie, is the only one lying wholly in Ross-shire. The scenery of the basin is varied, and as fine as anything to be seen in the Scottish highlands : towards the north the ground is low, but proceeding southwards it becomes more elevated, culminating on the south-western borders in several giant peaks exceeding 3000 feet in height, and on the south-eastern borders in mountains slightly less elevated. The district is a veritable sportsman's paradise, the deer-forests, grouse-moors, and fishings (both in river and loch) being of the best. Trout abound in nearly every loch, with salmon and *salmo ferox* in some of the larger lochs, and char in some of the smaller lochs lying to the east of Loch Ness; the fishing in most of the lochs is preserved.

Loch Ness (see Plates I. and II.).—Loch Ness formed the subject of discussion at a meeting of the Research Department of the Royal Geographical Society on January 18, 1904, and preliminary notes on the bathymetry, temperatures, and seiches were published in the *Journal* in October, 1904.* Since then many temperature and seiche observations and supplementary soundings have been taken, and the preliminary measurements and calculations have been carefully revised, the final results being given in this paper. Loch Ness is one of the best known of the larger Scottish lochs, since it forms a considerable part (nearly one-half) of the waterway known as the Caledonian canal, which occupies the great glen running in a north-east and south-west direction from the Moray Firth on the east coast of Scotland to Loch Linnhe on the west coast, thus cutting Scotland into two portions. Through the Caledonian canal thousands of visitors are carried each season on the route between Inverness and Fort William, and the splendid scenery of the canal and surrounding district has furnished a theme for many pens. The absence of islands in Loch Ness is a striking characteristic,

* *Geogr. Journ.*, vol. 24, p. 429.

and gives a touch of monotony to the grand and sombre scene, as one sails up or down; the little Cherry island, lying at the opening of Inchnacardoch bay near the head of the loch, is invisible except at close quarters. Castle Urquhart, on its rocky headland at the south side of Urquhart bay, forms a picturesque and noteworthy landmark.

In his journey to the Western islands of Scotland in the autumn of 1773, Dr. Johnston travelled along the shores of Loch Ness, which, he says, is in some places 140 fathoms deep, and he remarks further that "Natural philosophy is now one of the favourite studies of the Scottish nation, and Loch Ness well deserves to be diligently examined." After the lapse of 130 years this has been done, and it is proposed in this place to summarize the results obtained by the staff of the Lake Survey during their prolonged and "diligent examination" of Loch Ness.

The survey of Loch Ness was commenced on April 2, 1903, and by the end of that month the preliminary survey was completed, but subsequently, at various periods during the years 1903 and 1904, many additional lines of soundings and numerous isolated soundings were taken, some of them in connection with the work of collecting samples of the deposits from all parts of the loch, others in connection with the work of taking temperatures at various depths in different parts of the loch. The total number of soundings recorded is about 1700, but some of them have been omitted on the accompanying map to avoid overcrowding. On April 1, 1903, the level of the surface of the loch was determined from bench-marks as being 52·6 feet above the sea, and to this datum-level all soundings have been reduced. A levelling-staff was erected first at Fort Augustus, then at Invermoriston, Foyers, and Temple piers, and the height of the water on this staff was read daily during the progress of the survey, so that the variations in level from day to day, and the variations from the starting-point, were readily known. These staff readings showed that the water fell gradually but irregularly, and by April 15 it was 1 foot lower, and by the 18th it was 1½ feet lower, than on April 1.

Loch Ness proper may be said to extend from the head of the loch at Fort Augustus to the narrows at Bona ferry, a distance of 22¾ miles following the axis of maximum depth. This figure is inferior to the length of Loch Awe (25½ miles), and slightly in excess of the length of Loch Lomond (22⅔ miles); if we regard the small basin of Loch Dochfour, which is continuous with Loch Ness at its northern end, as forming part of the loch, then the total length, from the exit of the river Ness to the head of the loch, is about 24¼ miles.

In this place it is proposed to include Loch Dochfour in dealing with

Loch Ness; it is a basin about $1\frac{1}{2}$ miles in length, with a maximum depth of 50 feet in the wide central portion, whence it narrows towards the two ends, the southern narrows leading into Loch Ness, and the northern termination being divided into two branches, the eastern branch forming the river Ness, and the western branch the continuation of the canal. With a strong south-westerly wind there is a surface current from Loch Ness into Loch Dochfour through the narrows at Bona ferry, and, if long continued, the water becomes banked up in Loch Dochfour, and gives rise to a return current along the bottom into Loch Ness; with a strong wind from the north-east the surface current sets in the opposite direction, *i.e.* from Loch Dochfour into Loch Ness. Cut off from the western margin of Loch Dochfour, by embankments carrying the towing-path for the canal, are two small basins, one called Abban water, having a maximum depth of 9 feet, the other without a distinctive name, having a maximum depth of 23 feet; they stand at the same level as Loch Dochfour, the water evidently percolating through the embankments.

Loch Ness may be said to be fairly uniform in breadth, though varying to some extent, but on the whole its shore-line is very regular when compared with other large lochs. The upper portion between Fort Augustus and Foyers for about 10 miles is under a mile in width, except at the opening of Glen Moriston, where the breadth slightly exceeds a mile. The portion between Foyers and Castle Urquhart for about 5 miles is almost exactly a mile in width, while the lower portion between Castle Urquhart and Torr point for about 5 miles exceeds a mile in width. The widest part of the loch is at Urquhart bay, from the mouth of the river Enrick due east to the opposite shore, where the width is 2 miles. The portion of the loch from Torr point to Bona ferry for about $1\frac{1}{2}$ miles varies in width from a half to a quarter of a mile, and the central portion of Loch Dochfour is about a quarter of a mile in width. The mean breadth of the entire loch is nine-tenths of a mile, or less than 4 per cent. of the length; a smaller percentage of mean breadth to length has been recorded only in Loch Shiel and Loch Shin, with $2\frac{1}{2}$ and 3 per cent. respectively.

The waters of Loch Ness cover an area of nearly 14,000 acres, or $21\frac{3}{4}$ square miles. Among the Scottish fresh-water lochs this is exceeded only by Loch Lomond, which has a superficial area of nearly $27\frac{1}{2}$ square miles. As already stated, the area draining directly into Loch Ness is about 332 square miles, while its total drainage area, including the area draining into all the tributary lochs, is about 686 square miles—an area over thirty times greater than that of the loch.

The maximum depth observed by the Lake Survey staff in Loch Ness was 754 feet, about a mile due south of Castle Urquhart in the centre of the loch. A greater depth than this has been recorded in only one Scottish loch, viz. Loch Morar, which has a maximum depth of 1017 feet, and after Loch Ness come Loch Lomond and Loch Lochy, with maxima of 623 and 531 feet respectively.

The volume of water contained in Loch Ness is estimated at 263,000 millions of cubic feet, or $1\frac{3}{4}$ cubic miles. In no other Scottish loch does the bulk of water amount to a cubic mile, in fact Loch Ness contains about three times as much water as the two lochs which most nearly approach it in this respect, viz. Loch Lomond with 92,800 million cubic feet, and Loch Morar with 81,500 million cubic feet. The largest volume of water recorded by Dr. Mill among the lakes of the Cumberland district is only 12,250 million cubic feet. As far as we are aware, the volume of water contained in the large lakes of Ireland has not yet been carefully worked out, but, taking Loch Neagh, for instance, which is said to cover an area of 153 square miles (or seven times greater than the area of Loch Ness), and to have a maximum depth of only 48 feet, a rough calculation will show that the bulk of water in Loch Neagh must be less than that in Loch Ness. It seems quite possible, therefore, that Loch Ness may be the largest body of fresh water, not only in Great Britain, but in the United Kingdom.

Correlated with the enormous volume of water in Loch Ness is the high value of the mean depth, which works out at 433 feet for the entire loch. This far exceeds that of Loch Morar, viz. 284 feet, which comes next in this respect. The mean depth of Loch Ness is equal to 57·4 per cent. of the maximum depth—a higher percentage than has been observed in any other large deep loch, the nearest approach to it being in the case of Loch Avich, with a maximum depth of 188 feet and a mean depth of 98 feet, the percentage being 52·4. It is true that in some shallow flat-bottomed basins the percentage of mean depth to maximum depth exceeds that in Loch Ness; as, for instance, Loch Watten in Caithness (70 per cent.), and Loch Bruadale in Lewis (74 per cent.), but the maximum depths are here only 12 feet and 6 feet respectively. Except for Lochs Ness and Avich, in all the deep Scottish lochs, *i.e.* those having depths exceeding 100 feet, the mean depth is less than one-half of the maximum depth, the percentage varying from 19·4 in Loch Shiel, and 19·5 in Loch Lomond, to 49·4 in Loch Lungard, and 49·6 in Loch Suanival (Lewis).

It has been stated that the surface of Loch Ness stands about 52 feet above mean sea-level, so that by far the greater portion of its floor falls below the level of the sea.

An inspection of the bathymetrical map of Loch Ness shows (1) the comparative simplicity of the basin ; (2) the steep shore-slope throughout the greater part of the loch; and (3) the large area of the lake-floor covered by very deep water. The 100-feet, 200-feet, 300-feet, 400-feet, and 500-feet contours are continuous, and only the 600-feet and 700-feet contours are interrupted by a shoaling opposite the entrance of the river Foyers, probably due to the deposition of material brought down by that river. This shoaling is covered by 515 to 524 feet of water, and both to the north-east and south-west the bottom sinks to depths exceeding 700 feet.

The 100-feet basin is about $22\frac{1}{2}$ miles in length, the southern extremity approaching to within 100 yards from the shore at the entrance of the river Tarff, and the northern extremity extending into the narrow part of the loch beyond Torr point, approaching to within a quarter of a mile from Bona ferry.

The 200-feet basin is $21\frac{2}{3}$ miles in length, approaching to within 150 yards from the Monastery boat-house slip at Fort Augustus, and quite close to the south-western shore off the entrance of the river Oich, and extending beyond Torr point on the north to within less than a mile from Bona ferry.

The 300-feet basin is $20\frac{3}{4}$ miles in length, extending from less than 300 yards from the Monastery boat-house slip on the south to just beyond Torr point, or $1\frac{1}{2}$ miles from Bona ferry, on the north.

The 400-feet basin is 20 miles in length, distant over a quarter of a mile from the Monastery boat-house slip on the south, and about three-quarters of a mile from Torr point, or over 2 miles from Bona ferry, on the north.

The 500-feet basin is about $18\frac{1}{2}$ miles in length, distant less than a mile from the Monastery boat-house slip on the south, and about $1\frac{1}{2}$ miles from Torr point on the north. The southern extremity of this basin differs somewhat from the usual truncate form, partaking of a rectangular character.

The two 600-feet basins are separated by an interval of little over half a mile, and are almost exactly equal in length, both of them slightly exceeding 8 miles in length. The northern one is distant about 2 miles from Torr point, and the southern one less than 2 miles from the Monastery boat-house slip at Fort Augustus.

The two 700-feet basins are separated by an interval of nearly $2\frac{1}{2}$ miles, the northern one being nearly twice as long as the southern one, and including the maximum depth of the loch—754 feet. The northern basin is $6\frac{1}{3}$ miles in length, and distant about $2\frac{3}{4}$ miles from Torr point, while the southern basin is $3\frac{1}{3}$ miles in length, and nearly 6 miles distant from Fort Augustus. The maximum depth recorded in the southern basin was 739 feet near the southern end of the basin, while towards the northern end of the basin a depth of 735 feet was recorded, the intervening soundings being slightly shallower.

These details show how extremely symmetrical Loch Ness is in all its bathymetrical characteristics. All the contour-lines, except the deepest one, approach rather closer to the southern than to the northern· end of the loch, but in the case of the 700-feet contour this is reversed.

The shore-slope on both sides of the loch is nearly everywhere steep. Gradients exceeding 1 in 1 are of frequent occurrence, and in certain places the slope approaches the precipitous. Near the southern end of the loch, off the south-western shore at the entrance of the river Oich, a sounding in 204 feet was taken about 100 feet from shore, but the steepest slopes were observed off the north-eastern shore in the vicinity of the Horseshoe craig, where a sounding in 236 feet was taken about 100 feet from shore; another in 175 feet about 50 feet from shore; and, off what is known as the Cormorant rock, a sounding in 206 feet was taken about 50 feet from shore. This last-mentioned sounding gives a gradient exceeding 4 in 1, or an angle of about 15° from the perpendicular.

The steep shore-slope is further seen by the manner in which the contour-lines of depth as a rule hug the shores, leaving a comparatively very large area of the lake-floor along the central line of the loch covered by very deep water. This is strikingly shown by the fact that nearly one-half of the entire basin is covered by more than 500 feet of water, and over one-third by more than 600 feet of water. In the following table are given the approximate areas in acres between the consecutive contour-lines drawn in at equal intervals of 100 feet, and the percentages to the total area of the loch :—

Feet.				Acres.		Per cent.
0 to 100	...	...	...	1892	...	13·6
100 ,, 200	...	...	...	1340	...	9·6
200 ,, 300	...	...	...	1610	...	11·6
300 ,, 400	...	...	...	1121	...	8·0
400 ,, 500	...	...	...	1329	...	9·5
500 ,, 600	...	...	...	1627	...	11·7
600 ,, 700	...	...	...	2461	...	17·7
Over 700	...	...	...	2556	...	18·3
				13,936		100·0

This table brings out several interesting peculiarities when compared with the similar tables published for the other large Scottish lochs. The most remarkable point is that the two deepest zones are larger than any of the other shallower zones, the deepest zone of all, though the interval between the 700-feet contour and the maximum depth is only half the usual interval between the contour-lines, being the largest of all. Such a distribution of the depth-zones has not been observed in any other loch, and is a reversal of the usual rule of the shallowest zone being the largest one, though one or two exceptions to this rule have been recorded, as, for instance, in Loch Treig, where the zone between 200 and 300 feet is larger than either of the two shallower zones, and in Loch Lochy, where the zone between 100 and 200 feet is a little larger than the shore-zone. In the deepest of all Scottish lochs, Loch Morar, the shore-zone is equal to 42 per cent. of the total area, and the second zone between 100 and 200 feet is equal to 13 per cent., while of the deeper zones not one exceeds 9 per cent. of the total area. In Loch Lomond, again, the shore-zone is equal to 68 per cent. of the entire area, and the second zone between 100 and 200 feet is equal to $16\frac{1}{2}$ per cent., while the deeper zones are in each case less than 6 per cent. In Loch Ericht the shore-zone is equal to 34 per cent., the second zone between 100 and 200 feet is equal to 25 per cent., and the third zone between 200 and 300 feet is equal to 19 per cent. of the total area, the deeper zones in each case not exceeding 10 per cent. In Loch Tay there is a regularly decreasing percentage in the zones of depth from the shore into deep water, the numbers for each zone at intervals of 100 feet being respectively 30, $23\frac{1}{2}$, 21, $15\frac{1}{2}$, 9.

TABLE 10
The Lochs within the Ness Basin†

Loch.	Height above sea. Feet.	Number of soundings.	Length in miles.	Breadth in miles.		Mean breadth per cent. of length.	Depth.			Ratio of depth to length.		Volume in million cubic feet.	Area in square miles.	Drainage area.	
				Max.	Mean.		Max. Feet.	Mean. Feet.	Mean per cent. of max.	Max.	Mean.			Total in square miles.	Ratio to area of loch.
Ness ...	52·60	1693	24·23	1·96	0·90	3·7	754	433·02	57·4	170	295	263,162	21·78	686·31	31·6
Quoich ...	556·00	280	6·95	0·80	0·43	6·1	281	104·60	37·2	131	351	8,345	2·86	49·18	17·2
Poulary ...	[320 approx.]	37	1·46	0·20	0·10	6·7	47	9·90	21·0	164	779	39	0·14	82·18	587·0
Garry ...	257·00	272	4·90	0·56	0·36	7·3	213	78·00	36·6	121	332	3,794	1·75	137·33	78·5
a' Bhainne ...	[1060 approx.]	42	0·36	0·26	0·14	38·9	28	9·69	34·6	68	196	14	0·05	1·81	36·2
Lundie (Garry)	44·540	103	0·76	0·40	0·22	29·6	54	16·28	30·1	74	246	78	0·17	3·44	20·2
	[Aug. 18, 1869]														
Oich ...	106·00	195	4·02	0·30	0·19	4·7	154	41·78	27·1	138	509	890	0·76	170·96	224·9
Uanagan ...	118·20	56	0·52	0·12	0·07	13·5	43	16·80	39·1	64	163	18	0·04	1·21	30·2
Beag ...	605·20	27	0·30	0·22	0·13	43·3	29	11·80	47·2	63	134	13	0·04	20·40	510·0
Clunie ...	605·20	126	4·28	0·50	0·26	6·0	123	49·98	40·6	184	452	1,533	1·10	32·29	29·3
Lundie (Clunie)	681·50	28	0·46	0·18	0·09	19·6	25	7·80	31·2	97	311	9	0·04	0·95	23·8
West Loch Loyne	719·00	67	1·28	0·34	0·19	14·7	19	5·93	31·2	356	1,140	40	0·24	16·21	67·6
East Loch Loyne	706·10	123	2·75	0·30	0·15	5·6	35	10·32	29·5	415	1,407	123	0·43	23·87	55·5
An Staca ...	[1600 approx.]	85	1·02	0·40	0·25	24·5	51	15·52	30·4	106	347	110	0·26	1·23	4·8
Liath ...	1494·10	43	0·46	0·28	0·21	45·0	55	22·36	40·7	44	109	62	0·10	4·00	4·0
Nam Breac Dearga	[1570 approx.]	60	0·74	0·21	0·12	16·0	70	24·43	34·9	56	160	60	0·09	0·60	6·7
a' Vullan ...	[1750 approx.]	38	0·45	0·18	0·09	21·6	27	12·27	45·4	88	194	15	0·04	0·69	17·2
Meiklie ...	364·90	49	1·10	0·43	0·28	25·9	45	22·10	49·1	129	263	193	0·31	41·32	133·3
Aslaich ...	[1310 approx.]	38	0·35	0·14	0·09	26·9	26	10·91	42·0	71	169	10	0·03	1·62	54·0
Dubh ...	[1340 approx.]	20	0·18	0·11	0·07	38·9	18	7·00	38·9	53	136	2	0·01	0·17	17·0

Loch	Elevation													
Laide	859·80 [Aug. 4, 1869]	62	0·34	0·32	0·18	52·8	9	5·16	57·3	199	348	9	0·06	1·55	25·8
Tarff	956·20	80	0·69	0·60	0·36	52·5	89	23·89	26·8	41	152	136	0·21	1·20	4·8
Knookie	[nearly 700]	123	1·30	0·46	0·22	16·9	75	24·40	32·5	91	281	194	0·28	1·62	6·0
Nan Lann	[645 approx.]	56	0·70	0·34	0·15	20·8	109	37·03	34·0	34	100	105	0·10	3·69	36·9
Kemp	577·80	48	0·52	0·25	0·20	39·1	51	26·23	51·4	54	105	77	0·11	1·53	13·9
Nan Eun	[915 approx.]	29	0·48	0·18	0·11	23·6	21	9·90	47·1	121	256	15	0·05	3·81	76·2
Killin	[1044 approx.]	61	1·12	0·26	0·18	16·2	67	24·15	36·0	88	245	137	0·20	38·45	192·2
Nan Losganan	—	18	0·30	0·10	0·04	12·3	7	3·50	50·0	226	453	1	0·01	0·24	24·0
Mhor (Garth and Far-raline)	638·55	279	4·84	0·64	0·35	7·2	91	24·11	26·5	281	1,060	1,134	1·69	20·77	12·2
Bran	—	49	0·74	0·20	0·05	6·9	50	12·63	25·3	78	309	13	0·04	0·28	7·0
a' Choire	865·00	45	0·61	0·33	0·22	36·1	60	27·55	45·9	54	117	103	0·13	0·94	7·2
Ruthven	701·10	103	2·26	0·54	0·25	11·4	42	11·27	26·8	284	1,059	180	0·57	4·01	7·0
Ashie	717·75	50	1·60	0·44	0·33	20·4	57	21·26	37·3	148	397	309	0·52	2·83	5·4
		4385										280,923	34·25	689·14*	20·1

* With the exception of Loch Ashie, the drainage areas of all the lochs are included in that of Loch Ness.

†The "summary table" referred to on page 356 above is this Table 10, photo-reproduced from *The Geographical Journal*, vol. XXXI, no. 1, January 1908, pp. 50-51.

The Deposits of Loch Ness*
by G. W. Lee and L. W. Collet
with analyses of selected samples by A. Wilson

ABOUT sixty samples of the deposits covering the floor of Loch Ness were collected by the members of the Lake Survey staff from various parts of the loch, and were examined according to the methods used in the *Challenger* Office for the study of marine deposits.

They may be classed as follows :—

(1) *Dark grey mud*, from the deep basin opposite Urquhart bay ;

(2) *Ferrugineous mud*, from the part of the Invermoriston deep basin opposite Horseshoe craig ;

(3) *Peaty mud*, from the south-west end of the Invermoriston deep basin ;

(4) *Yellow-grey clay*, from off Inverfarigaig and off Cherry island ; and

(5) *Brown sand*, from shallow water off Urquhart bay.

(1) DARK GREY MUD.

The eleven samples of this mud are homogeneous and coherent when dry. A typical sample from 740 feet, opposite Urquhart bay, has the following mineralogical composition :—

Minerals (25 per cent.), mean diameter 0·1 millimetre. Of these particles quartz is the most abundant, often coloured red by a coating of iron oxide. Orthoclase, chloritic minerals, and limonite are also present.

Fine washings (75 per cent.), composed of vegetable matter (15·89 per cent.) and clayey matter (59·11 per cent.), with fine mineral particles and limonitic matter.

Chemical Composition.

Total silica	62·36
Ferric oxide	12·27
Alumina	9·38
Lime	tr.
Magnesia	tr.
Loss on ignition	15·89
	99·90

The high percentage of silica is due to the great proportion of quartz. The alumina is due to the presence of felspar and clayey matter. The defect 0·10 per cent. is probably due to the fact that the alkalies have not been estimated.

---

*From *The Geographical Journal,* vol. XXXI, no. 1, January 1908, pp. 58-61, Appendix III to article entitled "Bathymetrical Survey of the Fresh-Water Lochs of Scotland," subheaded "Part XIII.—Lochs of the Ness Basin. Third Part."

(2) Ferrugineous Mud.

This type of sediment is limited to the part of the Invermoriston deep basin opposite Horseshoe craig. One of the samples was found after examination to be composed of:—

Minerals (29 per cent.), essentially represented by ferrugineous grains, which are accompanied by quartz, orthoclase, chlorite, and hornblende. These mineral particles are angular, and have a mean diameter of 0·12 millimetre.

Fine washings (71 per cent.), composed of vegetable matter (18·46 per cent.) and fine minerals (52·54 per cent.), belonging to the species mentioned above.

Chemical Composition.

Total silica	37·44
Ferric oxide	24·48
Alumina	15·12
Lime	2·16
Magnesia	1·80
Loss on ignition	18·46
	99·46

The defect 0·54 per cent. is to be sought for in the alkalies.

As there is no clayey matter in this sediment, and as the microscopical investigation did not reveal the presence of many aluminous minerals, the high percentage of alumina, *i.e.* 15·12 per cent., is to be explained by the fact that the ferrugineous grains are not made up of pure iron oxide, but of a mixture of this oxide with clay.

Although manganese was not estimated in the above quantitative analysis, it was found to be rather abundant in another sample.

(3) Peaty Mud.

This type of mud occupies a large area of the floor of the loch in the south-west end of the Invermoriston deep basin.

In order to show the differences in composition due to increase of depth, two descriptions will be given here.

First Sample. Depth 300 feet.

Minerals (35 per cent.), angular, mean diameter 0·2 mm.: orthoclase and acid plagioclase, greenish chlorite in large flakes, quartz, hornblende, and ferrugineous matter.

Fine washings (65 per cent.), composed of vegetable matter (37·10 per cent.) and mineral particles (27·90 per cent.) belonging to the above-mentioned species.

Chemical Composition.

Total silica	47·88
Ferric oxide	5·58
Alumina	7·02
Lime	1·08
Magnesia	0·59
Loss on ignition	37·10
	99·25

Second Sample.   Depth 445 *feet.*

Minerals (10 per cent.), angular, mean diameter 0·12 mm.: orthoclase and acid plagioclase, quartz, chlorite, hornblende, and ferrugineous matter.

Fine washings (90 per cent.), composed of vegetable matter (25 per cent.) and fine mineral particles (65 per cent.) of the same species as those mentioned under the heading: minerals, but chlorite and decomposed felspar are relatively more abundant.

Chemical Composition.

Total silica	...	...	...	...	...	...	46·03
Ferric oxide	...	...	...	...	...	...	10·41
Alumina	...	...	...	...	...	...	7·61
Lime ...	...	...	...	...	...	...	9·64
Magnesia	...	...	...	...	...	...	1·60
Loss on ignition	...	...	...	...	...	...	24·65
							99·94

Comparing the results of the investigation of these two samples, it will be seen that as the depth increases both the percentage and the diameter of the minerals decrease, the proportion of vegetable matter also decreasing.

The high percentage of lime in the second analysis is probably due to fragments of shells.

(4) YELLOW-GREY CLAY.

One sample was taken off Cherry island in 95 feet, and eight samples off the south-east coast, east of Inverfarigaig, in 250 feet. This is very clayey in character, being soft to the touch and plastic when wet, coherent when dried, and taking in the latter state a light brown streak if rubbed with a hard smooth body.

The Cherry island sample is made up of—

Minerals (1 per cent.), angular, mean diameter 0·1 mm.: quartz, orthoclase, chlorite, and ferrugineous matter.

Fine washings (99 per cent.), composed of clay and very fine mineral particles

Chemical Composition.

Total silica	...	...	...	...	...	...	58·42
Ferric oxide	...	...	...	...	...	...	9·51
Alumina	...	...	...	...	...	...	24·58
Lime ...	...	...	...	...	...	...	0·52
Magnesia	...	...	...	...	...	...	3·74
Manganese	...	...	...	...	•••	...	2·11
Copper oxide ...	...	...	...	...	...	...	0·65
Loss on ignition	...	...	...	...	...	...	0·59
							100·12

One of the eight other samples is made up of—

Minerals (29 per cent.), angular, mean diameter 0·1 mm.: quartz and decomposed felspar, with a decomposed ferrugineous mineral.

Fine washings (71 per cent.), composed of vegetable matter (4·2 per cent.) and clay and mineral particles (66·8 per cent.).

Chemical Composition.

Total silica	...	...	...	...	...	...	50·94
Ferric oxide	...	...	...	...	...	...	14·76
Alumina	...	...	...	...	...	...	19·80
Lime ...	...	...	...	...	...	...	6·58
Magnesia	...	...	...	...	...	...	3·61
Loss on ignition	...	...	...	...	...	...	4·20
							99·89

In these analyses the lime and magnesia probably belonged to some ferro-magnesian mineral, which was subsequently transformed into what is given here as "decomposed ferrugineous mineral," the advanced state of decomposition preventing its determination.

(5) BROWN SAND.

To four samples of sediment dredged in 30 feet near the coast west of Urquhart bay we give the name of Brown Sand. One of the samples has the following composition :—

Minerals (69 per cent.), angular, mean diameter 0·2 mm., mostly made up of quartz, coloured reddish by a coating of iron oxide. Decomposed mica, hornblende, and plagioclase are also represented. The sand contains a few small fragments of rocks, 1 to 3 millimetres in diameter.

Fine washings (31 per cent.), composed of vegetable matter (4·4 per cent.) and fine mineral particles (26·6 per cent.). There is no clayey matter.

Chemical Composition.

Total silica	...	...	...	...	...	...	77·62
Ferric oxide	...	...	...	...	...	...	3·60
Alumina	...	...	...	...	...	...	5·20
Lime ...	...	...	...	...	...	...	5·88
Magnesia	...	...	...	...	...	...	2·20
Loss on ignition	...	...	...	...	...	...	4·40
							98·90

The alumina, lime, and magnesia are most likely due to the mica and hornblende, whilst the defect of 1·10 per cent. might represent the alkalies.

CONCLUSION.

Loch Ness includes two deep basins separated by a barrier formed by the delta of the Foyers river. The muds from the south-western or Invermoriston basin contain a large amount of vegetable or peaty matter, brought down the lake probably by the rivers Tarff and Oich, with mineral particles coming from the disintegration of the rocks, transported by the streams. Small concretions of peroxide of iron and dioxide of manganese were dredged at one station. The muds often gave the characteristic reaction of manganese. On the slopes the muds are sandy, and of a red-brown colour, due to the presence of oxide of iron.

The muds from the north-eastern or Urquhart basin contain far less vegetable matter than those from the south-western basin, which may be due to the Foyers barrier retaining the vegetable matter in the upper basin.   In the north-eastern basin the vegetable matter increases with the depth, which is contrary to what is observed in the south-western basin.   Off Urquhart bay the contour-lines approach each other very closely, and the vegetable matter brought down the lake by the river Enrick is carried towards the deeper part of the basin.   Great differences are observed in the muds from the slopes on the two sides of the loch.   On the north-western slope we find especially a red sandy mud, coming without doubt from the washing out of the shore, composed of Old Red Sandstone.   On the south-eastern slope we have a fine yellow clay, with fragments of rocks and large mineral particles without vegetable matter.   The deposition of the clay in this position may be due partly to the strong prevailing westerly winds of Loch Ness giving rise to waves and currents, which would carry the fine clayey matter brought down by the Inverfarigaig river towards the south-eastern shore.   Three stones from a depth of 100 feet, opposite Inverfarigaig pier, were covered with a dark ring of manganese dioxide, marking out the line between the mud and water, as was pointed out by Sir John Murray and Mr. Robert Irvine in their valuable paper : " On Manganese Oxides and Manganese Nodules in Marine Deposits." *

* *Trans. Roy. Soc. Edin.*, vol. 37, p. 721 (1894).

The Biology of the Lochs of the Ness Basin*
by James Murray

COLLECTIONS of plankton were made in twenty-seven lochs in this basin.   With the exception of the lochs in the Great Glen itself, most of these lochs are at a considerable elevation, occupying the high tableland on the east of Loch Ness, or the higher mountainous tract on the west.

The situation of the lochs in two alpine masses, separated by the deep cleft of the Great Glen, gives rise to some peculiarities in distribution, most marked in the species of *Diaptomus* and the more conspicuous plankton desmids.

A number of species were only collected on one side of the Great Glen.   These peculiarities are probably due to the fact that the lochs to the east of Loch Ness were surveyed in spring or early summer, when the water was still cold, while those to the west were surveyed after midsummer, when they were about at the maximum temperature.

*From *The Geographical Journal,* vol. XXXI, no. 1, January 1908, pp. 64-67, Appendix VII to article entitled "Bathymetrical Survey of the Fresh-Water Lochs of Scotland," subheaded "Part XIII.—Lochs of the Ness Basin. Third Part."

Diaptomus gracilis was here, as elsewhere, almost universal, but was not seen in several of the eastern lochs.

D. laticeps was in Loch Ness and the other lochs in the Great Glen. It was not seen in any loch to the west, but was frequent in lochs to the east of Loch Ness. In Loch Ness the blue *Diaptomus* (identified by Mr. Scourfield as *D. laticeps*) is somewhat small and pale in colour. In other districts, and especially in hill lochs, it is of larger size and brighter colours—blue or occasionally red. There is some doubt as to the identity in all cases, and naturalists have given different identifications of the Loch Ness animal.

D. laciniatus, in contrast to *D. laticeps*, was only found to the west of the glen, in lochs high above the sea. To the east, though it was not in any of the lochs surveyed, it was in some lochans at a great elevation on Carnahoulin.

Desmids.—The conspicuous plankton desmids, which constitute probably the most distinctive feature of the western Scottish plankton, are not very well represented in the lochs of the Ness basin. There are few species, but they include several of the largest and most beautiful. They show no marked preference for the one side of the glen more than the other, but the greatest number of species is in Loch Aslaich, which lies west of Loch Ness.

Micrasterias apiculata, var. *fimbriata*, was in Loch Aslaich, and the var. *brachyptera* was found only once in Loch Ness.

M. radiata, Hass (*M. furcata*).—This very local species was in Loch Aslaich.

Staurastrum furcigerum, Bréb.—In Loch Bran, at Foyers.

S. longispinum (Bail.).—In Loch Aslaich and several neighbouring lochs.

S. ophiura, Lund.—Loch Ness and Loch Aslaich.

S. sexangulare (Bulu.).—Loch Garth, near Foyers.

S. brasiliense, Nordst.—Loch Aslaich.

Euastrum verrucosum, Ehr., *Micrasterias papillifera*, Bréb., *Xanthidium antilopeum* (Bréb.), *Staurastrum gracile*, Rolfs, *Staurastrum lunatum*, var. *planctonicum*, West, and one of the beaked *Closteria*, which I identify as *C. setaceum*, Ehr., are the most generally distributed desmids in the basin.

Crustacea.—Apart from the Calanidæ, a few of the Crustacea appear to be local in the district.

Sida crystallina.—Only seen in Loch Ness and Loch Aslaich.

Diaphanosoma brachyurum.—Only noted in the lochs of the Great Glen and some lochs to the west. The eastern lochs were doubtless surveyed before its season.

Holopedium gibberum.—Noted in scarcely half the lochs, but those on both sides of the Glen and at all elevations.

Leptodora was only seen in the lochs of the Glen and Loch Tarff; *Polyphemus* in the Glen and some lochs to the west; *Bythotrephes* in the Glen and Lochs Tarff and Ruthven to the east.

Rotifera.—*Conochilus unicornis* was generally distributed; *C. volvox* only in Lochs Ness, Laide, and Knockie.

Floscularia pelagica.—Lochs Ness, Oich, and Uanagan.

Synchæta pectinata.—Lochs Oich and Uanagan.

Anopus testudo.—Lochs Ness and Uanagan.

Triarthra longiseta.—In five lochs on the east side of the basin; apparently a cold-water species.

Gastropus stylifer.—Loch Ness and five lochs to the east, and Loch Aslaich to the west.

Sarcodina.— Clathrulina was not seen except in the lochs of the Great Glen. *Nebela bicornis*, West, though found in Loch Ness, was not got in the plankton, but while dredging in the shallow water of Inchnacardoch bay.

Loch Ness.—Loch Ness was made the subject of a more thorough, though still far from exhaustive, biological investigation than any other Scottish loch. A very large proportion of all the lacustrine organisms known in Scotland have been found in this loch.

The great majority of the species in all the larger groups—Crustacea, Rotifera, Sarcodina—have been got in Loch Ness, the only large group not very fully represented being the desmids. Some of the small groups have hardly been studied, except in Loch Ness, and it is the only loch the abyssal fauna of which is fairly well known.

To give any detailed account of the hundreds of species found in the loch would traverse too much the same ground as the general report on the " Biology of the Scottish Lochs," now in preparation. There will therefore be given here simply an epitome of the biology, and a comparison with the other lochs in the Ness basin.

The Plankton.—The plankton is the average plankton of Scottish lakes, with a very small admixture of the more local species. It is very poor in species, and always very small in quantity. No approach to " flowering " of the water has been noted. The greatest quantity was collected in late autumn, 1903, during the night, when a considerable migration from the deeper water to the surface evidently took place, as the quantity collected during the preceding day was much less. The plankton varies little throughout the year, a fact probably correlated with the low annual range of temperature, which is less than 20°·0 Fahr., while the upper limit of about 60°·0 is rarely touched.

About half the species of Crustacea remain all the year round, those which are absent in winter being *Bythotrephes*, *Polyphemus*, *Leptodora*, and *Diaphanosoma*. *Holopedium* was noted by Mr. Scourfield, but was never found during the systematic investigation afterwards. *Diaptomus laticeps*, Sars., appears to persist all the year round, and was found carrying eggs in March, when the temperature is at its lowest. *Clathrulina* was generally present, and *Volvox* occasionally.

There is a great contrast between Loch Ness and Loch Lochy in the relative abundance of the phytoplankton. Loch Lochy is very rich, and Loch Ness very poor. The two lochs are only some 10 miles apart, and are apparently under almost identical conditions. Loch Lochy, being in an almost uninhabited district, should be purer than Loch Ness, but a slight pollution is generally favourable to vegetable growth.

Littoral region.—Though there are only a few sheltered bays in Loch Ness, where littoral vegetation can establish itself, the microfauna and microflora found among the larger vegetation are very considerable, and constitute, indeed, the chief part of the species in the loch.

A great many of the animals extend downwards to a very considerable depth, and about forty species (exclusive of Rhizopods), including many Crustacea, Rotifers, Tardigrada, Worms, and the larvæ of many insects, have been collected as far down as 300 feet. Shells of all the Rhizopods extend to the greater depth, and many live at greater depths than 300 feet.

In Inchnacardoch bay Mr. Scourfield found *Ophryoxus gracilis* for the first time in Britain; and the rare *Ilyocryptus agilis*, previously known in several places in England, was got in the same locality.

Abyssal region.—In Loch Ness a large proportion of the littoral species extend to about 300 feet in depth, probably because of the very steeply sloping sides. Those species only are considered as truly abyssal which are generally distributed over the mud, into the deepest part of the loch. A small association of animals is found thus distributed, and the abyssal region, being defined as the bottom where this association is found almost free of admixture, must be considered to begin at about 300 feet. Exclusive of Rhizopods, there are about a dozen animals constantly found in this region, comprising—1 Mollusc, *Pisidium pusillum*, Gmel.; 3 Crustacea, *Cyclops viridis*, Jurine, *Candona candida*, Müll., and *Cypria opthalmica*, Jurine; 3 worms, *Stylodrilus galretæ*, Vejd., *Monotus morgiensis*, Du Plessis, and an undetermined Oligochæte; 1 insect, *Chironomus* (larva); several Infusoria, parasites on the Molluscs and Crustacea.

Several other species occur casually at great depths, such as *Hydra*, *Limnæa*, *Lynceus affinis*, and *Proales daphnicola*.

A small char, *Salmo altinus*, was dredged at a depth of over 500 feet.

Larvæ of *Tanypus* and some other diptera are frequent, but less constant than *Chironomus*.

Rhizopods.—Dr. Penard has identified about forty species and varieties from depths of more than 300 feet. They thus constitute the greater part of the species in our abyssal region, but their presence there is of little special interest, and there are only some half a dozen species and varieties which are doubtfully supposed to be peculiar to deep lakes.

Summary of the Number of Species.

	Species.			Species
Mollusca	5	Dinoflagellata		3
Hydrachnida	1	Phanerogamia		33
Tardigrada	22	Equisetaceæ		1
Insects	6	Lycopodiaceæ		1
Crustacea	55	Characeæ		2
Rotifera	151	Mosses		6
Gastrotricha	2	Hepatics		2
Worms	12	Florideæ		2
Cœlenterata	2	Chlorophyceæ		46
Infusoria	11	Myxophyceæ (Report in preparation)		—
Sarcodina	67			
Mastigophora	3	Bacillariaceæ		20

We have thus a total of 453 species recorded for Loch Ness, excluding all Vertebrata, blue-green Algæ, and some other groups on which no work has been done. The Hydrachnida, Insecta, Worms, Infusoria, Chlorophyceæ, and Diatoms, have all been insufficiently studied, and the lists could be easily increased.

The Aquatic Flora of the Ness Basin*
by George West

FROM certain points of view, plants may increase in interest and value in ratio to their rarity; of equal worth philosophically are those plants that occur in great abundance. The former, being scattered as individuals, or as small associations over restricted areas, are possibly, at present, of but small import in the economy of nature. The commoner plants, however, by reason of their dominance and abundance, become important agents, not only as a plant-covering to the Earth, but also in the effect they produce in the physiography of a country: barren tracts become heath or forest by the extension of vegetation; lakes are converted into morasses, moors, or even into land suitable for agriculture by the accumulation of plant-remains. Such natural operations tend to increase the wealth and social prosperity of man. As examples on the other hand, the sudden increase of a baneful fungus may bring ruin to thousands of agriculturists, and carry famine to the million; or morasses in hilly districts may slide into cultivated valleys, and completely overwhelm sites of human activity and wealth. These and many other phenomena are brought about by the predominance of certain classes of plants. How great, therefore, are the interests awakened upon the fields of practical thought and knowledge by the abundant and dominant plants in their never-ceasing antagonism with one another and with other forces of nature!

It is chiefly with some of the factors that control the dominant water-plants of higher organization in the Ness area that the following remarks are concerned.

The two great factors that contribute towards the distribution of the plant-covering over the surface of the Earth, and through its waters, are food and climate. Notwithstanding the conditions for plant-life being so often remote from the ideal, yet the plastic power that plants possess of adapting themselves to the various combinations of edaphic and climatic conditions is so great that there are comparatively few spots in which some plant or other is not able to thrive and carry on its metabolic activities. With aquatic plants the influence of the substances, food or otherwise, held in solution in the water, is vastly greater than that of climate.

The edaphic conditions dominating the flora in the majority of the numerous lakes of the Ness area are indirectly influences of climate. Indeed, the rock-basins that contain the lakes are themselves chiefly the result of climatic effects, because they were scooped out during a former period of glaciation. The study of our lake flora brings us, therefore, to consider the cause of a glacial epoch, and is thus the usher to one of the most abstruse and sublime realms of thought that the human intellect has ever been able to grapple with, so complicated and interwoven are the modes of nature's working. But to our more mundane considerations.

The yellow-brown colour of the waters of our highland districts is a matter of common observation, and is due to the water-supply from the mountains percolating

*From *The Geographical Journal*, vol. XXXI, no. 1, January 1908, pp. 67-72, Appendix VIII to article entitled "Bathymetrical Survey of the Fresh-Water Lochs of Scotland," subheaded "Part XIII.—Lochs of the Ness Basin. Third Part."

enormous quantities of peat before reaching the lakes. This, then, would appear to be an edaphic influence; and so it is, but the existing conditions—the presence of peat on the mountains—have been brought about by direct climatic influence. The climatic conditions that obtain in the exposed portions of the highlands are more favourable to the natural production of moorland than of forest. The two formations—moor and forest—are antagonistic to one another, the tendency being for the moorland to extend from the higher situations over the domain of the natural forest of the lower altitudes. The principal natural causes for this victory of moor over forest are—(1) wind, which is much less antagonistic to moor plants than to trees; (2) the peculiar acid humus that is formed abundantly from the remains of certain dominant moor plants, and which acts inimically towards trees.* These natural conditions have undoubtedly been unwittingly hastened during the past two thousand years by the destructive influence of man on forest.

It is the presence of the peat extract in the water that is the dominating factor governing the aquatic flora of the Ness area. Its presence excludes directly a number of aquatic or semi-aquatic plants that might otherwise thrive. It obliterates any calcium carbonate that might be present, and thus renders the water untenable to calciphilous plants. On the other hand, certain calcifugal plants, having become accustomed to tolerate the presence of humic acids, abound. I scarcely know that one should say the latter thrive the better through lack of competition with the former, because commonly it is not that competition for available space is so great, as that the local conditions favour the dominant production of an individual species.

The peat extract darkens the water, and this restricts the depth zone to which submersed aquatics will grow, because they are unable to carry on photosynthesis beyond a very limited depth, owing to want of light. Therefore the photic zone throughout which there exists sufficient light for the proper development of the higher plants does not extend to a greater depth than about 30 feet in the lochs of the Ness area, and is often very much less than that. The extreme depth to which such plants as *Nitella opaca* and *Fontinalis antipyretica* will flourish in these lakes may roughly be estimated by multiplying by four the greatest depth at which one can see the brown gravel at the bottom, when looking over the shaded side of a boat about midday in the summer, when the sun is shining brilliantly, with the water perfectly calm, and the boat still. Such a depth in Loch Ness is from 7 to 8 feet.

This multiplier, however, does not hold where the multiplicand is considerably greater. Thus at Loch Fiart, on Lismore, one may see the bottom at a depth of 25 feet under the above conditions, but plants do not thrive at a greater depth than 40 to 45 feet. Possibly this is because the less refrangible rays of the spectrum, which are most necessary to photosynthesis, become insufficient at greater depths; although the rays of shorter wave-length may penetrate to greater depths in sufficient quantity to fulfil the requirements of the metabolic activities that are dependent upon them. It must be borne in mind that the yellow-brown colour of

---

* Space does not permit an explanation here of the involved complications brought about by these factors.

the peaty lakes probably neutralizes the photo-chemical action of the violet rays at no great depth. We know that Rhodophyceæ thrive in the sea at least to a depth of 250 feet, but in all probability their reddish colour accentuates the photo-chemical action of the very feeble yellow-green rays * that penetrate such a depth of water. In similar manner a photographic plate becomes more sensitive to certain rays when its film is stained with suitable colours. Thus a film stained with erythrosin becomes sensitive to green and yellow. Exact information on these points in various waters of Scotland is much needed.

By reason of the preserving action of humic acids, the organic remains about the shores of the lakes do not readily decay, but undergo a slow process of disintegration, and form a sort of liquid peat. Owing to this action, suitably situated shallow places about peaty lakes become reclaimed by the growth of land-winning plants quicker than in water that is free from humic acids.

The last glacial epoch, after destroying the vegetation of Scotland, immediately began the formation of more numerous lake-basins for the reception of a greater aquatic flora after its disappearance. Not only this, for we find other results of glaciation actually dominating the vegetation in certain of our lochs at the present moment. At Lochs Oich and Lochy, for example, the sides of the adjacent mountains are coated with glacial drift-gravel. This gravel is brought into the lakes by the numerous streams in great abundance, and deposited upon the shores. Under the erosive power of the waves, the constant movement of this gravel upon the littoral entirely prevents the growth of aquatic phanerogams over a considerable area of the margin of the lakes. Again, in many places a steep escarpment, due to glacial action, enters a lake immediately, so that water too deep for phanerogams occurs without any shore whatever; instance Loch Ness opposite Invermoriston, where a depth of 652 feet may be sounded at about 120 yards from the margin. Here we see the indirect effect of a past epoch upon the flora of existing lakes, the lakes themselves being the direct result of that period.

Climate also affects the local distribution of the plants in each loch more or less. The prevailing, and frequently strong, winds are westerly; consequently there is, upon the eastern shore of a lake, a very considerable and oft-recurring wave-action. Acting upon a rocky or stony shore, this erosive power entirely prevents the growth of the higher plants in the shallow water where its influence is felt (see Fig. 5, p. 48). Unless sheltered by adjacent hills, all the lakes will be almost, or quite, devoid of vegetation on their eastern shore, whilst the western shore, and bays sheltered from the prevailing wind, will have an abundant vegetation. The algæ of the seashore may be cited as an example, on the other hand, that plants can develop, and luxuriantly too, on a rocky shore subjected to powerful erosion, but the case is here entirely different. The seeds of phanerogams, excepting the tropical Podostemaceæ, have no power to firmly attach themselves to rocks and stones, as have the spores of seaweeds. Still we do find, even in exposed parts of our lakes, fixed rocks often covered with mosses, hepatics, algæ, etc.

Wind is an important factor in dwarfing the semi-aquatic vegetation about the

---

* The rays for maximum photosynthesis in the red seaweeds are the yellow-green; these penetrate water sufficiently for photosynthesis to about five times the depth that red rays do.

littoral region of the lakes; especially is this the case with those situated in the more elevated and exposed positions.

The sudden rise of water to any great or prolonged extent is inimical to the well-being of plants in the lochs, particularly so if the water is extremely peaty. This is very pronounced at Loch Mhor, where an ever-changing level—due to the rainfall on the one hand, and the water used by the British Aluminium Company at Foyers on the other hand—does not allow a flora to grow at all. Previously existing trees at the margin have been drowned by the raising of the water-level (see Fig. 2, p. 44).

In these peaty lakes the aquatic plants are usually remarkably free of epiphytic organisms, and also of mud; neither do they bear that deposit of calcium carbonate so common to aquatic plants in lakes that are devoid of the peat extract. Humic acids, and perhaps carbonic acid too, in the waters almost extinguish molluscan life. Consequently one does not find the aquatic vegetation destroyed by these creatures, as is commonly the case where certain of them, especially *Limnæa*, abound.

The great variation between the summer and winter temperature of the water of the higher mountain lochs doubtless affects the flora to a greater extent than in those of lower altitude. These hill lochs are often shallow, and the comparatively small body of water may become heated to 70° Fahr. in summer, and may be frequently covered with ice in winter and spring. The ice often remains upon such lochs until April. Before its final disappearance, large shoals of broken ice grind upon the shores with surprising power and noise, and would destroy any littoral vegetation within its influence. Considering that such floating ice shifts about the loch with every change of wind, it is scant wonder that one so often finds these hill lochs devoid of marginal vegetation. In the great body of water of the large and deep lochs of lower altitude the temperature is more equable, winter and summer records not varying more than 10° to 20° Fahr., and such lochs seldom freeze.

It has already been pointed out that these peaty waters contain little or no calcium bicarbonate. Consequently there is no incrustation of calcium carbonate upon the aquatic plants. A necessary corollary to such antecedents is that no lime deposit resulting from the metabolism of plants is being laid down in these peaty lochs, as is the case where the water is charged with calcium bicarbonate.

The mud occurring in the peaty lakes of the Ness area is seldom of the black evil-smelling kind, such as is commonly found in non-peaty lakes, *e.g.* Duddingston Loch, near Edinburgh. In the latter case the decomposition of organic matter takes place with far greater rapidity than in water charged with humic acids. After the first stages of rapid decomposition comes the formation, among other substances, of ammonia, carbon dioxide, and hydrogen sulphide. It is the last mentioned that gives the mud such an offensive odour when disturbed. In the presence of humic acids this rapid putrefaction does not occur. Instead, the disintegration takes place slowly by a kind of carbonizing process. At the bottom of Loch Ness vegetable remains first become brown, then black and brittle, gradually crumbling to powder, and apparently no obnoxious gas is generated. Putrefaction does not take place, but rather a kind of desiccation—if one may apply this term to a sub-aqueous process. Likewise the mud from the bottom of Loch Ness has not the slightest offensive odour, neither does it stain one's hands as the fetid kind does.

Many plants, *e.g. Phragmites communis, Sparganium ramosum, Alisma Plantago,* etc., always grow more luxuriantly when the mud is black and fetid;

but other species, *e.g. Sphagnum,* various sp., *Isoetes lacustris, Lobelia Dortmanna,* etc., are unable to endure that kind of mud, not directly because of its presence, but because other factors, *e.g.* difference in food-salts, are correlated with the presence of this or that kind of mud. A number of other plants are comparatively indifferent, *e.g. Castalia speciosa, Menyanthes trifoliata,* etc.

Again, the aquatic vegetation being restricted to the photic zone, the greater portion of the bottom of these deep lakes receives but a small supply of organic remains. The refuse-eating fauna existing at the bottom is consequently able to maintain an equilibrium between supply and demand, so that the lake-bottom consists largely of the non-fetid excrement of these creatures. In shallow non-peaty lakes, whose floor is wholly carpeted with vegetation, *e.g.* Duddington Loch, the supply of organic detritus is greatly in excess of any refuse-eating fauna that may exist, therefore fetid mud results from the process of unhindered decomposition.

From the foregoing statements, it will be readily understood that the flora of the lakes in the Ness area is subjected to many varying conditions, and in order to maintain a proper tone of health a plant has of necessity to respond in suitable ways to all the varying external impressions. A plant is therefore in a constant and continual state of change, owing to the never-ceasing mechanical, physical, and chemical changes of its unstable environment. The plastic nature of many plants enables them to modify their organs in reciprocation to any fairly constant set of environmental conditions; and it is in this endeavour to accommodate themselves for the maintenance of healthy existence in inhospitable places, that certain deviations from the normal forms of more kindly environments are to be accounted for. That such forms should receive definite specific or varietal names is open to grave doubt. Physiologists and experimental botanists are becoming more and more sympathetic towards the simplicity of the astute George Bentham; and whilst recognizing, as did Bentham, the numerous forms fixed and transient, such are regarded as unit forms of the phylogenesis, or of the retrogression of a species.

In many districts one may distinguish mountain lochs by the presence of certain plants, as, for example, *Isoetes lacustris, Lobelia Dortmanna, Potamogeton polygoni-folius, Sparganium natans, S. minimum,* etc., and by the absence of reeds at the margin. But in the Ness area the presence or absence of such plants and associations is certainly no criterion of the elevation of a loch. All the plants enumerated are to be found at so low a level as Loch Ness (52 feet above the sea); and a reedy margin is found at quite highland situations, whilst it is almost absent in such low-lying lochs as Oich and Ness. The reason is not one altogether of elevation for the presence or absence of certain plants, but is rather due to the supply of food-salts, and the amount of exposure of the water to winds, coupled with the nature of the shore. The mountain lakes usually drain a very small area, poor in food-salts and rich in acid humus; consequently, only those plants are found in them that can obtain their requirements from an apparently scanty food-supply, combined with the presence of humic acids. Such plants are those that have been associated with mountain lakes. Lowland lakes usually drain a wider area, and soils poor in peat and rich in food-salts, which, although indispensable to most plants, are poison to others. In the area of Lochs Ness and Oich there is but a small amount of soil rich in food-salts available for drainage, compared with the soil poor in food-salts and rich in acid humus. Consequently, the effect of drainage from a small, rich food-area is almost extinguished by the humic acids, and in such lowland lochs we find vegetation identical with that of the highest mountain lakes.

Again, in Lochs Oich and Ness (and, of course, others) we have practically no reedy margin, neither have we in many mountain lakes. The reason for this is the nature of the shore, combined with the erosive power of the waves, leaving altogether out of the question food-supply. On the other hand, in mountain lakes with a sheltered peaty or muddy shore, as in lowland lakes of like nature, we find a reedy or sedgy margin. Highland lochs are usually in situations fully exposed to the fierce winds, their shores rocky or stony; consequently, they have few plants about their margins. Their water, being poor in food-salts and rich in humic acids, has a restricted aquatic flora; but the same conditions may obtain in the lowlands, when the flora of the lakes will be similar. On the other hand, a highland loch having a supply of food-salts, with a suitable shore and sheltered from prevailing winds, may quite well have the character of a lowland loch regarding its flora.*

Mirages on Loch Ness*

A KIND of mirage is one of the most familiar phenomena on Loch Ness, especially in winter and spring. It is best seen in the morning. Distant objects, such as the steamers plying on the lake, appear as though raised above the surface and floating in the air.

The most constant feature of the Loch Ness mirages is seen at promontories some miles distant. The shore-line at the promontories, though really nearly parallel with the horizon, is caused by the mirage to appear to form an angle with the horizon. When this angle is great (say 60° or more), the promontories appear like overhanging cliffs. When the angle is very acute, they seem to be suspended over the horizon. Objects which are known to be below the horizon are brought into view. The receding steamer, after sailing out of sight, will reappear miles further away, raised high above the loch and looking very large. The promontory at Dores appears as a conspicuous island in the middle of the loch. The fathers in the Benedictine Monastery at Fort Augustus tell that on one occasion a snow-covered mountain appeared over the end of the loch. These phenomena are best marked at a distance of several miles from the observer. The steamer, sailing away from the observer, seemed, at the distance of a mile or more, to leave the surface of the loch and sail up into the air.

Signs of the mirage were sometimes to be distinguished at lesser distances. Standing on the deck of the Lake Survey yacht *Rhoda*, when the eyes would be

---

*From *The Geographical Journal*, vol. XXXI, no. 1, January 1908, pp. 61-62, Appendix IV to article entitled "Bathymetrical Survey of the Fresh-Water Lochs of Scotland," subheaded "Part XIII.—Lochs of the Ness Basin. Third Part."

7 or 8 feet above the water, there could often be seen on the rocks of the nearest parts of the shore a conspicuous horizontal line, looking just like a high-water mark.   In the reports of the Balatonsee Commission, mirages of a similar nature are discussed.   Von Cholnoky explains how they arise through the formation of a lower stratum of warmer air, heated from the lake.   In shallow lakes like Lake Balaton, the mirage is essentially a summer phenomenon.   The lake remains warm during the night when the air cools.

In Loch Ness the converse is the case.   The great body of water maintains a moderate temperature throughout the year.   In summer the lake rarely attains to 60°·0 Fahr., and so the air may frequently remain as warm as the lake, though mirages may occur after any cold night.   In winter the lake maintains a high temperature, rarely falling below 42°·0 or 43°·0 Fahr., and thus the air will fall to a much lower temperature almost every night, and a well-marked layer of warmer air be formed by morning over the surface of the lake, giving rise to the mirage.

APPENDIX L

Trapping the Loch Ness Monster

In a detailed 25-page document, Robert Love has described, drawn, and budgeted Loch Ness traps of his design which the LNIB and I think quite worthy of construction and use. From that Love proposal I summarize some of the salient features. In brief, his ingenious apparatus has the following characteristics and advantages: fabrication of heavy plastic tubing combines strength requirements with weight light enough to permit handling by a small crew without extremely heavy lifting tackle; capacity accommodates specimen up to 20 ft. long; self-floating construction (trap raised by displacing the water inside plastic tubing by compressed air) allows raising even in rough water with additional buoyancy lifting trap partially clear of water for towing; capable of 30 days of unattended operation by means of automatic system for bait dispensing and renewal, with radio alarms for malfunctions.

Surface conditions on Loch Ness can be formidable. Winds sometimes exceed 60 mph and are often over 20 mph. Substantial wave action results. Waves of 6-8 ft. can be expected about 10% of the time, of 5 ft. 20% of the time, of 3-4 ft. 50% of the time, and of less than 3 ft. only about 20% of the time. Under such conditions, servicing of moored equipment from a work boat is a challenge. Difficulties increase as the size of the surface unit increases and approaches that of the work boat, since neither vessel dominates the other. The problem is further complicated if frequent service of equipment is required or if the work boat must be tethered in close proximity to the surface unit for extended periods of time. (Cf. Chapter V, Illus. 2, 3.) Sub-surface conditions are unique, as noted earlier with reference to the internal seiche. (See Chapter V, Illus. 6.) The underwater currents change with time and wind conditions and affect the diffusion of bait essence into the water; this is one reason dual-ended traps may turn out to be more effective.

Trap construction. External trap dimensions are 18 ft. by 6 ft. by 6 ft. The configuration utilizes dual entry at either end with horizontally offset overlapping trigger compartments located centrally. Each section is separate and is closed by a sliding gate at its end. The trap framework is constructed of welded plastic pipe (Acrylonitrile Butadiene Styrene, 1.9 in. o.d.). This rigid material has a density only 20% greater than water and thus loses 83% of its weight when submerged. Diagonal truss bracing is employed to increase rigidity where required. Construction of large-diameter welded pipe has the benefit of providing an integral pipe volume of over 6 cu. ft. This volume can be flooded to submerge the trap or purged with air to float the trap on the surface; a purged trap will float with approximately 50% of its height above the water line. Calculated

382

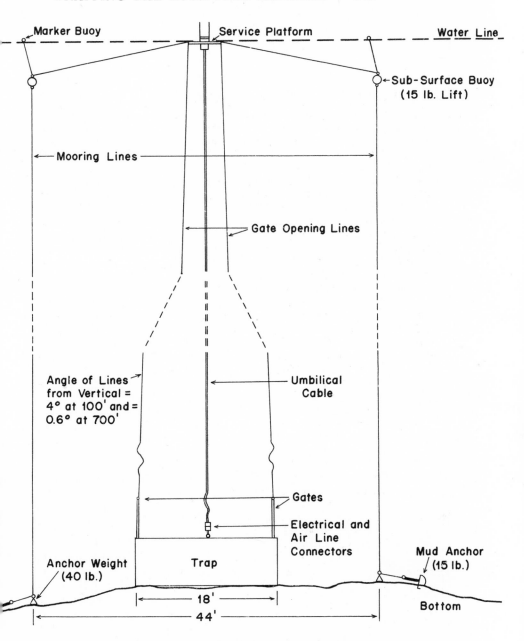

Marker Buoy   Service Platform   Water Line

←Sub-Surface Buoy
(15 lb. Lift)

←— Mooring Lines ——→

Gate Opening Lines

Angle of Lines
from Vertical =
4° at 100' and =
0.6° at 700'

Umbilical
Cable

Gates

Electrical and
Air Line
Connectors

Anchor Weight
(40 lb.)

Trap

Mud Anchor
(15 lb.)

|← 18' →|

Bottom

|← 44' →|

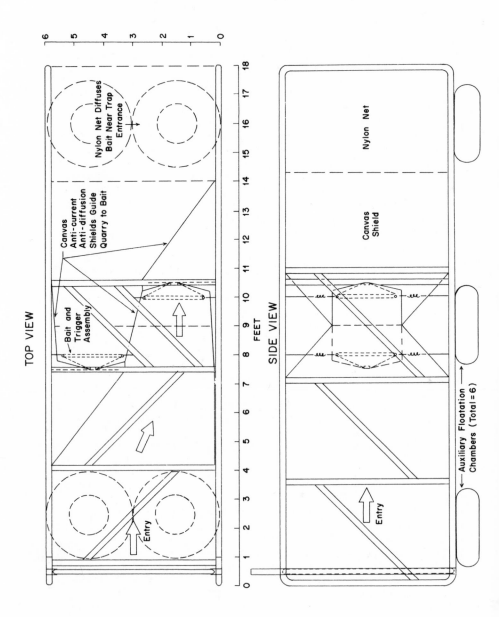

TOP VIEW

Nylon Net Diffuses Bait Near Trap Entrance

Canvas Anti-current Anti-diffusion Shields Guide Quarry to Bait

Bait and Trigger Assembly

Entry

FEET

SIDE VIEW

Nylon Net

Canvas Shield

Auxiliary Floatation Chambers (Total = 6)

Entry

weight of the trap and its operating mechanisms on land is about 230 lbs. This weight is manageable by a few men with light lifting equipment. Calculated weight of the trap when submerged with the pipe framework flooded is 78 lbs. This should be adequate weight to keep the trap in position on the bottom and to permit lifting the gates into the open "set" position by lines from the surface. Conversely it does not preclude the possibility of winching the trap to the surface if other systems fail.

The central area of both trap sections is covered with canvas to restrict diffusion of bait scent and to shield the trigger mechanisms from currents. Nylon netting of ½-in. mesh on the end section permits diffusion of bait scent near the open trap gates.

Bait. Our experience with eel traps (See Appendix G.) suggests a three-fold lesson: bait must be renewed frequently (almost daily) to remain effective; highly aromatic smoked baits such as kippered herring are most attractive; for maximum efficiency, bait essences must be introduced in a concentrated form (i.e. not decomposed by previous leaching by the water).

The proteinaceous bait material is partially emulsified by grinding with a natural fish oil to preserve its chemical essences. This bait fluid is stored in two flexible polyethylene "water containers" aboard each trap. Collapsing of the containers as bait is used eliminates pressure differential effects. These containers are rapidly replaced at the surface when empty. 5-gallon bait storage capacity released at 1 ounce per hour provides an automatic bait supply for about 30 days without rebaiting. Bait fluid is dispensed automatically for 3-5 seconds each hour by pumps controlled by an electrical time-clock mechanism. The pumps, when dormant, restrict the entry of water into the bait containers thereby providing a constant source of "fresh" bait fluid. Bait will be pumped from the containers into the water directly behind the trigger screen and diffuse into the water through the screen in a localized manner to induce probing by an animal against the screen.

Tripper mechanism. A trigger screen 2 ft. by 2 ft. is suspended at the inner end of the trigger compartment, 10 ft. inward from the trap gate. Pressure by an animal against any point of the screen trips a magnetic/electrical assembly and releases the trap gate for that section. Adjustment for different sensitivity of operation can be made to establish the minimum size threshold of animals capable of closing the trap.

Electrical energy. The primary power supply aboard the submerged trap is a 6-volt 4-amp-hour motorcycle storage battery in a sealed case which also houses the electrical circuitry. Short runs of cable from this local battery provide the high momentary current pulses for trap operation and testing. Secondary power supply aboard the service platform is a 12-volt 40-amp-hour automotive storage battery. A light electrical umbilical cable from the surface to the trap provides a continuous trickle charge to the submerged battery, maintaining it in a fully charged condition without need for frequent raising for exchange. The time interval for replacement of the surface battery is about 30 days, providing an

adequate margin to cope with the vicissitudes of Loch Ness weather. Replacement is easily accomplished during reasonable water conditions.

Automatic alarms. A small Citizens Band radio transmitter capable of being monitored from the shore or work boat is housed in the service platform above each trap. Each trap transmits on a unique channel, thereby identifying the trap reporting. Different audio tones, and on-off cycling of the tones, provide full information as to the operational condition of each trap on a continuous basis. Closure of one of the two gates on a trap transmits a continuous low frequency audio tone on that trap's radio channel. Closure of the second gate transmits a continuous high frequency audio tone. Design of the transistorized alarm circuity is "fail-safe" so that a switch failure or a broken connection in the umbilical cable automatically produces an alarm. If either bait system fails to dispense fluid when energized, a different bait alarm signal is automatically transmitted by radio. Flow failure is detected by flow switches in each line when the bait pumps are energized on the hour. While radio transmission is normally the indication that a trap requires service, a backup system is provided. A lamp, visible by night, is mounted atop the obstacle warning flagstaff on each service platform. This service alarm light will be automatically illuminated if any of the alarms should occur.

Service platform. The platform is designed to present a minimum profile to both wind and water movement. Use of foam floatation and a light plastic drum provides an enclosure which weighs less than 75 lbs. with all equipment installed. (Storage battery, control circuitry, etc.) Its small 2 x 4-ft. dimensions provide ease of access to equipment inside the drum. A platform of this size and weight can be secured to a work boat or, in an emergency, loaded on board by hand. Location of the storage battery below the water line provides ballast to assure stability. Connections to the trap below include the two trap gate setting lines, the electrical umbilical cable, and the air purging tube. The latter two are fastened together to minimize twisting and tangling.

Raising. Traps are raised by introducing air into the integral volume of the pipe framework via a ½-in. diameter flexible plastic purging tube. A portable air tank aboard the work boat provides the supply. A standard Scuba tank is sufficient to raise two traps from 700 ft. To raise a trap in rough water the work boat can approach the service platform, connect a 20-ft. air hose to the purging tube by a "quick disconnect" coupling, and then stand off at a distance while the trap is floated. Traps can also be winched to the surface utilizing the gate setting lines. Should both gates be closed, either the electrical cable or the purging tube has adequate strength for lifting the trap manually under calm conditions.

Biological and structural considerations. Since forward propulsion is produced by opposite flexure of alternate sections of the body, a swimming animal rarely occupies a longitudinal distance in the water as great as its extended body length. The 10-foot trap sections should be able to completely contain a swimming animal with a length of about 17 feet. However, to accommodate possible larger specimens, a few single-

compartment, 20-ft. traps will also be deployed. In practice, closure of a trap gate on the posterior section of a larger animal is likely to result in withdrawal of the tail into the trap and complete closure of the gate.

Large pelagic fish such as marlin and tuna, when hooked, appear capable of developing a propelling force approaching 25% of their weight. This force however, is partly inertial in nature, resulting from their high speed, and is not likely in close confinement. Nevertheless, the gates closing the ends of a trap and the central canvas panels are designed to withstand loads of about 1,000 lbs. with a safety factor of 2.

Forward propulsive forces are derived from muscular reaction of body and fin surfaces against the mass of water which, in turn, is directed rearward. The net force tending to move a trap, produced by an animal inside, is greatly reduced if both acting and reacting forces are contained within the trap. The design accomplishes this by employing canvas surfaces at either end. Thus reaction of water set in motion by the tail against the canvas-covered gate largely cancels the forward propelling force from the animal. Transverse forces can be exerted against members of the trap framework by an animal inside. The flexible canvas and net covering tends to distribute such loads, and the relatively large cross section of the design reduces the probability that large forces will be applied by body undulations. Internal and external trusses are included at frame sections most susceptible to such loads.

Maximum design loads have been calculated at typical locations utilizing a safety factor of 2. The 2-ft. spans between trusses will withstand a uniformly distributed pressure from an animal's body of 1,000 lbs. Under this load the deflection at the center of the span would be only 0.55 in. In the unlikely event that a fleshy animal could exert a concentrated load at a single point near the attachment of an interior truss, a force of 1,400 lbs. could be withstood. Maximum permissible force against the outer central 6-ft. spans is also 1,400 lbs. An animal capable of being contained in a trap of this size would not be expected to exceed these forces.

Bibliography

Adams, J. A., Fraser, J. H., Seaton, D. D., and Hay, S. J. "The Results Obtained from Plankton Sampling in Loch Linnhe and Loch Eil During a Study on the Effects of the Pulp and Paper Mill at Annat Point." Internal Report 73-1. Dept. of Agriculture and Fisheries for Scotland, Marine Laboratory, Aberdeen.

Agassiz, L. *1857 Contribution to the Natural History of the United States.* Boston, Little, Brown and Co. Vols. 1-4.

Andersen, H. T. (Ed.) *The Biology of Marine Mammals.* New York, Academic Press, 1969.

Annual Report, Loch Ness Investigation Bureau, London, 1967, 1968, 1969.

Augusta, J., and Burian, Z. *The Age of Monsters.* London, Paul Hamlyn, 1966.

————. *Prehistoric Sea Monsters.* London, Paul Hamlyn, 1964.

Baker, P. F. "Cambridge Loch Ness Expedition," 1962.

Barrington, E. J. W. and Jorgensen, C. B. (Eds.). *Endocrinology.* New York, Academic Press, 1968. See H. J. A. Koch.

Barron, J. "The Northern Highlands in the Nineteenth Century, Newspaper Index and Annals" (From the *Inverness Courier*) Inverness, Robt. Carruthers & Sons, Vol. I, 1800-1824 (1903); Vol. II, 1825-1841 (1907); Vol. III, 1842-1856 (1913).

Baumann, E. *Loch Ness Monster.* New York, Franklin Watts, 1973.

Bertin, L. *Eels: A Biological Study.* London, Cleaver-Hume Press, 1956.

————. "Les Larves Leptocephaliennes Geantes et le Probleme du Serpent de Mer." *Nature,* Paris, No. 3232, 312 (1954).

Bertram, G. C. L., and Bertram, C. K. R. "Bionomics of Dugongs and Manatees." *Nature,* 218, 423 (1968).

Beudant, F. S. "Memoire sur la possibilite de faire vivre des mollusques fluriatiles dans les eaux salees, et des mollusques marins dans les eaux couces, consideree sous le rapport de la geologic." *J. phy. chim. et. his. nat.,* 83, 268 (1968).

Blond, G. *Great Migrations.* New York, Macmillan, 1970.

Braithwaite, H. and Tucker, D. G. "Sonar Picks Up Monstrous Motions in Loch Ness," *New Scientist,* Vol. 40, No. 628 (1968).

Brett, J. R. "The Swimming Energetics of Salmon." *Scientific American* (August, 1965).

Brown, M. E. *Physiology of Fishes.* New York, Academic Press, 1957.

Burton, M. *The Elusive Monster.* London, Rupert Hart-Davis, 1961.

————. *Living Fossils.* New York, Vanguard, 1954.

Cahn, P. H. (Ed.). *Lateral Line Detectors.* Bloomington, Indiana University Press, 1967.

Cairns, D. "Life-History of the Species of New Zealand Fresh-Water Eel." *N. Z. Journal of Science and Technology.* B. General Section. Vol. XXIII, No. 2B (Sept. 1942).

————. "Life-History of the Two Species of Fresh-Water Eel in New Zealand." *N. Z. Journal of Science and Technology.* B. General Section. Vol. XXIII, No. 4B (Jan. 1942).

Camerano, L. *Monografia degli Anfibi Urodeli Italiana.* 1884.

Campbell, E. M. "Report of the Loch Morar Survey." Loch Morar Survey 1970

Committee, London, 1970.

Campbell, E. M. with Solomon, D. *The Search for Morag.* London, Tom Stacey, 1972; New York, Walker, 1973.

Carr, A. *Handbook of Turtles.* Ithaca, Cornell Univ. Press, 1952.

————. *So Excellent a Fishe.* Garden City, Natural History Press, 1967.

Carruth, J. A. *Loch Ness and Its Monsters.* Fort Angustus, Scotland, The Abbey Press, 1954, 1963.

Castle, P. H. J. "A Large Leptocephalid (Teleostei, Apodes) from off South Westland, New Zealand." *Trans. Roy. Soc., N. Z.,* 87, Parts 1 and 2, 179 (1959).

Cohen, D. *A Modern Look at Monsters.* New York, Dodd, Mead, 1970.

Colowick, S. P. and Kaplan, N. O. (Eds.). *Methods in Enzymology,* Vol. 6. New York, Academic Press, 1963. See S. Moore and W. H. Stein, p. 819.

Comfort, A. *Gerontologia,* 15, 248 (1969).

Costello, P. *In Search of Lake Monsters.* New York, Coward, McCann & Geoghegan, 1974.

Couch, J. *A History of the Fishes of the British Islands,* London, Groombridge and Sons, 1868.

Coulson, T. and Gibbinson, J. "In Search of Big Eels." *Fishing,* pp. 25-28 (March, 1966).

Craig, R. E. and Adams, J. A. "The Inverness and Beauly Firths." Dept. of Agriculture and Fisheries for Scotland, Aberdeen.

Crestfield, A. M., Moore, S., and Stein, W. H. *J. Biol. Chem.,* 238, 622 (1963).

Dean, B. "Changes in the Behavior of the Eel During Transformation." *Annals* of the New York Academy of Sciences, Vol. XXII, p. 321 (Dec. 5, 1912).

Dinsdale, T. *The Leviathans.* London, Routledge and Kegan Paul, 1966.

————. *Loch Ness Monster.* London, Routledge and Kegan Paul, 1966.

————. *Monster Hunt,* Washington, D.C., Acropolis Books, 1972.

Eastaugh, R. W. "Report of Freshwater Trials, Pisces Submarine, Loch Ness, 1969."

————. "Report of Submarine Research," in *Annual Report,* LNIB, 1969.

Fish, M. P. and Mowbray, W. H. *Sounds of Western North Atlantic Fishes.* Baltimore, Johns Hopkins Univ. Press. 1970.

Ford, C. *Where the Sea Breaks Its Back.* Boston, Little, Brown, 1956.

Frair, W., Ackman, R. G., and Mrosovsky, N. "Body Temperature of *Dermochelys coriacea*: Warm Turtle from Cold Water." *Science,* Vol. 177, pp. 791-93 (Sept. 1, 1972).

Frost, W. E. "The Age and Growth of Eels (*Anguilla anguilla*) from the Windermere Catchment Area," Part 1 and 2, *J. Animal Ecology,* 14, 26-36, 106-24 (1945).

Gadow, H. F. "Reptiles." *Encyclopaedia Britannica,* 11th Ed., Vol. XXIII, pp. 142-44 (1911).

Golder, F. A. (Ed.). *Bering's Voyages,* 2 vols. New York, American Geographical Society, 1925.

Gould, R. T. *The Case for the Sea-Serpent.* London, Philip Allan, 1930.

————. *The Loch Ness Monster and Others.* London, Geoffrey Bles, 1934.

Graham, D. H. *A Treasury of New Zealand Fishes.* New Zealand, A. H. Wellington and A. W. Reed, 1953.

Gray, J. *Animal Locomotion.* London, Weidenfeld and Nicolson, 1968.

Gregory, W. K. *Evolution Emerging.* New York, Macmillan, 1951.

Gregory, W. K., and Raven, A. C. "Studies on the Origin and Early Evolution of Paired Fins and Limbs." *Annals* of the New York Academy of Sciences,

Vol. 42, pp. 273-360 (1941-1942).

Gudger, E. W. and Smith, B. G. "The Natural History of the Frilled Shark Chlamydoselackus Anguineus," in the Bashford Dean Memorial Volume, *Archaic Fishes,* pp. 245-319, Museum of Natural History (1933).

Hay, O. P. "On a Collection of Upper Cretaceous Fishes from Mount Lebanon, Syria with Descriptions of Four New Genera and Nineteen New Species," *Bulletin* of the American Museum of Natural History, Vol. XIX, Article X, pp. 395-452 (1903).

Hammel, H. T., Caldwell, F. T., Jr., and Abrams, R. M. "Regulation of Body Temperature in the Blue-Tongued Lizard." *Science,* Vol. 156, pp. 1260-1262 (June 2, 1967).

Helm, T. *Monster of the Deep.* New York, Dodd, Mead, 1962.

Heuvelmans, B. *In the Wake of the Sea-Serpents.* New York, Hill and Wang, 1968.

Holcik, J., and Mihalik, J. *Fresh Water Fishes.* Spring Books, 1970.

Holiday, F. W. *The Dragon and the Disc.* New York, Norton, 1973.

_____. *The Great Orm of Loch Ness,* London, Faber & Faber, 1968.

Hubbard, S. J. "Hearing and the Octopus Statocyst." *J. Exptl. Biol.,* 845 (1960).

Hutchinson, G. E. *A Treatise on Limnology.* New York, Wiley, 1957.

Hyman, L. H. *Invertebrates,* Vol. VI, Mollusca I. New York, McGraw-Hill, 1967.

Itsuo, K. "Feeding Velocity of the Eel *(Anguilla japonica)." Bull. Jap. Sic. Sci. Fisheries,* 4, No. 5 (1936).

James, D. "Loch Ness Investigation." London, LNIB, 1968.

Johnston, R. "The Effects of a New Pulp Mill on Two Interconnecting Sea-lochs." Unpublished Typescript, Dept. of Agriculture and Fisheries for Scotland, Aberdeen.

Jones, F. R. H. *Fish Migration.* New York, St. Martin's Press, 1968.

Klein, M., Rines, R. H., Dinsdale, T., and Foster, L. S., *Underwater Search at Loch Ness.* Belmont, Mass., Academy of Applied Science, 1972.

Kooyman, G. L., "The Weddell Seal," *Scientific American* (Aug., 1969).

Kondo, H. (Ed.). *The Illustrated Encyclopedia of the Animal Kingdom,* Vols. 9, 10, 11, Danbury Press, 1972.

Kleerekoper, H. *Olfaction in Fishes.* Bloomington, Indiana Univ. Press, 1969.

Kulawas, C. "The Quest at Loch Ness." *Univ. of Chicago Magazine* (Sept.-Oct., 1968).

Leslie, L. A. D. "Monsters Reported in Irish Waters," *The Field,* December 23, 1965, p. 1353.

Liu, R. K. and Walford, R. L. *Nature,* 212, 1277 (1966).

Lockley, R. M. *Animal Navigation.* New York, Hart, 1967.

Love, R. M. *The Chemical Biology of Fishes.* New York, Academic Press, 1970.

Love, R. "Report of Sonar Research," in *Annual Report,* LNIB, 1969.

Lydekker, R. *Encyclopaedia Britannica,* 11th ed., Vol. XVII, 541-543; Vol. VIII, 647-648; Vol. XXIII, 280; Vol. XXV, 154-156.

Lyons, C. *Milestones in Ogopogosland.* Victoria, B.C., Canada, M. Pope, 1957.

Ley, W. *The Lungfish, the Dodo and the Unicorn.* New York, Viking, 1948.

MacGintie, G. E., and MacGintie, N. *Natural History of Marine Animals.* New York, McGraw-Hill, 1949.

Mackal, R. P. "Sea Serpents and the Loch Ness Monster." *Oceanology International.* (Sept.-Oct., 1967).

Martin, H. T. "Anguillavus hackberryensis." *Science Bulletin,* University of Kansas, Vol. 13, No. 7, pp. 95-98 (1920).

Maturana, H. F., and Sperling, S. "Unidirectional Response to Angular Acceleration Recorded from the Middle Crestal Nerve in the Statocyst of Octopus vulgaris." *Nature,* 197, 815 (1963).

Maxwell, G. *Seals of the World.* Boston, Houghton-Mifflin, 1967.

McGinnis, S. M., and Dickson, L. L. "Thermoregulation in the Desert Iguana Dipsosaurus dorsalis." *Science,* Vol. 156, pp. 1757-1759 (June 30, 1967).

Meek, A. *The Migrations of Fish.* London, Edward Arnold, 1916.

Meisenheimer, J. Pteropoda. Wissernsch. Ergebnisse Dtsch. Tilfsee Exped. Voldivia, 9 (1905).

Moore, J. A. *Physiology of the Amphibia.* New York, Academic Press, 1964.

Morton, J., et al. "Pelagic Mollusca, Swimmers and Drifters." *Nature,* 177, 1023 (1956).

Neilsen, J. G., and Larsen, V. Vidensk, Medd. Dansk Naturh. Foren., 133, 149 (1970).

Netboy, A. "Round Trip with the Salmon." *Natural History* (June-July, 1968).

Noble, G. K. *The Biology of the Amphibia.* New York, Dover, 1954.

Norman, J. R. *Great Fishes, Whales and Dolphins.* New York, Norton, 1938.

O'Donovan, V. T. *A Lough Monster of Southern Ireland.* London.

Olsen, C. R., Elsner, R., Hale, F. C., and Kenney, D. W., " 'Blow' of the Pilot Whale," *Science,* Vol. 163, pp. 953-955 (Feb. 28, 1969).

Orr, R. T. *Animals in Migration.* New York, Macmillan, 1970.

Oudemans, A. C. *The Great Sea-Serpent.* London, Luzac & Co., 1892.

Parker, T. J., and Haswell, W. A. *A Text-book of Zoology.* New York, Macmillan, 1963.

Parsons, P. A. *Complete Book of Fresh Water Fishing.* New York, Harper and Row, 1963.

Pearson, E. S. "A Further Development of Tests of Normality." *Biometrika,* XXII, 239 (1930-31).

Porter, W. H. "Sea Squirts: Sea Serpents and Ocean Monsters," *Oceans,* Vol. 4, No. 5 (Sept.-Oct., 1971).

Potts, T. H. *Out in the Open: A budget of natural history, gathered in New Zealand.* Christchurch, Lyttleton Times Co., 1882.

Pritchard, P. C. H. Florida State Museum *Bulletin,* 13, 85 (1969).

Regan, C. "The Osteology and Classification of the Teleosteam Fishes of the Order Apodes," *The Annals and Magazine of Natural History,* 18th Series, No. 58, Vol. 10. London, Taylor and Francis, 1912.

Rines, R. H., and Blonder, I. S. *Side Scan Sonar Investigation.* Belmont, Mass., Academy of Applied Science, 1970.

Romer, A. S. "The Appendicular Skeleton of the Permian Embolomerous Amphibian Archeria." *Contributions* from the Museum of Paleontology, University of Michigan, Vol. XIII, No. 5, pp. 103-159 (1957).

_____. "An Embolomere Jaw from the Mid-Carboniferous of Nova Scotia Breviora." Mueum of Comparative Zoology, Cambridge, Massachusetts, No. 87, pp. 1-7 (1958).

_____. "The Larger Embolomerous Amphibians of the American Carboniferous. *Bulletin* of the Museum of Comparative Zoology at Harvard College, Vol. 128, No. 9, pp. 415-454 (1963).

_____. "A New Anthracosaurian Labyrinthodont, Proterogyrinus Scheelei from the Lower Carboniferous Kirtlandia." Cleveland Museum of Natural History, No. 10, pp. 1-16 (1970).

————. "Review of the Labyrinthodontia." *Bulletin* of the Museum of Comparative Zoology at Harvard College. Vol. 99, No. 1 (1947).

————. *Vertebrate Paleontology.* Chicago, Univ. of Chicago Press, 1966.

Scheider, W., and Wallis, P. "An Alternate Method of Calculating the Population Density of Monsters in Loch Ness." *Limnology and Oceanography,* 18, pp. 343-346 (1973).

Schmalhausen, I. I. *The Origin of Terrestrial Vertebrates.* New York, Academic Press, 1968.

Schmidt, J. *Danish Eel Investigations During 25 Years: 1905-1930.* Copenhagen, Carlsberg Foundation, 1932.

————. "Eels and Conger Eels of the North Atlantic." *Nature,* Vol. 128, No. 3232. p. 602 (Oct. 10, 1931).

————. "The Fresh-Water Eels of New Zealand." *Trans. N. Z. Inst.,* Vol. 58, 379. Wellington (1927).

Shaw, E. "The Schooling of Fishes." *Scientific American* (June, 1962).

Sheldon, R. W., and Kerr, S. R. "The Population Density of Monsters in Loch Ness." *Limnology and Oceanography,* 17, pp. 796-798 (1972).

Sinha, V. R. P., and Jones, J. W. *J. Zool.* 153, 99 (1967).

Skjelsvik, E. "Norwegian Lake and Sea Monsters." Norveg Folkellinsgransking 7, Oslo (1960), p. 29.

Smith, D. G. *Copeia,* 1 (1970).

Spackman, D. H., Stein, W. H., and Moore, S. *Anal. Chem.,* 30, 1190 (1958).

Spector, L. F. "The Great Monster Hunt. *Machine Design,* Cleveland, Penton Publ. Co. (Sept. 14, 1967), pp. 44-52.

St. Adamnan, *Latin Life of the Great St. Columba,* Book 2, Chapter 27.

Stejneger, L. *Georg Wilhelm Steller.* Cambridge, Harvard Univ. Press, 1936.

Steller, G. W. Ausführliche Beschreibung von Sonderbaren Meerthieren, Hall, in Verlag, Carl Christian Kümmels (1753).

Svedjeland, Knut. "The Storsjö Monster." Mimeo copy Author's Collection.

Sweeney, J. B. *A Pictorial History of Sea Monsters and Other Dangerous Marine Life.* New York, Crown, 1972.

Walden, H. T. *Familiar Freshwater Fishes of America.* New York, Harper and Row, 1964.

Watson, D. M. S. "The Carboniferous Amphibia of Scotland," *Palaeontologia Hungarica,* Vol. I, Fasciculus 8, pp. 221-252, Budapest (1923).

————. "The Evolution and Origin of the Amphibia." *Philosophical Transactions* of the Royal Society of London, Series B. Vol. 214, pp. 189-257, London (1926).

Wilbur, K. M., and Yonge, C. M. *Physiology of Mollusca.* New York, Academic Press, 1964.

Williams, J. *Oceanography.* Boston, Little, Brown, 1962.

Williston, S. W. *Water Reptiles of the Past and Present.* Chicago, Univ. of Chicago Press, 1914.

Willums, J. "The Loch Ness Phenomenon: A Presentation of Scientific Facts." Xerox copy Author's Collection.

Witchell, N. *The Loch Ness Story.* London, Penguin, 1975.

Wood, F. G., and Gennaro, J. F. Jr. "An Octopus Trilogy," *Natural History,* Vol. LXXX, No. 3 (March, 1971).

Woodward, A. S. "Plesiosaurus." *Encyclopaedia Britannica,* 11th Ed., Vol. XXI, pp. 836-837 (1911).

Whyte, C. *More than a Legend,* London, Hamilton, 1957.

Young, J. Z. *The Life of Vertebrates.* Oxford Univ. Press, 1962.

Acknowledgments

First I wish to thank my wife who, in spite of my reluctance, persisted until I set pen to paper. I am most grateful to Robert E. L. Love, Jr. for his many contributions, not only as Field Director of the LNIB underwater search expeditions but also to this book. He deserves special credit for analyses of the Loch Ness food supply and the MacNab and Searle photographs, and for contributions to the sonar discussions and analyses.

I also wish to thank James Colvin, formerly of World Book Encyclopedia, for his invaluable dedication and support of research at Loch Ness and for his contributions to this book.

Special thanks are due to World Book Encyclopedia, LNIB, and the Academy of Applied Science for allowing generous use of visual material assembled by them or under their auspices. Acknowledgment is also extended for permission to use material published elsewhere: to John Wiley & Sons, Inc. (G. E. Hutchinson, *A Treatise on Limnology,* © 1957) for the diagram on p. 71 above; to Harper & Row, Inc. (H. T. Walden, *Familiar Freshwater Fishes of America,* illustration © 1964 by Carl Burger) for the drawing on p. 206 above; to Franklin Watts, Inc. (E. D. Baumann, *The Loch Ness Monster,* © 1972) for the map on p. 6 above. Some of the other non-photographic illustrations were done under my supervision by World Book Encyclopedia artists.

Two additional artists who worked so carefully under my direction, Charles Wellek and Mary Wall, must also be commended for the excellence of their illustrations.

I also wish to thank Mary Halaburt and Genevieve La Pinska for their heroic conversion of my handwritten text to typescript.

A special note of appreciation is also due Ron Mercer, Ivor Newby, Peter and Pauline Hodge, Holly Arnold, and Dick Raynor for their willingness to verify facts and check out various matters as they arose during the writting of this book.

Lastly I wish to thank the hundreds of people, including the local residents of Loch Ness, who have given me so much help in innumerable ways.

R.P.M.

Index

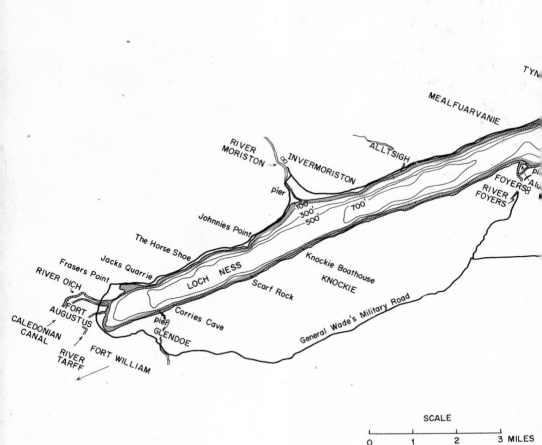

TYN

MEALFUARVANIE

RIVER
MORISTON   INVERMORISTON   ALLTSIGH

pier   pi

Alu

FOYERS
RIVER
FOYERS

Johnnies Point   100'
300'   700'
500'

The Horse Shoe

Jacks Quarrie   Knockie Boathouse

Frasers Point   LOCH NESS   KNOCKIE

RIVER OICH

Scarf Rock

FORT
AUGUSTUS   Corries Cave

CALEDONIAN   pier
CANAL   GLENDOE   General Wade's Military Road

RIVER   FORT WILLIAM
TARFF

SCALE

0   1   2   3 MILES